THOMAS WILLIAMS was a curator of the major international exhibition *Vikings: Life and Legend* in 2014 and is now Curator of Early Medieval Coins at the British Museum. He undertook doctoral research at University College London and has taught and lectured in history and archaeology at the University of Cambridge. He is the author of *The Tale of King Harald: The Last Viking Adventure*, a book for children retelling the saga of King Harald 'Hard-ruler', and numerous academic and feature articles.

Praise for *Viking Britain*:

'At once full of the most up-to-date archaeology and international scholarly thought, and full of the literary flourishes which bring the past most vividly to life for readers: dramatic reconstruction, physical scene-setting and authorial intervention. It is a great success'

RONALD HUTTON

'A highly readable, thoughtful and vivid book about the history of Scandinavian-British interactions in these islands'

CAROLYNE LARRINGTON, *TLS*

'Williams has written a fundamentally new history of the Vikings in Britain: authoritative, at times controversial, and above all a personal journey through the byways of life under Scandinavian military occupation ... A real pleasure to read'

PROFESSOR NEIL PRICE, Uppsala University

'Told with grand sweep, granular detail and terrific gusto, Tom Williams's book gives us a powerful sense of the violent and creative energies of this amazing time. Full of gripping images from the sources and vividly realised imaginative conjurings of events and landscapes, it gives us a wonderful sense of an age not just of war but of contacts and cultures'

MICHAEL WOOD

'Fresh, vivid and impeccably researched'

'Williams' infectiously enthusiastic book gives you everything you could want from a history of the Vikings; blood and thunder, Odin and Thor, sagas and sea voyagers, slavering berserkers and exquisite brooches ... An engrossing account ... Williams is scrupulous to avoid the easy pub-chat message. He writes fluently and with feeling'

'A lively, colourful book that explores in high definition what being a Viking really meant'

'Williams is a master at conveying the atmosphere of Viking Britain, at drawing prose pictures of its landscapes and at teasing out the complex strands of Dark Ages politics and recreating the early medieval mindset to give the reader an almost immersive experience ... Many historians similarly seek to stack facts in an easy to digest, if deceptive, order. Williams, conversely, glories in the chaos and jumble of the early medieval world, never pretending that motives or the simple successions of events can be easily captured'

'Brisk of pace and fresh of tone ... with a vividly atmospheric turn of phrase and a real momentum ... as ambitious and wide-ranging as the travels of the Vikings themselves, and as strange and enjoyable as any saga'

'An authoritative and up-to-the-minute account, told with verve and imagination'

# THOMAS WILLIAMS

# VIKING BRITAIN

## A HISTORY

WILLIAM
COLLINS

# FOR Z

William Collins
An imprint of HarperCollins*Publishers*
1 London Bridge Street
London SE1 9GF

WilliamCollinsBooks.com

First published in Great Britain in 2017 by William Collins
This William Collins paperback edition published in 2018

1

A catalogue record for this book is
available from the British Library

ISBN 978-0-00-817195-7

Maps by Martin Brown

Printed and bound in Great Britain by
CPI Group (UK) Ltd, Croydon

Storms break on stone-strewn slopes,
Snows falling, the ground enfettered,
the howling of winter. Then darkness awakens,
deepens the night-shadow, sends from the north
a harsh hail-harrying bringing terror to men.

*The Wanderer* (tenth century)[1]

# CONTENTS

# BRITAIN
## C. 800 AD

ATLANTIC
OCEAN

PICTAVIA

NORTH
SEA

DÁL RIATA

ALT CLUD

NORTHUMBRIA

IRISH SEA

GWYNEDD

POWYS

DYFED

GWENT

MERCIA

EAST
ANGLIA

ESSEX

WESSEX

KENT

SUSSEX

CORNWALL

ENGLISH CHANNEL

# BRITAIN

### C. 1000 AD

EARLDOM OF ORKNEY

SCOTLAND

MAN AND THE ISLES

ATLANTIC
OCEAN

NORTH
SEA

STRATHCLYDE

IRISH SEA

ENGLAND

GWYNEDD

DEHEUBARTH

MORGANNWG

ENGLISH CHANNEL

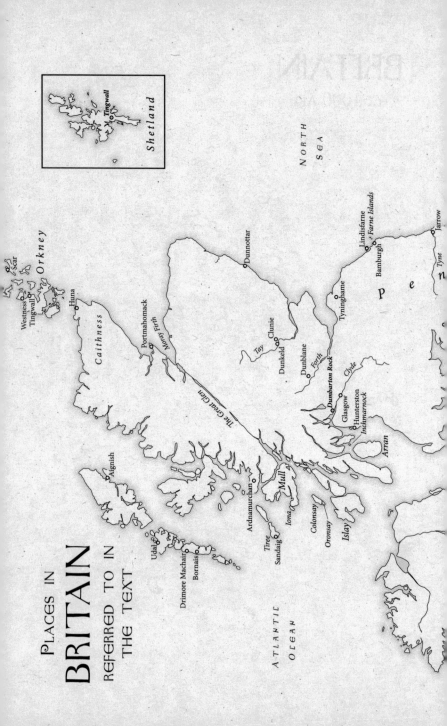

# PLACES IN BRITAIN
## REFERRED TO IN THE TEXT

Shetland

Tingwall

NORTH SEA

Orkney

Scar
Westness
Tingwall
Huna

Caithness

Portmahomack

Moray Firth

Dunnottar

Lindisfarne
Farne Islands
Bamburgh
Jarrow

P e n

Tyninghame

Tyne

Clunie

Tay

Dunkeld

Dunblane

Forth

Clyde

Dumbarton Rock

Glasgow
Hunterston
Inchmarnock

Arran

The Great Glen

Aignish

Ardnamurchan

Mull

Iona

Colonsay

Oronsay

Islay

Tiree

Sandaig

Udal

Drimore Machair

Bornais

ATLANTIC OCEAN

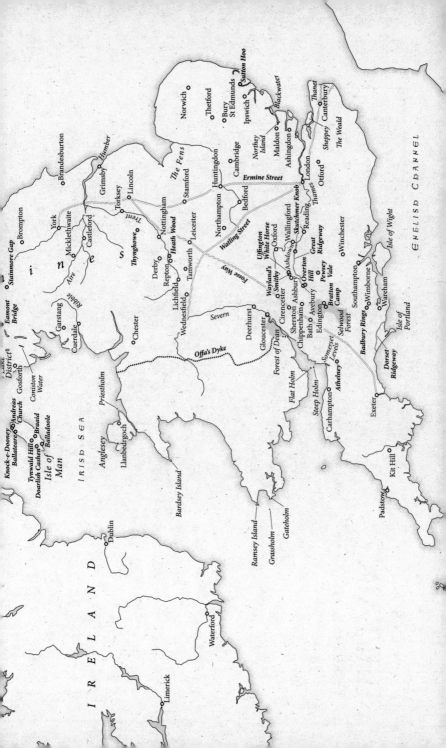

# PREFACE

In 2013–14 I was the project curator for the exhibition *Vikings: Life and Legend* at the British Museum. One of the first reviews, published in a major national newspaper, offered the following critique:

> There's no stage-setting. No gory recreation of the Lindisfarne raid, say, to get us in the mood [...] I felt like crying. Where were the swords? And if I was ready to bawl, what does this exhibition offer its younger visitors? It can't claim not to be for them. You can't put on an exhibition called Vikings without expecting some kids. The only way this exhibition could sound more child-friendly would be if it was called Vikings and Dinosaurs. But the austerely beautiful cases of brooches and golden rings and amber offer very little to fans of *Horrible Histories*.[1]

Leaving aside the issue of whether sensationalizing historical violence for the entertainment of children is ever appropriate (how about a 'gory recreation' of the Srebrenica massacre?), what these comments really reveal is an uncritical assumption that the Vikings have their proper place as players in a hilarious historical Grand Guignol, alongside head-chopping at the Tower of London. The Vikings, it seems to say, are a cheerful, bloody diversion for the kids on a wet bank-holiday afternoon, not a proper historical phenomenon. The indignation that springs from not having had these prejudices confirmed is palpable. Brooches? Women? Trade? BORING! Vikings are big men with swords, crushing skulls left, right and centre: the barbarian archetype writ large and red.

It occurred to me at the time that nobody would treat Roman history in this way. It is unthinkable, for example, that any art critic would yearn for lurid re-enactments of Roman soldiers cheerfully raping and murdering British women and children – least of all within the austere neo-classical precincts of the British Museum. The Romans, it is instinctively felt, are refined, have gravitas. They benefit from a cultural snobbery with extraordinarily deep roots (ultimately fastened in the smug imperial propaganda of the Romans themselves). Roman Britain, in particular, is widely presented in a solidly respectable way – epitomized in tiresome tropes of roof tiles and under-floor heating, good roads and urban planning, fine wine and fancy tableware. It is a period that can serve as an acceptable backstory to who we are and where we come from, a people 'just like us', who went to parties and wrote letters and had jobs. *Romanitas* – Romanness – means 'civilization'.

Few think of the age of the Vikings in those terms. Like other romantic curios they have been fetishized and infantilized, set apart from wider history alongside pirates, gladiators, knights-in-armour and, I suppose, dinosaurs. The Vikings are presented as cartoon savages who had a short-lived cameo rampaging around in the gloomy interlude between the end of Roman Britain and the Norman Conquest. It does them a grave disservice.

Between the conventional beginning of the Viking Age in the late eighth century and its close in the eleventh, Scandinavian people and culture were involved with Britain to a degree that left a permanent impression on these islands. They came to trade and plunder and, ultimately, to settle, to colonize and to rule. It is a story of often epic proportions, thronged with characters whose names and deeds still fire the blood and stir the imagination – Svein Forkbeard and Edmund Ironside, Ivar the Boneless and Alfred the Great, Erik Bloodaxe and Edgar the Pacifier – a story of war and upheaval. It is also, however, the story of how the people of the British Isles came to reorient themselves in a new and interconnected world, where new technologies for travel and communication brought ideas and customs into sometimes explosive contact, but which also fostered the development of towns and trade, forged new identities and gave birth to England and Scotland as unified nations for the first time. By the time of the Norman Conquest, most of Britain might justifiably be described as 'Viking' to varying degrees, and in language, literature, place-names and folklore the presence of Scandinavian settlers can still be felt throughout the British Isles, with repercussions for all those places that British culture and colonization have subsequently touched.

The Vikings have also retained their influence as a powerful cultural force in the modern world, and representations of the Viking Age in art, music and literature have had a profound impact on the western imagination. Indeed, much of what we imagine when we think of this period in British history – even the word 'Viking' itself – grew from political, literary and artistic currents that swelled in the nineteenth and early twentieth centuries. Here, too, a 'Viking Britain' came alive and, to the likes of William Morris and J. R. R. Tolkien, this was a place that seemed to lurk unseen just at the borders of their rapidly modernizing world. It was there not only in the writings and monuments that time had preserved, but also (and perhaps especially) in the elements themselves – the grey sea, the north wind and the very bones of the earth. In travel, art and literature, landscape became a way to commune with the people of the Viking Age – people who had seen the same red sun rising, felt the same cold wind on their necks, touched the same fissures in the smooth grey rock. This has in turn become a way to explore the mentality and world-view of a people with an intimate and profoundly imaginative relationship with the environment. For people living in the latter centuries of the first millennium, the landscape was teeming with unseen inhabitants and riddled with gateways to other worlds. Pits and ditches, barrows and ruins, mountains, rivers and forests: all could be home to the dead, the divine and the diabolical, haunted by monsters and gods.

Telling the story of the Vikings in Britain is therefore not a straightforward undertaking – it is the tale of a people who were not a people, who came to lands that were not yet nations. The historical record is patchy, the archaeology equivocal. Even the very words we use – 'Viking' most of all – slither away from easy definition. It is, moreover, the story not only of the three centuries leading up to (and overlapping) the Norman Conquest, but also of how that time has been remembered, recycled and reimagined by successive generations. It is, as earlier generations seem better to have appreciated, a world that is still tangible. The sense that the past is present in the landscape – that there is another world hovering just out of sight – has receded in step with modernity's alienation from the land. Against the advance of technology, urbanization and globalization, our imaginative connection to landscape continues to fight the long defeat. The land, water and sky have largely been disenchanted of the past, just as they were disenchanted of their elves and spirits during the enlightenment and industrial revolution. But the past can never be wholly erased, and the rivers, hills, woods and stones of Britain remain deeply imprinted with memories of the Vikings and their world.

It is a legacy that runs far beyond the confines of Britain itself. From the seventeenth century to the present, the English-speaking diaspora – of people, ideas, systems, values, laws and language – has had a transformative impact on the world, firstly through the expansion of Britain's Empire, and latterly through the ongoing dominance and global reach of North American culture and economic power. The memory of the Vikings may only be one small cell in the vast genome of Anglophone identity, but it is a tenacious and enduring one. Sometimes it appears overtly, in the simplified and bowdlerized versions of Norse myths and Viking stereotypes that penetrate popular culture, whether through the pages of comic books, the iconography of football teams or the covers of heavy-metal albums. But it also runs in deeper channels of thought and language, the serpentine ships that travel the dark rivers of the subconscious mind, a half-seen shadow of grim gods and thudding oars and dark pine forests wreathed in mist.

The chapters that follow tell the tale of the Vikings in Britain as a broadly chronological narrative. At times the story diverges as events begin to unfold simultaneously across Britain, but I have largely endeavoured to keep the overall momentum moving forward as much as possible. At the same time, however, this is also a book about ideas, objects and places. Through the physical remains and landscapes that the Vikings fashioned and walked – their runestones and ship burials, settlements and battlefields – it is possible to reach beyond the bare rehearsal of names and dates to explore the way that people in Viking Age Britain thought about their world and their place within it, and the way they have been remembered in the centuries since their passing: the stories they told and the tales they inspired, their fears, their fantasies, and the dooms they aspired to. Several themes recur throughout this book – in particular what being a 'Viking' really meant, how attitudes and identities changed over time, and what that meant for the ethnic evolution of the people of Britain – but in a general sense this book is about illuminating an influence on British history that has been profound and enduring, one that has shaped languages, culture and the historical trajectory of the British Isles and beyond for hundreds of years. In a small way, I hope, this book may help to restore to the Vikings some of the dignity that they have too often been denied.

There are, it must be acknowledged, some difficulties that attend the writing of a chronological history of this period; some parts of Britain – England especially – receive more detailed treatment than others, and not all of the evidence is discussed at equal length. In many cases this reflects the availability of source material: both the lack of it and – less often – its abundance. A complete inventory of all Viking-period archaeology found on the Isle of Man would run to many hundreds of pages; a compendium of all the contemporary written references to Viking activity in the same place would fit on the back of a small envelope. Frequently, however, the question of what to cover and what to leave out has been decided by me, and I make no apology for this: it reflects the fact that this book is a personal, at times perhaps idiosyncratic, exploration of the subject. It is intended to be neither definitive nor comprehensive – it cannot hope to be either, not within the covers of a book as slim as this. For all of the detailed regional surveys and the surfeit of books (of wildly varying quality) on the Vikings as a whole, a truly definitive compendium of evidence for the Vikings in Britain remains to be written: it would be a mammoth undertaking, probably running to multiple volumes. It would also, more than likely, be made less than definitive within days of its publication, as new data – much of it gathered by metal-detectorists – continues to roll in, week after week, and spectacular finds are made with some regularity.[2] At the same time, major research projects continue to transform our perception of Viking Age societies, their interactions and their evolutions; this too is unlikely to stop any time soon.[3]

This book has not been written with an academic audience in mind, but I am nevertheless deeply conscious of the need to provide signposts for the reader to the sources of the material from which this narrative has been constructed. Although it would be unnecessarily distracting to provide full scholarly citations, some textual references are necessary for the reader's orientation and to acknowledge sources that I have cited directly. I have chosen, in the main, to restrict these citations to primary written sources and archaeological reports – that is, to evidence rather than interpretation. However, where the work of individual scholars is referred to directly, or where a particular argument or line of reasoning is consciously derived from the work of others, I have also provided the appropriate citations. For brevity, a full citation is only provided the first time a work is referred to in the notes; thereafter, works are referred to by their author (or editor) and abbreviated title only. Primary sources that are referred to frequently have been abbreviated, and a full list of the abbreviations used and a full citation to the edition(s) relied upon in each case are provided in the endmatter. Where primary sources have been quoted in the text and the translation is my own, the citation in the Notes refers to an original language edition of the source in question. Where a translated edition of a source has been quoted, the citation in the Notes directs the reader to the translated edition relied upon. Exceptions are indicated in the Notes. A short summary of relevant further reading can be found at the end of this book. This is intended to direct the reader to the most accessible and up-to-date treatments and is intended only as a starting point to the vast literature that touches on the Vikings – in Britain and in wider perspective. In addition, a full bibliography of all literature cited can be accessed at tjtwilliams.com

## Acknowledgements

The ideas and opinions expressed in this book are – even where I believe them to be my own – indebted to a huge number of historians, archaeologists, linguists, numismatists, scientists and others, whose work I have read or with whom I have had the privilege of working, whether as a student, a colleague or a friend. Those people will know who they are, and may well recognize their own fingerprints on my thought-processes. Particular thanks are due to Gareth Williams (no relation), my colleague at the British Museum, and a man to whom I owe a great personal and intellectual debt. Neil Price at the University of Uppsala did me the honour of reading the entire book in draft. His comments have been both hugely encouraging and unerringly pertinent. My editors, Arabella Pike and Peter James, deserve many thanks indeed. Their ministrations – and, in the case of the former, great forbearance – have helped to ensure that the best possible version of this book was ultimately realized. My agents, Julian Alexander and Ben Clarke at LAW, also deserve fulsome thanks for their support and tireless efforts on my behalf. Tom Holland requires a special mention: if it had not been for a good-natured intervention on his part, my introduction to the aforementioned gentlemen would never have been effected, and this book may not have come into being at all.

My father, Geoffrey Williams, read every word of the manuscript as the chapters were produced and watched its slow gestation over many months. My discussions with him, and the innumerable errors identified and improvements suggested, have undoubtedly made this a better book. My mother, Gilli, produced (at exceptionally short notice and with remarkable facility) several of the fabulous line drawings in this book. For all of the help that both my parents have provided, as well as their unwavering love and support, my gratitude is profound.

And finally my wife, Zeena, has had to contend with an intrusive Viking presence in her life for longer now than she probably ever imagined. But she has weathered the storm and borne me up whenever I felt that I might sink. Nothing would have been possible without her. She is the best.

I cannot stress enough, however, that none of the people I have mentioned above can in any way be held responsible for my wilder flights of imagination, or for any errors that have made it into print: these are all my own.

### A Note on Names

There is a bewildering amount of variation in the rendering of personal names across this period, with the same name frequently appearing in wildly different spellings depending on the language of the written source in which it appears. As a rule of thumb, I have preferred to use the most contemporary and ethno-linguistically appropriate versions wherever possible. I have, however, made frequent exception wherever normalized modern spellings of names are likely to be more familiar to the reader: hence 'Olaf', rather than *Oláfr*; 'Eric', rather than *Eiríkr*; 'Odin', rather than *Oðinn*. Where variant forms are used (especially in quotations), I have provided the more familiar form in square brackets. Given the complexities and ambiguities of Viking Age onomastics, it is entirely likely that some inconsistencies remain: my apologies in advance if this is so.

In the text and Notes, 'ON' denotes Old Norse, 'OE' Old English and 'ModE' Modern English.

# 1

# OUTSIDERS
# FROM ACROSS
# THE WATER

When the watchman on the wall, the Shieldings' lookout
whose job it was to guard the sea-cliffs,
saw shields glittering on the gangplank
and battle-equipment being unloaded
he had to find out who and what they were. So he rode to the shore,
this horseman of Hrothgar's, and challenged them
in formal terms, flourishing his spear.

*Beowulf*[1]

In the days of King Beorhtric of Wessex (r. 786–802), 'there came for the first time three ships of Northmen from Hordaland',[2] and 'they landed in the island which is called Portland'.[3] '[T]he king's reeve, who was then in the town called Dorchester, leapt on his horse, sped to the harbour with a few men (for he thought they were merchants rather than marauders), and admonishing them [the Northmen] in an authoritative manner, gave orders that they should be driven to the royal town. And he and his companions were killed by them on the spot. The name of the reeve was Beaduheard.'[4]

'Those were the first ships of Danish men which came to the land of the English.'[5]

*

1

Looking south from the summit of the barrow, the land feels like it is slipping away, yielding itself to the ineffable splendour of the ocean. Away in the distance the dark bulk of Portland languishes, a last defiant redoubt set in the glittering sea. The world is wide here, the coast of England laid out in broad wings to east and west; on a bright clear day – the ozone hollowing out the sinuses – you feel weightless, as if you could step from the top of that mound and be lifted into the firmament, soar into that white light obliterating the edges of land, sea and sky, tumbling in the breeze.

The mound is known, for reasons now lost, as Culliford Tree. It is a tumulus, a Bronze Age burial mound – one of five running east to west – that had stood on the Dorset chalk for more than 2,000 years before it received a name in the English tongue. Like breakwaters in the surf, the mounds and their ancient dead have endured the battering tides of time, forcing history to shape itself around them. At some point after it was named, the barrow became the meeting place of Culliford Tree Hundred, the administrative district of which Portland formed part at the time of the Domesday Survey in 1086. It had probably served this purpose for hundreds of years prior to William the Conqueror's great national audit and by the end of the eighth century it was almost certainly a significant regional meeting place. It was in this place and in others like it that royal officials enacted the king's will and delivered his justice, adjudicating disputes and pronouncing verdicts which could include fines, mutilation and death. From the summit of the barrow, the landscape reveals itself to the watcher – a place from which the land could be claimed, authority enacted in the act of seeing.

On that day at the end of the eighth century when three ships came unasked to Portland, the man riding down to Portland strand might well have paused and looked back over his shoulder, looked for Culliford Tree. He might have sought comfort from the distant mound on the horizon – a dark beacon of antiquity and earth-fast custom, a symbol of territory and authority, of land and legitimacy. This man, Beaduheard, would have known that the barrow watched over him, lending him the power in the land, confirming the prerogatives of his office. He was reeve to the king of Wessex, Beorhtric, and as such he exercised the king's delegated authority. Reeves represented the king in towns, ports and sometimes across whole shires; the modern and medieval word 'sheriff' has its origin in these 'shire-reeves'. Beaduheard, therefore, was an important man – responsible, perhaps, for local government in Dorchester and the surrounding countryside, a man used to getting his own way.

Beaduheard arrives on Portland to find a group of travellers arrayed on the beach, their ships drawn up behind them, their backs to the sea. They are wary – frightened even. They are strangers in a strange land, conditioned perhaps to expect a frosty welcome. Beaduheard dismounts from his horse to receive them, others following his lead, shingle crunching beneath leather-shod feet. Words are exchanged but their meaning is lost – whatever mutual words they understood failing in the tension of the moment, drowned by the crashing of the waves. But Beaduheard is no diplomat, and the tenor of his words is clear enough. He 'admonishes' the newcomers in an 'authoritative manner', he attempts to 'drive them' to the king's residence ('against their will' as the chronicle of John of Worcester adds).[6] He knows his duty, and he knows the law.

The West Saxon edicts that are closest in date to these events are the laws of King Ine (r. 688–726). Clause 20 gives a sense of the sort of welcome that the unfortunate wanderer could expect in eighth-century Wessex: 'If a man from afar, or a stranger, goes through the woods off the highway and neither calls out nor blows a horn, he may be considered a thief, to be slain or to be redeemed [by paying his *wergild* ("man-price")].'[7] Britain's most southerly realm offered cold comfort to the lost.

In the Old English poem *Beowulf* – composed at some point between the early eighth and the early eleventh century – there can be found, expressed in the Reeve's own West Saxon tongue, a form of words that we might imagine Beaduheard speaking in his final hours: an echo of a lived experience.[8]

'What kind of men are you who arrive
rigged out for combat in coats of mail,
sailing here over the sea-lanes
in your steep-hulled boat? [...]

Never before has a force under arms
disembarked so openly – not bothering to ask
if the sentries allowed them safe passage
or the clan had consented [...]

So now, before you fare inland
as interlopers, I have to be informed
about who you are and where you hail from.
Outsiders from across the water,
I say it again: the sooner you tell
where you come from and why, the better.'[9]

In the poem, these words are spoken by the Danish coastguard to the eponymous hero and his men as they arrive from the realm of the Geats (southern Sweden) to lend their aid to Hrothgar, the Danish king. They are formalities, to be understood both by questioner and visitor: the back-and-forth ritual of arrival.

In the real-life counterpart to this scene, however, the newcomers on the Portland beach chose not to participate, not to play the game. Perhaps they did not know the rules.

The travellers, berated in a foreign tongue by an aggressive stranger, are frightened and frustrated – the instinct to fight or flee like a high-pitched whine, raised to intolerable pitch. In the heavy moments that follow, the confrontation develops the hypertension of a shoot-out: a bead of sweat running down the back of a sun-burnt neck, eyes darting left and right as time slows to dream-pace, measured out by the metronomic crashing of the surf. Perhaps a hand flickers towards a sword hilt; perhaps a horse stamps, a cloak billows, a gull shrieks ... When the spell finally breaks the violence

4

seems inevitable – preordained – as if only death can bring the world back into balance.

In the end, all that is left, in place of Beowulf's polite and formal replies, are huddled corpses on the strand, their blood swallowed between stones.

The arrival of these Northmen in Portland – the carbuncle that sprouts from Dorset into the English Channel – established the leit-motifs for Britain's early interactions with its northern neighbours: unanswered questions and sudden brutality, the fluid identity of the merchant-marauder, the collision of cultures at the margins of the land. For almost three centuries, seaborne marauders would return again and again – sometimes like the inevitable attrition of the tides, dissolving the most vulnerable shores one wave at a time, at others like a mighty storm that smashes sea-walls and wreaks devastation before expending itself exhausted. Sometimes it would seem more like the inexorable flood of a climate apocalypse, the waters rising and rising without respite, washing deep inland and bursting river banks deep in the interior of the land. Everywhere the crimson tide flowed and pounded, the history of these islands would be changed for ever, new channels and shapes scoured and moulded in the clay of British history.

The island that the crew of those three ships blundered into in the reign of King Beorhtric was still far from settling into its famil-iar modern grooves. Scotland, Wales and England did not exist, and the shifting patchwork of petty kingdoms that made up the political geography of Britain was fractured along cultural, linguistic, reli-gious, geographical and historical lines. Major fault-lines divided those parts of Britain that had once been exposed to intensive Roman colonization from those which had not, those which adhered to Roman and which to Irish forms of Christian liturgy, those who believed their ancestors were British from those who looked to a homeland in Ireland or across the North Sea. Landscape sundered highland zones from lowland zones; language divided speakers of Celtic languages from those who used a Germanic tongue; the sea brought an influx of foreign goods and ideas to some, while shutting others out.

The map of Britain at the end of the eighth century had developed slowly from conditions arising from the decline of the Roman Empire during the fourth century. In Britain, the removal of direct Roman administration and military defence around the year 400 coincided with changes to the cultural orientation of communities along Britain's eastern seaboard. Increasingly, their centre of gravity shifted from the Mediterranean world to the North Sea. Part of the reason for this was political and economic, but migration also played a major role. People from what is now northern Germany, southern Scandinavia and the Low Countries had been moving into eastern areas of Britain – particularly Kent, East Anglia and England north of the Humber – from at least the early fifth century. The numbers involved, and the nature of the migration, remains fiercely contested, but the impact was undeniable and dramatic.

By the early eighth century, the northern monk Bede was able to write with confidence about an 'English-speaking people' who were distinct from the native British. The key distinguishing characteristic of this group – as implied by Bede's phrase – was their tongue. These were people who spoke a different language from both Romano-British elites (for whom Latin was the ubiquitous written language) and the 'indigenous' Britons, who spoke varying forms of a Celtic language known as Common or Old Brittonic (or Brythonic). The newcomers, however, spoke a Germanic language known to modern scholars as 'Old English' (or, more rarely these days, as 'Anglo-Saxon') which was closely related to the languages spoken in the regions from which migrants across the North Sea had come.

While doubts hover over a great deal of Bede's narrative, and particularly his migration and conquest narratives (much of which is an elaboration of a vague, tendentious and ideologically motivated sermon written by the British monk Gildas in the sixth century),[10] the impact of the English language is not in doubt. Place-names and early vernacular written records attest that English became dominant and widespread at a remarkably early date. Moreover, these English-speakers (whatever their genetic ancestry) had, by Bede's day, become culturally and linguistically dominant in most of lowland Britain, forming a tapestry of greater and lesser kingdoms which had grown out of an inconsistent pattern of tribal groupings and late Roman administrative districts.

The most northerly of these English-speaking realms was Northumbria – literally the land north of the River Humber. By the late eighth century this kingdom covered a huge swathe of northern Britain, from the Humber to the Forth, cobbled together from a number of former British territories: Deira, Bernicia, Gododdin, Rheged and Elmet. For over a century, Northumbria had represented a high point of post-Roman achievement in scholarship and artistic culture, driven from major centres of learning such as Wearmouth-Jarrow (where Bede wrote, among much else, his *Ecclesiastical History of the English People*) and the island monastery of Lindisfarne. This extraordinary cultural flowering was also remarkable for its fusion of British, Irish, Anglo-Saxon and Mediterranean influences. The Lindisfarne Gospels – an illuminated manuscript of breathtaking beauty and craftsmanship – exemplifies the splendour, ingenuity and spontaneity of this northern renaissance, its famous 'carpet pages' weaving Celtic, Germanic and Coptic Christian themes into mind-bending symphonies of colour and cultural synthesis.

However, despite the cultural refinement and territorial muscle, Northumbria had been growing weaker throughout the eighth century, undermined by the incessant feuding of its aristocracy and the instability of its royal house. In 790, for example, around the time that the Northmen had arrived in Portland, King Osred II was deposed after only a year on the throne, forcibly tonsured and exiled from his kingdom. His replacement, Æthelred I, seems to have had powerful friends. It is likely that the coup was carried out with the support of Northumbria's large and belligerent southern neighbour: the kingdom of Mercia.

Covering most of the English midlands from approximately the modern Welsh border in the west to the borders of East Anglia in the east, and from the Thames valley in the south to the Humber and the Wirral in the north, Mercia dominated southern Britain and reached the apogee of its political dominance under King Offa (r. 757–96). In the last decade of the eighth century, Offa was at the height of his powers. From his power-base in the Staffordshire heartlands around Tamworth, Lichfield and Repton, the king exercised not only direct rule over Mercia, but political and military control over the neighbouring kingdoms of East Anglia, Essex, Kent, Sussex and Wessex. The greatest surviving monument of his reign is the massive defensive earthwork marking the western boundary of Mercia: Offa's Dyke. The scale of this engineering project is testament to the extent of the king's power and ambition, not to mention his ability to coerce his subjects into undertaking state-wide projects.[11] Offan statecraft was of the Corleone school of governance. When, for example, King Æthelberht of East Anglia attempted to assert a measure of independence (briefly minting his own coins), 'Offa ordered King Æthelberht's head to be struck off.' This sort of gangland authority was closely tied to the personal charisma of the king and, as it turned out, the Mercian supremacy unravelled shortly after Offa's death in 796.[12]

The decapitation of King Æthelberht wasn't enough to bring the kingdom of East Anglia to an end. Comprising at its core the ancient counties of Norfolk and Suffolk (the 'north folk' and the 'south folk' in Old English), the kingdom had, at the beginning of the seventh century, been an important power-broker. East Anglia had once boasted links to Scandinavia, the rest of continental Europe and beyond, and nothing better exemplifies the kingdom's cosmopolitan splendour than the great ship burial at Sutton Hoo near Woodbridge in Suffolk. The famous mustachioed helmet found at Sutton Hoo is the ubiquitous icon of the Anglo-Saxon age, an object which in its style, iconography and manufacture has its closest parallels among the grave goods buried with the military elite of southern Sweden. But the burial also contained – among other objects – silverware from the Byzantine Empire (the surviving eastern part of the Roman Empire, centred on Constantinople – modern Istanbul), coins from Merovingian Gaul (which comprised parts of France, Germany and the Low Countries) and weapons and jewellery embellished with garnets imported from India. Although East Anglia would never again achieve the influence it commanded in this glittering seventh-century heyday, it nevertheless maintained its independence long into the ninth century.[13]

The smaller kingdoms which had lain under Mercian domination during Offa's reign were, however, destined ultimately to becoming defunct as independent concerns. The royal dynasty of the East Saxons (with its core in Essex) and those of the South Saxons (Sussex) and Kent either disappeared or had been demoted to junior aristocratic rank by the early ninth century. The killer blow in each case was delivered not by Mercia but by another resurgent player in the English-speaking community: Wessex – the kingdom of the West Saxons.

Wessex had experienced a torrid eighth century. With its heartlands in Hampshire and Dorset, Wessex was an assertive force in southern Britain, extending north across Somerset, Wiltshire and Berkshire, and eating steadily westwards into Devon. During its heyday in the reign of King Ine (r. 688–726), West Saxon authority had also extended across Surrey and Sussex in the east. But more than sixty years of attritional warfare with the Mercians to the north had eroded its territories south of the Thames, created a militarized zone across the chalk uplands of Wiltshire and Berkshire and seen control of Sussex lost to Offa's Mercia. In 786, the pugnacious West Saxon ruler Cynewulf was killed in a power-struggle and the man who emerged as king, Beorhtric, was, it seems, Offa's man. The impression of Wessex in these years is of a beaten-down kingdom, exhausted by war and resigned to its subordinate status in Offa's new order. The man who would pick up the banner of West Saxon kingship from Beorhtric, however, was of a markedly different stamp. King Ecgberht (r. 802–39) would take the West Saxon kingdom to the peak of its power and prestige, overwhelming its smaller neighbours, restoring the pride and reputation of its royal house, and ultimately providing the self-confidence that future kings would need in the dark days that lay ahead. But all this was in the future. When the Northmen arrived on Portland, Wessex yet remained a weakened client state of the Mercian supremacy.

Although English kingdoms had been, and continued to be, dominant in lowland Britain, they were never the whole story, and in parts of Britain – notably the highlands and islands of what is now Scotland, Cumbria and the valley of the Clyde, the lands west of Offa's Dyke and the Cornish peninsula – a number of kingdoms of mixed provenance maintained distinct identities, languages, religious practices and cultural norms. Cornwall, beyond the south-western marches of Wessex, had been only lightly touched by direct Roman rule. At the western end of the kingdom of Dumnonia (Devon and Cornwall), the region had developed a distinctive culture that blended British and Irish influences and maintained maritime links with both Brittany and the Byzantine Empire. While Devon, the eastern part of Dumnonia, became subsumed by Wessex over the course of the eighth century – becoming thoroughly Anglicized in the process – Cornwall, for the time being, retained its independence.

Further north, the kingdoms of what is now Wales present an altogether more complex picture, and posed a greater challenge for their Mercian neighbours to the east. The scale of the threat is represented by the magnitude of the effort made by Offa, and perhaps his predecessors, to contain it (through the construction of the dyke), and a range of sources make clear that border raids into Mercian territory (and vice versa) were endemic.[14] The Celtic-speaking people of what is now Wales were no more unified, however, than their Anglophone rivals. The four main kingdoms, as established by at least 850, were Gwynedd (in the north and north-west), Dyfed (in the south-west), Gwent (in the south-east) and Powys (in the eastern and central regions). All of these, in one way or another, were based on the former Roman *civitates* of western Britain, themselves based on old Iron Age tribal groupings.[15] This, it must be admitted, is to simplify a complex and volatile pattern of tribal confederations, but it is evident that ruling Welsh elites clung to an idea of *Romanitas* even as it drifted ever further into the past. Latin and bilingual inscriptions on standing stones (stones deliberately erected as upright monuments) throughout Wales (and elsewhere in former Roman Britain) reveal a self-consciously Latinate identity that lasted into the ninth century and beyond. The bitter irony was that it was the heathen interlopers – the Anglo-Saxons – who, having adopted an explicitly Roman model of Christianity, would ultimately align themselves with the new mainstream culture of 'Latin' Europe; the British, despite having kept alive a vibrant, if idiosyncratic, Christian faith alongside the memory of their imperial heritage, were increasingly cast as the barbarians in this changing European landscape.[16]

The British kingdoms of Wales and Cornwall were by no means the only representatives of Brittonic-speaking culture to survive the Anglo-Saxon cultural takeover. Though some (such as Rheged, Gododdin and Elmet) had perished in the expansion of Northumbria, the British kingdom of Alt Clud ('the rock of the Clyde') still held out in the region bordering the Clyde. A shadowy kingdom of obscure origin, Alt Clud had its fortress capital at Dumbarton Rock. The kingdom had spent most of the eighth century fending off the unwelcome advances of its neighbours, and in 780 was burned (by whom, or why, is not known). One of the possible culprits was Alt Clud's neighbour to the north-east, the substantial and periodically powerful kingdom of the Picts (sometimes referred to as 'Pictavia'), a realm that had its heartland in northern and eastern Scotland, and which seems to have held sway (at least culturally) over the Orkney and Shetland islands. The most visible and dramatic monuments to Pictish culture are the symbol stones – slabs carved with images of beasts and enigmatic symbols that are most often interpreted as representations of the names of kings and aristocrats. By the eighth century, many of these objects displayed ostentatiously Christian iconography, and it is clear that Christianity had by that time become associated with expressions of power and status: a monastery at Portmahomack, on the Tarbat peninsula in Easter Ross, had been established as early as the sixth century, possibly with royal patronage.[17]

Pictish power was by no means unchallenged in northern Britain. The kingdom's main rivals were Northumbria, whose borders extended to the Forth, and whose armies it had repeatedly beaten back during the earlier part of the century, and the kingdom of Dál Riata, a Gaelic-speaking polity spanning the Irish Sea to include Argyll, Lochaber and the north-eastern part of Ulster. Dál Riata had its power-base at Dunadd near Kilmartin, an imposing hill-fort where its kings were believed to have been inaugurated – the impression of a foot, worn into the living rock, may have played a key role in the rituals that were enacted there. By the end of the eighth century, however, Dál Riata was coming under Pictish domination. In 736 Dunadd had been captured by the Pictish king Oengus (he underscored his dominance by dragging the sons of the Dál Riatan king back to Pictavia in chains), and by 811 Dál Riata was being ruled directly by the Pictish king Constantine (r. 789–820). By then, however, a new power was rising, and the Viking impact in northern Britain would have profound consequences for all of its regional players.

There is more that might be said. Ireland, the Isle of Man and the Irish monastic colonies of the Western Isles – Iona chief among them – are all stitched tightly into the events that followed the advent of the Northmen. Nor can the story of the Vikings in Britain be told without some reference to events in continental Europe. Nevertheless, the foregoing paragraphs sketch – in broad outline – the most important contours of British political geography at the time that three strange ships pitched up on the beach at Portland. Though nobody could have known it then, the death of Beaduheard marked the beginning of a series of cataclysmic upheavals that changed Britain for ever. Many of the places mentioned above will be revisited in the chapters that follow; many of the kingdoms will fall.

But before that story can be told, we must return to that beach in Portland, the dark sails receding into the distance. We watch them go, and the coastguard's questions replay in our minds, too late now for any hope of an answer: 'Outsiders from across the water […] the sooner you tell where you come from and why, the better.'[18]

There is no written source that tells these events in the words of the Vikings themselves. For the most part, the people of Scandinavia did not record their history in written form until long after the Viking Age is usually considered to have closed. The sagas and histories, produced in Norway and especially in Iceland, are products of the late twelfth century and later – sometimes much later. To say that the Vikings were illiterate is strictly false, however. As will be seen, they made use of their own runic script for inscriptions marking ownership or memorializing the dead. Moreover, poems composed during the Viking Age survived orally to be written down in later centuries. Nevertheless, very little of the Viking voice survives, and certainly nothing that will explain the identities, motivations and origins of those first violent pioneers. In the face of this Scandinavian silence we must turn and consider who the people of early medieval Britain thought these strangers were, where they had come from and what had driven them on to British shores.

The written sources for the Viking Age in Britain are not a straightforward guide to contemporary events. These were documents written for specific purposes, in different times and in different places, each one reflecting the views of the people who compiled or commissioned them. As such, they are partial and biased, limited by the range of knowledge which their authors possessed, though not by their imaginations. By far the most important sources for this period are the various manuscripts of the *Anglo-Saxon Chronicle*. The first, and oldest, of these manuscripts is normally referred to as the A text or, sometimes, as the 'Winchester Chronicle'. It was put together in the late ninth century – probably in the 890s

– as part of the intellectual scene that surrounded the court of King Alfred in Wessex. All later historians and chroniclers of the Middle Ages, including the other texts of the *Anglo-Saxon Chronicle*, rely on the A text to some degree.

The earliest record of the Viking arrival on Portland is found in the A text, and was therefore written down a century later than the events it describes. Although this *Chronicle* almost certainly contains real traditions and material from older sources, none of these survive for us to make a comparison. The suspicion therefore remains that the view of history which the *Chronicle* presents is coloured by a bleak century of Scandinavian plunder, conquest and colonization. In particular, one might justly raise an eyebrow at the chronicler's assertion that these 'were the first ships of Danish men which came to the land of the English [*Angelcynnes lond*]': quite apart from the vexed question of what exactly the chronicler meant by '*Angelcynnes lond*', one might well question how, 100 years later and from the perspective of Britain's most southerly realm, such knowledge could possibly have been possessed.[19]

The A text tells us, in no uncertain terms, that the newcomers were 'Danish' (*denisc*). While this might seem, on the face of things, to be a useful statement of origins, it is not at all certain whether that which seemed 'danish' to Anglo-Saxon eyes would necessarily appear 'Danish' to our own. As will be seen, the term *denisc* (along with other generic terms used throughout Britain) in fact came to be applied indiscriminately to people and things held to have emanated from the North. Far more promising is the statement that the newcomers were 'Northmen' (Norðmanna) from Hordaland (Hereðalande), now a county of western Norway centred on Bergen. Alas, this is surprisingly (and suspiciously) specific. The earliest record of this notice is found, not in the A text, but in the so-called 'northern recension' of the *Anglo-Saxon Chronicle*, and can be dated no earlier than the mid-eleventh century – at least 250 years after the incident at Portland. This reference may shed more light on the origin of eleventh-century Scandinavian settlers in Northumbria than it does on events in late eighth-century Wessex.[20]

In other words, the sources – so promising at first reading – really only tell us that the newcomers were foreigners, probably from somewhere across the North Sea. It is certain, however, that the people of Britain thought *something* when they encountered strangers on their beaches and imagined the worlds from which they had come. Understanding what that something might have been – what it meant – is bound up with how the people of early medieval Britain understood their own world, and their place within it.

# 2

# HEART OF DARKNESS

Then the Lord said unto me, Out of the north an evil shall break
forth upon all the inhabitants of the land.

JEREMIAH 1:15[1]

northwards lies the road to hell

SNORRI STURLUSON, *Gylfaginning* (early thirteenth century)[2]

*Ærest of swin forda upp andlang broces to ceolnes wyllan …*

('Go first up from the swine ford and along the brook to *ceolnes*
[Ceolwine's?] well')[3]

At the river's edge you pass a churl driving his pigs across the muddy
ford, hairy oinkers on their way to the wood pasture, eager to rootle
among *wyrttruma* ('woody roots') for acorns and beech mast; the
animal scent of sweat and pig shit, crumbly clods of dried mud
dropping from bristly bottoms. It is damp down here, soggy. Water
seeps into your shoes (stitched leather – hardly watertight) as you
turn to the north, away from the ford. Perhaps you slip a little on the
muddy path that runs beside the brook and stub a toe on a stone

– the dull throbbing adding injury to numbness in your cold feet; at least there are no midges (*mycgas*) at this time of year. You pause and place a bright glass bead on the flat mossy stone beside the spring where the brook wells up – you have heard from the monks how, long ago, a pilgrim called Ceolwine struck his ash staff on the stone and a rush of cold water sprang up to slake his thirst: a miracle they said. But an old man in the village told you this was rubbish: his grandfather had been a boy when the old gods still lived here and the folk made sacrifice, mounting the heads on ash poles and throwing the bones into the water; now their corpses haunt the marshy edgelands: 'you can hear them coming when the light fails boy: drip … drip … drip …'

Probably best to leave a gift either way.

*andlang hege ræwe to luttes crundele · þanon to grafes owisce ·*
*Andlang owisce to wege …*

('along the hedgerow to luttes [Lutt's?] pit and then on to the eaves of the grove; along the eaves to the road')

Reaching the hedgerow is a welcome relief: the land slopes slightly away from the brook here, the earth becomes firmer. As you walk alongside the broad band of bramble and blackthorn, you can hear the rustling of foraging birds: a blackbird (*ōsle*) probably, or a finch (*finc*). A streak of brown – a mouse (*mūs*), or a shrew (*screāwa*) perhaps – shoots across the path ahead and disappears rustling into the undergrowth: all are hunting for the last berries of autumn.[4] It is November (*Blōt-mōnaþ*: 'the month of sacrifice'), and the scent of damp earth mingles with the vinegar notes of rotten apples. You hurry past Lutt's pit – part stone quarry, part sepulchre (the word, *crundel*, is ambiguous): you have heard stories about this place too, but you would rather not dwell on them now, not until you are clear of the dark overhanging woods. You know you're being a baby – this is managed woodland after all – but you're glad when you reach the road all the same.

*… Andlang weges to æles beorge · nyþer on aler cumb · Andlang aler cumbes ut on afene · Andlang afene eft on swin ford.*

('along the road to æles [Ælle's?] barrow and down to alder-tree valley; along alder-tree valley and out to the Avon; along the Avon to the swine ford.')

From here it is an easier stroll on the compacted earth, compressed by the tread of generations of men and beasts. You need to watch where you're going, mind – sometimes dips in the path have allowed the rain water to gather. Here the plunge of heavy hoofs, and the ruts riven by the ox-wains, have churned the path into patches of slimy mud – you dance your way with giant steps, and try to keep to the green stripe that marks the middle of the track. When you eventually look up, you give an involuntary start: massing against the westering sky, the dark bulk of Ælle's barrow looms. The atmosphere thickens. This is a place of power; everyone knows it … even the monks, though they pretend it's all just superstition: heathen folly, you've heard them call it, although not in front of the reeve – he'll tell anyone who listens that his ancestor is buried under that mound, sleeping until the day his people call upon his aid in battle. It's not so different, now you think of it, to the stories the monks tell: of long-dead saints who return to help the living … Lost in thought you stroll through the alder trees and back down the valley, arriving at the river as the light begins to fail.

Standing on the banks you watch the ghost-white spectre of a swan glide past, the curve of its neck rising from its breast as the prow of a ship rises from its keel, carving the placid water, silent in its grace.

The fragments of Old English, translated above, are from what is known as a boundary clause, a description of the edges of a parcel of land. This one describes an area at North Stoke in Somerset. It was written down and added to a charter documenting a grant of land made by the West Saxon king Cynewulf (r. 757–86), Beorhtric's predecessor. Like many such clauses, it is written in English – the common tongue – but it is inserted into a document otherwise drafted in Latin, the officialese of ecclesiastical administrators. The implication is clear enough: while Latin was appropriate for the legal formulae of witness lists and the stern religious injunctions against violating the terms of the charter, the description of the land came straight from lived experience – from the mnemonic commitment of landscape to oral narrative.

A boundary clause circumscribes a place known at an intimately local level, swaddling a parcel of land with animals, plants and the bumps and wrinkles of the soil. In some cases these bounds can still be followed in the perimeters of modern parishes, and the 'beating of the bounds' – a communal ritual of remembering in which the bounds are not only walked, but the landmarks physically struck by the participants – has in some places endured to the present day. These texts provide more than a simple insight into local administrative geography, however. They show us a way of understanding the world, not with the false objectivity of the map-reader looking down from above, but as an actor and participant within it. Names and monuments emerge by the wayside: no one knows any more who this Ceolwine was or what he meant to the stream that bore his name; none can say what crawling things or shadow walkers (*sceadugangan*) might have emerged from Lutt's pit or Ælle's barrow in dark Anglo-Saxon dreams. What is beyond doubt is that places like these, all over England, were the punctuation points in the stories that rural communities told about their world: more than how to get from A to B (or, in the case of boundary clauses, how to get from A back to A), these were the tapestries of lived existence that were woven both in words and in the physical actions of human beings moving and interacting with the world around them.[5]

In a modern context, geographical knowledge tends to be represented in forms which are relatively static. We think of masses of land and water viewed from space, the contours of mountains, the reflective spatter of lakes, the ragged torn coastline of Norway – remembered by Slartibartfast in the *Hitchhiker's Guide to the Galaxy* for its 'lovely crinkly edges'.[6] We also think of neatly inked political boundaries, the nation states limned in pink and powder blue, or of roads and railways scored decisively across the page. These types of knowledge are essentially cartographical, known to us through abstracted, two-dimensional images. Whether carried in the imagination, drawn by hand or photographed from space, the map is the dominant means by which we understand our relationship to the physical world. And yet, in myriad ways, it is fundamentally flawed – made all the more misleading by the sense of omniscience it instils: maps, we feel, make gods of us. It takes only a little scratching to find the bloodstains under the cartographer's pastel palette. Enduring fault-lines of religion, language and politics are obscured; ancient pathways fade from view. Distances are rendered down to straight lines through empty space, continents grotesquely contorted through the amputation of their third dimension. The senses are cauterized: map-world is a place for the eyes alone. That we instinctively feel this sensory loss can be judged by the compulsive desire to run frustrated fingertips over the smooth surfaces of maps and globes, subconsciously seeking the missing textures of the earth.[7]

How inadequate – how *anaemic* – this would have seemed to Beaduheard's contemporaries, steeped in a geography that was personal, local, storied. For early medieval Britons, geographical knowledge was more than just a series of routes and landmarks; it was a series of signs and symbols that plumbed time, mythology and identity – moving through ancient landscapes could mean travelling backwards in time, while ancestral mythologies transported people to far-off realms.

Maps were not unknown, but their circulation was restricted to a handful of learned men and fulfilled very different purposes from their modern counterparts. A common form was the T-O map – a schematic diagram, or 'ideogram', that divided the world into three unequal segments: Asia (the top half of the circle), Africa (the bottom right quarter) and Europe (the bottom left). Jerusalem lay at the centre. The image was in part a means of concentrating the mind on the totality of God's creation, its symmetry and its unity. By superimposing the letters T and O on to its form, it also incorporated the initials of the words *terra orbis* (orb of the world; the globe) into the design. Needless to say, it was of limited utility to the disorientated traveller. Like boundary clauses, early maps and the base of knowledge from which they were derived were essentially concerned with circumscription – the gathering of what was known into (usually circular) plans, forming an 'inside' and an 'out there'. In the Greek and Roman worlds this had symbolized the distinction between civilization and *barbaricum*; in the Christian epoch 'inside' indicated, if not exactly Christendom, then the totality of that portion of the earth which lay within the orbit of potential salvation. Later medieval maps – such as the Hereford Mappa Mundi – depict Christ standing behind the world, literally embracing creation.[8]

That which lay beyond these borders was, in this conception, more dreadful than mere *terra incognita*. It was the abyss – the world beyond God.

A sense of how fearsome this outer world could seem is evident in Old English poetry and the cosmology it reflects: the Old English poetic retelling of Genesis, for example, paints the earth as a golden hall surrounded by a sea of darkness – the void a place of mist and sorrow beyond the light of God.[9] Other poems refine this image: the cold seas of *The Wanderer* and *The Seafarer* reflect both physical and spiritual desolation. It is *Beowulf*, however, that really drives this fear home:

> Grendel was the grim ghoul named,
> Famous edge-marcher, who held the moors
> The fen and fastness …[10]

The first part of *Beowulf* tells the story of how the eponymous hero came to Denmark from his home in the land of the Geats, drawn by tales of a monster – named Grendel – who for many years had menaced the hall – Heorot – of the Danish king Hrothgar. Beowulf defeats the monster, tearing off his arm and sending him fleeing back to die in his fenland home. But the real power and tension in this part of the poem follows the monster. Grendel is the border-walker, the dweller in shadow, the descendant of Cain and an avatar of jealous alienation. He is of the world 'outside' – *fifelcynnes eard*, literally 'monster-world' – and it is with horrible fascination that the poet follows him 'down over mist-slopes', creeping through the darkness, coming with the fog, greedy hands pushing at the hall door.[11]

'Heorot' literally means 'hart' (a male deer), but the word is derived from the same root as the Old English *heorte*, a word which means 'heart' in all its literal and figurative senses; and in *Beowulf* the hall is, indeed, the beating heart of human culture – a symbol of warmth and light, safety and security, community and the affirmation of bonds: it is fortress, pub and family home wrapped into one. The violation of that safety and sanctity is what gives the poem a psychological edge that cuts easily across the centuries – Grendel is the home-invader, the wolf in the fold, striking deep at the vitals of society.

In fact, Grendel and his kin are described in explicitly lupine terms by the *Beowulf* poet, a distinction they share with other malefactors of the Anglo-Saxon world. The term *wearg* (the origin of Tolkien's 'warg') meant both 'wolf' and 'criminal', and the label *wulvesheofod* ('wolf's head') was, by the eleventh century, used to define outlaw status. The Vikings who appear in the poetic account of the battle of Maldon in 991 are 'slaughter-wolves' (*waelwulfas*). These groups – monsters, criminals, outlaws, Vikings – posed threats to the ordered world represented by the hall: they were the wolves beyond the border, the slaughterers, raveners, stealers of property, of livestock, of children. In a world where terrors could be made horribly and suddenly real, it is small wonder that Ine's laws should have been so unforgiving to the outlander.[12]

Of all the compass points from which terror might emanate, there was one which held the greatest dread. This was not just because the sea had repeatedly disgorged boatloads of child-snatchers and hall-burners from precisely this direction, nor indeed because empirical observation demonstrated that this was the horizon over which the most wretched weather tended to hurtle, but because the Anglo-Saxons already knew full well that it was here that Satan had set his throne.

This was the medieval world's heart of darkness: the North.

Behind are the familiar paths and places of home, the songs in the hall, the fire, the harp. Out here there is only the dark, only the cold, only the biting north wind that screams over the barren hillsides. Rocky paths lie ahead, thin winding ways where death leers blackly from the fells below. A mist closes in, a wolf howls ... Down through the mist-bands, a glimmer of light flickers – ghostly, ethereal, unnatural: a sheen of dark water, witch-fires burning on its surface. Beyond the water a bleak forest looms, glowering from gloomy cliffs. Branches encrusted with rime and hoarfrost drag skeletal fingers through the frigid air; roots like serpents quest over slimy banks towards the rotting stagnant tarn. In the reeking water nameless things writhe and wriggle. Monsters dwell here – among the 'wolf-slopes, windy headlands, dangerous fen-tracts'.[13] To go further would be to risk soul and sanity: here the laws of nature are perverted and upended – the burning black water rushes upwards towards the heavens and gouts of ice and flame entwine. From the sky comes a deadly hail, lashing from the roiling clouds, and amid the black mist comes the beating of wings in the darkness, like clouds of leathery moths searching for prey to pluck into the storm-wracked heavens. Further northwards, and deeper down, lies the abyss itself: sometimes a foul cavern beneath the waves, infested with serpents and other filthy wriggling things, sometimes a grim bastion wreathed in smoke and fume, 'evil spirits running about amid the black caverns and gloomy abysses'.[14]

Other than the T-O ideograms, very few maps date to the eighth century or earlier, and the northern world is all but absent from them. It seems that, at the beginning of the Viking Age, what learned British monks knew of classical scholarship implied that Britain was, itself, at the ends of the earth: about lands further north, classical and Christian learning was vague, and it is uncertain how much of this knowledge was even accessible to British monks. The image they would have had was one of vaguely drawn islands floating in sluggish seas: of the isle of Thule and the land of the Hyperboreans (the dwellers 'beyond the north wind'), of men with bestial bodies and others with the heads of dogs – a dwelling place of monsters.[15] In this, it was not unlike any of the unknown regions of the earth, but the theme of the North as a specifically satanic realm also manifested itself in the literature of medieval Britain. Often this can be found in ways clearly derived from biblical narratives, but at others it appeared in vivid and idiosyncratic form.

In the tale of St Guthlac, written at the monastery of Crowland in Lincolnshire in the 730s by a monk called Felix, the treatment meted out by a demonic horde to the unfortunate anchorite is described in vivid terms. After a relentless campaign of physical and psychological punishment,

> they began to drag him through the cloudy stretches of the freezing skies to the sound of the horrid beating of their wings. Now when he had reached the lofty summit of the sky, then, horrible to relate, lo! the region of the northern heavens seemed to grow dark with gloomy mists and black clouds. For there could be seen coming thence to meet them, innumerable squadrons of foul spirits. Thus with all their forces joined in one, they turned their way with immense uproar into thin air, and carried the afore-named servant of Christ, Guthlac, to the accursed jaws of hell.[16]

Nor is this the only northern tradition to riff on the biblical theme of the diabolical North. The vision of St Paul, as told in late Anglo-Saxon England, recounts that 'St Paul was looking at the northern part of this world, where all the waters go down, and he saw there above the water a certain grey rock, and there had grown north of that rock very frosty woods, and there were dark mists, and under that rock was a dwelling place of water-monsters and wolves; and he saw that on that cliff there hung in those icy woods many black souls, tied by their hands, and their foes, in the guise of water-monsters, were gripping them like greedy wolves, and the water was black ...'[17]

That these ideas had deep roots in the northern psyche is implied by striking similarities between this description of the monster-haunted North and the *Beowulf* poet's description of the home of Grendel and his mother. The two descriptions are almost certainly related.

Though no comparable tales survive from the Celtic-speaking areas of Britain, the Irish life of St Brendan – written in the seventh century – describes boiling northern seas and an island of flame and tormented howling: 'the confines of Hell' as the saint puts it.[18] Even the people of Scandinavia themselves knew that *niðr ok norðr liggr Helvegr* ('netherwards and northwards lies the road to hell').[19] The word 'hell' itself has no Latin-Christian origin. It is older than that, reflecting fragments of a shared vision that haunted the darker dreams of the Anglo-Saxons and their contemporaries: a nightmare North of the early medieval imagination.

The human inhabitants of this world, if known at all, would have been distinguished for their heathenism – their rejection of Christian norms and values, their bloodletting and their weird rites. It would have been natural to imagine them, to use the historian Eric Christiansen's memorable phrase, as 'robot agents of Satan's foreign policy', flesh and blood avatars of the monster-world beyond the pale.[20]

When the men of the North next appeared in the written record, in all their dreadful pomp and fury, they more than lived up to the fevered imaginings of their victims. In 793, the North disgorged its innards in lurid tones, and chroniclers responded with imagery that came easily:

> In this year dire fore-bodings came over Northumbria and miserably terrified the people: there were immense whirlwinds and flashes of lightning, and fiery dragons were seen flying aloft. Those signs were soon followed by a great hunger, and a little after that in the same year, on 8 June, the harrying of heathen men wretchedly destroyed God's church on Lindisfarne, with plunder and slaughter.[21]

Of all the religious centres of northern Europe, there were few that could rival the cultural muscle of the island priory of Lindisfarne. Its peripheral location, tied to the Northumbrian coast by the narrow umbilical cord of its tidal causeway, belied the wealth and status that it had accrued since its foundation in the early seventh century. Much of this flowed from the stories told of its most famous bishop, Cuthbert (c. 634–87). Cuthbert – a monk originally from Melrose who had later been appointed prior of the community at Lindisfarne – was elevated to bishop in March 685. For perhaps as long as nine years, Cuthbert lived in self-imposed exile from Lindisfarne as a hermit on Inner Farne, a wildly bleak outcrop of grey granite stacks, jutting gloomily from the sea.[22] It was a life of hardship, solitude and self-denial modelled on the penitential attitudes of the desert fathers – St Anthony in particular. His elevation to bishop did little to change his temperament – by 687 he had returned to his hermitage, determined to live out his last in solitude.

On Inner Farne, Cuthbert – like St Anthony – encountered devils in the wilderness. The accounts of his struggles are brief – he fought them with 'the helmet of salvation, the shield of faith and the sword of spirit which is the word of God' – and the vanquished demons are left to the imagination.[23] But it is perhaps justifiable to imagine them in the same way that Felix depicted the diabolical horde that appeared in his life of St Guthlac:

they were ferocious in appearance, terrible in shape with great heads, long necks, thin faces, yellow complexions, filthy beards, shaggy ears, wild foreheads, fierce eyes, foul mouths, horses' teeth, throats vomiting flames, twisted jaws, thick lips, strident voices, singed hair, fat cheeks, pigeon breasts, scabby thighs, knotty knees, crooked legs, swollen ankles, splay feet, spreading mouths, raucous cries […] they grew so terrible to hear with their mighty shriekings that they filled almost the whole intervening space between earth and heaven with their discordant bellowings.[24]

The effect is cumulative. What starts out as absurd – comical even (shaggy ears? wild foreheads?) – becomes ever more grotesque and horrible, one perversion heaped on top of another, until the vision devolves into a squamous mass of deformed, unnatural depravity. If this is what early medieval people saw when they dreamt of wild places, then their dreams must have been dark indeed.

Whatever Cuthbert saw or did not see on Inner Farne, he conquered his little wilderness, living out the brief remainder of his life in self-imposed exile: eating, sleeping, fasting, praying. It is easy to picture him, like the figure in Caspar David Friedrich's famous painting, gazing sadly at the cold grey ocean that embraces him: a last outpost of human life, wearily defiant before the uncaring gulf and his own mortality.

When he died, Cuthbert's body was taken by boat to Lindisfarne. A great crowd received it, psalms were sung, and it was carried to the Church of St Peter and buried in a stone coffin beside the altar. Miracles were reported and he was canonized, his tomb becoming a place of pilgrimage. When, eleven years later, his resting place was deemed inadequate, he was exhumed for translation to a more exalted shrine. His body was apparently found uncorrupted, as pristine as the day he had passed away. The story only confirmed his sanctity and his legend spread, the monastery growing in size and wealth, its scriptoria producing illuminated gospels which – like the Lindisfarne Gospels (commissioned to ornament

Cuthbert's shrine-tomb) – are some of the greatest treasures of their age.

We might be justified in imagining that, for later generations of monks, the monastic life became rather more comfortable than Cuthbert and his forebears would have approved of. By the time of the raid on Lindisfarne, contemporaries – as we shall see – had already begun to voice their opinion on these matters, and it is likely that there really was a drop in standards in the century after Cuthbert's death; or, rather, that the monks gained access to temptations that their forebears had not enjoyed. Even so, the same cold sea would have lapped at their heels and the stories of the devils of Inner Farne would have been told again and again. For the monks living out their lives on the edge of the world, the sea would have been omnipresent – a wide and brooding, raging wilderness stretching out to eternity. Empty, but alive.

When the Vikings came it must have seemed to the monks as though something dreadful had finally stirred from its century-long slumber. What horrors did their bleary eyes see rushing up the moonlit shore, what gargoyles leered from the prows of the great black leviathans looming at the edge of the shadowed water? Did they see devils in the shadows – lit red in the glare of blazing torches? Were they 'ferocious in appearance' and 'terrible to hear with their mighty shriekings'? Did they possess 'filthy beards' and 'fierce eyes', 'foul mouths' and 'strident voices'?

Against the blood-red glare cast by fire, the dragon-headed prows of the ships stand in silhouette, grim spectators of the unfolding chaos. Like oars striking water, the axes rise and fall, biting into timber, bone and flesh; blood splatters across blankets and altar-cloths, burgundy smears in firelight. Brightly coloured shards of ruined gospels flutter among glowing embers, like butterflies and fireflies dancing together in the thermal draughts. A sea-cold breeze whips off the water, lifting the iron tang of blood and metal with the brine, the stink of death and burning carried deep into the land.

The attack on Lindisfarne in 793 has become the iconic moment that defines the engagement of Britain's inhabitants with their neighbours across the North Sea. A sudden seaborne assault on a renowned centre of Christian learning, it was an event that sent shockwaves through Europe. From the court of Charlemagne across the Channel, the English cleric Alcuin wrote a series of letters to his brethren in England in response to this unprecedented tragedy. To him, a terror from the North should have been foreseen, particularly in the light of 'the bloody rain, which [...] we saw fall menacingly on the north side' of St Peter's Church in York 'though the sky was serene'. Therefore one should not be surprised, he adds, 'that from the north there will come upon our nation retribution in blood, which can be seen to have started with this attack'.[25]

A sense of the psychological impact these raids had in the communities they visited can be found in one of the more unsettling objects to have survived them. A carved stone – cracked at its base, rounded at its top – was discovered on Lindisfarne and first mentioned in the 1920s. It numbers among more than fifty tombstones – many of them decorated with Anglo-Saxon carvings and inscribed with names – that have been unearthed on the island. This one, however, is unique. On one side, figures are depicted gesturing towards the sun and moon which ride the sky together on either side of an empty cross. It is an image evoking the passage of time, the transition of day into night, mediated by the risen Christ – a reminder of the judgement to come when night finally falls over the earth.

On the other side of the stone are depicted seven men, all facing forward, their arms raised. Weapons are held aloft by five of them

– three swords and two axes – and their clothing is distinctive. If the stone is taken as a whole, it seems to be a representation of the apocalypse, the armed men perhaps a representation of the wrath of God in corporeal form – a form that English monks would recognize. As we shall see, ecclesiastical commentators found it easy enough to imagine the Vikings as an instrument of divine justice. The stone was probably carved in the late ninth century, and there is no way of knowing whether these armed men are intended to depict Vikings rather than any other armed group, but it is hard to dispel the feeling that the trauma inflicted in Lindisfarne left psychological scars that would trouble the imaginations of generations of monks, colouring their apocalyptic visions.[26]

Lindisfarne was the first raid of this type to be recorded, but it was by no means the last. The years around the turn of the ninth century saw waterborne raiders attacking and pillaging poorly defended monasteries and settlements all around northern Britain and Ireland, as well as elsewhere in continental Europe, and for those on the receiving end it must have been a dreadful experience – made all the more terrifying by the primal horror that a heathen assault inspired.

Alcuin's words, very often ripped from their context, are found at the beginning of many treatments of the Viking Age: 'the pagans have desecrated God's sanctuary,' he lamented in his letter to Bishop Higbald of Lindisfarne, 'shed the blood of saints around the altar, laid waste the house of our hope and trampled the bodies of the saints like dung in the street'. One has to wonder whether Higbald and the monks needed reminding. Indeed, one could easily forgive the torrent of Anglo-Saxon invective that we might imagine issuing from the good bishop's lips upon reading the rest of Alcuin's letter, for it is not – as one might think appropriate – a warm-hearted missive expressing sorrow, solidarity and offers of practical assistance. It is, instead, a lecture on the assumed defects of Higbald's authority and the sub-par behaviour of his monks: they are accused of having asked for it through their drunkenness, vanity, lewdness, degeneracy and – most unfairly of all – lack of manliness ('you who survive, stand like men').[27]

In a similar letter to King Ethelred of Northumbria, Alcuin wrote the words which have led many to imagine the heathen storm breaking on the shores of Britain like lightning from a clear sky:

> Lo, it is nearly 350 years that we and our fathers have inhabited
> this most lovely land, and never before has such terror appeared
> in Britain as we have now suffered from a pagan race, nor was it
> thought that such an inroad from the sea could be made.
> Behold, the church of St. Cuthbert spattered with the blood of
> the priests of God, despoiled of all its ornaments …[28]

Once again the expat cleric used the opportunity to castigate the monks, this time for wishing to 'resemble the pagans' in their 'trimming of beard and hair'. With this stern intervention into the hairdressing habits of his former colleagues, however, Alcuin inadvertently alerts us to something potentially more significant than Northumbrian fashion trends, something which challenges and complicates the image of the North as a hellish realm and its peoples as the devil's imps.

While learned attitudes to the North seem certainly to have emphasized the diabolic qualities of its inhabitants, comments such as Alcuin's imply a measure of contact and even, in some cases, admiration or nostalgia for the Scandinavian world and its denizens: a contradiction at the heart of Anglo-Saxon ideas about the wider northern world. On a simplistic level, in order to copy heathen haircuts, the monks must have been exposed to and favourably impressed by them – and presumably not when ducking a swinging axe. It seems highly probable, if not yet provable, that Scandinavian traders had become a feature at some of the new trading settlements of eighth-century England (as well as, perhaps, in the Northern Isles and Pictish Scotland as well).[29]

It is certainly the case that the Viking Age emerged against a background of increasingly sophisticated European trade. A new type of specialized trading settlement had grown up around the North Sea during the eighth century, exploiting and facilitating long-distance trade. These settlements – known to historians and archaeologists as 'emporia' – included Southampton (Hamwic), London (Lundenwic), Ipswich (Gipeswic) and York (Eoforwic) in England, as well as trading settlements at Quentovic (France), Dorestad (Netherlands), Hedeby and Ribe (Denmark), Birka (Sweden) and Kaupang (Norway) among others. It seems inconceivable that every exchange of goods between Britain and Scandinavia in the eighth century was conducted through continental middlemen.

Whatever the realities of direct trading relationships in the decades leading up to the earliest Viking raids, archaeology suggests that contacts across the North Sea in the preceding centuries had been close. A famous example (referred to in the preceding chapter) serves to illustrate the point. The great masked helmet (the Old English word, rather wonderfully, is *grimhelm*) that was excavated from the boat grave found beneath Mound 1 at Sutton Hoo in Suffolk finds its closest parallels in the highly elaborate boat graves from the cemeteries at Vendel and, later, Valsgärde in Sweden; the parallels, in both the style of artefacts and the manner of their burial, demonstrate elements of a cultural identity that spanned the North Sea. This, and a great deal of other evidence (not least the transformation of lowland Britain from a Romano-British-speaking population to one which used the western Germanic 'Old English' language), broadly supports the stories which the Anglo-Saxons told about their own origins.[30] On this point, the Northumbrian monk and scholar Bede – writing at Jarrow in the early eighth century – was quite explicit:

> In the year of our Lord 449 [...] the Angles or Saxons came to
> Britain at the invitation of King Vortigern in three long-ships
> [...] They [...] sent back news of their success to their
> homeland, adding that the country was fertile and the Britons

cowardly [...] These new-comers were from the three most
formidable races of Germany, the Saxons, Angles, and Jutes.[31]

The first group, the Saxons, came from a region identified by Bede
as 'Old Saxony' – now north-west Germany. The Angles and the
Jutes originated in the Jutland peninsula, occupying land which, by
the time Bede was writing, lay within the kingdom of the Danes.
Quite how true this story is remains unknowable (though it is
certain that significant migration from the continent did occur).
But what is critical is that the Anglo-Saxons themselves believed it
to be true.[32]

By Bede's day, the 'Anglo-Saxons' had been in Britain for the best
part of 300 years (by his reckoning), and had been Christian, in
most cases, for several generations. By the late eighth century, they
had formed a number of independent kingdoms, each with its own
cultural and geographical peculiarities. Nevertheless, the tribes
from whom they claimed descent were (and, in the late eighth
century, remained) pagan peoples, part of a wider northern
European heritage that had stood beyond the limits of Rome's
continental frontiers. As receivers of that heritage, the Anglo-
Saxons were torch-carriers for traditions, tales, words and images
from a legendary world. That world, though its shapes and contours
grew ever more indistinct, yet blazed brightly in the imaginations
of poets and storytellers. The earliest genealogical lists of Anglo-
Saxon royal houses typically extend via Woden, the pagan deity
equivalent to Odin (ON Oðinn) in Old Norse mythology, through
Finn (a legendary Frisian king) to Geat, the eponymous ancestor of
Beowulf's own Scandinavian tribe.

Even a century of Viking attacks failed to dampen enthusiasm
amongst the Anglo-Saxons for their northern heritage. By the end
of the ninth century, royal genealogies had expanded to include
Bældæg (the Old Norse god Balder), Scyld (the legendary progen-
itor of the Danes) and possibly Beowulf the Geat himself.[33]
Negotiating the evidence for the ways in which the Anglo-Saxons
identified with this heritage is complex and sometimes bewildering.

Much of what remains is reduced to the blank names of kings and heroes – names which must once have conjured great arcs of narrative, laced with the myths of the pre-Christian past, but whose owners now stand mute guard at the entrance to pathways which can never now be trod.

The perpetuation of this fascination with the ancestral North did not, however, go unchallenged. Writing in around the year 800, our friend Alcuin was so incensed by this sort of thing that, in a letter to another Anglo-Saxon bishop, he demanded to know 'what has Ingeld to do with Christ?' We know only a single anecdote about Ingeld, king of the Heathobards – a gloomy story about how he burned Hrothgar's hall, Heorot, and was thereafter a target of the Danish king's vengeance. The story is alluded to in *Beowulf* and mentioned in passing in another Old English poem, *Widsith*. Alcuin's reference to Ingeld pops up in a passage in which he lambasts his fellow ecclesiasts for listening to music and 'inappropriate' stories at dinner-time and for laughing in the courtyards (he presumably didn't get invited to many parties). It is of particular interest, however, because it suggests that even in what should have been a thoroughly Christian environment, the old stories were still popular – and this at a time when, in Alcuin's own words, the 'bodies of the saints were being trampled like dung' by the living descendants of Hrothgar and his kin.[34]

Rather less is known about attitudes to the ancestral North in other parts of Britain. One tradition, reported by Bede, held that the Picts – the people inhabiting the highland and island regions of what is now Scotland – had originated in 'Scythia'. This land had been believed by classical authorities to have existed in an ill-defined region somewhere, seemingly, in northern Eurasia. Whether the Picts themselves believed this to be true – and if they did, what they thought of it – is less than clear. The Welsh, on the other hand, had their own distinct boreal traditions: to them, Hen Ogledd ('the Old North') referred to those parts of Britain from which their ancestors had been ejected by Anglo-Saxon incomers in the sixth and seventh centuries. It was an altogether more insular sense of northernness, and can only have compounded the sense that northern lands beyond the sea were a place whence nothing much good ever came.[35]

Among the English-speaking peoples, however, we are left with an apparent paradox – a set of attitudes to the North that painted it as both shining ancestral homeland and infernal monster-infested wasteland, its inhabitants as both cousins and aliens. As a result, the Viking has emerged as a Janus-faced figure, constantly at war with himself in our imaginations: poet or plunderer, merchant or marauder, berserker or boat-builder, kinsman or kin-of-Cain. The reconciliation of these themes and the resolution of these identities is in large measure the story of Viking Britain. It is a process of negotiation that continues to this day, and begins with the fundamental question of who we understand the Vikings to be.

# 3

# MOTHER NORTH

Huge warriors with golden beards and savage eyes sat or lounged on
the rude benches, strode about the hall, or sprawled full length on the
floor. They drank mightily from foaming horns and leathern jacks,
and gorged themselves on great pieces of rye bread, and huge chunks
of meat they cut with their daggers from whole roasted joints [...]
All the world was their prey to pick and choose, to take and spare
as it pleased their barbaric fancies.

ROBERT E. HOWARD, 'The Dark Man' (1931)[1]

When I was growing up, my idea of what a 'Viking' should be
was not, I presume, very different from that imagined by
anyone else of my generation.

My grandmother – who lived in Glastonbury, Somerset – was a
full-time carer and companion to a (to my young eyes) elderly disa-
bled gentleman whom I knew only, and affectionately, as 'Venge'. An
Italian by birth, who in truth luxuriated in the name Bonaventura
Mandara, Venge was an exceptionally kind and gentle man, with a
love of brandy, cigars, cards and horse-racing: he was, in other words,
a jolly fine fellow. He would often encourage me, sprog that I was, to
clamber on to his bad leg (always propped up horizontally in front
of him, encased in a steel and leather contraption that both frightened and fascinated) and read me the cartoon strips from the back
of his newspaper. Only one of these left any kind of impression.

*Hägar the Horrible* – a comic strip drawn by the American cartoonist Dik Browne – was probably my first encounter with a Viking. The eponymous Hägar fulfilled all the stereotypes: an unruly faceful of red beard, an unashamedly horned helmet, a flagon of foaming ale, an aversion to bathing. In essence he remains the classic 'Viking as barbarian', essentially indistinguishable from the cartoon caveman. That was fine with me. Hägar and his frequent anachronistic assaults on large medieval stone castles were a happy complement to early childhood visits to Glastonbury spent rampaging around the ruins of the medieval abbey and staring through the windows of King Arthur themed crystal shops.

When I was a little older, I remember being taught about the Vikings – the only time I ever encountered the subject in compulsory education. I must have been about eight, and although perhaps not best equipped to appreciate the significance of what I was learning, I remembered that lesson when all else had faded away. The thing that stuck, the one key message that lodged most firmly in my brain, was that no Viking ever wore, possessed – or perhaps even imagined – a horned helmet.

The absence of horns on Viking helmets invariably comes as a blow to those who aren't prepared for it. Many is the occasion on which I have been obliged to plunge in this particular knife; it is remarkable to witness, in fully grown adults (in fact, especially in adults), the visible shrinking of the spirit that accompanies the unexpected death of an image formed in childhood. There may well be, and I apologize for it, readers of this book who are right now experiencing the bewildering combination of anger and disbelief that accompanies the detonation of this fact-bomb.

To a small boy weaned on *Hägar the Horrible* the news was, well, horrible. I still remember the frustration of it all – if the Vikings didn't have horned helmets, why had I been lied to? Thankfully my young mind was still fertile enough to bounce back from this mental napalm. The blow was also softened slightly by the discovery that the helmets they did wear were *almost* as cool (or so I tried to convince myself) as their cornigerous surrogates. The evidence for helmets of any kind, however, is slim. Aside from scattered fragments, only one complete Scandinavian helmet of the Viking Age has ever been found. This is the famous Gjermundbu helmet (named after the place in Norway where it was buried, along with its owner), an arresting object defined by the sinister half-facemask that was intended to protect the eyes and nose. Its owl-like visage – cold, impassive and predatory – was the face presented by at least one Norwegian warrior in his battle-cladding.[2]

Outside Scandinavia, other helmets have been found in graves that may, on the strength of their form or contents, have been the burial places of Vikings – or, at least, of people with a cultural affinity to Scandinavia. But none of these – most of which have been found in what is now Russia and Ukraine – is distinct from the material culture of the (non-Viking) local populations. Are these Viking helmets? If the only qualification is that a person of Scandinavian extraction might once have put one of these things on his head then the answer must be yes. But these helmets are radically different to the Gjermundbu helmet: open faced, conical, distinctly eastern – and worn by all sorts of other people who were definitely not Vikings. So perhaps these were just helmets that some Vikings happened to wear – not 'Viking' helmets at all. Perhaps these were no more 'Viking' helmets than the Volga salmon they ate for dinner was 'Viking' fish. But, of course, that is equally true of the Gjermundbu helmet as well – simply putting it on didn't make the wearer a Viking, and we can't even be certain (no matter how probable it may be) that it was made by, or even worn by, someone born and bred in Scandinavia. As we shall see, material culture can be a most treacherous guide to ethnicity.

The problems lie both in the semantics (the word 'Viking') and in the underlying premise that 'the Vikings' were a 'people' whose characteristics can be listed like a Top Trump card or tabulated like a character-class in a role-playing game. It is fair to say that Vikings, in this sense at least, never existed.

Most modern academics have an uneasy relationship with the term 'Viking', and reject the idea that it can be used as an ethnic label. Its original meaning is disputed. It could mean people who hung around in bays getting up to no good (from ON *vik*, meaning 'bay or inlet') or perhaps people who frequently showed up at trading settlements (from OE *wic*); there are, also, other possibilities. However, its original derivation is largely irrelevant – what is important is what people thought they meant by it when (and if) they used the word. As a common noun (in its Old Norse and Old English forms Vikingr and Wicing respectively), the word was used rarely during the Viking Age and was applied only to a minority, not all of whom were Scandinavians. In Old Norse poetry composed in praise of Viking kings (known as skaldic verse), much of which dates to the Viking period, the word was as likely to be applied to the enemies of Scandinavian kings as to home-grown marauders. Indeed, one of the rare English uses of the term is found in Archbishop Wulfstan's lament, *c.* 1014, that slaves were running away from their English lords to become 'Vikings'.[3] Who the Vikings were, therefore, could be a relative concept. It was never an ethnic category, and in most cases it seems to have been used disapprovingly, suggesting that 'Vikings' could prove as much a menace to Scandinavians as to their victims elsewhere.[4]

Runestones – memorials to the dead erected during the Viking Age and inscribed in the runic alphabet that was used to render the Old Norse language in written form – also record a number of instances of the word. In most of these cases the word appears as a personal name, and this phenomenon is known from Viking Age Britain as well: a man called 'Wicing' was minting coins in Lydford (Devon) on behalf of King Cnut in the eleventh century.[5] The implication is that the term 'Viking' wasn't necessarily negative, and although we can't know for certain if these were names given at birth, it accords well with a society in which individuals revelled in tough-guy epithets.[6] Indeed, the abstract form of the noun (ON *viking*), particularly as encountered in later Icelandic literature, meant a seaborne mission involving adventure, violence, plunder and risk, and was a normal and honourable means by which a man might make his name.

The poetry of the tenth-century Icelander Egil Skallagrimsson – contained in the thirteenth-century saga of his life – sums up, in words which just might originate with Egil himself, a view of the indulgent nature of Viking parenting:

My mother said to me
That they would buy for me
A ship and lovely oars
To go away with Vikings,
Standing in the stern,
Steering the glorious ship,
Then putting into ports,
Killing a man or two.[7]

In this sense, 'Viking' was fundamentally something that one *did* or was a part of, and there is very limited evidence that the word was used in this way during the Viking Age. A runestone erected by a mother in Vastergotland (Sweden) implies that to engage in 'Viking' activity (in this case in the west – that is, in Britain and Ireland) could be considered praiseworthy: 'Tóla placed this stone in memory of Geirr, her son, a very good valiant man. He died on a Viking raid on the western route.'[8]

However, there seems to have been an expectation that a man (it was almost certainly an overwhelmingly – if perhaps not exclusively – male occupation) would, at some point, settle down. Supported by the wealth accrued during his Viking days, he might set himself up as a farmer and landowner, the head of a family, with a good reputation among his peers. He might take on some public duties at legal gatherings, and he would use his wealth to patronize poets and craftsmen and perhaps even organize trading expeditions. He would become, in other words, respectable. Inevitably, however, there were always individuals who were sufficiently bloodthirsty, marginalized, restless, irresponsible, fame-hungry, greedy or outcast to make the Viking lifestyle a permanent occupation – these outsiders would have been among those who self-identified as Vikings, and it is for these people that the disapproval of Scandinavian skalds seems to have been reserved. This distinction between being and doing was perhaps a little like the different attitudes that a young person might encounter if he or she were to state an ambition to become 'a traveller' rather than merely to 'go travelling'.

All of which is rendered somewhat irrelevant by the unavoidable observation that hardly anybody was ever called a Viking during the Viking Age itself: they were referred to across Europe and beyond as Danes, Dark Heathens, Dark Foreigners, Fair Foreigners, Foreign Irish, Gentiles, Northmen, Pirates, Pagans, Rūs, Scythians and Varangians, but hardly ever – in Old English – as Vikings (*wicings*). As we have seen, the *Anglo-Saxon Chronicle* tends most frequently to speak of 'Danes', despite considerable evidence to indicate that many of the Vikings who found themselves in Britain came from all over the northern world: various Viking leaders can be shown to have had Norwegian origins, runestones commemorate the death of Swedish Vikings in Britain, and even the Viking dead themselves, through analysis of the oxygen isotopes in their teeth, can be shown to have grown up as far afield as Estonia, Belarus and high latitudes beyond the Arctic circle.

The early English had form when it came to conflating complex cultural phenomena into a homogeneous 'them' – the diverse inhabitants of much of Celtic-speaking Britain had been labelled *wealas* ('foreigners', whence the modern 'Welsh') and treated as a largely undifferentiated rabble since at least Bede's day. Likewise, 'Danish' seems to have become a convenient catch-all term for people who predominantly spoke Old Norse, wherever they actually came from.[9]

One might expect that modern historians would have long ago developed more subtle approaches to complex issues of identity and cultural affiliation. And yet, until relatively recently, it was widely assumed that past 'peoples' could be identified as essentially unchanging racial blocs with cultural traits that were stable, heritable and identifiable through language, behaviour, skull-size and material culture. This 'culture-historical paradigm', accompanied by racist bricolage of varying offensive shades, was driven by the twin engines of misapplied Darwinist logic and the German revolution in philology (which had demonstrated the interconnections between Indo-European languages and the mechanics of linguistic development). Social, cultural and racial development was soon seen to be as predictable as vowel mutation and as inexorable as evolution.[10] It was only during the second half of the twentieth century that these views began to change and mainstream academia started thinking more critically about past ethnicity.[11]

It is no coincidence that in Anglophone scholarship this shift coincided with the loss of Britain's Empire and the country's diminution as a global power. The culture-historical model shared many features with the system of racial classification that had been used by academics and administrators to reinforce the discriminatory structures of the British Empire – and in particular the position of white English men at the pinnacle of the world order they had invented. It was a classic circular argument – the fact of Empire proved the superiority of the British, the innate genius of whom had made British global supremacy inevitable. At the time, the obvious implication was that the greatness of Britain had been present in the genes; for, if cultural traits were – like DNA – handed down the generations, then surely the seeds of that greatness lay in the blood of mighty ancestors. And, of course, they found greatness in abundance: in the Romans whose civilization prefigured their own Empire, in the Anglo-Saxons whose Germanic origins had (in their minds) brought law, democracy, freedom and a distinctively 'English' Christianity to Britain, and, increasingly, in the Vikings.[12]

As the nineteenth-century children's author R. M. Ballantyne wrote in 1869, 'much of what is good and true in our laws and social customs, much of what is manly and vigorous in the British Constitution, and much of our intense love of freedom and fair play, is due to the pith, pluck and enterprise, and sense of justice that dwelt in the breasts of the rugged old sea-kings of Norway!' A stirring message for the Empire's future administrators.[13]

The British Empire was in essence a maritime concern. From Francis Drake to Horatio Nelson its greatest heroes and progenitors had been seamen. Even Alfred, the ninth-century king of Wessex, was fêted (on the strength of very little evidence indeed) as the founder of the English navy.[14] The Vikings, as a seafaring people, seemed to embody and prefigure all the greatest traits and achievements of the British: the spirit of commerce and adventure, the cutting-edge maritime technology, the suicidal bravery on land and sea, the discovery and settlement of new and exotic lands, the rattling of sabres in the faces of savage natives – even the cheerful pillaging of Catholic Europe with a gusto of which Drake would have been proud. The thought that these qualities had been reproduced in the British – not only by the example but in the very blood of the Vikings – was a tremendously exciting one in the intellectual climate of the late nineteenth and early twentieth centuries. Here was a myth of origins that did not rely on the Mediterranean parallels and exempla that had been the staples of classical education since the Renaissance; the Old North was real and palpable in the cold salt spray of home waters, and the roar of Boreas carried the family ghosts with it.

So, out of half-digested Icelandic sagas, Wagnerian wardrobe cast-offs, classical ideas of barbarian virtue and a good dose of romantic nationalism, the classic image of the Viking was born: blond and bare-chested, lusty and bold, a noble savage for the north

European soul. This, incidentally, was also the crucible in which the horned helmet was forged, a fantasy propagated and popularized through book illustrations. Thomas Heath Robinson's illustrations for the English retelling of Frithiof's Saga, published in 1912, have a lot to answer for in this respect, and Arthur Rackham's drawings accompanying the translated libretto of Wagner's *Ring* cycle didn't help either; even though the *Ring* wasn't 'about' Vikings, the valkyries, gods, dwarves and other paraphernalia of Norse myth placed it in the same milieu. Most importantly of all, it was in the latter part of the nineteenth century that the word 'Viking' came popularly to be applied to these people, their culture and their age.[15]

In the light of modern attitudes towards Britain's imperial project, it is now hard to view the enthusiasm of men like Ballantyne without cynicism. The approving comparisons made by men of the nineteenth century between themselves and their Viking forebears now carry a grim irony. Shackles and collars have been excavated from major Viking commercial centres at Dublin and elsewhere along the trade routes to the slave-markets of central Asia; they are functionally and technologically identical to those used in the African slave-trade that underpinned much of Britain's vast imperial wealth. The greed, brutality and callous disregard for the art and culture of others that the British were periodically to display across the globe were aptly prefigured in the rapacious Viking lust for silver, slaves and tribute. The qualities that some in the past saw as 'manly vigour' might very well strike us today as psychopathic tendencies – whether manifested in the eleventh-century Norwegian king Harald Hard-ruler or the nineteenth- and twentieth-century British general Horatio Herbert Kitchener. And, as Britain's Empire unravelled in the decades following the Second World War, misty-eyed nationalist eulogies to the North became ever more absurd, and comparisons with the recently humiliated Nordic countries increasingly unwelcome.

The marchers move with a practised military discipline, boots polished to a high shine, brass buttons gleaming. At the front march the Rikshird (the State Troopers) in navy blue, followed by the Kvinnehird (the women's brigades) and the various youth groups gathered together under the banner of the Nasjonal Samling Ungdomsfylking ('National Unity Youth Front'). Everywhere there are shining eyes and waving banners, gold crosses on red fields, eagles and swords. They move like an army, down from the plain little whitewashed church towards the barrow cemetery. The hump-backed mounds rise and plunge in the grass, like leviathans playing in the shallows of Oslo fjord, the glittering waters spreading out to the east.

A pouchy-looking fellow, with limp sand-coloured hair and slightly bulgy eyes, is standing at a podium. As he begins to speak, the faces of the young men and women assembled before him look up in rapture, glowing with the promise of a golden dawn.

> 'Norwegian women, Norwegian men. Today, we are gathered in a historic place, at a historic time in the lives of our people … It was from here, where the Yngling dynasty has its graveyard, that – with thought and deed acting in concert – Norway became united […] Was it not the Viking kings, the Ynglings resting here, the strong Nordic men, who one thousand years ago drove forward the will of the Norwegian people […]?'[16]

The speaker was Vidkun Quisling, leader of the puppet regime that governed Norway under close supervision from Nazi Germany between 1942 and 1945, and chairman of the Norwegian fascist movement Nasjonal Samling ('National Unity'). Between 1935 and 1944, Nasjonal Samling held meetings during the Pentecost holiday at the Borre national park in Vestfold, near Oslo.[17] The park is the setting for a cemetery of forty surviving grave-mounds, the largest of which are 23 feet tall and up to 150 feet in diameter. In 1852, one of the mounds was demolished by the Norwegian Public Roads Administration for the purpose of gravel extraction. In the process, the remains of an elaborate Viking Age ship burial were discovered. Although the excavations were botched and most of the evidence of the ship itself was lost, the treasures that were found accompanying the burial were spectacular. Gilt-bronze bridle fittings, with their knot-work and zoomorphic decorations, gave rise to the definition of a new Viking art-form: the 'Borre' style.[18] These were some of the first artefacts that allowed Norwegians to imagine the splendour of Viking Age power, and historians eagerly took up the Borre site as emblematic of national origins – a powerful symbol in the period around 1905 when the independent kingdom of Norway formally came into being after more than 500 years of political and dynastic union with Denmark and (latterly) Sweden. In 1915, Professor Anton Wilhelm Brøgger sensationally claimed that the ship burial was the grave of Halfdan the Black, father of Harald Finehair (*c.* 850–*c.* 932) – the man credited as the first king of a unified Norway. This built on medieval traditions that considered the Borre mounds to be the cemetery of the legendary Yngling dynasty, from which Halfdan and Harald ultimately sprang.

These elaborate confections of folklore and invented tradition have disintegrated under scrutiny in recent decades. But, in the political climate of post-independence Norway at the beginning of the twentieth century, a national myth of such potency went unchallenged. In 1932, with Brøgger as its indefatigable cheerleader, Borre became Norway's first national park – a sacred site, as he saw it, in the birth of Norwegian nationhood.[19]

These were the myths that Quisling, and men like him, eagerly embraced. Borre was not the only Viking Age site that Nasjonal Samling commandeered for their propaganda – they also met at the iconic battle-sites of Stiklestad and Hafrsfjord where Quisling told his audience (wrongly), 'Norwegian kings sat on Scotland's throne and for almost four hundred years Norwegian kings ruled Ireland,' pointing out too (and stretching the truth almost as much) that 'Ganger Rolf [Rollo], who was a king of Norwegian birth [he wasn't], founded a kingdom in Normandy [he didn't] which was so powerful that it conquered England [150 years later].' The promotion of the archetypal Viking image – the aggression, the expansionism, the machismo – became a powerful recruiting tool for the Nazis and their fascist allies. Numerous propaganda images (the majority produced by the Norwegian artist Harald Damsleth) featured lantern-jawed Nordic types riding the decks of dragon-prowed long-ships, alongside more sophisticated and esoteric uses of runic scripts and mythological allusions. These fostered a spurious sense of continuity between the Viking Age and the National Socialist project. The deep roots and time-hallowed legitimacy that these symbols implied lent the ultra-modern ideology of racist nationalism a gravitas that helped it to transcend its inherent novelty and absurdity.[20]

It was the latter quality that fascist movements in Britain never quite managed to escape: P. G. Wodehouse's brilliant lampoon of the British politician Oswald Mosley and his British Union of Fascists, or 'Blackshirts' (with Roderick Spode's 'Blackshorts'), proved that the British capacity to laugh at anything was a useful barricade against the pompous po-facedness of fascist demagoguery.[21] But the ultimate failure of British fascism is perhaps also testament to the fact that, by the mid-twentieth century, the medieval (including the Viking) past – so relentlessly plundered by nationalist movements across Europe – had already been integrated into British national culture in forms which were harder to bend into totalitarian shape. Nevertheless, the degree to which the Nazis successfully co-opted the image of the Vikings into National Socialist propaganda can be measured in the long-term and widespread contamination of northern European heritage. J. R. R. Tolkien's deeply held loathing for 'that ruddy little ignoramus' Adolf Hitler rested in no small part on his recognition of the damage done by 'Ruining, perverting, misapplying, and making forever accursed, that noble northern spirit, a supreme contribution to Europe, which I have ever loved, and tried to present in its true light'.[22]

It remains the case today that too warm an enthusiasm for the 'Germanic' past can raise suspicions (often justified) of unsavoury politics: the subject remains a fecund repository for the imagery of racist propaganda. This taint is one of the quietest, most tenacious and most ironic legacies of the Third Reich.[23]

This squeamishness about the Vikings and their world would lead ultimately to a thorough reappraisal of the Viking Age in the decades following the Second World War. Pioneered by the British archaeologist Peter Sawyer, revisionist histories sought to downplay the lurid violence and warrior ethics of the Vikings, emphasizing instead their artistic, technological and mercantile achievements.[24] There is no doubt that it was a necessary corrective, rebalancing the Viking image and dispelling a plethora of myths and falsehoods that had stood unchallenged since the Middle Ages. However, far from liberating the Vikings from nationalist captivity, the new narratives provided a fresh palette with which revivalists and nationalists could embellish what had previously been a relatively two-dimensional image. Viking ancestors became pioneers without equal, craftsmen and poets, engineers and statesmen – as well as remaining the warriors and conquerors they had always been. All of which was true of course, at least of some individuals at certain times and in different places. But the desire to demystify the Viking Age also brought in train a new myth: that the Vikings – with their storytelling and home-making, their pragmatism, their games and their shoe-menders – were essentially the same as we are, but fitter, stronger, clearer of purpose, uncorrupted by modernity. Peering into the Viking world, some have found a mirror reflecting back all that they would wish themselves and the modern world to be: simple, undiluted, purified …

But, as we shall see, the Vikings *were* strange. They were strange to their contemporaries and they should be strange to us too. Theirs was a world in which slaves were raped, murdered and burned alongside the decomposing corpses of their dead owners, a world where men with filed teeth bartered captive monks for Islamic coins, where white-faced women smeared their bodies in fat and human ash and traversed the spirit world in animal form: it is not the template for a brave new world that I, for one, would choose. Thus 'the Vikings', to us now and to their contemporaries in their own time, could represent something both familiar and alien: they could be weird and remote, monstrous even, but also bound tightly into narratives of who the English-speaking peoples have felt themselves – wanted themselves – to be. It is a complex and enduring problem, and shifting emphases in the presentation of the Vikings and their homelands, from the eighth century to the present day, illuminate the preoccupations of the modern psyche just as much as they do the realities of the Viking Age itself.[25]

All of which is to say that the whole idea of the 'Viking' needs to be handled with care. As it is used in a modern sense (and in this book), the word is largely employed as a term of convenience. It is used to define a period, the seaborne warriors whose activities characterized that period, and the shared cultural connections, ideas and art-styles (mostly, but not exclusively, of Scandinavian origin) that both bound people together and spawned new identities. It is important to recognize that – like the reality of all human life – what we mean by the term is chaotic, contestable and imprecise, resisting easy definition. How that chaos is, and has been, negotiated is in part what this book is about. And thinking about it is important, because the stereotypes can be deadly.

In the 1940s, hundreds of young Norwegian men, stirred by images of their 'Viking' heritage and convinced by nationalist propaganda of the threat from Russian Bolshevism, signed up for the 'Norwegian Legion'. They were promised that they would be fighting in the interests of a free and independent Norway. Instead they found themselves, barely out of training, ordered by German officers into the meat-grinder of Hitler's Eastern Front. A hundred and eighty of them (around 20 per cent) were killed before the legion was acrimoniously disbanded. Those few who remained committed to the Nazi cause were integrated into the SS Nordland Division, a force of mainly Scandinavian volunteers which had

VAR
ÆRE ER
TROSKAP

Norwegian propaganda for the SS

formerly constituted a part of the SS Wiking Division. These were the men who were inspired by the Viking-themed propaganda images churned out by the Reich and who had listened misty-eyed to Quisling's fantasies in the supposed burial ground of Halfdan the Black. The men of SS Nordland, convinced of the superiority of their Viking blood, would go on to commit atrocities in eastern Europe which were equal to the crimes of any of their Nazi peers.[26]

# 4

# SHORES
# IN FLAMES

Bitter is the wind tonight,
it stirs up the white-waved sea.
I do not fear the coursing of the Irish sea
by the fierce warriors of Lothlind [Vikings].

Irish monk (ninth century)[1]

If the raid on Lindisfarne in 793 remains the apocalyptic touch-stone for the Viking Age in Britain, it was only the first of many similar attacks that were to rage up and down the coastlines of Britain and Ireland in the years around 800. Viking raiders struck at Iona in the Western Isles in 795, at Jarrow (former home to the monastic scholar Bede) in 796, at Hartness and Tynemouth in 800, at Iona again in 802 and 806.[2] The earliest raids in Ireland fell in 795 on Rathlin Island, Co. Antrim (almost certainly the same group that had already hit Iona in that year), at St Patrick's Isle (Co. Dublin) in 798 and at Inishmurray (Co. Sligo) in 798 and 807.[3] The record is patchy and incomplete; but what is certain is that people died and people suffered. There is not much direct evidence of the impact of these early Viking raids, no clear indication of the human cost exacted – of the people, possessions and lives that were snatched away. But there are traces – objects and remains that give terror and plunder a weight and substance that even the purplest of ecclesiastical prose fails to convey. It is here, in the material traces of the Viking Age – in stone and bone and metal – that something of the original purpose and the impact of the Vikings in Britain can be seen.

A grim and bearded head lies within the collection of the British Museum.[4] It is small, made of bronze and dated to the eighth century – a piece of Scottish, Irish or Northumbrian workmanship. It was probably intended to depict the face of a saint (it is strikingly similar to the depiction of St Mark in the Lichfield Gospels). Discovered near Furness Abbey in Cumbria (a region, as we shall see, of later Scandinavian settlement), the head has been adapted as a weight in a manner typical of Viking traders. Stuffed with lead, it has been turned to a new use in the hands of owners more concerned with personalizing their belongings than with piety. The little head, severed from its body, hacked from whatever piece of ecclesiastical treasure it had once been intended to decorate, is a reminder of the material consequences of Viking raids – of the treasured possessions that were broken and stolen, the human heads that were detached from their bodies, of the people taken away from their homes and disposed of far away.

Direct evidence for the sort of violence recorded by monastic writers is rare and often equivocal; a number of skeletons excavated from the ditch of an enclosed settlement at Llanbedrgoch on Anglesey, for example, were long believed to be local victims of Viking raiding until chemical analysis of the remains revealed several of them to have grown up in Scandinavia: not, in itself, any reason to believe that they were not the victims of raiding, but enough to complicate the narrative considerably.[5] In only one place in Britain – at the former monastery at Portmahomack in Scotland – has good evidence for the violence of Viking raiding been uncovered; it is a place, moreover, that is not mentioned in any written source that has survived from the Viking Age.

*

'The further north you go in the island of Britain, the more beautiful the scenery becomes, the hills wilder, the skies wider, the air clearer, the seas closer. Even for those not born in Scotland, you feel as if you are driving towards your beginnings.'[6] This is how Professor Martin Carver described his journey to Portmahomack. The small fishing settlement lies at the north-eastern tip of the Tarbat peninsula: a finger of land that points emphatically north-east, separating the Moray and Dornoch Firths. It is the shard of crust marking the end of the Great Glen, the weirdly rectilinear fracture that shears a diagonal fissure through Scotland, scoring a damp line that puddles along its length into Loch Ness and Loch Linnhe before dispersing into the Firth of Lorne. There is a sense up here, as elsewhere in the far north of Britain, of land dissolving at the margins, like the edge of pack ice giving way to the ocean, splintering and drifting into ragged and provisional forms. To travel there is to a find a place of transitions and embarkations, not journeys ending.

The monastery that Carver discovered at Portmahomack was revealed in a series of archaeological investigations between 1994 and 2007. It is, just for the fact of its existence, a supremely signif-icant addition to our knowledge of the early medieval north. No record of it exists in any written source, and it is – so far – the only monastery discovered within the notional bounds of the Pictish kingdom; indeed, it lies close to its heart. At the height of its wealth and productivity in the eighth century, the monastery was produc-ing prodigious quantities of vellum for the production of manu-scripts as well as high-quality liturgical metalwork such as chalices and pyxes (containers for holding the consecrated bread used in the Eucharist). There was obviously a limit to the number of such objects (particularly of the latter sort) that a single church required, and so the workshops probably served newer, start-up monasteries elsewhere in Pictland and perhaps beyond. It is precisely this sort of wealth and activity that drew attention to Portmahomack and probably sealed its fate. For at that time, and in that place, the attention of outsiders was something that no one would have wanted to attract; at some point around the year 800, the monastery burned.

The parts nearest the sea went first, the blaze ripping through the workshops of the vellum-makers, immolating timber, straw and heather. The severity of the fire can be judged by the condition of stone fragments, cracked and reddened in the heat of the burning. Carver's team discovered that most of these stones, strewn on top of the fire, had been part of a great cross-slab (a flat rectangle with a cross carved upon it in relief). The stone, which had originally stood at the edge of the monastic graveyard, had been toppled and obliterated – pulverized with a calculated malice more reminiscent of the violence done by Islamic fundamentalists to ancient artefacts than of any casual vandalism. This was destruction with a purpose – the work of people with motive and intent, who had an understanding (whatever that was) of what such a monument stood for. It was not the only one: other stone cross-slabs (at least one, probably three) were broken down and shattered on this site.[7]

A famous example of the sort of thing that was broken at Portmahomack can be seen just 5 miles away at Hilton of Cadboll. The stone that stands near the chapel there is an imposing monument, nearly 8 feet tall and 4½ feet wide, heavy and overbearing. The images that decorate its surface – like those discernible among the fragments from Portmahomack – are stunning in their quality and execution, renderings in stone of the types of imagery more familiar from illuminated manuscripts like the Book of Kells. It is a replica, the original stone having been moved from here in the mid-1800s and ultimately finding its way to the National Museum of Scotland in Edinburgh.[8] The imagery that survives on the original monument is almost all on one side. Scenes of aristocratic life – hunting dogs and a deer run to ground, mounted men with spears and others blowing horns, a woman riding side-saddle – are surrounded by a frame of twisting vines and interlacing animals. Surmounting it all are the idiosyncratic hieroglyphs known as 'Pictish symbols' – in this case the 'crescent and V rod' and the 'double-disc and Z rod', as well as the 'comb and mirror', tucked into

The Hilton of Cadboll stone

the corner of the figurative hunting scene. Nobody really knows what these symbols represent, but they certainly had their origins in a distant past. The best guess at present is that they signify the names, and perhaps ranks or affiliations, of Pictish aristocrats.[9]

Missing from the original Hilton of Cadboll stone is the feature that, at the time of its making, would have been its definitive attribute: the huge and elaborate cross that once decorated its eastern side (a reconstruction of this cross can now be seen on the replica, sculpted by Barry Grove). This cross was deliberately defaced, methodically, carefully and totally; but not by Vikings. In 1667, or a little later, the redressed stone was inscribed with a memorial to one Alexander Duff and his three wives (one assumes that these were consecutive, rather than concurrent, relationships). In the febrile religious climate of seventeenth-century Scotland, it seems possible that the ostentation of this cross was enough to make it a target for iconoclasts. No one knows whether it originally carried an image of the crucified Christ; if it did it would have been even more offensive to Protestant sensibilities – nothing says 'Popish' quite like an enormous ornamental crucifix embellished with vine scrolls and animal interlace. At the very least it was clearly not considered worth preserving such an object, pregnant as it was with associations that ran counter to prevailing cultural, political and religious norms.[10]

In 1640, the Aberdeen Assembly (the General Assembly of the Church of Scotland) determined that 'in divers places of the Kingdome, and especially in the North parts of the Same, many Idolatrous Monuments, erected and made for Religious worship are yet extant' and should be 'taken down, demolished and destroyed, and that with all convenient diligence'. Such stones, in other words, in the seventeenth century, were inescapable reminders of a regional, native identity that was partly defined and sustained by its religious affiliations. For the men of the Aberdeen Assembly, such reminders were intolerable – on religious grounds, certainly, but perhaps also as memorials to an aristocratic, kin-centric and local way of life, deep-rooted and old-fangled things that lay far beyond the systems and controls of civic assemblies, national government and kirk. At the time of their making, however, these stones were billboards proclaiming the political and cultural dominance of the prevailing local dynasties, and clearly could be no less provocative. Around the year 800, not long after the monuments at Portmahomack and Hilton of Cadboll were erected, a new power was plying the coastal waters of Pictland. This power, founded in raw military strength and impressive maritime technology, was unimpressed by the strictures, injunctions and symbols of the British Christianity it encountered. Moreover, it had a vested interest in challenging the strident Pictish identity that those stones gave voice to. It was a power determined to frame the landscape in its own terms, without reference to local landmarks and the bigwigs who had built them. For Viking warlords – seeking, perhaps, to consolidate their spheres of influence – the Pictish monuments of Portmahomack may have represented an intolerable challenge to their mastery of the northern oceans. This perhaps was the reason why they suffered so badly.[11]

It was not, of course, only the stones that suffered. Although it is the damage done to buildings and to things that endures in the archaeological record, and although it is the irretrievable loss of cultural heritage that grieves the historian most acutely, for the monks who were present at the monastery on the day it burned there were corporal and existential issues at stake. Excavation of the monastic cemetery revealed the skeletons of three men who had suffered extreme personal violence. One of them (number 158 in the excavations report) was struck in the face with a sword, a wound which cleaved through his flesh and into the bones of his skull. Somehow he survived to die another day. Another monk, number 152, received three blows to the head with a heavy bladed weapon. He was less fortunate than his brother. 'As two of the cuts were on the back of the head,' Carver explains, 'it is likely that the assailant attacked from behind. Given that one of the fractures was on the crown of the head, the individual may have been below the assailant at one point (e.g. kneeling). As injuries with larger weapons are more likely to produce terminal fractures, it is possible that a weapon such as a large sword may have been used to produce these fractures.'[12]

Here are the Vikings we think we know – hacking apart the head of a fleeing monk, shearing open his skull from behind as he drops to his knees. Did he stumble in his flight – driven by the burning terror that had spewed up out of the ocean? Or did he drop to his knees in prayer, facing death as a martyr with the *Pater Noster* on his lips? This we cannot know. What we can say with certainty, however, is that someone cared enough about him in death to remove his bloody corpse from the smoking ruins and inter it with dignity within the confines of the monastic cemetery. These were hardly likely to be the actions of his killers. They, presumably, were long gone, in ships laden with silver chalices and the gilded covers of holy manuscripts, their precious painted vellum leaves left to burn in the smouldering wreckage or used to stoke the camp-fires at their next stop along the coast. Not that the Vikings would leave this corner of Britain alone. There were other islands, and other sources of wealth, to be won.[13]

The island of Inchmarnock, lying off the Scottish coast among the other islands of the Clyde, is not much of anything really, not now at any rate: a smear of wooded hillside between the coast of Bute and the Kintyre peninsula, a few fields caught napping when the tide came in too fast. These days it is privately owned by Lord Smith of Kelvin, who breeds highland cattle on the island; there are no other human residents.[14] Twelve hundred years ago, however, Inchmarnock was thriving. Excavation in and around the medieval ruins of St Marnock's church has revealed evidence of early medieval metalworking, and – most significantly – of what has been interpreted as a monastic schoolhouse. Dozens of fragments of slate, scratched with graffiti, patterns and text, seem to be the work of students, copying or practising writing and carving: a longer Latin text in a neat insular minuscule is perhaps an exemplum – passed around for copying – and fragments of cross-slab monuments imply the ultimate intended expression of the artistic skills being taught here.

One can imagine a clutch of young boys, seated cross-legged on a hard earth floor, stifling their yawns as an older monk tries patiently to explain the importance of making sure their half-uncials are all the same height. A little way from the main group, one boy sits apart. He doesn't join in with the covert attempts of the others to turn their practice slates into gaming boards,[15] or to flick pebbles at the brother's back when he gets up to go for a piss. Instead he silently persists in his own project, scratching at the lump of grey schist he keeps tight in his left hand, pressing down hard, his muscles taut. He hasn't been long on the island – he came with some older monks from Iona; something had happened there, apparently, but the other boys weren't told what. The new boy won't speak, and the monks won't tell them. 'Just keep on eye on the sea,' they say, 'just watch the sea.'

Among the slates found on Inchmarnock, one stands out as utterly unlike anything else found there.[16] It depicts four figures, all in profile, facing to the right as if moving together resolutely in the same direction. Three of them – only one of which is complete (the upper-right portion of the image has broken away and is presumably lost, or perhaps still somewhere under the surface of Inchmarnock or in the foundations of its ruinous buildings) – appear to be armed men dressed in mail shirts, the cross-hatching on their legs perhaps indicating the tight wrappings that were worn to gather the loose material of fabric trousers. They surround the image of a ship, its multitude of oars giving it the appearance of an unpleasant, scuttling invertebrate. The central figure in particular dominates the composition – large and commanding, a shock of long hair streaming from his bristly, oversized head. He leans forward slightly, propulsive and determined, in total contrast to the pathetic figure behind him. Stunted and unfinished, his head is barely outlined – just a jumble of lines; he is indeterminate, without identity: a nobody, a blank. What gives him purpose is the object attached to him, shackled to him in fact, hanging from an arm that pushes forward, reaching out. There is something terribly poignant about the gesture – drawn so clearly, where the face is absent, the fingers delineated and the hand open. It is on the object, however, that interpretation of the image turns. It could be a lock or a manacle; several such objects have been discovered in Ireland and around the Baltic. The object seems to be chained to the body of the figure in some way, and perhaps to the waist of the warlike central figure as well. Lines extending from the shoulder of the latter figure also seem to imply a captive being dragged into bondage – dragged, perhaps, to the waiting ship and a long journey east.[17]

If the object is not a manacle, it is most probably a depiction of a portable reliquary shrine. These little house-shaped objects are a familiar component of ecclesiastical culture around the Irish Sea; containing the relics of a saint, they would have functioned both as containers for holy objects and as portable focal points for devotion. As such, they were often highly decorative and valuable. Surviving examples, like the Scottish Monymusk reliquary, give an indication of the craft and precious materials with which such treasures were invested. As such, they made tempting targets for robbers – especially robbers with scant regard for Christian sensibilities. Substantial quantities of ecclesiastical metalwork, including house shrines, from northern Britain and Ireland in particular, have been found in Scandinavian graves and settlements – often adapted for use in new ways. A casket of exactly this type, manufactured in the eighth century in Ireland or western Scotland, was discovered in Norway, eventually entering the royal collections of the Danish–Norwegian royal family and from there into the collections of the National Museum of Denmark. It is empty, long having lost the relics it was built to house, but on its base is scratched an inscription in Old Norse, the letters formed in the distinctive runic alphabet used in south-west Norway and in the later Norse colony of Isle of Man: 'Rannveig owns this casket.'[18]

The noise is deafening. The sail cloth beats and rumbles like barrels tumbling over cliffs, and the ship's timbers scream in the rending hands of wind and water; above it all comes the shrieking gale, the thousand voices that howl together, raging and vengeful as they pour unending out of the blackening sky, riding on the salty arrows of the storm. He fights to bring the sail in, to stop the oar holes, to secure the provisions. He thinks he can hear the howling – the wolf that will swallow the sun; he thinks he can feel the thrashing of coils – the serpent that encircles the earth; he thinks he can see the shadow of the ship, *Naglfar*, built from the fingernails and toenails of the dead.[19] His right hand reaches up and grips the hammer that hangs around his neck. He forces his thoughts homeward, to the bright hearth and the cows in the byre. He thinks of his boys playing on the hillside, and the carvings around the hall door; he thinks of his wife, sitting by the fireside, her head bowed, weeping. Suddenly the storm is dying, the rain reducing to great globs of water that strike hard but sparingly, the rage of the wind expended, quietened now to a whispered lament. A ray of sunlight breaks through the fortress of black clouds in the east, a golden glimmer spreading on dark water. An arch begins to form, building itself from the ether into a bridge of colour linking the heavens with the earth. He smiles: it is a good omen. Bending down to open the chest that serves as a rowing bench, he begins to rummage among the clinking metal objects within. Eventually he produces a house-shaped box. It is small but exquisite, gleaming with gilt bronze. He wipes a ruddy-brown stain from the lid with a corner of his cloak and opens it up, peering inside and grunting. Standing, he upends it over the edge of the boat and towards the disgruntled water, shaking its contents into the breeze. Scraps of fabric, little brown bones, a fragment of wood, tumble into the slate-grey sea and are swallowed in darkness. He closes the box again, turning it in his big, scarred hands, the fugitive light glinting from its golden edges; he thinks of his wife, sitting by the fireside, the casket in her lap; she looks up, and she smiles.

Rannveig is a woman's name, and there is every possibility that the casket that bears it was brought back from a successful campaign of raiding in the west, its holy contents dumped without ceremony, repurposed as a lavish gift from a father, husband or suitor. An Irish annal of 824 describes the fate that befell the bits and pieces that had once been or belonged to St Comgall: 'Bangor at Airte was sacked by heathens; its oratory was destroyed and the relics of Comgall were shaken from their shrine.'[20]

Of course, Rannveig might well have acquired such an object by other means before marking her ownership in writing; Viking women were not dependent on men for their status and possessions.[21] But it is hard to imagine how such an object could have been liberated from its keepers and divested of its holy cargo without the application or threat of violence, and this – in the overwhelming majority of cases – was the preserve of men.

It may well be, therefore, that the Inchmarnock stone depicts the abduction of valuables both human and material, shackled together, shrine and guardian hauled off into bondage as one. The drawing was made – on the basis of its context and the style of the lettering found on its reverse side – around the year 800, the same time that the monastery of Portmahomack burned. It seems highly likely, given what else we know of events in that region in those years, that Viking raids on Iona and the coast of Ireland, as well as further away to the west, furnished the imagery and impetus for someone to scratch this odd graffito on to stone. With its menacing ship and exaggerated, trollish warriors, it calls to mind those heartbreaking drawings produced by the child survivors of wars and atrocities – crude images in which men, their weapons and their vehicles loom huge and all powerful, the visual manifestation of unhealable mental scars. As always, of course, there are competing interpretations (as with the apocalyptic gravestone at Lindisfarne, we can never know for sure what this scene was intended to convey), but it is easy to see how the arrival of murderous waterborne marauders could have jolted those on the receiving end into novel spasms of creativity.[22]

Thus we come to perhaps the most lucrative and plentiful source of wealth that the Viking raiders targeted – plunder that leaves little trace in the archaeological record, but which defined the activities of people from the north in the eye of those they encountered. In the early tenth century, the Arab traveller Ahmad ibn Rusta described the activities of Vikings in eastern Europe (the Rūs). He explained how they raided their neighbours, 'sailing in their ships until they come upon them. They take them captive and sell them in Kharazān and Bulkār (Bulghār) […] They treat their slaves well and dress them suitably, because for them they are an article of trade.'[23] Being treated well, however, was – for a slave – a relative concept. For women and girls, the experience was as horrific as could be expected, and frequently far worse. Another Arab writer, Ahmad ibn Fadlan, describes his encounters with a group of Rūs travellers, making their way from the north along the Volga towards the markets of central Asia and the Middle East. In an extended description of the funeral of the Rūs chief, ibn Fadlan describes how a slave girl – owned in life by the dead man – 'volunteered' to die and accompany him to the grave. After a lengthy ritual, the girl was stupefied with alcohol, repeatedly raped, stabbed with a dagger and strangled with a cord. Once dead, she was burned upon the funeral pyre with the dead man, his horses and his hounds.[24]

These accounts are from the east, where the Viking trade routes came into contact with the Abbasid Caliphate, the Byzantine Empire and the flowing riches of the Silk Road.[25] But the goods they brought to trade were harvested far away; all and any of the people who could be preyed upon by sea might find themselves shackled and transported. Descriptions of the seizure of people are commonplace – particularly in the Irish chronicles. The year 821, for example, saw the 'plundering of Etar [Howth in Dublin] by heathens; from there they carried off a great number of women'. Ten years later, in 831, 'heathens won a battle in Aignecha against the community of Armagh, so that very many were taken prisoner by them'. In 836 came 'the first plunder taken from Southern Brega by the heathens […] and they slew many and took off very many captive'.[26]

Monks may have been of less value as sex-slaves, and men were probably valued primarily as manual labour, often carried back to Scandinavia to work the farms of landowners where they, as well as female slaves, would have been expected to undertake the hardest and foulest work. Recent research has even suggested the institution of slave 'plantations' in parts of Scandinavia, where imported workers were housed in cramped conditions and forced to mass-produce textiles for the export market.[27] There they were known in Old Norse as þrælar ('thralls'), a word which survives in modern English with something close to its original meaning (to be in 'thrall' to something is to be captivated by it). The low regard in which these unfortunate folk were held can be gauged by a poem, written down – in the only surviving version – in the thirteenth or fourteenth century, but probably preserving a much older text and ideas.[28] It describes the mythologized origins of social castes in Scandinavia and lists the sort of pejorative names and menial tasks thought suitable for the children of a thrall ('slave'; ON *þræll*) or thrall-woman (ON *þír*):

> I think their names were Big-mouth and Byreboy,
> Stomp and Stick-boy, Shagger and Stink,
> Stumpy and Fatso, Backward and Grizzled,
> Bent-back and Brawny; they set up farms,
> shovelled shit on the fields, worked with pigs,
> guarded goats and dug the turf.
>
> Their daughters were Dumpy and Frumpy,
> Swollen-calves and Crooked-nose,
> Screamer and Serving-girl, Chatterbox,
> Tatty-coat and Cranelegs;
> from them have come the generations of slaves.[29]

Slavery was an institution across Europe, as it had been in the days of the Roman Empire, and persisted into the Norman period. In 1086, some 10 per cent of the English population was recognized as being unfree, and Anglo-Saxon slave-owners had the power of life and death over their slaves until the late ninth century.[30] The capture of defeated enemies was also a feature of inter-kingdom warfare in both Britain and Ireland before and during the Viking Age. In 836 (the same year that Vikings took captives from Brega), Fedelmid mac Crimthainn, king of Munster, attacked the oratory at Kildare 'with battle and weapons', taking the abbot Forindan and his congregation captive: they were shown, according to the chronicler, 'no consideration'.[31]

What was different about the Viking slave-trade was its integration into long-distance commercial networks that connected the

Irish and North Seas with the Baltic, Black, Caspian and Mediterranean Seas. No longer could slaves taken in Britain and Ireland expect to remain within a reasonable radius of their erstwhile homes, surrounded by people who differed from them little in speech or custom, and who respected social and cultural norms that were mutually understood. Instead they faced the possibility – if they weren't shipped directly to Scandinavia or to more local Viking colonies – of being transported like livestock over vast distances, to be sold in the markets of Samarkand or Baghdad, or – perhaps – to meet a horrific death on the banks of the River Volga. If they survived that journey and made it to market, they may well have found themselves, prodded and manhandled, forced to watch as their price in silver was carefully measured out – the scales tipping with the heft of weights, gleaming with ornaments ripped from the books and treasures that had once adorned their homes and churches.

# 5

# BEYOND THE
# NORTH WAVES

What is a woman that you forsake her,
And the hearth-fire and the home-acre,
To go with the old grey Widow-maker?

RUDYARD KIPLING, 'Harp Song of the Dane Woman' (1906)[1]

Explaining the beginnings of the Viking Age is to enter into difficult and contentious territory. We can observe the Vikings' arrival in the written sources, and glimpse what they wanted and how they went about getting it. But to question why people from northern Europe suddenly began to risk their lives on the wide ocean and brave the unknown dangers of foreign lands is another matter. To make progress on this front requires consideration of where the Vikings came from – not just geographically, though this is important for understanding the economic and political pressures that affected them, but also culturally. The structure of society in the pagan north, the shared values and beliefs – these were critical factors in pushing people towards the 'Viking' way. Ultimately, these are questions to which there can be no firm answers, only suggestions and reconstructions and ideas placed in the minds of people we cannot hope to know, but by doing so we can perhaps inch a little closer to understanding what made the Vikings tick.

Despite the very limited information provided by the written sources, it is clear that the people who were raiding Britain at the turn of the eighth century came from somewhere in the 'Danish'-speaking (that is, Old Norse-speaking) north-east and – most importantly from the perspective of Christian writers – were heathens. In the year 800, the Baltic was a pagan lake. The people who had turned their attention to Britain came from the west of this region – from what is now Denmark, Norway and Sweden – but all of the neighbouring lands to the east were also inhabited by pagan peoples, by Baltic and Slavic tribes in (moving clockwise around the Baltic coast) modern Finland, Russia, Estonia, Latvia, Lithuania, Russia (again), Poland and Germany. It would be wrong to draw very firm distinctions or borders between these groups – as in Britain, it is better to try to forget everything we know about the way that the storms of history have left their tide lines on the map. The formation of modern north-eastern Europe – its political geography and its religious and ethno-linguistic fault-lines – has been the result of more than a millennium of often catastrophic upheaval that lasted well into the second half of the twentieth century. The people who formed Viking raiding parties could have been (and in later centuries demonstrably were) drawn from all over this wider region.[2]

To the south and west was the Carolingian Empire, a great swathe of Europe – corresponding to most of modern France, northern Italy, western Germany and the Low Countries – united under a Frankish king (the Franks were a Germanic tribe who had begun to settle the Roman province of Gaul in the fifth century and who give their name to the modern nation of France). That king, in the same year, had been crowned emperor of the Romans by Pope Leo III, a title that confirmed him as the sanctioned champion of an aggressive Christianity and the successor to the authority of the long-defunct Roman Empire in the west (the eastern, or Byzantine, Empire, centred on Constantinople – modern Istanbul – remained a going concern). That king would come to be known as 'Karolus Magnus': 'Charles the Great', or Charlemagne. By the time he received the imperial crown, Charlemagne had already redrawn the boundaries of Christendom in western Europe. In particular, a series of bloody campaigns against the pagan Saxons of northern Germany – effectively completed in 797, though revolts continued until 804 – had brought the boundaries of Frankish Christian Europe into contact with the pagan Scandinavian and Slavic tribes of the Jutland peninsula and western Baltic littoral. These wars had been exceptional for their combination of extreme brutality with religious zeal. In 772 Charlemagne ordered the destruction of the Irminsul, a holy tree or pillar central to Saxon worship.

Ten years later, in a particularly notorious incident, he had 4,500 Saxon prisoners beheaded on the banks of the River Weser near the town of Verden, apparently in retribution for their involvement in a revolt against Frankish domination. This was followed by laws that made death the penalty for refusing baptism.[3] The violence of Charlemagne's Christian mission prefigured the Crusades by three centuries.

Whatever the precise nature of the religious beliefs of the Saxons, it is likely – as we shall see – that they were shared, at least in part or in outline, by their neighbours to the north in what is now Denmark. Indeed, an inconsistent but interconnected network of beliefs, stories and rituals extended from the borders of the Frankish world throughout the Baltic world, linking together people of markedly different linguistic and cultural backgrounds through broadly compatible world-views and systems of social hierarchy. It is certain that Charlemagne's bellicose Christian foreign policy would have sent ripples of alarm shuddering out across the Baltic. Kings, chieftains, priests and priestesses would have wondered how long it would be before their traditional way of life and their political independence would be snuffed out beneath the hooves of Frankish horsemen, how soon they would see their timber halls burning and their sacred groves falling beneath the axes of Christian missionaries.[4]

This fear and uncertainty prompted a range of reactions. Some, like the Slavic Obodrites, did a deal with the superpower to their west, accepting Charlemagne as nominal overlord, providing the Empire with military aid and, in return, maintaining a level of political and religious freedom. They did this, admittedly, under duress: Charlemagne had invaded their territory and taken hostages. The Danes, for their part, provided shelter to Charlemagne's enemies and took steps to defend their landward border with Saxony by reinforcing the ditch and rampart structure – the Danevirke (literally the 'Dane-work') – that divided Germania from the Jutland peninsula.[5] As Charlemagne's conquests in Saxony became established geopolitical facts, Danish kings increasingly found themselves having to deal directly with Frankish power.

In 804, the Danish king Godfred arrived with his fleet and 'the entire cavalry of his kingdom' at Hedeby (Schleswig) on the Danish border.[6] It was a show of strength and, after a diplomatic exchange with the emperor, he departed – feeling, presumably, that he had roared loudly enough to convince his Frankish neighbours that the Danes were not to be trifled with. In 808, however, he apparently changed his mind, this time crossing with his army into Obodrite territory to the south-east, sacking a number of Slav settlements and burning the coastal trading settlement at Reric. The Obodrite inhabitants of the town, on the Baltic coast east of Jutland (close to the modern German town of Wismar), may have been accustomed to paying tribute to the Danish king. If so, the alliance with Charlemagne put an end to that, and also gave the Frankish Empire a friendly port on the Baltic. It was probably for both these reasons that Godfred, after destroying the town, deported its traders to Hedeby, placing them – and their tax revenues – firmly within his own sphere of control.[7]

Charlemagne hardly leapt to the defence of his allies. The *Frankish Royal Annals* describe how he sent his son Charles to wait at the banks of the Elbe to make sure that no one entered Saxon territory; the Obodrites were left to their fate. Once the Danish army had withdrawn, the Franko-Saxon army crossed the river and burned the fields of those Slavic tribes who had allied themselves with the Danes (and who had probably done so in order to avoid similar treatment from the Danish king; this has ever been the fate of small tribal communities – the weakest always suffer the most).

Some fairly empty diplomacy followed in 809 – conducted, so it would seem, to give both sides an excuse to shore up the loyalty of their various Slavic allies. Godfred, however, had not finished baiting the Empire.

In the summer of 810, Charlemagne was at the great palace complex he had commissioned at Aachen (now in Germany), the new capital of his hard-won realm. The cathedral at Aachen still incorporates a building – the Palatine Chapel – built as part of the original palace in the 790s by the architect Odo of Metz. The extraordinary scale and lavish attention to detail of the building, with its many-coloured marble floors and tiers of rounded portals – the eight sides of the central vestibule surrounded by the sixteen-sided outer perimeter – are the monumental vestiges of the staggering wealth and imperial grandeur of Carolingian power at its apogee. Gleaming white stone, green porphyry and blood-red Egyptian granite, frescos and mosaics, marble and bronze – the remains of great civilizations of the past were being gathered together, literally building a new empire.[8]

In 787, Pope Hadrian I wrote to Charlemagne agreeing to let him take from Ravenna 'mosaic and marble and other materials both from the floors and the walls', and the emperor's biographer – Einhard – describes him having marbles and sculptures brought from Rome and Ravenna to adorn the palace at Aachen.[9] The most startling of all the surviving fixtures of the Palatine Chapel, however, is the throne. Raised on a dais of six steps, the simple and unadorned seat exudes a living presence from the vaulted shadows. Though it has been sat upon by thirty-one German kings since Charlemagne's day, it is indissoluble from the memory of its first master, the first Holy Roman Emperor. It is easy to indulge the imagination by picturing the great ruler brooding here amid the magnificence of his rule, chin resting on one hand as he gazed on the holy altar to the east, considering the price of power and the promise of salvation.

In June 810 Charlemagne's eldest daughter, Hruodtrude, died and the emperor may well have found himself in sombre and reflective mood; whether he ever burst from his throne in rage or retreated to it in search of holy guidance can never be known, but the events that followed can have done little to improve his mood:

> he received the news that a fleet of two hundred ships from Denmark had landed in Frisia, that all the islands off the coast of Frisia had been ravaged, that the army had already landed and fought three battles against the Frisians, that the victorious Danes had imposed a tribute on the vanquished, that already one hundred pounds of silver had been paid as tribute by the Frisians, and that King Godofrid [Godfred] was at home.[10]

The chronicler, evidently concerned that his Frankish readership would find this all rather hard to swallow, felt compelled to affirm that 'that, in fact, is how things stood'. As if this were not bad enough, the elephant which Charlemagne had been given by Harun al-Rashid, caliph of Baghdad, died suddenly soon afterwards: a bad summer indeed.

Charlemagne, of course, was not prepared to let Godfred's belligerence stand. He began to raise an army and would no doubt have pursued his opponent with all of his customary zeal, had not the Danish king died as suddenly as the elephant, apparently murdered by his own people (who would, understandably, have been worried that their king's pathological warmongering was leading them into the teeth of Charlemagne's war machine; before his death, Godfred had reportedly boasted that he was looking forward to fighting the emperor in open battle). What the *Annals* fail to conceal, however, is the extent to which the Frankish Empire had been rattled; Godfred, one might say, had given even Karolus Magnus the willies.

This may all seem like something of a digression: what, one might ask, do the border wars of Frankish kings have to do with the story of Viking Britain? But the story of Godfred and his dealings with the emperor brings a number of issues into perspective. Firstly, it highlights the critical point that, at precisely the same time as the first Viking raids in Britain were taking place, continental Europe was dominated by a mighty superpower at the height of its strength. Charlemagne's Empire was economically and militarily superior to any other regional power, and its presence fundamentally affected the way in which rulers dwelling in its shadow (including Anglo-Saxon kings) could operate. Faced with the prospect of poking the monster on the doorstep, some Scandinavian warlords may have been prompted to exploit new avenues of adventure away to the west. Secondly, it highlights the political and economic importance of towns and trade and the maritime technology by which these could be exploited, defended and harassed. Places like Reric, Hedeby and the coastal settlements of Frisia formed part of a much larger network. Such networks, and the opportunities for long-distance trade they presented, opened new frontiers for the most ruthless and entrepreneurial individuals – particularly those with access to effective maritime technology.[11]

Finally, the belligerent career of Godfred indicates that by the late eighth and early ninth century there were individuals in parts of Scandinavia who were able to wield resources and military power that had the potential, at the very least, to disrupt and dismay even their most powerful neighbours. They were, moreover, human beings (not merely the demonic hordes of clerical imagination) – people who dealt in the pragmatic realities of early medieval politics and trade. They were people with aspirations towards lordship and power on an increasingly grand scale; and, to achieve and maintain it, they would need the trappings, the wealth, the loyalty and the prestige that society demanded of them.

At over 260 feet in length, the house at Borg on Vestvågøy is – by any standard – a massive structure. Dark, squat and muscular, the great hall holds fast to the Norwegian soil, its eaves reaching almost to the ground. It is a dwelling of the earth, rooted in the soil, rising from it like the gently arching back of some giant slumbering beast. In winter, if the snows come – despite the latitude, the Gulf Stream keeps the Lofoten Islands relatively warm – it is given back to the landscape: one more gentle mound among undulating drifts of white – betrayed, perhaps, only by the thin drift of wood smoke that rises from the roof-spine. And though massive, it represents an utterly different expression of power from that expressed by Charlemagne's palace at Aachen. Where the Palatine Chapel soars, tiers of columns and arches reaching upward to heaven, the long-house at Borg spreads in the horizontal, hugging the skyline, long, low and narrow (only around 30 feet wide). Aachen is an expression of a cosmopolitan outlook, its stylistic cues taken from the architecture of Rome and Byzantium, its fixtures literally transplanted from elsewhere – signifiers of a pan-continental imperialism, rendered in imported stone. Borg, on the other hand, is a creature of the vernacular. Its form – the long, bow-sided plan and gently curving roof-line – is peculiar to early Scandinavian architecture, an evocation perhaps of the curving keels of the ships which defined northern life. More fundamentally, the hall itself is built from the very tissue of the land: the trees that were felled to raise its skeleton, the turf blocks that were cut and stacked to flesh it and to bind it to the earth. The hall is fashioned from its environment, moulded into a new form, clinging to the shores of a sheltered tidal estuary (Inner Pollen), the glittering peaks of Himmeltinden and Ristinden looming to the west.

The traveller rides from his ship on the lakeside, up, past outbuildings and over fields, to the great house hunkered in the snow, atop the low hill before the mountains. There are four doors along its eastern side, but the southernmost entrance is grander than the others, with its pillars and lintel carved with the images of writhing creatures, biting and twisting and gripping each other in a tangle of sinuous limbs and gaping mouths. The traveller dismounts and a thrall-boy appears from another door; he runs to take the reins of the horse, leading it away towards the north-easterly end of the building. The traveller follows for a few steps, catching the soft shuffle of heavy feet inside, a low whinny, the hot stench of dung and warm animal bodies. Cattle and horses, pungent and comforting: a homely smell. He smiles and turns back to the carved portal, ducks his head and passes through.

Inside the cold violet of the Lofoten dusk gives way to a deep orange glow of firelight, bouncing from tapestries and the rich umber of the timber walls. The flames cast shadows that set the carved beasts wriggling on the pillars that run in two aisles down the length of the building. Between them the long hearth lies sunken in the floor, flames licking up to light the rafters, heat filling the hall that extends to the right of the door. There are older men seated at benches along the sides of the hall, and they rise as he enters, bringing the wide world indoors, shaking the smell of winter from his cloak.

The long-house, as experienced today, is a reconstruction of the building as it may have looked between the early eighth century when it was constructed (on the site of an earlier, sixth-century building), and the mid-tenth century when it was demolished. The original hall lay a few hundred yards to the east; the position of its timber pillars, long since rotted away, are marked now with modern posts, its outline clearly visible from the air. At nearly 270 feet, the building was 30 feet longer than Westminster Hall. Unlike that great sepulchral eleventh-century chamber, however, the hall at Borg was the social hub of a whole farming community, and saw all of life swirling through its portals. Archaeological investigation of the site suggests that the building was divided into five rooms. The largest of these – at the north-east end of the building – was a cattle byre and stable-block, a home to precious animals over the cold, dark winter months and a source of living warmth to the human inhabitants of the building. Perhaps for obvious reasons, the slope on which the building stands drops away to the north-east, meaning that the north-east end of the building lies around 5 feet lower than the part of the building that contained the domestic and human-centred areas – nobody wants a river of shit pouring through their living room all winter.[12]

Objects found in the rest of the building give clues to the various uses to which the apparently communal spaces were put: whetstones and spindle whorls, sword fragments, iron tools and arrow heads indicate the sorts of activities that men and women would have undertaken from and in the building – weaving, hunting, farming and preparations for the possibility of violence. There were also a number of what are known in archaeological circles as *gull-gubber* – thin gold foils struck with images that are most commonly believed to depict mythological scenes – leading to the suggestion that the communal activities that took place here included religious or ritual functions as well as social and practical ones.[13] The evidence seems to suggest that, unlike the hierarchical and authoritarian structures of the Christian Church, with its professional priesthood and purpose-built temples, Viking religion – at least at the beginning of the Viking Age – was personal and domestic. It is probable that, at places like Borg and elsewhere (such as Lejre in Denmark or Gamla Uppsala in Sweden), the principal heads of individual estates would have adopted the role of cult leader alongside their more prosaic responsibilities, perhaps taking the lead in making sacrifices of animals (*blót*) and in depositing the valuables that have been discovered in earth and water in these places. *Gullgubber*, precious objects already invested with mythic symbolism, would have made appropriate offerings.[14]

It has been suggested, with varying degrees of emphasis, that religion played a role in the violence doled out to churches, monasteries and Christian communities – that the Vikings, aware of the impending threat posed by aggressive Christian nations, turned on the most visible and accessible symbols of this religion in a sort of pre-emptive strike (or not so pre-emptive if, as one might argue, Charlemagne's Saxon wars were regarded as the first demonstration of what awaited all their pagan neighbours). In such a war of cultural self-preservation, it would have mattered little whether the churches and monasteries were situated in Frankia or in Britain. The symbols were the same, and thus – it is argued – the political identity of their creators would have been regarded as part of a homogeneous bloc, a united threat to tribal culture and independence. Indeed, such was Charlemagne's power that the whole of Christian Europe, Britain included, can in some respects be seen as lying within a Frankish sphere of influence.[15] It is hard to imagine how the events of the late eighth and early ninth century could have failed to leave a deep and negative impression on communities around the Baltic, particularly about the nature of Christian faith and the character of its practitioners – violence, terror and subjugation would have seemed the inescapable outriders of the cross.

The destruction of the cross-slabs at Portmahomack can, from this perspective, be seen as evidence for an ideological component to Viking raiding. Just as a raiding army might harass the lands and dependants of an enemy king in order to force a confrontation, the Vikings – it could be argued – were directly and deliberately targeting the houses of God and his personnel. It is, it must be said, easy to get carried away with the idea that the Viking Age began as a pagan religious war. But as even the most frequently cited exponent of this thesis – Bjørn Myhre – has pointed out, Christianity should be seen in the light not just of its spiritual content but of the political affiliations it affirmed.[16] For Charlemagne, as for many other European monarchs, Christianity represented a powerful toolkit of symbols, hierarchies and rituals through which he could emulate the political and military achievements of the Emperor Constantine and, by extension, Roman imperial power as a whole; simple soul-food it was not. Cultural vandalism directed by pagans towards those same symbols (if that is what Carver uncovered at Portmahomack) might therefore be better interpreted as a statement of defiance against rampant Frankish imperialism – not anything 'anti-Christian' in the strictly religious sense.

However, what seems to have been much more important than any of this was the acquisition of wealth. This term is a little abstract – in modern culture 'wealth' tends to be measured by fairly crude standards: the amount of money in a bank account, the relative value of share prices, projected tax receipts, quantity and quality of property, land, assets.[17] 'Wealth' in the early Viking Age, however, can be seen as a rather more expansive concept. Luxury goods – such as the English and Frankish glassware also discovered at Borg – were highly prized for their intrinsic quality and usefulness, and ownership of them was, as now, one index of achievement. But such assets also performed key social functions, and their ownership hinted at broader networks or the potential to forge them. In the early Middle Ages, gift-giving between lords and their retainers (as well as between rulers) was the basic agent of social cohesion and a measure of relative political substance; in return for weapons, jewellery and luxury items (and the expectation of more), men would pledge loyalty to their lords as warriors. This relationship was the fundamental basis of the war-band, and bonds thus forged were subsequently invested with and cemented by solemn oaths and a code of heroic ethics.

The system was very similar in Britain and had endured for centuries: the Old Welsh poem *Y Gododdin* (describing events of the fifth century, but written any time between the sixth and thirteenth centuries), for example, describes the operation of a war-band of this nature – its constituents paid in advance for their loyalty and support in battle with mountains of food and rivers of booze.[18] In Old English and Old Norse poetry, however, this relationship had developed into a material exchange, driven in part by the desirability of the goods being produced in Frankish and, to a lesser extent, Anglo-Saxon workshops. By the Viking Age this had crystallized into a general expectation of the role of a monarch, expressed most succinctly in Old English maxims ('the king belongs in his hall, sharing out rings'),[19] but also repeated through a mind-boggling number of 'kennings' in skaldic verse – an economical means by which to emphasize the virtue of any given ruler:

'lofty ring-strewer'; 'thrower of gold'; 'eager, wolf-gracious bestower of friendly gifts' …[20]

The ownership of precious objects was thus a symbol of the quality of one's social connections – not merely personal riches, but a visible symbol of the patronage of a powerful lord; perhaps even, ultimately, signifying the potential to dole out gifts to one's own dependants. The ability of important individuals to acquire prestigious objects was, therefore, an absolute prerequisite to the exercise of power, and generosity was seen as one of the two fundamental pillars of exemplary lordship. The other pillar, however, perhaps less immediately appealing to modern sensibilities, was the ability to provide an unending diet of human corpses to satisfy the sanguine cravings of wolves, ravens and eagles.[21] The king or warlord who could demonstrate himself to be both open- and bloody-handed was likely to cement his reputation – ideally in verse – and the ownership of portable wealth spoke to both of these qualities.

Happily, these two traits dovetailed neatly. It is quite obvious how a Viking warlord, seeking to improve both his reputation and the size of his war-band, could kill two birds with one stone by violently extracting wealth from foreign shores and doling it out among his followers. Such a socio-economic system, however, has its drawbacks. Though its mechanisms are straightforward, its demands necessarily mushroom: increasing war-bands require increased resources, increased resources require larger and more frequent raids, larger and more frequent raids require larger war-bands, and so on.[22]

Of course, there are other ways of acquiring portable wealth, and it seems that Scandinavian traders were pioneers in exploiting the trade networks that had developed around the North Sea during the eighth century. We have seen already the keen interest that Godfred took in securing access to Baltic and North Sea trade, but there is no reason to separate the acquisition of goods through trade from the violence enacted elsewhere. Books, exhibitions and school textbooks often make a great deal of the characterization of

Vikings as either 'raiders' or 'traders', with the public encouraged to view the Vikings through one or other of these lenses. This irritating meme is, in essence, a product of the academic debates of the 1970s and 1980s – debates which, while important at the time, have tended to perpetuate the wrong sorts of questions. It is obvious, of course, that raiding and trading were never mutually exclusive phenomena; the Viking slave-trade is the most obvious manifestation of this false dichotomy. The burning, killing and plundering that accompanied Viking activity around the coasts of Britain and Ireland were carried out by the same individuals who might have been found weeks later hawking their captives in the Hedeby slave-market or peddling bits of plundered church furniture in the bazaars of central Asia. Nevertheless, the evidence for peaceful trading is plentiful, and Scandinavian traders must have been a familiar sight at major emporia like Ipswich, York and Southampton. Indeed, it is probably as a result of such trading expeditions that Scandinavians came to be aware of the wealth of Anglo-Saxon kingdoms, the geography of the British coastland and the location of monasteries and the wealth they housed. It also, presumably, allowed for an insight into local political fault-lines that ambitious men might hope to exploit.[23]

None of this can really diminish the possibility that the earliest raids were the outcome of individual initiative, with their subsequent popularity among Scandinavian seafarers a reflection of the ease and profitability with which monasteries could be divested of their valuables. This comes close to a Victorian view of Viking derring-do, a tendency to explain the Viking Age by the hot-blooded 'pith and pluck' of Nordic men that drove them to adventure. But it cannot be denied that human agency would have had a disproportionate impact in an age when populations were small, and when stories of young men returning from overseas, their boats sitting low in the water with treasure and slaves, would have spread fast and far. To the farming communities of Norway, stretched out along the narrow strip of cultivable land, eager for the social and economic capital to resist political pressure from the south, such apparently easy wealth would have seemed to present opportunities on a scale previously undreamt of. There is unlikely to have been a shortage of volunteers for future expeditions, or a dearth of ambitious chieftains planning new adventures. Perhaps the lord of Borg was one of them.

# 6

# THE GATHERING STORM

... The bird cries,
grey-coat screams, battle-wood resounds,
shield to spear-shaft replies. Now shines the moon
drifting into dimness. Now deeds of woe arise
that will propel this peoples' malice.
But awake now, warriors of mine,
Seize thy linden-shields, dwell on courage,
Fight at the front, be fierce and bold!

*The Fight at Finnsburg*[1]

Although Viking raids would continue to afflict Ireland with almost absurd frequency throughout the 820s and 830s, there is a gap of twenty-nine years after the third raid on Iona in 806 before a Viking raid is again recorded in Britain.[2]

For historians, knowing what was to come, this can seem like a trivial span of time, a brief hiatus before the hammer would fall with all its force. But for people living at the time it would have seemed very different; they did not know that they were living in the 'Viking Age'.[3] Many of those who were aware of the attacks on Lindisfarne, Jarrow and Iona, including some of the survivors, would have lived out the rest of their lives with the impression that this diabolical onslaught had burned itself out – passing, perhaps, like the fiery whirlwinds and bloody rain that had presaged its arrival. Indeed, for more than a generation after the appearance of the first Vikings in the written record, the overwhelming fear – in southern Britain at least – would have been that, if violence were to come, it would come from people who spoke familiar (if not shared) languages, who lived similar lives in recognizable landscapes and who worshipped the same god in broadly compatible ways.

In 798, for example, King Ceolwulf (newly king of Mercia after Offa's death in 796) ravaged Kent and captured its king, Eadberht. Eadberht was dragged to Mercia in chains where he had his eyes gouged out and his hands cut off.[4] In 815, King Ecgberht of Wessex raided the 'west welsh' (that is, the Cornish) from 'east to west'.[5] Ten years later, the same king defeated the Mercians at a place called Ellendun (now somewhere underneath the western suburbs of Swindon), 'and a great slaughter was made there'.[6] A fragment of poetry recalls that 'Ellendun's stream ran red with blood, was stuffed up with corpses, filled with stink'.[7] In the same year King Beornwulf of Mercia was killed by the East Angles (it was a bad year for the Mercians). These violent convulsions all took place during a period that saw a steady shift in the centre of political gravity in southern Britain, focusing power around the kingdom of Wessex at the expense of Mercia and some of the smaller southern realms. In this reorientation – which would have huge repercussions later on – the Vikings were of little consequence. In the early ninth-century brutality league they would have struggled to make the play-offs.

Ultimately, however, this state of affairs did not hold. The first black clouds reappeared in 835, when 'heathen men' raided across the Isle of Sheppey, but even darker days lay ahead. In 836, a fleet of thirty-five ships (one version of the *Anglo-Saxon Chronicle* says twenty-five) arrived at Carhampton on the Somerset coast, and the formidable King Ecgberht – bane of Mercians and Cornishmen – was there to face them. The fighting that ensued was the first setpiece battle (that we know of) that pitched a Viking army against British foes. Once again, and not for the last time, the *Chronicle* provides the gloomy observation that 'a great slaughter was made there', and from what little else is known about it, it seems indeed to have been a grim day's work. If the number of ships is taken at face value, a Viking army numbering 1,500 men would be a conservative estimate, and it is probably fair to assume a similar number assembled to fight them. Three thousand men engaged in brutal hand-to-hand fighting with axe and sword would have made for a terrifying spectacle.[8]

Although Anglo-Saxon chroniclers reveal little about the realities of early medieval battle, their poets were less reticent:

> The horror of battle materialized. There was cracking of shields, attacking of warriors, cruel sword-chopping and troops dropping when first they faced a volley of arrows. Into that doomed crowd, over the yellow targe and into their enemies' midst, the fierce and bloody antagonists launched showers of darts, spears, the serpents of battle, by the strength of their fingers. Relentless of purpose onwards they trod; eagerly they advanced. They broke down the shield barrier, drove in their swords and thrust onwards, hardened to battle.[9]

The opposing armies would have faced up to one another in close formation, huddling together so that each man might benefit from the protection afforded by the large, round timber shield held by the man to his right. The defensive barrier thus created – a sort of clinker-built fence of human-held timbers – is known by poetic convention in Old English and Old Norse poetry as the 'shield-wall'. Its importance as a military concept has probably been over-stressed by modern historians – it was a product of fear and necessity as much as it was ever a formalized battlefield tactic, its description in poetry a function of conventional semantics (like other evocative constructs such as *wíhagen*, 'war-hedge') – but there is no doubt that an army arranged this way presented a formidable face to the enemy. The shields would have been brightly painted, probably carrying religious symbols or depictions of beasts designed to intimidate enemies and provide courage to those who sheltered behind them. Ninth-century examples, excavated in Norway with their timber still surviving, are around 3 feet in diameter and painted black or yellow. Rimmed with iron, these shields were augmented with a large semi-circular metal boss riveted to the centre. This protected the hand (which gripped the handle attached behind it), but could also blunt the edges of misplaced weapon-strikes or smash the face of an enemy once the shield-wall had broken down into the series of individual duels and knots of vicious combat that the battle would inevitably devolve into.[10]

The smashing of one's own face was, obviously, something to be avoided wherever possible. Helmets, like the one discovered at Gjermundbu, were probably more common than their rarity in the archaeological record might imply; the simple psychology of self-preservation would suggest that some sort of head and face protection would be desirable. An Anglo-Saxon helmet, found during the Coppergate excavations in York in the late 1970s, suggests the sort of thing that might have been available to the wealthiest warriors. Although it would have been old fashioned by the 830s (it was probably made in the third quarter of the eighth century), it seems to have remained in use until the first half of the ninth century. Old fashioned it may have been, but it was of exceptional craftsmanship and quality – not least the creatures that are woven into an intricate lattice in the decoration of the brazen nose-guard, and the eyebrows terminating in the heads of fanged serpentine creatures. The equipment of warriors in this period would have been far from homogeneous, and military gifts and heirlooms could be prized symbols of lineage, affiliation and religious persuasion. The Coppergate helmet carries an inscription on the brass crest that runs over the top of the helmet, an invocation to commend protection of its wearer – a man named Oshere – to the care of the saints.[11] The inscription enhanced the helmet's protective capabilities, transforming it into a magical item that conferred mystical as well as physical protection: a reminder that, to the warriors of the Viking Age, supernatural forces could play a critical role on the battlefield: 'IN NOMINE DNI NOSTRI IHV SCS SPS DI ET OMNIBUS DECEMUS AMEN OSHERE XPI' ('In the name of our Lord Jesus Christ and of the Spirit of God, let us offer up Oshere to All Saints. Amen').[12]

Other helmet fragments, like an eyepiece discovered at Gevninge on Zealand (Denmark) and dated to the cusp of the Viking Age, imply that the finest helmets might still have resembled those recovered from the Vendel, Valsgärde and Sutton Hoo cemeteries. These objects, with their full-face coverings of mask or mail, their swooping dragons and coiling serpents, their images of riders and spear-shakers, are objects to inspire awe and terror in equal measure. They rise up darkly from an age of legend, conjuring images of heroes and kings – dripping with antiquity and the glamour of mighty forebears. If helmets like these did indeed appear on the battlefields of the Viking Age, it would have seemed to contemporaries as though the ghosts of the mighty dead strode among them still, time collapsing amid the blood and chaos of battle, the eternal raven wheeling overhead.[13]

Several high-ranking West Saxons fell in the fighting at Carhampton: the ealdormen Duda and Osmod (ealdormen were senior nobles, subordinate to the king and often in charge of a shire or, later, groups of shires) and the bishops Herefrith and Wigthegn. They were surely the tip of a bloody iceberg, but the *Anglo-Saxon Chronicle* was never much concerned with the deaths (or the lives) of the average warrior. Of their enemies we know even less. All we are told, in a phrase that would roll out with grim regularity on the parchment leaves of the *Anglo-Saxon Chronicle*, is that *þa Deniscan ahton wælstowe geweald*: 'the Danes had possession of the place of slaughter'. In other words, they were victorious.[14]

The attack at Carhampton was a major incident, and it represented a sea-change in how Viking raiders related to the people of Britain. No longer content with the small-scale smash-and-grab raids which had defined Viking activity in the early ninth century (and which had picked up again in Ireland and Frankia from the 820s), the Vikings who attacked Carhampton seem to have done so with a heightened sense of what might be achieved through violence. A settlement of some importance, with archaeological traces dating from the fifth to the eighth centuries, Carhampton seems also to have been the site of an early monastic church

– associated with the Celtic saint Carantoc. It may, therefore, have been a place of pilgrimage and a major centre of wealth, and in this it would fit the pattern of the targets of earlier Viking attacks, both in Britain and abroad.[15]

However, Carhampton was also the site of a royal estate (it is included in the will of Ecgberht's grandson, Alfred, drawn up sixty years later) and was later the administrative centre for the hundred in which it sits – all of which suggests that it was an important political centre. This might, in part, explain why King Ecgberht himself was there to deal with the Viking threat – for if a king couldn't hold his own, how could he be expected to defend an entire kingdom? His failure to do so in this case may well have emboldened the people who had sailed against him. Victory against the fearsome king of Wessex can only have awakened Viking warlords to their ability not only to wrest wealth from hapless coastal communities, but also, through sheer force of arms, to win glory, fame and – perhaps – power and dominion of their own.

In 838, King Ecgberht brought his army to Hengestdun, now known as Kit Hill in Cornwall. He had come to head off a new threat to his growing hegemony – an army of Cornishmen and their 'Danish' allies who had marched east to contest with the West Saxon king for control of their borders and to make a stand against his increasingly domineering approach to the south-west. The battle that ensued was significant, not so much because of its outcome, but because – for the first time that we know of – a Viking army had chosen to involve itself in the internal politics of Britain, making common cause with the Cornish to fight against the West Saxon king.

It is not known why the Vikings chose such involvement. Perhaps they fought as mercenaries, seeking a share in the spoils, or perhaps they had been promised land or trading rights in whatever new arrangement could be wrested from the English king. Whatever the reason, it was a sign of things to come: over the course of the ninth century, Viking war-bands would increasingly use their military muscle to redraw the map of Britain. On this occasion it came to naught. Ecgberht, as we have seen, was not a king to be trifled with (his heavy-handed treatment of the Cornish in the 820s had perhaps gone some way to inspiring the events of 838). When the king 'heard of that [the alliance between the Vikings and the Cornish], he then went there with his army and fought against them at Hengestdun, and put both the Britons and the Danes to flight'.[16]

Rising to the impressive height of 1,096 feet, Kit Hill dominates the valley of the Tamar from which it rises, standing aloof from its comrades that huddle together in the uplands of Bodmin Moor. Up here you can see for miles. From Bodmin to Dartmoor to Plymouth Sound, a vast swathe of Britain's south-western peninsula opens itself to the eye: rime-scoured boulders and ancient field boundaries, rough delvings and crook-backed pollards, the scars of a tussle between the tough, wilful landscape and its human wranglers that has been fought over millennia. To the south the sea glints in a cleft cut into the horizon by the broad silver band that snakes through green pastures on its way from the hills. It is no doubt the combination of its commanding position and its accessibility by sea and river that gave this place the strategic importance that it seems to have had in the ninth century; whoever held this place could, with good reason, consider himself master of the Cornish borders.

The significance of the formative battle that was fought here was not lost on early English antiquarians. Of the many earthworks and monuments that litter the sides and summit of Kit Hill, one of the most prominent is a five-sided enclosure of low walls, with bastions at four of the five intersections. It looks like the shaggy remains of a fortress. This curious structure was long interpreted as a Civil War-era fortress (1642–51) on the strength of compelling similarities with the plans of other, better-documented forts around England. However, appearances were deceptive. On 27 June 1800, Sir John Call, who owned the adjacent estate and manor at Whiteford, wrote in his will that he desired a 'tomb of Cornish granate [sic] alias Moorstone' to be made on top of Hingsdon Down or Kit Hill 'within or adjoining to the Inclosure of the Castle I have built there'.[17]

'[T]he late Sir John', William Betham explained in the fourth volume of his *Baronetage of England* (1801–5), 'erected something like an old Saxon castle on the summit, with large stones of granite found there in great plenty'. It seems likely that this peculiar endeavour (though not untypical of the folly-building extravagances of his peers) was intended to evoke the battle that was fought there in 838 – a battle of which he seems to have been dimly aware: 'a Battle was undoubtedly fought at the bottom of that hill some time between the 7th and 8th century [fought in 838, it was in neither of these centuries]'. It is perhaps surprising that Sir John should have been so sketchy about the details – he was, from 1785, a fellow of the Society of Antiquaries, the learned society set up in 1707 to cater for the growing interest of certain well-heeled gentlemen in the physical evidence of the past. In its early days, the Society seems to have been largely a drinking club for like-minded men of a particular sort, and there were no formal entry requirements. Sir John, for example, seems to have been admitted on the strength of some interesting lithographs he had picked up in India. He had worked there as a military engineer, planning the fortifications at Madras – this, of course, being the reason for his 'Saxon fort' looking more like a typical post-medieval redoubt than the Anglo-Saxon stronghold he intended.[18]

When I visited Kit Hill with my wife and parents, it was a disconcerting experience. Thick banks of dreary mist swamped the landscape and shut down visibility to 20 feet in every direction. I felt as though, rather than standing at the summit of a massive Precambrian abscess on the sedimentary bedrock, we had been washed up on the shores of some weird fog-bound island, its coarse cliff-top vegetation concealing innumerable pits and fissures from which some Cornish Caliban could spring at any moment. The atmosphere was distinctly alien – a landscape stripped of all familiarity; even the cagoule-clad ramblers seemed vaguely sinister. At the highest point a great masonry tower rises through the white shrouds of clinging ether like a star-gazer's tower, the haunt of some Prospero, rising – to use Mervyn Peake's immortal words – 'like a mutilated finger [...] pointed blasphemously at heaven'.[19] Or, perhaps, like the funnel of some fantastical steamship, ploughing onwards through fog-bound oceans, on its way to a lost world.

This tower is, indeed, a chimney, unusually ornamental for its purpose. An obsolete monument to the industrial mining operations of the second half of the nineteenth century, it once exhaled the by-products of the steam engine which pumped water from the deep delvings below. Mining took place on Kit Hill from the Middle Ages until the early twentieth century, and the seemingly random gouges in the upper slopes are memorials to the earliest, open-mining phases of this activity. In subsequent centuries, workings grew deeper and more elaborate, as miners began seeking out the veins of tin and copper that had seeped into fissures in the granite in some unimaginably ancient epoch, and now the hill is riddled with shafts and tunnels, their lethal openings hidden amid gorse and bracken. These borings reached their climax in the 1880s with the Excelsior Tunnel, an 800-yard gallery driven horizontally into the side of the hill, like the passage to some improbably vast tomb. It was, in fact, constructed to mine the deepest lodes, and was extended on a few occasions in the early twentieth century. In 1959–60, however, the tunnel was taken over by the UK Atomic Energy Authority for bomb testing. Despite rumours to the contrary, these tests never involved any nuclear material, although – despite modern radiation tests confirming the Ministry of Defence's assurances – rumours to the contrary inevitably persist.[20]

In the ninth century, Kit Hill was known for other reasons and, as we have seen, by a different name – Hengestdun, the hill of Hengest – and a wisp of its memory still clings to its lower eastward slopes in the tautological place-name Hingsdon Down ('don' and 'down' both derive from OE *dun*, meaning 'hill').[21] The name is important. Hengest would have had a dual meaning in Old English. It means 'stallion'. But it was also the name of the legendary founding father of the English-speaking people – one half of the alliterative duo who, according to Bede, arrived in three ships from across the North Sea in the mid-fifth century. Landing in Kent, Hengest and his brother Horsa (and later his son Æsc) defeated the unfortunate Vortigern and his sons and began the process of clearing out the degenerate Romano-British order, founding the royal house of Kent in the process.

The story raises all sorts of red flags. The idea of a duo named 'Stallion' and 'Horse' paving the way, through the might of their arms, for a whole new set of nations, has 'foundation myth' written all over it (despite its continued acceptance as fact in some quarters). It may well be that Hengest and Horsa were, originally, a pair of pre-Christian deities who were turned from gods into human ancestors by Christian writers and given prominent roles in the authorized version of English origins. Whatever the reality, it is clear that the name had a great deal of potency attached to it by the ninth century.[22]

Early medieval battles were often fought at places associated with the names of gods and heroes, some of them burial mounds, others – like Hengestdun – massive hills that might have been imagined in some way to house the oversized remains of superhuman occupants. These were places where the past dwelt and where the memories of mighty warriors could be imagined to confer an aura of legitimacy, rootedness and martial prowess on those who fought in their shadow. These were also, conversely, places where ancient English claims could be challenged and new (or older) associations of landscape inscribed or resurrected – places where symbolic blows could be struck in the struggle for hegemony.[23] It must be partly for these reasons (as well as for its strategic significance) that when the Cornish wished to challenge the supremacy of the West Saxon dynasty, it was here that they came to meet King Ecgberht in battle.

The defeat of the Cornish cemented West Saxon authority over the south-west, but it did little to deter future Viking war-bands from chancing their arm in Britain. For the rest of the century, a rising tide of violence was directed towards the Anglo-Saxon kingdoms. Some of them were raids, directed – just as they always had been – towards concentrations of wealth. However, the battles of Ecgberht's reign, fought at places of symbolic significance like Carhampton and Hengestdun, signalled a shift in the level of engagement that the Vikings displayed towards their adversaries. From this point onwards, Viking armies were to display an increasingly sophisticated understanding of how power was articulated within the kingdoms of Britain, exploiting, undermining and appropriating the political and physical landscape until they themselves became an integral part of it.

# 7

# DRAGON-SLAYERS

This is a very old story: the Danes who used to fight with the
English in King Alfred's time knew this story. They have carved on
the rocks pictures of some of the things that happen in the tale, and
those carvings may still be seen. Because it is so old and so beautiful
the story is told here again, but it has a sad ending – indeed it is
all sad, and all about fighting and killing, as might be expected
from the Danes.

ANDREW LANG, 'The Story of Sigurd' (1890)[1]

In 850, the *Anglo-Saxon Chronicle* reports, 'heathen men stayed over the winter for the first time'. Although this notice passes without commentary in the *Chronicle*, dropped in almost as though it were an afterthought, the over-wintering of the heathens was the breath of wind that carried off the first leaves of autumn from the old Anglo-Saxon kingdoms. It was the harbinger of a storm that would not only strip those old oaks bare, but tear many of them up by their roots.[2]

Viking attacks had been increasing in volume and severity since the 830s, particularly in Wessex and the south-east. Between 840 and 853, this part of Britain was attacked at least fifteen times, and an attack is also recorded as taking place in Northumbria in 844 – resulting, disastrously, in the death of the king and his heir.[3] The first raids on Lundenwic (London) occurred in 842 and 851,[4] and there were attacks on Southampton and Portland (840), Romney Marshes (841), Rochester (842), Carhampton again (843) and Canterbury (851).[5] Many of these seem to have started off as raids with, presumably, economic motives, and most seem not to have encountered serious resistance. On occasion, however, Viking raiding armies were intercepted by shire levies raised by local leaders or by the king, resulting in pitched battles in which Viking armies often took a serious mauling.

At the mouth of the River Parrett in 848, the men of Dorset and Somerset – led by their respective ealdormen, Osric and Eanwulf, and Ealhstan, bishop of Sherborne – 'made a great slaughter' of a Viking war-band.[6] The Vikings were defeated again in 850 at a place called Wicga's Barrow by Ealdorman Ceorl and the men of Devon,[7] and in the following year King Æthelwulf of Wessex and his son Æthelbald routed the Viking army at a place called Aclea where they 'made the greatest slaughter of a heathen horde that we have ever heard tell of'.[8] Achieving a crushing victory over his heathen foes would have brought the king great personal satisfaction. In 843 he had gone to Carhampton with the intention of defeating a Viking army at the very place where humiliation had befallen his father, Ecgberht, in 836. But at the second battle of Carhampton, Æthelwulf too had been outfought. The victory at Aclea in 851, therefore, avenged both his own and his father's shame, ending it the way that Anglo-Saxon feuds had always traditionally been settled: in blood.[9]

After this robust West Saxon response, Viking war-bands seem to have become wary of assaulting Wessex directly, with raids in southern Britain confined to Kent for the rest of the decade. But the Viking winter camps of 850 – or at least the concept of such camps – were never abandoned. It became possible for Viking armies to mount raids throughout the year, as seems to have been the case in the early 850s, and by living off the land they could keep large numbers of warriors permanently in arms. Reinforcements from overseas could join them unimpeded, and the numbers of men and the size of their fleets could therefore grow unchecked. Unlike the Anglo-Saxon warriors they faced, there was no imperative for them to return to their fields for the harvest, or – like their compatriots in Scandinavia – to stay at home when North Sea storms kept their ships moored over the winter.[10]

Conflict between Anglo-Saxon kingdoms had always been, to a certain extent, a ritualized activity. The phrase 'ritual war' is an unfortunate one, implying something lacking in severity (what one anthropologist has compared to 'over-enthusiastic football'),[11] and in truth there is no reason to believe that Anglo-Saxon battles were not brutal and serious affairs. But they rarely resulted in lasting political change. Warfare seems generally to have followed a traditional pattern that was mutually understood, and battles – as we have seen – were often fought at places that held a mutual significance. Conflict was also limited by the natural constraints of the agricultural year. Campaigns took place during summer, before the harvest, while the weather was at its best and the roads were most passable; fortifications were seldom used, the Anglo-Saxons seeming to have preferred to face their enemies in the open, an opportunity – whether in victory or defeat – to carve out a legend that would be worth remembering.[12]

The Vikings, however, seemed – in the beginning at least – to be breaking all of these rules.[13] They had no respect for the traditional patchwork of allegiances and loyalties, the ancient boundaries or the conventions of war. They were perfectly happy to dig themselves in to fortified harbour-sites on major rivers, and their focus on portable food and wealth meant that much of their violence fell on settlements, monasteries and royal halls. They avoided pitched battles where they could and were able – thanks to their ships – to strike quickly and quietly into the very heart of Britain, regardless of the state of the roads. Places that had been far from any border now found themselves, as a result of a coastal or riverine position, exposed to war in a way that they had not been in the past.[14]

'They have no cultivated fields,' one contemporary Islamic writer observed of the Rūs he encountered travelling through eastern Europe and central Asia. Instead, he went on, 'they live by pillaging the land of the Saqāliba'.[15] These (the Rūs) were men who had chosen a different path to prosperity, and their harvest lay before them, to be reaped on the battlefield: 'When a son is born,' the same writer elaborated, 'the father throws a naked sword before him and says: "I leave you no inheritance. All you possess is what you can gain with this sword."'[16]

Entrepreneurial values like these, arising in a society that praised highly the fruits of memorable feats of violence and bravery, bred dangerous men with a single-minded determination to get rich quick or die trying. They were not going home to stack hay and muck out pigs, at least not empty-handed. And this meant – for the kingdoms of Anglo-Saxon England – a threat unlike any they had previously had to face.

In 865 an army appeared in East Anglia that was described in the *Anglo-Saxon Chronicle* as a *micel hæðen here* – 'great heathen horde'. *Here* is a difficult word to translate. It is clear that, in general terms, it meant army – the numerous 'herepaths' and 'herefords' that can be found among the place-names of England testify to its common usage in describing militarized infrastructure. However, the word normally used of Anglo-Saxon armies in this period is *fyrd*, and presumably *here* originally had other connotations. A clue to what these were can be found in the laws of King Ine, which explain how *þeofas* ('thieves') appropriately describes a group of up to seven individuals and *hloð* ('band') a group of more than seven but fewer than thirty-five. Any more marauders than this should, according to the laws, be called a *here*. A *here* therefore, in this context, was just a large group of thieves all working together – as good a definition as any for a Viking army operating unlawfully within the bounds of an Anglo-Saxon kingdom, without regard to life, property or the king's laws.[17]

What is less debatable is that this particular *here* was *hæðen*, and that it was *micel*. Although numbers are problematic (as Ine's laws make clear, a *here* need have been no bigger than three dozen – the number needed to crew a single vessel the size of the ship discovered at Gokstad, near Oslo in Norway), the Viking forces that had menaced Carhampton had numbered perhaps as many as 1,500 men – enough to defeat West Saxon royal armies on two separate occasions. It is probably safe to assume that the 'great heathen horde' was considerably bigger; as we shall see, archaeological traces of Viking camps of this period in Britain imply sizeable groupings.[18]

What happened next is not altogether clear, but it seems that the *micel hæðen here*, having spent the winter in the East Anglia, took horses and rode north. Once out of East Anglia, they may have used Ermine Street – the 'Great North Road' – that climbs the country between the Pennines and the Fens, linking London with York. It seems likely, though the sources do not tell us this, that the Viking fleet shadowed the progress of the mounted army as it made its way north, carrying supplies and reinforcements and providing the means for a quick getaway if things turned out badly. Certainly this would have allowed the land-based force to travel faster and more lightly than would otherwise have been possible, while at the same time removing the constraint on manpower that a purely amphibious offensive would have entailed.[19]

Out in the countryside, the inhabitants of the timbered hamlets and farmsteads would have been woken, if they were lucky, by dark news riding hard up the Great North Road: they would have grabbed what they could and fled, the Viking army sweeping through deserted settlements, taking the wheat and slaughtering the livestock, ransacking the church and burning the homes. The horde swept into Northumbria, a sudden blitzkrieg that took the kingdom off guard. Before any resistance could be mustered, the Vikings were already within the walls of Eoforwic (York), the heart of Northumbrian power and the seat of the second most important ecclesiastical diocese in Britain.

\*

By the mid-ninth century, Northumbria was no longer the beacon of Christian learning and sainted warrior kings that it had once been; the lustre of its golden age had dulled considerably by the time of the first raids on Lindisfarne and Jarrow. Civil wars and endemic feuding had weakened the kingdom, and Viking attacks had taken a toll on its ruling class, killing its king in 843 and disrupting the succession. And, although the kingdom was by no means a spent force, there can be little doubt that the sacking of its monasteries – international powerhouses of wealth, learning and industry – had been a setback to Northumbrian culture and economy, disrupting trade and creating the insecurity in which political fragmentation was ever more likely.[20]

Northumbria's rivals seem to have sensed its weakness. In 828, Ecgberht of Wessex had led a huge army to Dore (literally 'door' or 'narrow pass'), part of a continuum of features that marked the northern borders of Mercia.[21] The result of the meeting at Dore was that Ecgberht received the 'submission and concord' of the Northumbrians, and was recognized (in the Wessex-produced *Anglo-Saxon Chronicle* at least) as 'Bretwalda' – overlord of Britain.[22] Forty years on and the situation had not improved; the Northumbrian king, Osberht, had been deposed in favour of a rival named Ælle, of whom very little is known, other than that – from the perspective of later chroniclers – he was an 'unnatural king' (that is, he was perceived as a tyrant without a legitimate claim to the throne).[23] It is unlikely, given the precedent of Northumbrian politics over the previous century, that this had been a peaceful transition of power, and it is probable that murders and civil war had taken a toll on the aristocracy and the fighting capacity of the kingdom. It may have been, in some respects at least, a weakened state, unprepared to face a ruthless and opportunistic enemy seeking to take advantage.[24]

The Viking capture of York in 866 seems initially to have stunned the Northumbrians into inaction, and it took months for them to organize a response. Part of the delay was probably diplomatic, for when an Anglo-Saxon army was eventually gathered, both the rival claimants to the Northumbrian throne were present. The idea, presumably, was to set differences aside until the existential threat had been overcome. For Ælle and Osberht, however, the reassuring familiarity of their former enmity was gone for ever.

The Anglo-Saxon counter-attack on York was, at first, dramatically successful. The old Roman walls, reduced in height but still largely intact, had been reinforced with wooden ramparts by the ninth century. Nevertheless, it seems the Northumbrian forces were able to break into the city with little difficulty. The exuberance of this head-on assault, however, seems to have been the undoing of the Northumbrians; having smashed their way in, they swiftly found themselves trapped inside the city. Surrounded and outnumbered, with no means of retreat, the vanguard was annihilated.

No one knows what happened within the walls of York in 867. But the remnants of the Northumbrian army must have looked on in horror as the Viking army emerged from a city that remained resolutely in their grip. Perhaps the Vikings jeered at the survivors, or hurled foul abuse; perhaps they bared their arses or displayed the severed heads of fallen Northumbrians on the points of their spears.[25] Whatever the case, Northumbrian resistance was broken. Fighting continued, but by the end of the day 'an immense slaughter' had been made of the Northumbrian army, and both Ælle and Osberht were dead.[26]

The capture of York left a deep impression. The story of its fall and the events that led to it and flowed from it were told and retold over the centuries, the form the story took in the Old Norse saga literature of the Middle Ages colouring the way in which the historical events – and the conduct of the Vikings in general – have been perceived. By way of backstory to the capture of York, the sagas offer up the character Ragnar Loðbrók, the supposed father of the leaders of the *micel here*. Ragnar Loðbrók – which is to say, Ragnar Hairy-pants (ON *brók* is from the same Germanic root as the

English word 'breeches') – is of indeterminate historicity, and his exploits, as recounted in several sagas and a twelfth-century history written by the Danish cleric Saxo Grammaticus, tend towards the implausible.[27] His deeds, and his death, were used to frame an epic story of revenge and super-human prowess, a tale that flowed from deep seams of myth.

It all begins with the tale of how Ragnar gained his nickname. What follows is my version of the story, rationalized from the various sources in which it is told, embellished a little, but still leaky with plot-holes.

Jarl Herruð of Gautland[28] (the land of the Geats, in southern Sweden) had a daughter named Þóra; she was the most beautiful woman of whom any had heard tell. Her father had made for her a fenced hideaway in which she dwelt. One day, the Jarl gave to his daughter a small serpent – a baby – and she kept the snake in a box of ashes upon a mound of gold. But babies, as they are wont to do, grow bigger, and so it was with the snake.[29] Larger and larger the serpent grew, and the gold multiplied beneath it, until the serpent was so big that it coiled around Þóra's dwelling, its tail eventually meeting with its head, lying upon a huge heap of treasure. None could approach it, so fierce and deadly had it grown, and every day it devoured a whole ox – no doubt to the great upset and impoverishment of the folk thereabouts. Jarl Herruð could see that this state of affairs could not continue, and let it be known that whosoever would rid him of this menace could take his daughter as wife and claim all the gold that lay beneath the serpent's belly. When this news reached Ragnar, the son of Hring, king of Denmark and Sweden, he determined to slay the monster and win for himself the fame, riches and marriage that Herruð had promised. In preparation he fashioned for himself a suit of shaggy clothes of fur and wool. These he boiled and soaked in tar and dipped in sand to harden them (though others say that he drenched them in water and froze them in the snow until they were ice-clad: a glittering suit of crystalline armour, jagged and deadly). Thus attired, Ragnar took up his shield, spear and sword and sought the beast.

When Ragnar reached the lair of the serpent, it was quickly roused against him. Rearing up to a fearsome height, it hung in the air above its challenger, swaying ominously from side to side, fangs bared and dripping with venom. Suddenly, it vomited its poison, but the foul bile was futile against the strange armour Ragnar wore. Enraged, the serpent darted forward, an emerald blur, its great jaws gaping wide, seeking to rend and tear. But Ragnar held his shield steady in front of him and rushed forward to meet the creature, thrusting with his spear. The jaws of the snake closed uselessly around the iron-banded shield, gouging at the wooden boards, snapping on the metal boss; but the spear struck home, biting into the serpent's neck and through its spine into the ground beyond. The thrashing of the beast in its death-agony shook the earth and made the pillars of Þóra's hall tremble like the forest trees when the storms come. But Ragnar was unafraid; he drew his sword and raised it high, before bringing it down with all his strength, hacking through the sinewy neck and striking the serpent's head from its body. The maimed coils flung themselves from left to right, the tail beating on the ground, black blood pouring on to the earth. When at last it lay still, and Ragnar was sure the beast was dead, he departed. But he carried away only the shaft of his spear and left behind the spear-head where it stood, still upright, pinning the head of the serpent to the soil.

The next day, Jarl Herruð marvelled at the carnage that had been wrought and listened to his daughter's tale. She suggested that he call a great assembly – a *thing* – to which all men should be commanded to attend. In this way, she thought, the man whose spear-shaft matched the spear-head that had been left in the ground would be discovered, and the mystery of the hairy slayer solved. On Herruð's orders this was duly done, and – on the appointed day – Ragnar arrived at the gathering, clad as before in his strange suit of shaggy clothes. He stood apart from the other men at the edge of the *thing* and watched as each hopeful suitor – many of them great earls and powerful warlords, clad in fine embroidered cloaks of bright colours and with silver rings jangling on their arms – came and tried to fit his spear-head to their spear-shafts. None of them, of course, could make the spear-head fit. At last it was Ragnar's turn and he stepped from the shadows, still stinking with the serpent's gore and venom. There was a murmuring among the disappointed suitors: how dare this foul-smelling vagrant think to claim such a fair prize? Ragnar cared not: he duly presented his spear-shaft. Þóra lifted the spear-head and slipped it on to the end: it fitted – of course it did – and a gasp went up from the assembled throng. But then Ragnar pushed the fur hood from his head, and suddenly all could see that it was the son of King Hring who was the serpent-slayer. The embarrassed silence lasted for long seconds, but it was broken by Herruð, who let out a great bellow of mirth: 'My son-in-law shall you be, Ragnar Hringsson, but all shall know you now as "Hairy-pants"!' At this, all those who were gathered fell about laughing, and Herruð commanded that the *thing* become a wedding feast. Ragnar and Þóra were duly married, and with her by his side, Ragnar in time returned home to rule his father's realm as king.

The plot-holes are inevitable really, as all of the surviving versions have their internal inconsistencies and none of them agree. Saxo's version, for instance, has Þóra receiving a clutch of snake-babies that grow up to rampage around the countryside wreaking havoc. But that the story is an old one is confirmed by the fact that the tale seems already to have been well established by the twelfth century, appearing not only in Saxo's *Gesta Danorum*, but also in the first lines of a poem called *Krákumál* – purportedly Ragnar's death-poem, but written long after his death:

We struck with our swords!
So long ago, it was:
we had gone to Gautland
for the *ground-wolf*'s slaughter.
Then we won fair Thora;
thus the warriors named me
Loðbrók, when I laid that
*heather-eel* low in battle,
ended the *earth-coil*'s life
with inlaid shining steel.[30]

*Krákumál* makes use of a number of kennings to describe the serpent: 'ground-wolf'; 'heather-eel'; 'earth-coil'. All describe the same thing: a writhing snake-like beast of monstrous size – a *wyrm* in Old English, *ormr* in Old Norse – a thing of soil, and ground-dwelling. Although these verses perform a subtle linguistic dance around the issue, we understand intuitively the true nature of the monster. It is the creature that has haunted the imaginations of human civilizations from the moment they were able to express themselves: the oldest terror of all. Dragon.

The Geats of Gautland had already suffered their share of dragons in the literature of northern Europe. *Beowulf* famously concludes with the hero's fight – as king of the Geats – against a beast far more terrible than the earth-bound *wyrm* that Ragnar faced. Beowulf's dragon is airborne and fire-spewing, like those which presaged the arrival of the Vikings at Lindisfarne, a harbinger of apocalyptic devastation:

The dragon began to belch out flames
and burn bright homesteads; there was a hot glow
that scared everyone, for the vile sky-winger
would leave nothing alive in his wake.
Everywhere the havoc he wrought was in evidence.
Far and near, the Geat nation
bore the brunt of his brutal assaults

and virulent hate. Then back to the hoard
he would dart before daybreak, to hide in his den[31]

Nevertheless, like others of his kin, this dragon is also at heart an earth-dweller: the 'harrower of the dark [...] who hunts out barrows [...] driven to hunt out hoards underground, to guard heathen gold through age-long vigils'.[32] This gold-hoarding habit of dragons is a common theme and was regarded as self-evident in Anglo-Saxon verse – the gnomic poem *Maxims II* presents the idea that the 'Dragon must dwell in the barrow, cunning, proud of its treasures' as a fact equivalent to the truth that 'fish must dwell in water'.[33]

The dragon's jealous and possessive attitude towards hoarded treasure seems to have operated in both Old English and Old Norse literature as a symbol of the pernicious and destructive vice of avarice, to be contrasted directly (as it is in *Maxims II*) with the dictum that 'the king belongs in his hall, dealing out rings'. The gold-hoarding serpent was thus – as well as being an embodiment of flaming Armageddon – a more subtle nemesis of ordered life, a poison gnawing at the roots of society, breaking the bonds that held people together; it was the duty of heroes and kings to fight them, even if the entropic forces they represented could never be truly defeated.[34]

These characteristics of the monstrous serpent were well represented in the most epic streams of Norse mythology. Niðhöggr ('spite-striker') and Jörmungandr ('mighty-wand', aka Midgarðsormr – lit. 'Middle-earth-serpent') were creatures of another order of magnitude altogether. The former gnawed at the roots of the world tree, literally undermining the pillar of creation. In the end of days Niðhöggr would, it was foretold, herald the doom of the world:

Then there comes there the dark dragon flying,
the glittering snake up from Moon-wane hills,
it bears in its wings – and flies over the plain –
dead bodies: Spite-striker [Niðhöggr]; now she must sink.[35]

Jörmungandr – the world-serpent – was a being of yet more profound cosmological significance: he was the mighty *wyrm* whose body encircled the mortal realm, separating the human world from chaos. He, too, would break his bonds at the end, when the denizens of Utgarð (the 'out-world') would thrust the world into oblivion at *Ragnarök* – the 'doom of the gods'. To contend with such a menace, no mortal champion would suffice: Thor the Thunderer, protector of gods and men, would be the one to shoulder the futile burden; his many contests with the world-serpent were told in tales that travelled far and wide across the Viking world.

Although mention of more 'mundane' dragons in Old Norse literature is fairly common, serpents of Beowulfian splendour are, to quote Tolkien once again, 'as rare as they are dire'.[36] The template for them all, however – the ur-dragon – is Fáfnir, the creature slain in one of the most important cycles of Old Norse hero-tales by Sigurd the Völsung – the godfather of all dragon-slayers. The tale begins as follows:

When Otr, while swimming in the guise of (no surprise) an otter, was killed by the god Loki, recompense was paid in treasure to his father, Hreidmar, and his brothers, Regin and Fáfnir. The treasure, however, as treasure often does in such stories, worked an evil spell upon the brothers, partly as a result of a cursed ring that Odin had added to the treasure hoard at the last moment. The brothers conspired and murdered their father, but Fáfnir betrayed his brother and stole the treasure for himself. He fled with it to a place called Gnitaheiðr, where he became transformed into a dreadful serpent, there to guard his hoard jealously. Regin, meanwhile, plotted his vengeance, becoming skilled in smithcraft and adopting a young man named Sigurd as his protégé. In time Regin forged a deadly sword, which he called Gram, and set Sigurd on the quest to which his life hitherto had led. Sigurd went to Gnitaheiðr and dug a hole for himself, waiting for Fáfnir to slither overhead. The dragon duly returned and Sigurd drove the sword upwards through the serpent's body.

Fáfnir took a long time to die, and conversed long with his murderer, but die he eventually did, and – as Regin had instructed him – Sigurd cut out the dragon's heart and began to roast it on a stick over the fire in order that he should serve it up to his master. Anxious not to deliver undercooked organs, Sigurd tested the meat with his fingers, burning his thumb. He stuck the thumb into his mouth and tasted the dragon's blood that was smeared there. Instantly, Sigurd gained the ability to understand the speech of birds. Seven such creatures, so it transpired, were conversing in the trees above him and were taunting him for his apparent stupidity, explaining that Regin had tricked and used him to enact this vengeance, and that he intended to claim the dragon's treasure all for himself. On hearing this, Sigurd promptly sought out Regin, and lopped off his head with Gram, the sword Regin himself had forged.[37]

That is the end of the dragon-slaying part of the tale, though it is not by any means the end of the Sigurd legend. This segment, and the convoluted story of thwarted love and vengeance between kinsfolk that follows, was told and retold throughout the Middle Ages, finding epic form in the thirteenth century in the Old High German *Nibelungenlied* and the Old Norse *Völsunga saga*, medieval poems that would ultimately inspire Richard Wagner's *Der Ring des Nibelungen*, a series of operas – *Das Rheingold*, *Die Walküre*, *Siegfried* and *Götterdämmerung* – first performed as a cycle in 1876. The original costume designs for these operas, by Carl Emil Doepler, alongside Arthur Rackham's illustrations for the English-language version of Wagner's libretti, would prove to be enormously influential for Victorian imaginings of Norse mythological themes; Thoma's winged helmets and bronze bustiers set a template for how Wotan (Odin) and his valkyries should be presented that has proved remarkably resilient.[38]

The Völsung legend, however, would also find its way into the British (and global) psyche through a less overt but equally influential route. In the closing years of the nineteenth century, a small boy living with his mother in a village close to the outskirts of industrial

Birmingham made a discovery. Towards the end of the *Red Fairy Book*, the second of British writer and critic Andrew Lang's compendia of fairy-tales, a young J. R. R. Tolkien found 'The Story of Sigurd'. It affected him deeply. 'I desired dragons with a profound desire,' he recalled in 1939; '... the world that contained even the imagination of Fafnir was richer and more beautiful, at whatever cost of peril.' It would have a seismic effect on his imagination, shaping a lifelong enthusiasm.[39]

In 1914, having won the undergraduate Skeat Prize for English at Exeter College, Oxford, Tolkien would use his winnings to purchase the 1870 translation of *Völsunga saga* produced by the great artist, writer, craft pioneer and medievalist William Morris (who was also an important figure in the nineteenth-century Viking revival) and his friend the Icelandic scholar Eiríkr Magnússon.[40] In tone, plot and subject matter, the legend of Sigurd would inspire a great deal of Tolkien's oeuvre: both directly, in a poem that he wrote in the traditional English alliterative metre (published posthumously as *The Legend of Sigurd and Gudrún*) and indirectly, in myriad elements of his tales of Middle-Earth: from the slaying of the dragon Glaurung by the hero Turin Turambar (like Sigurd, from beneath) in *The Silmarillion*, to the gold-madness of Thorin Oakenshield in *The Hobbit* and, of course, the cursed ring that defined *The Lord of the Rings* trilogy.[41]

William Morris, for his part, also produced his own epic retelling of the Sigurd story that was separate from the translation undertaken with Eiríkr Magnússon. Now largely forgotten, the 10,000 lines of rhyming hexameters that comprised *The Story of Sigurd the Volsung and the Fall of the Niblungs* (1876) was once an object of high praise, and its author considered it his finest poetic achievement. George Bernard Shaw, for one, was filled with enthusiasm, gushing that with *Sigurd the Volsung* Morris had 'achieved the summit of his professional destiny by writing the greatest epic since Homer'. According to Shaw, Morris 'was quite aware of the greatness of this work, and used to recite passages from it, marking its swing by rocking from one foot to another like an elephant. After one of these recitations he sat down beside me. I said "This is the stuff for me; there is nothing like it."[42]

In the longer term, *The Story of Sigurd the Volsung* suffered from the inevitable comparisons that were drawn between it and Richard Wagner's monumental work on the same theme. The four operas of the *Ring* cycle were first performed together at Bayreuth in 1876, the same year that Morris' poem was published, and caused a sensation in Europe. It was not a comparison that Morris would have welcomed. His own opinion of Wagner's work, indeed, of opera in general, was not a charitable one: 'I look upon it as nothing short of desecration to bring such a tremendous and world-wide subject under the gas-lights of an opera; the most degraded and rococo of all forms of art – the idea of a sandy-haired German tenor tweedledeeing over the unspeakable woes of Sigurd, which even the simplest words are not typical enough to express!'[43] This is probably unfair to Wagner who, after all, had his own axes to grind about the state of theatrical music. But Morris, by almost any sane measure, is a more sympathetic character than the great German maestro, so I hesitate to intervene in the latter's defence.

Thus the Sigurd narrative has been – and continues to be – an incredibly potent force in shaping our conceptions of northern mythology and the tone and texture of modern fantasy. This potency, however, arises from and builds on the defining role this legend played in the world-view of northern peoples from an exceptionally early date. As the archetype for many other human dragon-slaying heroes, Beowulf and Ragnar included, Sigurd represented an important and popular figure of early medieval folk culture.[44] Images of the hero stabbing the dragon in its soft underbelly – alongside other scenes from the tale – have been found as far afield as Tatarstan.[45] The most famous depictions are found cut into standing stones in eastern Sweden, with particularly striking examples at Ramsund and Gök in Södermanland. In these carvings, the body of the serpent coils in an oval loop around the stone, an attenuated ribbon that carries an inscription incised in runes – a message to commemorate the dead. This is commonplace on the

Viking Age runestones of Scandinavia – as though the names conveyed by the runes could somehow shimmer into serpentine life, to be carried into immortality on the backs of dragons. But in these examples, down below the runes, an intrusive figure lurks, his sword jutting upwards, piercing the body of the *wyrm*: here is Sigurðr Fánisbani – Sigurd Fáfnir's Bane – striking the heroic, cowardly blow that defines him.[46]

Sigurd imagery also found its way to Britain during the Viking Age: four Christian runestones erected on the Isle of Man by communities of Viking origin display imagery from the Sigurd legend, and an iconographic scheme that depicts the roasting of Fáfnir's heart and Sigurd sucking his thumb was carved into a standing cross at Halton in Lancashire.[47] One of the Manx stones contains a rare detail, found in only a handful of other depictions of the story. This is the image of Gunnar in the snake-pit; a scene from later in the story – pithily summarized in the thirteenth-century *Völsunga saga*. Gunnar, who with his brother Högni had murdered Sigurd in order to claim the treasure for themselves, fell foul of their brother-in-law, Attila the Hun, who – having invited them over for dinner – had Högni's heart cut out and Gunnar thrown into a pit of snakes. The latter brother was able to fend off death for a short while by playing a harp with his feet: all of the snakes fell asleep, except for one, which delivered the fatal bite.

Ragnar Loðbrók was in many respects a reinvention of his dragon-on-slaying antecedent Sigurd; it was even said (with cavalier regard for chronology) that Ragnar's second wife, Aslaug, was the daughter of Sigurd himself (with the valkyrie Brynhildr). Ragnar and Aslaug even had a son they named 'Sigurd', a young man who, it was said, had the image of a snake biting its own tail swirling in his iris: for obvious reasons he became known as Sigurd 'snake-in-the-eye' (*ormr í auga*).[48]

Ragnar may never have existed, and if he did, almost nothing we are told of his life in the sagas is true. His death, as recorded in the sagas and in *Krákumál*, is pure fantasy. He was said to have died languishing at the bottom of a snake-pit – consigned to this improbable death by Ælle, one of the two kings of Northumbria killed by the *micel here* in 867. (The similarity to the treatment of Gunnar in *Völsunga saga* is obvious and probably deliberate.) What is clear, however, is that when Scandinavians of the later Middle Ages came to write about the deeds of Ragnar and his sons they saw them in the light of the most heroic figure of all: Sigurd the dragon-slayer himself. This alone should tell us something about the high regard and wide-ranging fame that attended the reputations of the men who took York in 867. But what is also clear is that it was felt necessary to provide some sort of explanation for the Viking invasions of Britain in the 860s, a compelling origin tale to explain what happened, to justify all the violence and the bloodshed, to explain the appalling deeds and doings of a cast of individuals who (or some of whom at least) have a far better claim to historicity than their supposed father.[49]

# 8

# EAGLES
# OF BLOOD

Do you know how to cut? Do you know how to read?
Do you know how to stain? Do you know how to test?
Do you know how to invoke? Do you know how to sacrifice?
Do you know how to dispatch? Do you know how to slaughter?

*Hávamál*[1]

Björn Ironside, Halfdan Whiteshirt,[2] Ubbe, Sigurd Snake-in-the-Eye and Ivar the Boneless.

The recitation of their names has a poetry about it, like the ritual summoning of Viking ghosts. Most of these individuals – if not all of them – were, unlike their supposed father, real people. Of the five, three of them – Ubbe, Halfdan and Ivar – had a major role to play in Britain during the ninth century. In the stories that were written about them in later centuries, the relationship with their father, Ragnar Loðbrók, was crucial – not least in establishing a motive for their violent intrusion into England.

The vengeance that they (and Ivar in particular) were believed to have wrought on King Ælle for supposedly dumping their dad into a snake-pit has been held up for centuries as the epitome of Viking savagery and pagan cruelty. 'Ivar and the brothers', so the story is told in *Ragnarssona þáttr* ('The Tale of Ragnar's Sons', written *c.* 1300), 'had the eagle cut in Ella's back, then all his ribs severed from the backbone with a sword, so that his lungs were pulled out'.[3]

This grotesque performance has become known as the 'blood-eagle'. Saxo Grammaticus, writing at least a hundred years earlier than the author of this account (though still 300 years after the event) gives a version of something similar, but his description is 'milder' in that the outline of an eagle is simply incised into Ælle's back; no messing around with ribs and lungs flapping about all over the place (although Saxo does introduce some literal salt into the wound: 'Not satisfied with imprinting a wound on him, they salted the mangled flesh').[4] More pressing than the disagreement between these sources, however, is the fact that the only contemporary account of Ælle's death implies that it occurred during the Northumbrian attempt to recapture York in 867. Even if we imagine this unpleasant spectacle taking place in the immediate aftermath of victory, one might expect that something so outlandish would have received a passing mention, even in a document as famously laconic as the *Anglo-Saxon Chronicle*.

The earliest Old Norse reference to the killing of King Ælle comes in verse form. In a stanza of one of several skaldic poems composed in praise of King Cnut in the eleventh century (known collectively as *Knútsdrápur*), the poet Sigvatr Þórðarson wrote:

Ok Ellu bak,
At lét hinn's sat,
Ívarr, ara,
Iorví, skorit.[5]

Translated literally, this turns out as:

And Ella's back,
at had the one who dwelt,
Ivarr, with eagle,
York, cut.[6]

To say that skaldic verse is an economical art-form would be something of an understatement, and the particular form that the *Knútsdrápur* took (a metre known as *tøglag*) was particularly compressed. Most pertinently, the relationship of the elements within the stanza is as ambiguous in Old Norse as it is in modern English. It *can* be translated as 'Ivar, who dwelt at York, had an eagle cut into Ælle's back' – the implication being that Ivar cut the *image* of an eagle into Ælle's back. This seems to have been how medieval writers understood it, and modern historians have tended to accept the interpretation of Saxo and the saga-writers.

However, the verse could equally well mean 'Ivar, who dwelt at York, caused an eagle to cut Ælle's back.'[7] Or, if one is to fill in the subtext: 'Ivar, having captured York, defeated and killed King Ælle: which meant, to everyone's general satisfaction, that eagles were able to gouge the flesh of his corpse as it lay face down and naked in the mud: hooray for Ivar, feaster of eagles!' This, the reader may remember, is very much the sort of thing that Viking aristocrats enjoyed being praised for. Good kings were those who could claim particular success in turning their enemies into fleshy morsels for raptors and carrion creatures (especially the wolf, raven and eagle). In other words, it is utterly conventional, and precisely the sort of thing we should expect a skaldic poet to come out with.[8]

The elaborate and inconsistent descriptions of gory rituals contained in Saxo's history and in the sagas seem, when seen in this light, to have been the product of a medieval misunderstanding, one which has been compounded by a tendency among modern translators to approach the poetry through the prism of those later embroideries.

The supposed 'rite of the blood-eagle' seems, therefore, to be a myth of Viking barbarity conjured up in later centuries by antiquarians enthralled by the exoticism of their forebears and titillated by their gory antics. As Roberta Frank, the incomparable scholar of Germanic languages and literature, put it: 'Medieval men of letters, like their modern counterparts, could sometimes be over-eager to recover the colourful rites and leafy folk beliefs of their pagan ancestors.'[9] This should not be allowed to obscure the fact that the pagan people of northern Europe did indeed engage in practices which – from our perspective – appear horrific and bloodthirsty.

In a famous passage in his *Gesta Hammaburgensis ecclesie pontificum* ('Deeds of the Bishops of the Church of Hamburg-Bremen'), the eleventh-century German chronicler Adam of Bremen decided to give an account of what he called 'the superstition of the Swedes'. After an extraordinary (and frankly somewhat unlikely) description of a temple at Uppsala, he goes on to explain that:

> each of their gods have appointed priests to offer up the
> sacrifices of the people [...] The sacrifice proceeds as follows:
> nine males of every living creature are offered up, and it is
> customary to placate the gods with their blood: their corpses
> are hung in the grove next to the temple. That grove is so sacred
> to the heathens that every single tree is considered to be divine,
> thanks to the death or rotting carcass of the sacrificed; they
> hang dogs and horses there alongside men.[10]

There are plenty of details in Adam's account that provoke sceptical beard-stroking – the grandiose scale of the temple and its associated rituals, as well as the obvious Christian agenda of the author, are paramount among these.[11] But even if the details are dubious – indeed, even if there never was a temple at Uppsala[12] – evidence from elsewhere in the Viking world suggests that sacrifice, perhaps including human sacrifice, was very much a part of pre-Christian religion in the north. In 1984, remodelling of Frösö Church in Jämtland, Sweden, led to an archaeological investigation of the chancel. Beneath the altar, the excavators discovered the stump of a birch tree, cut down before the church was built. In the dark earth surrounding the tree were found the bones of animals – cattle, goat, sheep, pig, horse, dog, chicken, grouse, squirrel, deer, elk and bear – scattered in profusion, disarticulated, broken and cut. The remains of humans were also found: two adults (possibly more) and two children – one between three and five years old, the other a baby of less than six months. All of the bones, human and animal, can be dated broadly to the Viking Age. The evidence from Frösö strongly suggests that the tree was a focal point for sacrificial offerings, and it is possible that humans and animals (or parts of animals) were hung from branches – in a manner similar to that described by Adam of Bremen – until they were cut down and buried, or rotted and fell to the earth below.[13]

Other images and texts from the Viking Age seem to corroborate Adam of Bremen's tale – at least in part. Ibn Fadlān explained that, in gratitude for supernatural intervention and assistance, animals were slaughtered and their remains offered to the idol. The offerer 'hangs the heads of sheep or cows on the wooden stakes which have been driven into the ground'.[14] Ibrâhîm ibn Ya`qûb al-Ṭurṭûshî, a Jewish merchant from Islamic Spain, reported that in Hedeby, 'When a man kills a sacrificial animal, whether it be an ox, ram, goat, or pig, he hangs it on a pole outside his house so that people will know that he has made a sacrifice in honour of the god.'[15] It must have made for a grisly street scene.

A fragment of tapestry, woven in the ninth century, was preserved in a ship burial at Oseberg near Oslo in Norway. It seems to depict a strange tree laden with corpse-fruit while a procession of wagons, horses, women and warriors passes beneath it. Finally, the famous Stora Hammars picture stone from Gotland appears to show something more elaborate: a small figure lies face down on a small structure. Behind, to the right, stands a bearded man, leaning forward, wielding a spear. Behind him and above him, two large birds are depicted – ravens, perhaps. To the left of the scene an armed man hangs from a tree, to the right a crowd wave their weapons in the air.[16] No one knows what this scene is intended to convey (a mythological scene, a legendary narrative, a depiction of contemporary practices?), but the impression of blood-ritual is unmistakable and a connection to the cult of the god Odin entirely plausible.

One of the most evocative of medieval embellishments was that which transformed the supposed rite of the blood-eagle from a sadistic and vengeful act into a religious ritual. This notion of cultic sacrifice has its origins in the only other saga account of the practice – a description in the thirteenth-century *Orkneyinga saga* which insists that Halfdan Long-leg (a son of the ninth-century Norwegian king Harald Finehair) 'had his ribs cut from the spine with a sword and the lungs pulled out through the slits in his back' by Einar, Earl of Orkney, who 'dedicated the victim to Odin as a victory offering'.[17] The saga is deeply flawed as a guide to historical events, its grisly details as unreliable as the sources discussed above. In one detail, however, the saga may preserve a real aspect of the relationship between death and ritual during the Viking Age: an association with the lore and cult of Odin, Lord of the Hanged (Hangadrottinn).

There is no escaping the fact that Odin, as we know him from Old Norse poetry, as well as from later medieval writings, is a troubling and sinister deity. Among the most ominous of the huge number of names by which he was known are Valföðr ('father of the slain'), Skollvaldr ('lord of treachery'), Hjarrandi ('screamer'), Grímnir ('the hooded one'), Hildolfr ('battle-wolf'), Bölverkr ('evil worker'), Draugadróttinn ('lord of the undead'), Hengikeptr ('hangjaw') …[18] His portfolio is a broad one: magic, warfare, rune-craft, fate, poetry, prophecy, dissimulation, power and death seem to have been considered his main areas of interest. Odin's multifaceted nature makes him a difficult god to characterize. But in all his guises there runs a skein of darkness, an intimacy with death that hangs off him like a cloak of shadow that obscures and obfuscates – a dark and tattered mantle.

Odin's association with bloody rituals is bound up with the god's repeated acts of self-sacrifice in the pursuit of hidden or forbidden wisdom. His one empty eye socket – the god's most unambiguous distinguishing feature – was the result of his thirst for a draught from the well of Mímir, the fountain of wisdom and intellect presided over by its eponymous guardian. To gain access to the well, Odin plucked out his own eye and gave it to the waters – an exchange of sight for insight.[19] When Mímir the guardian died, decapitated during a war between the gods, Odin took possession of the severed head. He carved runes into it, spoke charms over it. Ever after it would speak with him, whispering him secrets, telling of other worlds. Here is Odin the necromancer, conversant with corpses.

The knowledge of runes and charms came about as the result of an even greater sacrifice – the god's dedication of himself to himself:

> I know that I hung on that windy tree,
> spear-wounded, nine full nights,
> given to Odin, myself to myself,
> on that tree that rose from roots
> that no man ever knows.
>
> They gave me neither bread, nor drink from horn,
> I peered down below.
> I clutched the runes, screaming I grabbed them,
> and then sank back.[20]

The tree from which Odin was hung is probably to be identified with the world tree, Yggdrasil. The spear with which he was wounded is probably his own dwarf-forged spear, Gungnir. Unlike the loss of his eye, given as surety to a third party, this was a more profound sacrifice – one which acknowledged Odin himself as the highest power to which an offering could be made, himself to himself, an ordeal of transcendental suffering – the primal bargain of power for pain.

The initial Viking capture of York came towards the end of 866, and the calamitous Northumbrian counter-attack didn't materialize until March of 867.[21] The delay meant that the Vikings were probably able to celebrate their victory in synchronicity with the mid-winter festival, a time of drinking, feasting and sacrifices known, in Old Norse, as *jol* – or, as we know it, Yule. As is so often the case, we only have much later writers to rely on for any sense of what this festival involved. And, almost as predictably, it is the Icelander Snorri Sturluson in his great historical cycle *Heimskringla* who provides the detail. This comes, firstly, in *Ynglinga saga*, where he explains that sacrifices were made at mid-winter for a good harvest (a provision which makes sense if one imagines mid-winter as marking the rebirth of the sun – the start of the solar year – and the beginning of a new cycle of growth),[22] and, secondly, in *Hakonar saga góða* (the saga of Hákon the Good). Hákon (King of Norway between 934 and 961) is principally remembered for his role in promoting Christianity in Norway, and one of the ways he apparently tried to achieve this was by aligning the Yule festival with the dates of Christmas. As Snorri explains, 'previously observance of Yule began on midwinter night (12th January), and continued for three nights'. He goes on:

It was an ancient custom, when a ritual feast was to take place, that all the farmers should attend where the temple was and bring there their own supplies for them to use while the banquet lasted. At this banquet everyone had to take part in the ale-drinking. All kinds of domestic animals were slaughtered there, including horses, and all the blood that came from them was called *hlaut* ('lot'), and what the blood was contained in, *hlaut*-bowls, and *hlaut*-twigs, these were fashioned like holy water sprinklers; with these the altars were to be reddened all over, and also the walls of the temple outside and inside and the people also were sprinkled, while the meat was to be cooked for a feast. There would be fires down the middle of the floor in the temple with cauldrons over them. The toasts were handed across the fire, and the one who was holding the banquet and who was the chief person there, he had to dedicate the toast and all the ritual food; first would be Odin's toast – that was drunk to victory and to the power of the king – and then Njǫrð's toast and Freyr's toast for prosperity and peace. Then after that it was common for many people to drink the *bragafull* ('chieftain's toast'). People also drank toasts to their kinsmen, those who had been buried in mounds, and these were called *minni* ('memorial toasts').[23]

Although this description is generic – it could apply to any festival – the fact that it follows Snorri's reference to Yule implies that he expects it to be read in that context. Much of it evokes a familiar yuletide scene – families gathered together around the fire, plenty of booze and roasted meat, companionable glasses raised to family and absent friends, to peace and good fortune. From a modern perspective, however, this cheerful tableau of comfort and joy is somewhat compromised by the torrent of gore applied liberally to walls, floors and guests. Still, if we believe Snorri (and his description is disarmingly artless and non-judgemental), this is the sort of scene that we can imagine Ivar, Ubbe and Halfdan enjoying over the York festive period during the winter of 866/7.

Snorri Sturluson, as imagined by the
artist Christian Krohg in 1899

After consolidating their initial victory by defeating and killing Osberht and Ælle, the Viking army was soon making provision to move on. By the end of 867, the great heathen horde was in Mercia, bedding down for another winter and, perhaps, a new round of Yule sacrifice. This, understandably, was not to the liking of the Mercian king, Burhred, though there seems little he could do about it. He was compelled to send south – to Wessex – and request the assistance of his brother-in-law, King Æthelred (Burhred had married Æthelswith, the daughter of the old West Saxon king Æthelwulf in 853). The following year, 868, the West Saxons, led in person by Æthelred and his brother Alfred, joined forces with the Mercians and advanced on Nottingham where the Viking army, 'protected by the defences of the fortress, would not give battle'.[24] This was probably not what the English had expected; pitched battles – not sieges – had long been the preferred Anglo-Saxon way of war. This new-fangled use of fortifications set an unwelcome precedent.

We don't know a great deal about the realities of siege warfare during the early medieval period, and what we do know is often derived from continental contexts where continuity with late Roman military strategy and technology was arguably stronger. Even so, offensive strategies against fortified positions were, in the words of one distinguished historian of early medieval military affairs, 'usually conducted with a minimum of finesse'.[25] In the ancient world, siege technology had been impressive. A great Assyrian relief carving produced in the early seventh century BC depicts the capture of the walled Hebrew city of Lachish in 701 BC by the Assyrian king Sennacherib. That siege, which took place 1,500 years before the Viking Age, involved massed archers, scaling ladders, siege towers and battering rams – the latter encased in a contraption with more than a passing resemblance to a tank.[26] Compare this to the images depicted in relief on the early eighth-century AD 'Franks' casket, a remarkable whalebone box crafted in Northumbria and now housed (apart from a single panel in the Bargello Museum in Florence) at the British Museum. On its lid, a single archer is depicted defending a fortified enclosure, firing arrows from the only point of egress – presumably the door. Ranged against him is a motley band which, compared with the mighty hordes of Sennacherib, seems woefully underprepared for the task in hand (although, to be fair, the scale of the undertaking hardly appears comparable).

Techniques of siege warfare seem to have been rudimentary at best. In the absence of any evidence in Britain for siege engines, the assumption has to be that assaults were typically conducted using the 'direct approach'; such seems to be the implication of the few indications that survive.[27] In 757, an internecine feud within Wessex resolved itself in a kerfuffle at the royal hall at Meretun (unidentified). The episode concluded with fighting that took place 'around the gates', until a faction loyal to the (slain) king, Cynewulf, 'forced their way in' and did for the would-be usurper, Cyneheard. In 917, when Æthelflæd, 'the lady of the Mercians', captured Derby from the Vikings, 'four of her thegns [lesser Anglo-Saxon noblemen], who were dear to her, were slain within the gates', implying that – 150 years later – barrelling through the front door was still the principal method for gaining access to fortified places.[28] These are the occasions on which such tactics worked: when they went wrong – as at York in 867 – they could be catastrophic. More often than not, however, the sieges reported in the *Anglo-Saxon Chronicle* seem to have ended in something rather more bathetic. Engagements of this nature probably resembled the first attempt on the French castle in *Monty Python and the Holy Grail*: a futile charge, a pelting with a range of unpleasant objects, and an ignominious retreat.

Of course, we don't know for sure that the siege of Nottingham was quite as calamitous as all that. Nevertheless, it does seem to have been a bit of a damp squib. 'There occurred no serious fighting there,' the *Anglo-Saxon Chronicle* offers, rather feebly. John of Worcester adds limply, 'the Christians were not able to breach the wall'.[29] In the end, the Mercians 'made peace' with the Viking army; in other words, with no end to the stand-off in sight, and the troops grumbling about their fields and families, the English bought the Vikings off.

All parties went their separate ways – the Vikings back to York, Æthelred and Alfred back to Wessex (presumably). The whole affair has the appearance, if not of cock-up, then certainly of anti-climax. Nevertheless, the episode is significant for several reasons: firstly, it demonstrated how weak Mercia had become since its heyday a hundred years earlier. Not only had Burhred failed to deal with the Viking threat, but he had been forced to turn to his brother-in-law (and, probably, nominal overlord) to dig him out of the hole – unsuccessfully, as it turned out.[30] Secondly, it highlighted the willingness, as we have seen, of the Vikings to make use of fortifications in a way which left their enemies off-balance and struggling for military solutions. Finally, and related to the last point, it points to the strategic choice to which Anglo-Saxon kings would resort over and over again when faced with this sort of Viking aggression: they reached for their metaphorical chequebooks, rather than their swords, frequently with disastrous consequences.

Burhred was not the first to pay the Vikings to go away. The East Anglian king, Edmund, seems to have done much the same when the *micel here* turned up on his doorstep in 865; the horses and provisions the Vikings had taken in his kingdom on that occasion were almost certainly rendered up by the East Anglians in order that they might avoid any further unpleasantness.

In 870, however, the Vikings returned to Edmund's kingdom. They 'rode over Mercia into East Anglia and took up winter settlement at Thetford.' This time there were no deals to be made. 'And that winter,' the *Anglo-Saxon Chronicle* relates, 'King Edmund fought with them, and the Danes took victory, and slew the king and took all the land.'[31]

This brief notice represents effectively everything that is known of the Viking conquest of East Anglia: no battle, no deed of heroism or cruelty, no desperate resistance or punitive vengeance has survived to be passed on to us. All we know is that, 450 years after the Anglian settlement of eastern England, 300 since the South folk and the North folk had recognized a single king to rule over them, 250 since the occupant of Mound 1 had been laid to rest at Sutton Hoo in a ship filled with the treasures of the age, and only 40 since the East Anglian king Æthelstan had slain two Mercian kings in battle.[32] Anglo-Saxon East Anglia had fallen to new rulers.

Like the capture of York and the death of King Ælle, however, the conquest of East Anglia and, particularly, the killing of King Edmund were to leave a lasting imprint on the early medieval imagination, eventually developing a significance that would reverberate through the centuries. And, as with Ælle, this would hinge almost entirely on the way that Edmund's death was later reported.

The first – and fullest – account of Edmund's death, the *Passio Sancti Eadmundi*, was written in Latin during the second half of the tenth century by a man called Abbo, a Frankish Benedictine monk from the Abbey of Fleury (in modern France). Probably aware that the century-long gap between Edmund's death and his account might raise issues of credibility, Abbo was particular about establishing the provenance of his tale. He claimed that he had heard it from Archbishop Dunstan, who had himself heard it told to King Athelstan (of Wessex) by an ancient who had served as King Edmund's armour-bearer. Believe that if you will – there is no way to prove it either way. Suffice it to say, however, that there are aspects of Edmund's death (and subsequent undeath) that present certain difficulties.

Abbo starts, in time-honoured fashion, to establish some familiar tropes (I quote at length to give a flavour of his idiosyncratic waffle). He reminds us:

> that from the north comes all that is evil, as those have had too good cause to know, who through the spite of fortune and the fall of the die have experienced the barbarity of the races of the north. These, it is certain, are so cruel by the ferocity of their nature, as to be incapable of feeling for the ills of mankind; as is shown by the fact that some of their tribes use human flesh for food, and from the circumstance are known by the Greek name

A ninth-century gravestone from the monastery at Lindisfarne depicts the onslaught of armed men

The late-tenth-century Gjermundbu helmet, the only complete Viking Age helmet ever found in Scandinavia

A lead weight, adapted from a piece of ecclesiastical metalwork

The Inchmarnock 'hostage stone'; a graffito that appears to depict a slave-raid in progress

The reconstructed Viking Age long-house at Borg, Lofoten (Norway)

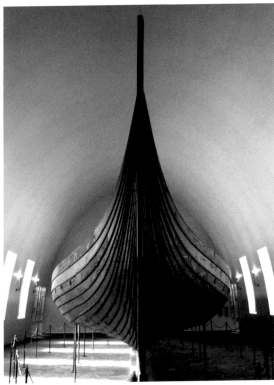

The Gokstad Ship, built c.890, now housed in Oslo

*Opposite:* This image, from a twelfth-century life of St Edmund, depicts Ivar and Ubbe setting sail for England

The Coppergate Helmet, a Northumbrian helmet forged between 750 and 775

Sigurd pierces the body of the dragon Fáfnir from beneath on a runestone from Ramsund, Södermanland (Sweden)

Wayland's Smithy in *c*.1900, before restoration of the barrow took place in the 1960s

When the Somerset levels flood, the early medieval landscape is briefly restored. The village of East Lyng is to the left, attached to the Isle of Athelney, the strip of green extending diagonally up and right from the centre of the photograph

*Opposite:* A reconstruction of the Viking camp at Repton

Wayland's Smithy in *c.*1900, before restoration of the barrow took place in the 1960s

When the Somerset levels flood, the early medieval landscape is briefly restored. The village of East Lyng is to the left, attached to the Isle of Athelney, the strip of green extending diagonally up and right from the centre of the photograph

*Opposite:* A reconstruction of the Viking camp at Repton

An Anglo-Saxon font, carved in the ninth century, at Deerhurst in Gloucestershire

The early medieval crypt of St Wystan's Church at Repton

A reconstruction of the Viking camp at Torksey

Anthropophagists. Nations of this kind abound in great numbers in Scythia, near the Hyperborean Mountains, and are destined, as we read, more than all other races, to follow Antichrist, and to batten without compunction on the agonies of men who refuse to bear on their foreheads the mark of the beast.[33]

Vikings, Abbo wants us to understand, are a very bad thing.

He continues, in this wonderfully circumlocutious way, to elaborate the arrival of Ivar ('a tyrant who from sheer love of cruelty had given orders for the massacre of the innocent') and Ubbe ('his associate in cruelty') in East Anglia and the hideous and horrible atrocities they carried out there. All of which is mere preamble to the real point of Abbo's story – the description of the gruesome and absurdly sadistic killing of King Edmund, drawn out in lingering, almost eroticized, prose. Edmund, stoic in his refusal to fight, was bound in chains, mocked, beaten and tied to a tree. He was lashed and tortured, 'but unceasingly called on Christ with broken voice'. Irritated by this, the Vikings 'as if practising at a target' discharged a forest of arrows into the hapless king until he resembled 'a prickly hedgehog' (asper herecius). Somehow, this was not enough to finish off the defiant Edmund, or even to silence him (his people may have wished that he had shown the same backbone on the battlefield). This was apparently the final straw for Ivar. Edmund, barely able to stand, 'his ribs laid bare by numberless gashes', prepared for the killing blow: 'while the words of prayer were still on his lips, the executioner, sword in hand, deprived the king of life, striking off his head with a single blow'.[34]

In the past, some historians have attempted to argue that Abbo's lurid descriptions are an essentially accurate illustration of a ritualized killing, a garbled retelling of the sacrificial rite of the blood-eagle. This is manifestly absurd. For one thing, the Passio Sancti Eadmundi should be judged precisely as it is titled. It is a Passio (a 'passion'), a story modelled on the Passion of Christ, a martyrdom story explicitly intended to elicit empathy and sympathy from its audience for its anguished protagonist – an overwrought exhortation for reader or listener to wallow in second-hand suffering, to facilitate mental excoriation in order that the audience can better comprehend the corporal self-sacrifice that God inexplicably demands from his most devout followers. It is also, of course, modelled explicitly on the sufferings of Christ and of St Sebastian, that other famous Christian pin-cushion. Abbo is not trying to fool us. 'In his agony', he patiently explains, Edmund resembled 'the illustrious martyr Sebastian'. To argue that the *Passio* is a description of an offering of royal blood to Odin, with Ivar officiating as fanatic pagan priest,[35] betrays a gross misunderstanding of the conventions of martyrological literature, as well as a failure properly to challenge the dubious provenance of the tale.

Other details more fundamentally undermine the *Passio*'s credibility. After the killing, Edmund's severed head was taken into the woods and thrown into a bramble patch. Dismayed, those loyal to the dead king resolved to find it and bring it back for burial alongside the rest of his remains (which, Abbo delights in reminding us, were 'bristling with grievous arrows, and lacerated to the very marrow by the acutest tortures'). However, not even decapitation could stop Edmund from babbling:

The head of the holy king, far removed from the body to which it belonged, broke into utterance without assistance from the vocal chords, or aid from the arteries proceeding from the heart. A number of the party, like corpse-searchers, were gradually examining the out-of-the-way parts of the wood, and when the moment had arrived at which the sound of the voice could be heard, the head, in response to the calls of the search-party mutually encouraging one another, and as comrade to comrade crying alternately 'Where are you?' indicated the place where it lay by exclaiming in their native tongue, Here! Here! Here! In Latin the same meaning would be rendered by Hic! Hic! Hic! And the head never ceased to repeat this exclamation, till all were drawn to it. The chords of the dead man's tongue

vibrated within the passages of the jaws, thus displaying the miraculous power of Him who was born of the Word and endowed the braying ass with human speech.[36]

The search party duly discovered the garrulous head in the bushes, where it was being guarded by a monstrous wolf. 'Lifting up, therefore, with concordant devotion the pearl of inestimable price which they had discovered, and shedding floods of tears for joy, they brought back the head to its body.'[37] They were accompanied by the wolf, who – having seen the head safely entombed – wandered placidly back into the forest.

The *Passio* was, transparently, a carefully crafted piece of promotional literature – a puff piece for an ineffective king, elevated to sainthood on account of his death at the hands of an ungodly horde. The cult of St Edmund developed in East Anglia remarkably quickly after his death, but it was Abbo's writings that really got it off the ground. Shortly after it was written it was translated into Old English (in a mercifully abridged – and far more elegant – form) by the prolific writer and abbot of Cerne, Ælfric of Eynsham. With new-found interest beyond East Anglia, and a compelling myth with which to sell it, the cult grew during the latter half of the tenth century and into the eleventh. By the reign of Cnut, the shrine of the saint-king was receiving significant investment and royal patronage. Enthusiasm for the saintly Edmund continued beyond the Norman Conquest and grew throughout the Middle Ages: Edward I's younger brother (1245–96) was named after him, and St Edmund also appears on the Wilton diptych as a patron and guardian of the angel-faced Richard II (r. 1377–99), alongside John the Baptist and Edward the Confessor. Although his prominence declined after the adoption of St George as the patron of Edward III's Order of the Garter in 1348, Edmund's tomb-shrine ceased to be a major place of pilgrimage only when it was destroyed in 1539 during the reign of Henry VIII. Nevertheless, the town and the abbey which housed it still bear his name – Bury St Edmunds: the *burh* ('stronghold') of St Edmund.[38]

Edmund's story reminds us that the Christian Anglo-Saxons had their own notions of sacrifice, their own notion of the power of holy blood. And of course, like the Vikings, Christians had their own corpse-god, and their own spiritual mysteries to unravel. Like Odin, Christ had also hung upon a windy tree (in Old English, *treow*, 'tree', was a ubiquitous simile for 'cross'), pierced in the side by a spear. And, like Odin's auto-sacrifice, Christ's semi-permanent death on the cross was also – in its own confusing way – an offering of self to self: the sacrifice of a son by a father, both of whom were indivisible parts of a triple-faceted deity.[39] These similarities are unlikely to be coincidental. The story of Odin's sacrifice may well have been influenced by Christian theology (bearing in mind that all the written sources pertaining to the god date – in the form they survive – from the Christian era). Conversely, both stories, Christian and pagan, may have derived some of their content and their cultural capital from yet more ancient mythic stock. What is certain, however, is that the Vikings shared a range of fundamental religious, moral and supernatural ideas with the Christian Anglo-Saxons with whom they came into contact, not least concerning the transcendental value of self-sacrifice. They saw it in the stories of their god, and they also found it in the way that human beings met their own ends.

# 9

# WAYLAND'S BONES

From hence he little Chawsey seeth, and hastneth for to see
Faire Reading towne, a place of name, where Cloths ywoven be.
This shewes our Aelfrids victorie, what time Begsceg was slaine
With other Danes, whose carcasses lay trampled on the plaine …

WILLIAM CAMDEN, *Britannia* (1607)[1]

We are treading on heroes. It is sacred ground for Englishmen, more
sacred than all but one or two fields where their bones lie whitening.
For this is the actual place where our Alfred won his great battle, the
battle of Ashdown ('Æscendum' in the chroniclers), which broke the
Danish power and made England a Christian land.

THOMAS HUGHES, *Tom Brown's School Days* (1857)[2]

'Probe with bayonets,' Lenin is famously supposed to have advised. 'If you encounter steel, withdraw. If you encounter mush, continue.'[3] If the Vikings in England had a strategy in the years that followed the death of King Edmund, this may have been it. Northumbria and East Anglia had fallen, Mercia revealed as decidedly soft. Only Wessex was yet to be properly tested, and the *micel here* was preparing to thrust the bayonet.

In 870, a Viking army struck suddenly up the Thames valley and seized the settlement known as Readingum (Reading) at the confluence of the Thames and Kennet rivers. It was mid-winter, and Reading may have been a tempting target, a depot, perhaps, for provisions gathered against the season. Local resistance, however, did not collapse entirely. Soon after the Vikings had captured Reading, a Viking raiding party – presumably foraging for supplies – managed to fall foul of the Berkshire levy, led by their ealdorman, Æthelwulf. A Viking *jarl*, Sidroc, was killed in the fighting. The engagement was fought just west of Reading, at a place called Englafeld (somewhere near the small village of Englefield, Berkshire, about a mile south of the M4). It was, in all likelihood, a minor skirmish, fought between a provincial militia and a small band of raiders (who had probably expected little resistance from the terrified peasantry). Nevertheless, it was the first time – so far as we are aware – that the *micel here* had suffered any sort of reverse in England since its arrival in 866. It was the first time that the bayonet had struck anything like steel.

The Vikings withdrew to their foothold in Reading, and began to prepare for the inevitable West Saxon counter-offensive. They constructed a rampart to join the two rivers, creating a fortress assailable only from the west, and waited for the Anglo-Saxon army to arrive.[4]

The West Saxon king, Æthelred, and his brother, Alfred, had already had experience of facing a dug-in Viking army when they had failed to dislodge the force that had captured Nottingham in 868. This time, however, they were defending their own kingdom. Arriving at Reading, they once again decided to pursue the direct approach, 'hacking and cutting down all the Vikings whom they had found outside' until they reached the gates of the stronghold. The assault on Wessex might have turned out rather differently if the Vikings had trusted to their ramparts, sitting it out until the West Saxons had been forced – as at Nottingham – to cut some sort of deal. However, for whatever reason, the Vikings chose not to wait it out. Perhaps they did not have sufficient supplies to endure a siege (Æthelwulf's victory at Englefield may have undermined efforts to acquire adequate provisions) or perhaps the fortifications – which must have been constructed at speed – were insufficient to inspire any feelings of security. Whatever the reason, the Vikings, trapped and with no means of retreat, decided to go on the offensive: 'like wolves they burst out of all the gates and joined battle with all their might'.[5] Fighting was fierce, and 'a great slaughter was made on both sides',[6] but in the end, 'alas, the Christians eventually turned their backs, and the Vikings won the victory'.[7]

The battle at Reading, from a West Saxon perspective, was a fiasco. Ealdorman Æthelwulf, the hero of Englefield, died in the fighting, and the royal house had been defeated and humiliated. There were, however, three feeble rays of light that broke through the dark cloud that was now hanging over Wessex – though it is doubtful whether anyone could perceive them at the time. Firstly, the king and his brother had survived the debacle. Had they not, it is likely that the kingdom would have collapsed as quickly as East Anglia and Northumbria had. Secondly, Æthelwulf had proven that the Vikings of the *micel here* could be beaten, a reminder that West Saxon armies – as recently as the 850s – had punished Viking intruders in the past. Finally, the *micel here* was no longer quite so *micel* as it had been.

The juggernaut that had rolled over Northumbria, Mercia and East Anglia with such contemptuous ease in the 860s was now, almost certainly, beginning to fragment. It is likely that sizeable contingents remained in Northumbria and East Anglia to retain their grip over the local populations, even as their more entrepreneurial comrades turned west – after all, supply lines needed to be established and maintained, ships guarded and provisions gathered, new recruits absorbed, equipment repaired, camps and fortifications constructed. Although the written sources reveal very little of these processes, archaeology is beginning to provide enormous quantities of new data regarding the way in which these armies operated in England; nevertheless, we are still largely in the dark about the personnel and make-up of the army that invaded Wessex. It appears, however, that of the sons of Ragnar Loðbrók only Halfdan accompanied the army that advanced from Reading. He was one of two 'kings', along with another chieftain named Bacsecg, whom the English sources refer to by name.

None of this would have provided much comfort to King Æthelred as he led his beaten and demoralized army away from the confluence of the Kennet and the Thames. They travelled along the river, the Viking army in close pursuit, into the marshlands that sprawled along the river banks. The Anglo-Norman poet-chronicler Geoffrey Gaimar, writing in Norman French in the 1130s, provides considerable – if slightly confusing – detail about the direction of the West Saxon army's flight. According to Geoffrey, they went (somewhat counter-intuitively) east – away from the West Saxon heartlands. 'Æthelred and Alfred were driven back to Whistley [Wiscelet],' Gaimar explains, 'a ford in the direction of Windsor [Windesoures] across an expanse of water in a marsh. This is where one of the Danish armies turned back to, but they were not aware of the ford over the river here. The ford to which the Danes withdrew was Twyford [Thuiforde], as it has always been called, and this is how the English escaped, but not without suffering many casualties and mortalities.'[8]

It was deep winter. Forced to take the most difficult way, armoured men would have struggled through the sucking mud of frigid swollen bogs, their shields and weapons discarded as freezing mist and brackish water saturated woollen clothes and leather shoes. The weakest would have come quickly to grief – those who dropped behind, wounded or exhausted, left to drown in the mud or be speared like eels, wriggling in the shallows. For the battered survivors, although the northward crossing of the river would have meant a brief respite from the threat of imminent death, there would have been little opportunity to catch their breath. Only four days after the flight from Reading, Alfred and Æthelred would be forced to fight the Viking army again, at a place called Ashdown (Æscesdun).

The main source for the battle – and for Alfred's career in general – is the *Vita Ælfredi regis Angul Saxonum* (the 'Life of Alfred king of the Anglo-Saxons'), written by Asser, bishop of Sherborne, a

Welsh monk, originally from the community of St David's in Dyfed (Wales), who was invited to join the learned circle that surrounded King Alfred in the 880s. The life was written in 893, and shares much of its detail with the *Anglo-Saxon Chronicle*, the earliest version of which (the A recension, or 'Winchester Chronicle') was also written in the 890s in the court of King Alfred. They were, therefore, products of the same time and place and written under the patronage of the same individual: Alfred (King Alfred, as he was by the time they were written). We should then expect them to have been based on first-hand knowledge when dealing with events from Alfred's life, to be accurate and specific when making reference to named places, to share the same West Saxon biases and positive attitude towards their patron, and to agree on most fundamental details. In general these expectations are met. Both sources identify the location of the battle as a place called Ashdown. The fighting took place '*on Æscesdune*' according to the *Anglo-Saxon Chronicle* and Asser gives the same English name, adding helpfully, '*quod Latine "mons fraxini" interpretatur*' ('which in Latin means "hill of the ash-tree"'). The good bishop was in this, as in much else, exceptionally well informed.[9]

His description of the conflict itself is remarkable – the fullest contemporary description of an early medieval battle before 1066:

> the Vikings, splitting up into two divisions, organized shield-walls of equal size (for they then had two kings and a large number of earls), assigning the core of the army to the two kings and the rest to all the earls. When the Christians saw this, they too split up the army into two divisions in exactly the same way, and established shield-walls no less keenly. But as I have heard from truthful authorities who saw it, Alfred and his men reached the battlefield sooner and in better order: for his brother, King Æthelred, was still in his tent at prayer, hearing Mass and declaring firmly that he would not leave that place alive before the priest had finished Mass, and that he would not forsake divine service for that of men; and he did what he said.

The faith of the Christian king counted for much with the Lord, as shall be shown more clearly in what follows.

But Alfred could only wait so long, and eventually – while Æthelred 'was lingering still longer in prayer' – Alfred was forced to take matters into his own hands: 'acting courageously, like a wild boar, supported by divine counsel and strengthened by divine help, when he had closed up the shield-wall in proper order, he moved his army without delay against the enemy.'

The fighting took place around a 'small and solitary thorn-tree' (which Asser noted, 'I have seen for myself with my own eyes'):

> the opposing armies clashed violently, with loud shouting from all, one side acting wrongfully and the other side set to fight for life, loved ones and country. When both sides had been fighting to and fro, resolutely and exceedingly ferociously, for quite a long time, the Vikings (by divine judgement) were unable to withstand the Christian onslaught any longer; and when a great part of their forces had fallen, they took to ignominious flight. One of the two Viking kings and five earls were cut down in that place, and many thousands on the Viking side were slain there too – or rather, over the whole broad expanse of Ashdown, scattered everywhere, far and wide: so King Bacsecg was killed, and Earl Sidroc the Old, Earl Sidroc the Younger, Earl Osbern, Earl Fræna and Earl Harold; and the entire Viking army was put to flight, right on until nightfall and into the following day, until such time as they reached the stronghold from which they had come. The Christians followed them till nightfall, cutting them down on all sides.[10]

These were the first links to be forged in the armour of Alfred's formidable later reputation, and they were cunningly wrought. But despite the length and apparent detail of the account, Asser's narrative differs markedly from other key sources in one critical area – the role of the king.

Reading Asser's account, one would be forgiven for thinking that Æthelred did not show up for the fight at all, spending the whole battle mumbling his paternosters in pious ineffectitude. And yet the *Anglo-Saxon Chronicle* is clear: 'Æthelred fought against the kings' force, and there the king Bagsecg was killed.' Later historians of the twelfth century supplied even more detail. William of Malmesbury (d. 1143) gives the firm impression that it was Æthelred's late intervention that saved the day for the West Saxons. By downplaying Æthelred's military role, Asser was deliberately emphasizing Alfred's exceptional martial skill, fortitude and porcine courage at Æthelred's expense; he had, however, managed to do so while still emphasizing the former king's laudable piety – this, Asser asserts, was also key to victory ('it counted for much with the Lord'), by ensuring that Alfred was able to act with holy sanction, direction and support – a conduit for the stern judgement of the Lord on a pagan people. Getting this balance right was difficult, and politically sensitive.

By the time Asser was writing his account, in the 890s, Alfred had become king of Wessex. He had succeeded after Æthelred's death in 871, a few months after the battle of Ashdown. Alfred, like his brother, derived his claim on the West Saxon throne from his father – King Æthelwulf – reinforced by the important role he had played as right-hand man to his brother, King Æthelred. Alfred, therefore, had an interest in upholding the legitimacy of the West Saxon dynasty and the previous incumbents of its throne. So Asser was careful to stress King Æthelred's efficacious religiosity and the divine aura this conferred on the West Saxon crown. The 'solitary thorn-tree' around which the battle was fought was also probably intended to make the same point. Trees symbolized the cross in Anglo-Saxon thought, and the thorn tree – in providing the material from which Christ's mocking 'crown of thorns' was made – had particular significance; whether or not there really was such a tree at Ashdown, Asser's reference to it was clearly intended to double down on the idea that the appropriate divine powers had been invested in the battle.

Bothering God, however, was only part of the job description for an early medieval king, albeit an important part. Kings also needed, perhaps more than anything else, to be effective war-leaders: virile protectors of their lands, treasures and people. The subtext of Asser's narrative, therefore, carried a subtle but clear message: Æthelred may have had the ear of the Lord, but Alfred was his strong right arm; and that, ultimately, was what counted.

No one knows for certain where the battle of Ashdown was fought. It is known *roughly* where – somewhere on the high chalk uplands of the Berkshire downs – but the specific place is supposedly lost.[11]

Until the early twentieth century, it was generally believed that the battle was fought near a village called Ashbury, now in Oxfordshire but formerly in Berkshire (prior to the 1974 county boundary changes). An earthwork near the village was already known as 'Alfred's Castle' in 1738, and the association could conceivably be older.[12] The connection between this part of the downs and Alfred's battles against the Vikings was fixed in the imagination by a belief that the White Horse of Uffington, the massive equine figure carved into the chalk roughly 2 miles to the east of Ashbury, probably Iron Age, was originally fashioned as an Anglo-Saxon monument to victory.[13] Despite being utterly fallacious, this notion was popularized by Thomas Hughes in his wildly successful novel of 1857, *Tom Brown's School Days*. Hughes imagined that after his victory 'the pious king [Alfred, Æthelred having been quietly ejected from the story], that there might never be wanting a sign and a memorial to the countryside, carved out on the northern side of the chalk hill, under the camp, where it is almost precipitous, the great Saxon white horse which he who will may see from the railway, and which gives its name to the vale over which it has looked these thousand years and more'.[14]

You can still see the White Horse from the railway today, galloping along the southern rim of the vale that takes its name. Those who have frequently 'travelled down the Great Western Railway as far as Swindon' (as I have done and Thomas Hughes evidently also did) will, if they 'did so with their eyes open, have been aware, soon after leaving the Didcot station, of a fine range of chalk hills running parallel with the railway on the left-hand side as you go down and distant some two or three miles, more or less, from the line'.[15] The White Horse has galloped across those chalk hills since long before any Viking or Anglo-Saxon pondered its perplexing outline against the upland grasses.

Ashbury's fall from favour as the location of the battle of Ashdown is largely attributable to the work of the renowned place-name scholar Margaret Gelling and her demonstration that Æscesdun (Ashdown) could not convincingly be associated with any single place. She drew attention to the indisputable fact that, from at least the tenth century, the term 'Ashdown' was used to refer to the whole of the Berkshire downs.[16] This is highly unusual: as Gelling admitted, no other tree-hill compound place-name is used to describe such a wide area. Nonetheless, the evidence that the term was used in this way is entirely sound. However, it seems to me likely, in the context of descriptions of the battle of Ashdown, that Asser and the *Anglo-Saxon Chronicle* intended the place-name to have a specific geographical meaning.

One reason for this is that in no other instance does Asser or the anonymous Anglo-Saxon chronicler fail to identify with precision the location of a battle fought by Alfred. Moreover, on each occasion they associate Alfred's battles with royal estate-centres. There are many reasons why this might be so: for example, royal halls may well have served as muster-points and supply depots for West Saxon armies, and the practical exigencies of campaigning meant that battles were often fought at or close by them.[17] But Alfred's interest in promoting flattering accounts of his reign, alongside his promotion of literacy (it was, after all, no good commissioning biographies and chronicles if nobody could read), is suggestive of the king's concern with shaping his own legacy – a desire to propagate his legend through the work of Asser and the chronicler. It may be that, faced with a largely illiterate populace, Alfred's circle set about deliberately linking the king's most memorable achievements with well-known places – particularly those which already had royal associations. In that way, Alfred's legend could be insinuated into the very fabric of his kingdom, the list of place-names a mnemonic tally of his martial exploits, stitched into the landscape.

It should follow that if a *specific* place known as Æscesdun, particularly one known to have been in royal hands around the time of the battle, could be located within four days' march from Reading, it would have a sound prima facie claim to being close to the site of the famous battle. Judged against these criteria, Ashbury – the traditional location of the battle – has a compelling claim.

The village is referred to in a charter of 840 which describes the grant of land at Ashdown (Asshedoune) from King Æthelwulf (Alfred's and Æthelred's father) to a man named Duda. The charter is headed with the place-name 'Aysheburi' (Ashbury), implying that Ashbury was known to be the centre of an estate in which land at Ashdown was located.[18] Over a hundred years later, in 947, the West Saxon crown was again giving away land at Ashdown (Aysshedun); in this charter, land was given by King Eadred to a chap called Edric which this time included a manor '*quod nunc vocatur Aysshebury*' ('which is now called Ashbury'). This charter also contains an Old English boundary clause, which described the perimeter of the parish of Ashbury, or at least its western half.[19] Taken together, these two documents tell us that, when used in a legal sense, the term Ashdown was understood to refer to a specific area of the Berkshire countryside surrounding the manor of Ashbury (which later gave its name to the modern parish); and that Ashbury was an estate in West Saxon royal ownership by 840, and remained so until 947 when the manor was transferred to a nobleman called Edric. Given their knowledge of West Saxon toponomy, tendency towards specificity, and interest in crafting Alfred's legend in explicable, geographical terms, it seems more than likely that, when Alfred's writers used the term Ashdown, it was Ashbury in particular that they meant.

Early medieval battle-sites frequently have a number of other characteristics in common. Established meeting places are one, and Ashbury is close to the meeting place of the defunct Hildeslaw hundred.[20] Proximity to major roads is another, and many battles were fought along the Wessex Ridgeway that passes to the south-east of the village.[21] But the most evocative feature of the places where men came to fight and die in early medieval Britain, in Wessex at any rate, was the presence of prehistoric monuments. Alfred's Castle, the Bronze Age univallate hill-fort that lies to the north-west of the Ridgeway, has been mentioned already. But there are other, older monuments in this landscape, and one in particular – brooding on the high chalk – that would have worked a dark spell on the West Saxon imagination.

My wife and I came to Ashbury in late afternoon, the sun already beginning to signal its long retreat. We sat for a few minutes in our defiantly out-of-place Nissan Micra, eating cheese rolls and sipping coffee. If you were to ask Google about Ashbury, you would be presented with images of the quintessential English village: the Christmas-card-perfect Norman church, sixteenth-century public house and half-timbered buildings, thatched cottages surrounding the village green. It is the sort of place where it's all too easy to imagine John Nettles bimbling about, investigating the death of a parson in the vicarage potting shed. English rural settlements aren't really like that, of course, not entirely – except, perhaps, here and there in the swamp of affluence that pools along the Thames valley corridor, from Richmond in the east to Cirencester in the west. In this attractive stripe of southern Britain, the combination of influential Tory constituencies, a convenient commuter route to Paddington, coachloads of Japanese tourists and a surfeit of substantial pensions combine to provide the conditions and incentives that make places like Witney and Bibury so improbably manicured and photogenic. Most English villages, however, away from their village greens, are not so neat and tidy: plastic bus shelters with their small rusty waste-bins and resolutely brutalist lamp-posts, rusting corrugated-iron lean-tos and discarded tarpaulins, unlovely post-war architecture spilling into the surrounding countryside – most villages and small towns in the UK boast their own tatty hinterlands, miniature frontiers where human habitation gives out untidily into the woods and farmland beyond. It's always been that way, the lived-in contingency that blurs the boundaries between private, public and wild space.

The lay-by where we sat with our Thermos was at the edge of the village: a yellow grit silo, a bollard, gardens and concrete houses stuttering out into farmland. We got out of the car and began to walk, up a footpath towards the east, climbing the chalk ridge. I can't remember what we were arguing about – we were both tired; a misunderstanding about a buzzard I think, or something to do with sheep … maybe both. I know that I broke my umbrella in a fit of pique – the spike was stuck in the earth when I kicked it, and it bent beyond repair. I had to carry the useless thing around with me for the next hour as a badge of shame. It was forgotten though, when we got to the top of the chalk and started along the Ridgeway. The afternoon was beginning to thicken. Darkness was a way off yet, but the atmosphere was changing, deepening; the shadows between the trees were blacker, distances subtly distorted. We arrived at the monument suddenly, and silence fell like a heavy shutter; the dark bulk of the orthostats caught the low oblique sunlight that spilled in ribbons through the beech trees. A mist was rising in the valley behind us.

The Neolithic chambered tomb, constructed around 5,500 years ago, wouldn't have looked to Alfred as it appears to us now. Its modern arrangement is a restoration of something approximating its original (or, rather, final) appearance. The four huge sarsen stones that dominate the southern end of the long-barrow were set upright after excavations carried out in the early 1960s by the archaeologists Stuart Piggott and Richard Atkinson; there were originally six of them, silent guardians flanking the dark burrow of an entrance – a portal, unmistakably, to another world.[22] Photographs taken in the early twentieth century show the monument as it looked before any restoration had taken place: a tumble of overgrown stones, wilder and weirder – if a little less grandiose – than it appears now. This, or something close to it, would have been how the people of early medieval Britain encountered the monument.[23] What the Romano-British called it, we do not know. Speakers of English, however, had called it *welandes smiððan* – Wayland's Smithy – from the middle of the tenth century, and probably long before.[24]

The association between this tomb and the work of a legendary smith endured for a staggeringly long time. In an eccentric letter of 1738 to one Dr Mead, Francis Wise, keeper of the Oxford University archives, repeated the legend of Wayland's Smithy that he had heard from 'the country people': 'At this place lived formerly an invisible Smith, and if a traveller's Horse had lost a Shoe upon the road, he had no more to do than to bring the Horse to this place with a piece of money, and leaving both there for some little time, he might come again and find the money gone, but the Horse new shod.'[25] If Wise's account does genuinely preserve a folk tradition attached to the long-barrow (rather than a flight of Francis' admittedly over-stimulated imagination), it would suggest that stories of Wayland had continued to circulate in the Berkshire hills for at least eight centuries.[26]

Alfred knew who Wayland was. In the Old English translation of Boethius' *De consolatione philosophiae* – usually attributed to Alfred's court, and perhaps to Alfred himself – the phrase '*Ubi nunc fidelis ossa Fabricii manent?*' ('Where now lie the bones of faithful Fabricius?') is translated as '*Hwaet synt nu þæs foremeran* ['and'] *þæs wisan goldsmiðes ban Welondes?*' ('Where now are the bones of the wise and famous goldsmith Weland [Wayland]?').[27] They weren't in Ashbury, that's for sure, although archaeologists did find plenty of bones in the barrow when they excavated it.[28] But the Anglo-Saxons hadn't called it *welandes beorg* or *welandes hlæwe* (Wayland's Barrow) – they had called it a smithy, and such – in their imaginations – it presumably was, the workshop of a craftsman both famous and wise: 'Wise, I said, because the craftsman can never lose his craft nor can it be taken easily from him – no more than the sun may be shifted from its place. Where are the bones of Weland now, or who knows now where they were?'

It is interesting that the Boethius translator should pause and digress on the value of craft at this point in *De consolatione*. The passage into which Wayland was inserted is a meditation on the transience of mortal life and the futility of earthly fame in the face of death and the passing of generations – topics which, as we have seen, appear to have weighed heavily on the Anglo-Saxon imagination. But Alfred seems also to have been uncommonly fixated by his own legacy, with crafting a kingdom that would outlive him. Indeed, the word 'craft' (OE *cræft*) has been recognized as one of the most important in Alfredian literature, invested with connotations not merely of skill but also of virtue, and other works attributed to Alfred are replete with the imagery of construction and labour: his version of St Augustine's soliloquies, for example, frames the gathering of knowledge as a great building project, detailing the collection of timbers and materials to construct a new and better world and the skill involved in their assembly.[29] The metaphor was matched in the physical construction of towns and ships that would occupy his later reign and those of his children and grandchildren. Alfred, in other words, seems to have been determined to challenge – through craft, fame and wisdom – the fatalistic pessimism of Boethius.

Wayland, however – the craftsman whose skill was as everlasting as the sun – was an uncomfortable avatar to invoke. Old English poetry makes a few references to him. *Beowulf* refers approvingly to a Wayland-forged mail-shirt, and the poem *Deor* – one of the oldest in the canon – gives voice to the tale of Wayland in a highly abridged and allusive, but relatively complete, form.[30] The most complete account of the myth, however, is found in Old Norse verse – a poem called *Völundarkvida* ('the song of Völund [Wayland]') – demonstrating that Wayland was an entity whose tale, like so much else, was shared across the North Sea. It is a thoroughly unpleasant story, which culminates in the eponymous hero – who had been captured and hamstrung by the wicked King Nídud (OE Nithhad) – raping and impregnating the king's daughter, murdering his sons, fashioning cups from their skulls, jewels from their eyes and brooches from their teeth (which he presents to their oblivious parents), and then escaping on the wing like some vengeful Nordic Daedalus. At least one scene from the legend decorates the 'Franks' casket: a bearded figure holds out a cup he has forged, a mysterious object gripped in a pair of tongs in his other hand. Below the work-bench a headless body lies. As *Völundarkvida* has Wayland explain to the horrified Nídud:

> 'Go to the smithy that you set up:
> there you'll find bellows spattered with blood;
> I cut off the heads of those small cubs,
> and in the mud beneath the anvil I laid their limbs.'[31]

This is not the workshop of the benevolent, elvish tinker imagined by the folk of eighteenth-century Berkshire. Perhaps it was the sight of Neolithic bones protruding from the earth that suggested to the Anglo-Saxon mind the association of the long-barrow with Wayland. It was a dark place, a bloody place – sown with corpses, seeded with bones.

The story of Wayland hints at a tension in the Anglo-Saxon psyche. It reminds us that while Asser paints the Viking wars as a binary struggle between godless heathen and the Christian warriors of Wessex, older and darker things yet lurked in the Anglo-Saxon mind – skeletons in the closet. Alfred and his circle wanted to leave the impression that they were building a new world, a world of craft and learning and Christian enlightenment. But somewhere, down in the mud beneath the anvil, down among the roots of Alfred's new England, the bones of Wayland still lay – a pagan past that the English had never properly come to terms with: a past with its roots in the old North, in stories of rape and mutilation, transmutation and supernatural flight, of vengeance and violence.

The archaeologist Neil Price has suggested that the Anglo-Saxons reacted in such a visceral way to the heathen Vikings appearing suddenly in their midst not only because of their violence and their paganism, but also because of a dreadful familiarity – a familiarity born of an ancient kinship and a shared web of stories and ways of seeing:

> The Anglo-Saxons [...] knew that this Viking world-view was not so far removed from what theirs had been not so long before, and maybe, under the surface, still was [...] The Vikings were not only conventionally terrifying, they were a dark mirror held up to the image of what the English needed to believe themselves to be.[32]

The Anglo-Saxons, looking into that mirror, saw things that they preferred not to confront – felt as though they stood unsteadily on the brink of the howling abyss of pagan savagery from which they had lately hauled themselves. The Vikings were, therefore, in Freudian terms, *unheimlich* ('uncanny'). They were that which 'ought to have remained secret and hidden but has come to light', a manifestation of 'something which is familiar and old established in the mind and which has become alienated from it'.[33] Freud's concept of the *unheimlich* has been productively employed to explain the potency in supernatural horror of the dislocation of the familiar and the mundane – the chair that moves in the empty room, the child that begins speaking in tongues ... It has also been invoked to explain the frisson of archaeology, the uncovering of that which should remain hidden. The frequent recourse to archaeological themes by the writers of weird literature – M. R. James, H. P. Lovecraft, Robert E. Howard, Clark Ashton Smith, Arthur Machen, Algernon Blackwood – stands testament to the thrill and horror of uncovering unspeakable hidden knowledge, places and things. But, for the Anglo-Saxons, the 'uncanny' had a horrible and malevolent reality, marauding across the countryside with axe and flame. The lost English homeland – 'emptied of its people', as Bede had believed, at the time of the fabled Anglo-Saxon migrations – had shown itself to be far from depleted. This lost world, romanticized in fireside tales where the monsters were remote and the heathen gods glossed with Christian ethics, was spewing forth a revenant nation, reaching out a rotting hand to drag the English screaming back into the mire.

The Anglo-Saxons may have thought they had escaped their past. But now their sundered kinsmen, their gods and their beliefs were rising up out of the darkness, borne on black tides from a world beyond the pale.

Ashdown may have been a major victory for the West Saxons, but it was hardly a decisive one – the exception rather than the rule. Probably this is why Asser made such a big deal of it: the years that followed marked a pretty desperate start to Alfred's reign as king.

In 871, Æthelred and Alfred fought the Viking army at Basengum (probably Old Basing in Hampshire). They were defeated. Later in the year they fought again at the unidentified Meretun; despite putting up a stiff fight, they were defeated again with serious casualties (including Heahmund, bishop of Sherborne). After Æthelred's death later that year, Alfred fought the Vikings again at Wilton (Wiltshire). The Vikings, once again, 'had possession of the place of slaughter'.[34] Exhausted by the fighting (the *Anglo-Saxon Chronicle* notes that there had been nine *folcgefeoht* – literally, 'folk-fights', probably battles involving shire levies from across Wessex, rather than single local militias – as well as innumerable raids and skirmishes) and presumably demoralized by the succession of losses, the West Saxons agreed terms in 871. The Viking army, led by Halfdan, withdrew – first to Reading and then to London.[35]

Once again, the Vikings had been bought off by their victims.

# 10

# REAL MEN

A Geat woman too sang out in grief;
with hair bound up, she unburdened herself
of her worst fears, a wild litany
of nightmare and lament: her nation invaded,
enemies on the rampage, bodies in piles,
slavery and abasement. Heaven swallowed the smoke.

*Beowulf*

The sun is low, striking sharply against the earthen furrows, deepening them to chasms of peaty black between golden brown ribs of soil. The oxen have stopped at the edge of the water meadow; they stare listlessly ahead, snorting white clouds of spectral vapour into the frigid air. Steam rises from their great ruddy backs. The man stands by the plough, ready to move the animals and reharness them, ready for the return journey back up the next strip of land, back towards the village and a welcome fire. It is winter, and the river has flooded the water meadow, waterlogging it, leaving no trace of the rampaging cowslip and cranesbill that will saturate the field with colour in the spring. Now the silver water lies pale under skeleton trees, their roots breaking the surface like tentacles. Alder and goat-willow screen the water. Later in the winter the villagers will cut withies for poles and baskets, but for now the willow pollards march beside the river with their misshapen bodies and wild upright hair: a throng of trolls mustering on the river bank. Beyond them the sun is raising the ghost of a fog. There is a sudden plop, perhaps an otter taking to the water, then a sudden rush of wings – a thrush startled into flight, the clumsy crash of a wood pigeon. There is something out there, a presence on the river. The man squints, trying to squeeze his vision between the withies, into the silver twilight between the trees. He sees nothing, just the gathering mist, but a sound comes. A gentle swish of oars and, buried in it, a low pulse like a muffled heartbeat. He can feel sweat beginning to bead at the back of his head, prickling on his top lip, like insects crawling at the roots of his hair. Something is coming – something big – real and tangible, gliding into the November sunlight: sightless eye, immobile jaws gaping, a monster of oak carving through the land. And then it is gone, back into the mist.

The image of the Viking ship in full sail on the open sea, emerging blackly on the wide horizon, is a reasonably familiar one. Less commonly pictured in the mind's eye is the glimpse of the carved bestial prow glimpsed through the trees on a quiet river bank. Yet it was the exploitation of England's river routes – made possible by their light and shallow-draughted ships – that provided Viking armies with a means of swift and efficient movement through Britain's interior that vastly increased the range of their attacks and the extent to which they were able to destabilize Anglo-Saxon kingdoms in the second half of the ninth century.

There are few places in Britain that are further from the sea than Repton in Derbyshire, a quiet, pretty village of smart Georgian and Victorian houses and shopfronts, running in a ribbon of red brick away from the southern bank of the River Trent. Repton is further now from the river than it was a thousand years ago when it lay at the heart of the kingdom of Mercia, but the Trent is still capable of flexing its muscles in the faces of the villagers. In 2012, flood waters swamped the fields that fill the plain to the north of the village, between the river's old bed and its new route skirting the southern edge of neighbouring Willington. A wide band of English countryside, almost three-quarters of a mile across in places, was transformed into a gloomy dystopian landscape, spindly bare trees and bedraggled hedgerows standing proud of the brown and brackish water, watched over by bleak concrete ramparts – the monstrous cooling towers of Willington power station.

The rising water stopped mercifully short of Repton itself; although the sports fields of Repton School were submerged, the swollen river's creep was checked at the perimeter of St Wystan's churchyard by the banks of the stream – the Old Trent Water – that still follows the ninth-century course of the river. When Repton Abbey was founded as a double-monastery (a monastery with a twin community of monks and nuns) in the seventh century, the rising ground to the south had probably ensured that the community was safe from all but the most extreme flooding, despite the river running perilously close. It was here that a young, bellicose nobleman called Guthlac had come to take monastic vows in the late seventh century, before embarking on a new career as a spiritually obstinate, demon-defying fenland hermit. It was evidently a secure and amenable environment, allowing the monastery to become the recipient of considerable investment in subsequent centuries. The Church of St Wystan as it appears today is mostly the product of the thirteenth and fourteenth centuries, but hidden beneath the high medieval gothic spires can still be found the crypt of the Mercian church, built in the early eighth century.

It is quite extraordinary, the physicality of the atmosphere in this small and dingy subterranean cube. John Betjeman described the space as 'holy air encased in stone', a turn of phrase which perfectly encapsulates the curious sense of *substance* that one encounters on descending into the gloom, the shadowed vault supported on four candy-twist columns, like rustic Tudor chimney pots. It is a place rank with religion, the air thickened by the ineffable weight of antiquity and prayer, as though something has been trapped down here, entombed for centuries. This aura is compounded, perhaps conjured, by the knowledge that this crypt once housed the bones of Mercian kings. The first of these (and the one for whom it may have been constructed) was King Æthelbald, who was interred in the crypt in 757. His bones were later joined by those of King Wiglaf (died c. 839) and Wiglaf's grandson Wystan who, though he declined to take the crown in favour of a religious life, was nevertheless done in by his relations in 849.

As John of Worcester reported it, Wystan – or St Wystan as he became in death – 'was carried to a monastery which was famous in that age called Repton, and buried in the tomb of his grandfather king Wiglaf. Miracles from heaven were not wanting in testimony of his martyrdom; for a column of light shot up to heaven from the spot where the innocent saint was murdered, and remained visible to the inhabitants of that place for thirty days.'[1]

Twenty-four years later, the men and women living in the precincts of the church that still bears his name may well have wished that Wystan's left-over parts could have produced some new and impressive miracle – preferably, this time, something with a more practical application. For the river had finally proved a risk to the religious community and the relics of the saints and kings it curated; in the winter of 873/4, however, it was not the water that threatened to sweep Repton away, but the deadly flotsam that it bore.

When the Vikings left Wessex in 872 after making terms with Alfred, they first found their way to London where, the *Anglo-Saxon Chronicle* recounts, the Mercians 'made peace with them'.[2] The Viking army spent another winter there before moving on, travelling to Lindsey (a region within what is now Lincolnshire) in 873 and establishing a new camp at Torksey, 10 miles north-west of

Lincoln. The Mercians, once again, 'made peace'.[3] If the Viking bayonet was probing for steel, it was finding little of it. When spring came, the *micel here* was on the move again. From Torksey the River Trent offered an inviting artery that led straight to the heart of the Mercian kingdom. The sources tell us very little – even by their own stingy standards – but the impression given is of a swift and surgical intervention that brought the once glorious kingdom to its knees at a single stroke: 'the horde went from Lindsey to Repton and took winter-quarters there, and drove King Burhred across the sea [...] and occupied that land'.[4]

In the *Anglo-Saxon Chronicle*, Burhred comes across as a hapless king: thrice he had come to terms with the Viking great army (in 868, 871 and 872), only to find himself ejected from his kingdom, and his people subjugated with humiliating ease (he died in Rome, and was buried at St Mary's Church in the city's English Quarter).[5] The contrast with the way that Viking progress in Wessex was described should be obvious: there the Viking army is depicted as encountering resistance at every step, suffering defeats at Englefield and Ashdown and grinding out hard-won victories elsewhere (although we should remember that Alfred had also, in 871, paid the Vikings to go away).

It is tempting to read the sources at face value, and to see the West Saxons as the defiant epitome of the bulldog mentality, a striking contrast to the flaccid appeasement practised by the Mercians: Alfred playing Churchill to Burhred's Chamberlain. To do so, however, is to be corralled by channels of thought dug by Alfred's own propagandists. There is simply no way of knowing how hard the Mercians fought to preserve their kingdom and eject the Viking menace. As we shall see, at least one Viking warrior came to grief on Mercian soil.

The subtle disparagement of their Mercian neighbours that we can perceive in the West Saxon sources served Alfred's political ends. By the latter part of his reign, when these documents were compiled, Alfred was increasingly concerned with claiming a hegemony than extended far beyond Wessex. His own military reputation (which was patchy at best before the late 870s) was bolstered by having his contemporary monarchs painted as battle-shirking weaklings. More importantly, by painting the last independent kings of Mercia as weak, ineffective and lacking credibility, the claims of Alfred and those of his offspring to rule in Mercia appeared more legitimate than they otherwise might have done.

At some point, not long after Repton was taken under new management, a ditch and rampart were dug, closing off an area to the north of the church and forming a D-shape against the river bank – a space providing unimpeded access for ships to moor but offering landward protection, the direction from which danger was most likely to arrive. The church building itself was incorporated into the defensive circuit, a masonry gate-house through which access could be controlled. Instead of Mercian royalty, monks and devout pilgrims, Viking warriors now breathed the holy air of St Wystan's crypt. At around the same time, the first of a number of graves were dug around the church, many of them decidedly unconventional for ninth-century Mercia.[6] One man was buried with a gold ring on his finger and five silver pennies, all of which can be dated to the mid-870s; his grave, which lay adjacent to the church wall, was cut through a layer of burnt stone and charcoal – an indication that the church had been severely damaged, broken rubble and burnt timber strewn where they had fallen after the upper parts of the building had burned. As at Portmahomack, a monolithic stone cross was shattered and discarded, its fragments buried in a pit to the east of the chancel.

The most famous of these burials is Grave 511. Like several others, the man in this grave was buried with weapons – in this case a sword and knife. He had died, it would appear, unpleasantly. Following a blow to the head, he had suffered a deep cut to the left femur where it connected to the pelvis – probably from a sword or axe. The blow was administered when the victim was already on the ground, and it would have severed the femoral artery resulting in massive blood loss; it would also have deprived him of the soft parts that had once dangled between his legs. In an apparent attempt to compensate for this loss, those who buried him placed the tusk of a boar in the appropriate position. And, if any doubt were to remain about the cultural affiliations of the deceased, this man had been laid in the grave with, among other objects and pieces of metal-work, the hammer of Thor about his neck.

Odin and Thor were the most popular and powerful gods of the Norse pantheon, but in many ways they were diametrically opposed to each other in character. Where Odin was subtle and sinister, the patron of poets, sorcerers and kings, Thor presented a less compli-cated personality. He was a proponent of what we might call the direct approach – more action, fewer words; less brain, more fist. He is often (as we see him in the stories that survive of him) a bit of an oaf. Most of these tales features the god smashing things up, shouting, getting drunk, breaking things and hitting people. He is a 'mannish' god – a god of farmers, fishermen and fighters (as the runologist R. I. Page put it, 'the everyday Viking [...] the man-in-the-fiord').[7] He is precisely the sort of god we would expect to feel particularly embarrassed about a misplaced member, and whose devotees might have felt the need to make showy compensation for their comrade's missing man-parts.

In the *Prose Edda*, a medieval primer on Norse mythology and one of the most valuable sources for pre-Christian belief in Scandinavia, Snorri provides a potted outline of the god's key attributes:

Thor [...] is the strongest of all gods and men [...] [He] has two male goats called Tannigost [Tooth Gnasher] and Tannigrisnir [Snarl Tooth]. He also owns the chariot that they draw, and for this reason he is called Thor the Charioteer. He [...] has three choice possessions. One is the hammer Mjollnir. Frost giants and mountain giants recognize it when it is raised in the air, which is not surprising as it has cracked many a skull among their fathers and kinsmen. His second great treasure is his Megingjard [Belt of Strength]. When he buckles it on, his divine strength doubles. His third possession, the gloves of iron, are also a great treasure. He cannot be without these when he grips the hammer's shaft.[8]

The story that best sums up Thor's character is recounted in the eddic poem Þrymskviða ('the Song of Thrym'). Unlike the dark and difficult texts with which it was compiled in the Codex Regius (poems, for example, like Völuspá and Grímnismál), Þrymskviða is a fairly light-hearted romp. Nevertheless, like all good satire, it gets to the heart of the matter (in this case Thor's character) with pointed efficiency. It runs thus: Thor woke up one morning to find his magical hammer, Mjölnir, missing. Loki, the trickster god, was deputed to find out where it was and flew to the hall of the giant, Thrym. Thrym admitted to having stolen it and claimed to have hidden it 'eight leagues under the earth', adding that 'No one shall have it back again unless he brings me Freyja as bride.'[9] On receiving this news, Thor was keen to take the giant up on the bargain ('these were the first words he found to say: "Freyja, put on your bridal veil"'). Freyja, unsurprisingly, was less enthusiastic ('Freyja was enraged, and gave a snort, so that the gods' hall trembled, and the great Brísings' neck-ring tumbled: "You'd think I'd become the maddest for men if I drove with you to Giants' Domain [Jötunheimr]"').

Eventually, the god Heimdall came up with a cunning plan:

'Let us put Thor in the bridal veil,
let him wear the great Brísings' neck-ring!

Let us have keys jangling beneath him,
And women's clothes falling round his knees,
and broad gem-stones sitting on his chest,
let us top out his head with style.'

Then Thor spoke, the strapping god:
'The gods will call me a cock-craver,
if I let myself be put in a bridal veil.'[10]

Thor's protests notwithstanding, Heimdall's scheme was put into action. Thrym, evidently not the brightest of characters, was easily bamboozled by the cunning disguise; nevertheless, his suspicions were eventually aroused by his bride-to-be's table habits: 'Freyja' (Thor) packed away a whole ox, eight salmon, all the food laid out for the women and three casks of mead. Loki (in the guise of a maidservant) was forced to claim that the false bride had not eaten for eight days because of her excitement at the approaching nuptials (Loki, unlike Thor, apparently had no qualms about cross-dressing). Finally the moment of the wedding ceremony arrived, and Thrym called for the hammer Mjölnir to be brought forth to hallow the union. Thor needed no more encouragement than this: his heart 'laughed in his chest' as he grasped the hammer and set about venting his anger and humiliation:

Thrym, lord of ogres, was the first one he felled,
before battering all of the giant-race.[11]

*Þrymskviða* is a tale that, at least in its received form, postdates the Viking Age – possibly by some margin (the manuscript in which it is found – the Codex Regius – was compiled in the latter part of the thirteenth century). The poem may have been intended to parody the absurdities of past beliefs; perhaps transforming the mighty Thor into a berserk Widow Twanky was one way to tame the unsettling residue of a none-too-distant pagan heritage.[12] Nevertheless, several themes in the poem resonate with much of what else we know or is implied about Viking attitudes to sexuality and Thor's place in the pantheon.

The term which Andy Orchard, regius Professor of Anglo-Saxon at Oxford University, provocatively translated as 'cock-craver' is the Old Norse word *argr*, which is normally (and euphemistically) rendered as 'unmanly'.[13] In reality, *argr* (and its cognate form *ragr*) was an insult which, when directed at both men and women, implied some sort of unusual enthusiasm for being penetrated. When directed at a woman, therefore, it suggested promiscuity; when directed at a man it ascribed a passive homosexuality. It was a particularly rude charge to level at one's (male) counterparts, and to insult someone in these terms could constitute a potentially lethal slight. The earliest Icelandic law codes are clear that no intervention or recompense could be expected if those bandying unsubstantiated slanders came to violent grief as a result of their impertinences.

The Norwegian Gulathing law was specific about what constituted the worst sorts of insult:

> Concerning terms of abuse or insult. There are words which are considered terms of abuse. Item one: if a man say of another man that he has borne a child. Item two: if a man say of another man that he has been homosexually used [*sannsorðenn*]. Item three: if a man compare another man to a mare, or call him a bitch or a harlot, or compare him to any animal which bears young.[14]

This, however, wasn't a moral abhorrence of homosexuality in the sense that the Christian Church would later seek to formulate it, and the law codes and sagas – all of which date to the post-conversion epoch – have to be read carefully in this light. What, instead, the Vikings seemed to find upsetting was the feminized role of the *ragr-mann* (gently translated: 'unmanly-man'). Indeed, using men for sex – particularly in a punitive way – seems to have incurred no moral judgement. To bugger one's enemies was a manly way to humiliate a vanquished foe: the latter, by contrast, would then be considered *argr/ragr*, *rassragr* ('arse-*argr*'), *stroðinn* or *sorðinn* ('sodomized') or *sansorðinn* ('demonstrably sodomized').[15]

The problem, it seems, was not so much being gay as being thought to be 'unmanly' in some way. Indeed, other typically female behaviour could also attract accusations of *ergi* (unmanliness), suggesting that it was the adoption of inappropriate gender roles that Vikings objected to, rather than homosexual liaisons per se.[16] Even the gods could be susceptible to these imputations – Loki, in the most extreme example, gave birth to Odin's eight-legged horse Sleipnir after an intimate moment with the frost-giant's stallion Svaðilfari ('Unlucky Traveller'); Loki was in the guise of a mare at the time. Odin too, though more indirectly, was labelled *argr* because he practised a form of sorcery – *seiðr* – that was explicitly considered the preserve of women. As Loki pointed out:

> 'It's said you played the witch on Sámsey,
> beat the drum like a lady-prophet;
> in the guise of a wizard you wandered the world:
> that signals to me a cock-craver.'[17]

This, however, is a very specific image of effeminacy, and one to which we shall return. The picture it conjures (Loki's crude insult aside) is an indefinably eerie one – another thread in the weft of Odin's surpassing weirdness.

It is this fear of effeminacy (or, rather, the fear of being seen as effeminate) that Thor expresses in *Þrymskviða*. In the end, he is forced to erase the threat to his manhood in the only way a deity with limited subtlety of mind could manage: by beating all and sundry to a pulp. This image of Thor fits easily into our conception of this god of warriors and working men, an unreconstructed he-man who responded to danger, irritation and humiliation with brute force – problem-solving with a hammer. Certainly, the cult of Thor seems to have become extremely popular in the late Viking Age. By the time Adam of Bremen was describing the temple at Uppsala, Thor was regarded – from a Christian perspective anyway – as the major deity. Hundreds of Thor's-hammer pendants and rings (from which small hammers and other amulets were suspended) have been found throughout the Viking world, from Iceland and Ireland to Poland and Russia – many, though by no means all, in graves.[18]

And yet, despite all this, when we start to probe the details of the cult of Thor a surprisingly complex picture begins to emerge. For one thing, the vast majority of individual Thor's-hammer pendants found in graves (as opposed to the rings and the disassociated finds) are found in the graves of women.[19] This fact alone is enough to suggest that there was more to the invocation of the god than the doom-brained muscle-cult we may have been led to expect by sources like *Þrymskviða*. Moreover, runic inscriptions invoking Thor's blessing of monuments implies that his role could be imagined as a broader responsibility to preserve and protect those things that people held valuable.[20] His hammer could even (if *Þrymskviða* can be trusted) be used symbolically to seal a marriage ceremony.[21]

Grave 511 at Repton, with its Thor's-hammer pendant, is therefore a reminder of the heathenism of the Vikings who comprised the *micel here*, and allows us to begin to imagine the social mores and attitudes of the people who found themselves here in the winter of 873/4. But the presence of the boar's tusk and the humerus of a jackdaw among the grave goods suggests that, woven into the machismo of the Viking way of life, were ideas and attitudes that remain alien to us, and whose significance is irrevocably lost. The part of the Repton excavations that makes this latter point most dramatically, however, is another grave – this time a mass grave – that remains as strange, unique and compelling as it was when it was first broken open in 1686. In an account given to the antiquarian researcher Dr Simon Degge in 1727, a man called Thomas Walker described how he had dug into a large mound that stood west of St Wystan's Church:

> About Forty Years since cutting Hillocks, near the Surface he
> met with an old Stone Wall, when clearing farther he found it to
> be a square Enclosure of Fifteen Foot: It had been covered, but

the Top was decayed and fallen in, being only supported by
wooden Joyces. In this he found a Stone Coffin, and with
Difficulty removing the Cover, saw a *Skeleton* of a *Humane
Body Nine Foot* long, and round it lay *One Hundred* Humane
Skeletons, with their feet pointing to the Stone Coffin. They
seem'd to be of the ordinary Size.[22]

Walker went on to confess that 'The Head of the great Skeleton he
gave to Mr. Bowers, Master of the Free-school.' Dr Degge made
further enquiries with the son of the aforementioned Mr Bowers,
who said at the time that 'he remembers the Skull in his Father's
Closet, and that he had often heard his Father mention this Gigantic
Corps …'[23]

Wonderful as this all is, we would be right to be sceptical, and a
later generation of fascinated antiquarians were determined to
prove the case one way or another. Excavations in 1789 and 1914
followed, the former – despite finding the Gigantic Corps absent –
confirmed the presence of 'vast quantities of human bones'.[24] It
wasn't until the 1980s, however, that a systematic programme of
excavation was undertaken. The results of that campaign revealed
one of the most shocking and enigmatic burials ever excavated in
the British Isles.

The mound had been constructed over a twin-celled stone building dated to the seventh or eighth century, undoubtedly part of the
religious complex on the site. Prior to its final repurposing it had
been used as a workshop, although it may originally have been built
as a chapel or mortuary. To construct the mound, the walls of the
building had been dismantled to ground level, leaving only the
subterranean part of the building in situ. The floor of the eastern
cell was covered with a layer of red marl, and a stone cist had been
erected in the centre. All traces of the body which this contained, as
described to Dr Degge, had disappeared – as had most evidence for
the cist itself (unsurprising, given the repeated, and mostly inex-
pert, prior interventions). What did survive, however, were the
other bones: 1,686 of them to be precise, the disarticulated remains

of 264 people, strewn about in charnel chaos, a disordered landscape of death. Among the bones, objects were discovered – a
Scandinavian-style axe-head, sword fragments, two long single-
bladed knives (seaxes), a key and a range of decorative fragments of
metalwork dating to the seventh or eighth centuries. Amid all this
were five silver coins, four of them dated to 872, one of them to
873/4. These last artefacts were a critical, and astoundingly fortui-
tous, discovery, for they dated the construction of this extraordinary monument, with exceptional precision, to the period when
Repton was under occupation by the Viking *micel here*.

Although the scene uncovered by the excavators was one of
morbid disarray, this was all as a result of the rough treatment the
burial had received at the hands of Thomas Walker and his ilk. It
soon became apparent that the bones had originally been carefully
sorted by length and stacked neatly around the central grave.
Moreover, most of the small bones (hands, feet, vertebrae) were
absent, suggesting that the skeletons had been moved, reinterred in
the mound after an initial period of burial elsewhere – long enough,
it would seem, to ensure that the remains were free from fleshy
parts. Carbon dating of a small sample brought back a range of
dates between the seventh and the ninth centuries, and the general
absence of trauma to the bones complicates an interpretation of
these skeletons as the remains of battle-damaged Vikings of the
*micel here* or their victims.

Debate continues about who they were and why they were
interred in this way, and ongoing analysis seeks to clarify their
origins. It may be – as the excavators believed – that some of the
bones are Scandinavian, the remains of the followers of some great
lord gathered up to lay beside him in death. On the other hand, it
may be that some of the disarticulated bones are the remains of
Mercian monks, nuns and aristocrats whose bones were disturbed
by the digging of the ditch and the clearing of the mausolea.[25] It may
even be the case that the bones of the Mercian kings – Æthelbald
and Wiglaf – were jumbled in among them, as well as, perhaps, the
holy remains of St Wystan himself:[26] the carefully conserved relics

of a proud nation, reduced to morbid trophies in a ghoulish heathen catacomb.

Who, then, was the missing occupant, the '*Humane Body Nine Foot* long' who had once been laid in the central grave in such grim splendour? Although we can be pretty certain that his or her physical stature was exaggerated, this was clearly the grave of an important individual, afforded a rare and imposing memorial. We know with more certainty who it was not. The movements of the Viking leaders Halfdan and Ubbe are mentioned in the years following the over-wintering at Repton; other leaders of the army – Guthrum, Oscetel and Anwend – led a part of the army to Cambridge in 874 and were also clearly still alive. Bacsecg was killed at Ashdown in 871, and it seems unlikely that even the most devoted of followers would have been prepared to carry a ripe corpse around England for three years. There is only one other Viking warlord active in England whose name we know, but whose fate and movements in the years after 870 are uncertain. The evidence is contradictory, but the excavators make a good case that the mound at Repton was raised for Ivar the Boneless.[27]

Two and a half miles west and slightly south of Repton, on high ground overlooking the valley of the Trent, yet more mounds were being raised to the dead in the years following 873. The cemetery at Heath Wood comprised fifty-nine barrows, hillocks of earth that once stood on open heathland – like the workings of an army of giant moles. These were monuments that marked the places where the ashen remnants of the dead had been interred, fifty-nine memorials to occasions when the earth of Derbyshire had been dug and reformed to cover the cremated fragments of human beings and animals, swords and shields, buckles and spurs, nails, pins and melted treasures. These were the graves of pagan people whose community practised a rite of burial long abandoned by the Christian English, laying out the dead upon a funeral pyre, draped with jewellery or girded with weapons, surrounded by sacrificial offerings, immolated.

Snorri explained that 'Óðinn [...] ordained that all dead people must be burned and that their possessions should be laid on a pyre with them. He said that everyone should come to Valhǫll with such wealth as he had on his pyre, and that each would also have the benefit of whatever he himself had buried in the earth. But the ashes were to be taken out to sea or buried down in the earth, and mounds were to be built as memorials to great men.'[28] Although we would be right to be dubious of the specificity with which Snorri describes the thoughts and motivations of people who lived hundreds of years before his own time, his words nevertheless resonate not only with the archaeology, but with other more contemporary accounts. Here once more is ibn Fadlan, describing the funeral of a Rūs chieftain:

They dressed him [the dead man] in trousers, socks, boots, a tunic and a brocade caftan with gold buttons. On his head they placed a brocade cap covered with sable. Then they bore him into the pavilion on the boat and sat him on the mattress, supported by cushions. Then they brought *nabīdh* [alcoholic drink], fruits and basil which they placed near him. Next they carried in bread, meat and onions which they laid before him.

After that they brought in a dog, which they cut in two and threw into the boat. Then they placed his weapons beside him. Next they took two horses and made them run until they were in lather, before hacking them to pieces with swords and throwing their flesh on to the boat. Then they brought two cows, which they also cut into pieces and threw on to the boat. Finally they brought a cock and hen, killed them and threw them on to the boat as well.[29]

After a lengthy ritual, the slave-girl was finally killed, having been laid beside the dead man:

Then people came with wood and logs to burn, each holding a piece of wood alight at one end, which they threw on to the wood [that was piled below the boat]. The fire enveloped the wood, then the boat, then the tent, the man, the girl and all that there was on the boat. A violent and frightening wind began to blow, the flames grew in strength and the heat of the fire intensified.[30]

This was a grand funeral for a great man. The burning of boats, like their burial, was probably uncommon,[31] but the broad outlines of the pomp and sacrifice – and their explanation – would have been familiar across the Viking world. As they stood on the banks of the river watching the burning, one of the Rūs party spoke to ibn Fadlan's interpreter. 'You Arabs are fools!' he apparently exclaimed. 'Why is that?' ibn Fadlan politely enquired through his interlocutor. 'Because you put the men you love most, and the most noble among you, into the earth, and the earth and the worms and insects eat them. But we burn them in the fire in an instant, so that at once and without delay they enter Paradise.'[32]

The rites practised at Heath Wood may have replicated – albeit on a smaller scale – the scenes witnessed by ibn Fadlan on the Volga; similar funerals are also known to have taken place in Scandinavia – Norway and Sweden especially – during the Viking Age.[33] Nevertheless, in England, obviously 'Viking' burials are rare discoveries. Despite the development of new Scandinavian-inflected identities and socio-economic change that occurred in the decades following the 870s, the graves at Heath Wood and Repton remain the only places where good evidence exists for a whole community behaving in a way that was significantly divergent, obviously heathen. These were the people of the *micel here*, and here – for the first time – they were putting their roots into English soil. They would run deep: although their funerals would become less distinctive – less visible in the archaeological record – Viking sculpture, found at Repton, attests to a more than transient Scandinavian presence in this part of Britain. And, in time (or perhaps straight away), Old Norse names were bestowed on the neighbouring villages, names which speak eloquently of perceived ethnic difference in the first phases of Viking settlement. They are still the names these villages bear today: Ingleby – the 'farm of the English'; Bretby – the 'farm of the Britons'.

In 874, according to the *Anglo-Saxon Chronicle*, the great Viking army that had first arrived in England in 865 broke apart, never again to operate as a unified force in England. (Perhaps the death of whoever lay in the Repton mound snapped the last thread of unifying authority binding together the confederation of chieftains and warlords that made up the *micel here*. Perhaps the raising of that mound to their fallen leader was a last symbolic act of triumph and remembrance – the interment of a Viking hero at the symbolic heart of England's once mightiest realm, left to slumber on among the skulls of conquered kings.) Guthrum and the others went east. Halfdan, however, went back to Northumbria to assert some measure of authority in the northern part of that kingdom. He wasted no time in getting on with the traditional occupations of Northumbrian rulers by harassing the Picts and Strathclyde Britons ranged along his northern and western borders. What was recorded under the year 876, however, was much more significant. The *Anglo-Saxon Chronicle*, in one of the most understated but consequential remarks in the recorded history of early medieval Britain, notes that 'Halfdan divided up the land of Northumbria', and his people 'were ploughing and supporting themselves'.[34]

By 875, the land was changing – utterly and irrevocably. And not merely in the terminal collapse of age-old kingdoms; the Vikings had insinuated themselves into the very marrow of England. The soil was being ploughed by Viking hands, and their dead were laid to rest in it. The earth was being worked and mounds raised; even the bones of the English dead, perhaps even their kings, were now being co-opted into the graves of warriors born in Denmark, Norway or beyond. In every part of these islands, the children of Viking men were being born to native mothers. And, perhaps most profound of all, the names of things had begun to change: places that had borne English names for 400 years or more were shedding them as a new lexicon established itself in the wake of settlement: Norse words, Viking words. This was no longer a harrying, nor even a simple conquest, the exchange of one ruling dynasty for another. This was colonization, with all the cultural, linguistic, geographical and political upheaval such a process brings in train. Its impact can still be felt today.

# 11

# THE RETURN OF THE KING

And naught was left King Alfred
But shameful tears of rage,
In the island in the river
In the end of all his age.

In the island in the river
He was broken to his knee:
And he read, writ with an iron pen,
That God had wearied of Wessex men
And given their country, field and fen,
To the devils of the sea.

G. K. CHESTERTON, *The Ballad of the White Horse* (1911)[1]

In March 878, seeking refuge, King Alfred came to Athelney, a hidden spit of land, rising gently from the bleak expanse of the Somerset Levels.

He had led his battered court to this remote place in the short dark days of January and February, 'leading a restless life in great distress amid the woody and marshy places of Somerset'.[2] The language of the *Anglo-Saxon Chronicle*, with its woods (*wuda*) and moor-fastnesses (*mór-fæstenas*), recalls the monster-haunted wildernesses of *Beowulf* and *St Guthlac*, drawing, with allusive economy, a world at the margins of human life – a place of estrangement and shadow-life. Asser tells us that the king 'had nothing to live on except what he could forage by frequent raids, either secretly or even openly, from the Vikings as well as from the Christians who had submitted to the Vikings' authority'. Alfred was a king turned *wulvesheofod* ('wolf's head'), his tenure in the wilderness an inversion of the order of Anglo-Saxon life. Alfred, like Grendel, had become the *sceadugenga* – the 'shadow-walker' – the wolf beyond the border 'who held the moors, the fen and fastness ...'[3]

These days, Athelney is a nondescript lump of ground, surrounded by the flat fields of the Somerset countryside. But when the flood tides come – as they did in with devastating effect in 2012 and 2014 – we can see it again as Alfred saw it: white sky and white water, the sheet of pale gauze split by the black fingers of the trees, torn by sprays of rushes, limbs of willow lightly touched with sickly green, catkins swinging like a thousand tiny sacrifices. Off in the distance a heron hauls itself skyward, spreading wide black pinions, beating a lazy saurian path across the Levels. The other birds carry on their business, snipe and curlew boring surgical holes into the shallows. The plop of a diving frog adds percussion to the throaty chorus of his fellows, lusty young bulls emerging bleary-eyed from their winter beds, seeking out mates to tangle with in the mud.

Later in his life, Alfred would invest in Athelney by founding a monastery there, perhaps in gratitude and recognition for the role it had played in his career, or perhaps as part of his campaign of self-mythologization. 'Æthelingaeg' is how Asser spells it, though the manuscripts of the *Anglo-Saxon Chronicle* present various different iterations. It means 'isle of princes' (Æðeling 'prince' + *eíg* 'island'), an auspicious name for a royal refuge and one which we might suspect was bestowed only after it had played its part in Alfred's story. He would also establish a stronghold there, a 'formidable fortress of elegant workmanship' connected to the island by a causeway, the genesis of the modern village of East Lyng.[4] But at the time he came there in 878 it was an isolated place – cut off amid the swollen waters of the Levels, an island, 'surrounded' as Asser explained 'by swampy, impassable and extensive marshland and groundwater on every side'.[5]

In 878, Athelney was a place where Alfred could hide from his Viking enemies and plan his attacks against them – attacking them 'relentlessly and tirelessly'.[6] It would briefly become for him the seat of a guerrilla government in exile, of a king without a kingdom, an Avalon unto which the king would pass and where he would be reborn.

It had taken several years for the situation in Wessex to reach this sorry pass. By 875, Northumbria and East Anglia had fallen to Viking armies, and Mercia was riven by faction and war, its ancestral tombs ransacked and defiled. Only Wessex had weathered the Viking storm and remained intact: the military resolve of Alfred and his people had delivered four years of peace. That peace, however, was now over and in 875 the king's warriors fought (and won) a maritime skirmish with a raiding fleet. One Viking ship was captured and six (Asser says five) were driven off. This, however, was only the opening move in a new war for the West Saxon kingdom.[7]

In 876, the army that had been led to Cambridge from Repton by Guthrum, Oscetel and Anwend moved suddenly into Wessex and occupied Wareham, a fortified convent in Dorset. Crisis seemed initially to have been averted through negotiation – hostages were exchanged and the Viking army swore holy and binding oaths – but it transpired that this Viking force had no particular intention of leaving Wessex. The army slipped away from Wareham by night, executing the hostages granted by Alfred (we can imagine that the Vikings held by the West Saxon army suffered a similar fate in return) and moved on to occupy Exeter in Devon. Alfred gave them good chase, but once again the limitations of early medieval siege-craft sucked all the momentum from the campaign: the king 'could not overtake them before they were in the fortress where they could not be overpowered'.[8] Had it not been for the weather, things might have looked bleak for Wessex – 120 Viking ships were lost in a storm near Swanage, preventing them from linking up with their comrades at Exeter.[9] The result, yet again, was a stalemate, and once more hostages were exchanged (none of whom can have felt very optimistic about his future) and oaths sworn; this time, perhaps sapped of confidence as a result of the failure of their planned pincer-movement, the Viking army did indeed withdraw. They went, in fact, to Mercia, where they formally carved up Ceolwulf's kingdom, leaving the latter a rump part, and saw out the winter in Gloucester.[10]

This occurred in 877, and we know nothing of what befell Ceolwulf and his subjects in that, presumably depressing, period. It is likely, however, that the time spent in Mercia was used by the Viking army to consolidate their land-taking and to gather reinforcements. Soon after Twelfth Night (7 January) in the deep winter of early 878, the Viking army rode south into Wessex, to the royal estate at Chippenham in Wiltshire. They probably came via Cirencester, joining the Fosse Way and cutting through southern Gloucestershire like a dagger, before turning to the south-east. No early sources record whether Alfred was himself present at Chippenham, or whether he fought the Vikings there. All we are told (to give Asser's version) is that 'By strength of arms they forced many men of that race [West Saxons] to sail overseas, through both poverty and fear, and very nearly all the inhabitants of that region submitted to their authority'.[11]

Chippenham was occupied by Guthrum's army and Alfred began his period of exile in the wilderness. It was approximately ninety years since the first recorded Viking raids on England had taken place; in that short time, every one of the Anglo-Saxon kingdoms had been broken.

*

In later days in was said that St Cuthbert appeared in a vision to Alfred on Athelney. The speech that the king received was the stuff to put fire in the belly of any dynastic ruler: 'God will have delivered to you your enemies and all their land, and hereditary rule to you and to your sons and to your sons' sons. Be faithful to me and my people because to you and your sons was given all of Albion. Be just, because you have been chosen as king of all Britain.'[12] The story was added to the Alfred myth after the king's death, in either the mid-tenth or mid-eleventh century,[13] and Asser makes no mention of it. It seems likely to have been a tale spun during the reign of Alfred's grandson to prop up his political ambitions and solidify the standing of the cult of St Cuthbert. Nevertheless, had Cuthbert been looking down from his cloud in the 870s, he would have seen plenty of things which might have given him cause to visit destruction on the Vikings – not least the disturbance of his incorruptible slumber. The sack of his former monastery at Lindisfarne in 793 was, by then, a story from another age, but the arrival of the *micel here* in Northumbria was another matter. Heathen warlords were now in positions of power across the north, their people settling and dividing up the land. The reappearance of Halfdan on the Tyne in 875, 'devastating everything and sinning cruelly against St Cuthbert',[14] seems to have been what galvanized the monks to remove Cuthbert's precious bones from their resting place on Lindisfarne. According to the *Historia de Sancto Cuthberto*, so began seven years of wandering for Cuthbert's corporeal remnants, a terrestrial Odyssey of northern Britain designed, perhaps, to spare these relics the indignities that had befallen the dead of Repton. They finally came to rest at Chester-le-Street where they remained until 995, when they were disturbed once more.

If it was not Cuthbert's discorporate exhortations, it may be that something else galvanized Alfred to action. Perhaps it was the news that Odda, ealdorman of Somerset, had destroyed a Viking army that had arrived with twenty-three ships in Devon. His victory came at an unidentified hill-fort called 'Cynwit'.[15] In the fighting, the Viking leader Ubbe, slayer of King Edmund, son of Ragnar Loðbrók and brother to Halfdan and Ivar the Boneless, was killed.[16] Moreover, the *Anglo-Saxon Chronicle* notes, 'ðær wæs se guðfana genumen þe hie hræfn heton' ('there was taken the banner that they called Raven').[17] A later gloss on this passage adds that the banner had been woven by three sisters, the daughters of Ragnar Loðbrók, in a single day: when the banner caught the breeze and the raven's wings flapped, then victory in battle was assured; if it hung lifeless, defeat was in the offing.[18] There is a great deal that might be said about ravens and banners, weird sisters and weaving, and their place on the Viking Age battlefield. For now, however, it is sufficient to note that the seizure of such a banner would have been a considerable morale boost to the West Saxons. Although the defeat of Ubbe at Cynwit may have left Guthrum's army in a more vulnerable position than either he or his enemies had expected, its most important consequence may have been to demonstrate to the West Saxons and to Alfred that the Vikings could be beaten, that God was on the side of the English, and that his assistance – whether mediated through St Cuthbert or not – was more than a match for any heathen battle magic.

Whatever the catalyst, Alfred began to prepare. Messengers must have gone from Athelney to the ealdormen and thegns that remained loyal to him, into the shires to spread the word that the king was preparing to fight. We know that the shires had a well-developed system of hundred and shire assembly places, many of which would have been in use in Alfred's day and probably for long ages before. It is likely that these formed the hubs for military assembly, and that to them, all over Wessex, armed men would have made their way when they received the call of their reeve, ealdorman or king. So little is known, however, of the precise mechanisms by which a West Saxon army assembled – let alone in strange circumstances like those of 878 – that any attempt to reconstruct the movements or constituents of Alfred's army, beyond what Asser and the *Anglo-Saxon Chronicle* reveal, can only ever be informed speculation; indeed, the subject of how armies were raised in Anglo-Saxon England has long been a subject of intense academic scrutiny and debate.[19]

But we can imagine the little beginnings, the woman watching anxiously as the reeve's messenger rides hard away, mud splattering up from the puddles of spring rain; the grave expression on her husband's face as he walks back towards the house; the old sword he gives to his eldest son, still just a boy, to defend the farm when he is gone. We can imagine the tears and the parting, the lonely trudge past familiar fields, a spear over one shoulder, a sack over the other. On towards the hall of the thegn, to meet with other freemen of the hundred; he knows these men, has drunk with them, played games with them as a boy, one is his brother-in-law. They embrace each other and renew their friendships, ask after children and lands and livestock, tell bawdy jokes, ask dirty riddles;[20] but they don't stay long. They are nervous, though companionship helps them hide it. They need to keep moving, a small band now, singing the old songs as they go, songs of Wayland, Finn and Hengest.[21]

There are others on the road, little knots of armed men, some on horseback, others on foot, some in fine armour handed down from their grandfathers, garnets glittering on sword belts, gold on their horse bridles, others with little more than a padded jacket and a rusty spear. They make their way over hills and by herepath, through forests and over moors, by swift-running brooks and stagnant meres, coming together at the barrows and trees, the old stones and muddy fords – the ancient meeting places of Wessex. First the hundred, where local men were met and accounted for and news distributed, the king's summons made plain. Then they are back on the road, a war-band now, heading for the shire-moot, to join the reeve or ealdorman – to form the *fyrd* ('levied army'). As they go, further now from home, they begin to see tongues of flame shooting up from the hillsides, like the breath of dragons in the dusk: at first they think of burning villages, the harrying of Danes, before they recognize the signal fires, beacons calling the men to battle.[22]

When morning comes they see the camp spread out before them, the ealdorman's war banner fluttering, gold thread glittering in the sun. But there is no time to rest and swap stories, to renew old acquaintances. News has reached them that the king is on the move.

Presently, in the seventh week after Easter he [Alfred] rode to Egbert's Stone, which is in the eastern part of Selwood Forest (*sylva magna* ['great wood'] in Latin, and *Coit Maur* in Welsh); and there all the inhabitants of Somerset and Wiltshire and all the inhabitants of Hampshire – those who had not sailed overseas for fear of the Vikings – joined up with him. When they saw the king, receiving him (not surprisingly) as if one restored to life after suffering such great tribulations, they were filled with immense joy. They made camp there for one night. At the break of the following dawn the king struck camp and came to a place called Iley [*ASC*: *Iglea*, 'island wood'], and made camp there for one night.

When the next morning dawned he moved his forces and came to a place called Edington, and fighting fiercely with a compact shield-wall against the entire Viking army, he persevered resolutely for a long time; at length he gained the victory through God's will.[23]

Walking on the northern rim of Salisbury Plain feels like clinging to the edge of the world – the land drops away 300 feet below the earthen banks of the fortress that crown the hillside like a circlet of turf-grown soil. The ramparts belong to Bratton Camp, a massive Iron Age hill-fort that encloses the long, mutilated hogback of a Neolithic long-barrow at its centre. Walking the perimeter, the wind rips across man-made canyons, forcing the breath back down my throat. I find that I am leaning at almost 45 degrees into the gale, and am suddenly, uncomfortably, aware of the fathoms of empty space to my right, a vast ocean of air; the plain sweeps to the north, a swathe of open country laid bare for leagues. I briefly see myself tossed like a leaf, spinning into oblivion – just another piece of organic matter on the breeze. My gut flips at the sudden feeling of vulnerability, and I begin to tack back towards the long-barrow; the sharp smell of sheep shit hits me in the nose. As I get closer to the mound an old ram with a sad face stares at me reproachfully. I ignore him, and some of his ewes go bouncing off from their grazing patch on top of the barrow, scattering in dim-witted panic.

From up here the strategic significance of the place is obvious, and it is likely that Bratton Camp was once a look-out post. The name of the ground that slopes off to the south of the hill-fort is 'Warden Hill', a swell of upland that runs hard up against the bedyked confines of the hill-fort. The name 'Warden' may very well be a development from the Old English *weard* ('watch') and *dun* ('hill'). From here one can look across to the east, around 2½ miles along the line of the chalk ridge, to Tottenham Wood, the site of another Neolithic long-barrow. There are lots of English place-names with elements like 'tut', 'toot' or 'totten' forming part of them; though often difficult to interpret, many may originate in Old English constructions like *tote-hām* or *tōten-hām* meaning 'house near the look-out station' or 'house of the watchman'.[24] Both Bratton Camp and Tottenham Wood boast commanding views over the low countryside to the north, casting a watchful gaze from the rim of the plateau; down below, 2 to 3 miles from both putative look-out sites, is the meeting place of Whorwellsdown Hundred at Crosswelldown Farm.[25]

Looking south from the farm, Salisbury Plain rises up like a great green cliff edge, the low sun casting its man-made terraces and earthen banks into horizontal bands of undulate chromatism, like a great green tsunami surging northwards to consume the plain. Riding on that crest, both Bratton Camp and Tottenham Wood are clearly visible from the old hundred meeting place – three land-marks, each one visible to and from the others, enclosing the land-scape in a triangle of watchfulness. Between them, hugging the base of the escarpment are the villages of Bratton and Edington, the latter a place that takes its name from the bleak hillside that looms over it: Eþandun – 'the barren hill'.

Centuries before Alfred led his armies here, before the West Saxons had become Christians, they had brought their dead to Bratton Camp, to cut their graves into the ancient barrows, to lay them down among the more ancient spirits of the land. Three early

Anglo-Saxon burials, revealed by nineteenth-century excavators, were dug into the long-barrow, and even earlier excavations uncovered the remains of a warrior buried with axe and sword, interred in the top of a Bronze Age round barrow that stood at the southern entrance to the camp.[26] Most thought provoking of all, perhaps, was the evidence of a cremation platform discovered at the long-barrow – the remains of a pyre where the pagan West Saxons had once burned their dead.[27] Up here, up on the heights, the smoke and the flames would have been seen for miles.

The theatre of such events would have impressed themselves on the imagination in ways that would not have been easy to forget, passing into folklore. *Beowulf*, as so often, evokes the majesty and spectacle of the ritual in ways which charcoal and fragments of burnt iron cannot:

> The Geat people built a pyre for Beowulf,
> stacked and decked it until it stood foursquare,
> hung with helmets, heavy war-shields
> and shining armour, just as he had ordered.
> Then his warriors laid him in the middle of it,
> mourning a lord far-famed and beloved.
> On a height they kindled the hugest of all
> funeral fires; fumes of woodsmoke
> billowed darkly up, the blaze roared
> and drowned out their weeping, wind died down
> and flames wrought havoc in the hot bone-house,
> burning it to the core. They were disconsolate
> and wailed aloud for their lord's decease.[28]

One can only speculate how long the memory of the ancestors burned and buried here would have lingered in the collective memory, what associations this landscape may have held for Alfred and his contemporaries; but it is hard to believe, even if the ancient funerals were forgotten, that the monumental remains of Bratton Camp and the numerous barrows of the chalk ridge did not exert a pull on the West Saxon imagination. The names of the long-bar-rows at Bratton Camp and Tottenham Wood – if they ever boasted them – are lost. But, given the evidence of Anglo-Saxon boundary clauses elsewhere, it is highly probable that names or legendary material of some type had accumulated at these monuments by the late ninth century. Places like these were deliberately sought out as venues for battle or military assembly – it was surely deliberate, for example, that Alfred should have chosen to muster his army at Egbert's Stone before moving on to Iley Oak and Edington; it was Ecgberht (Egbert), Alfred's grandfather, who had returned Wessex to pre-eminence among the Anglo-Saxon realms – a military hero whose memory was an appropriate one to invoke ahead of a battle that would determine the fate of his own dynasty and the future course of British history.[29]

There are other reasons why Edington might have been impor-tant to Alfred and why he led his army here. His father, Æthelwulf, had come here in the 850s, the place-name Edington appearing as the place of ratification for a charter granting land in Devon to a deacon called Eadberht.[30] Alfred himself later bequeathed the estate at Edington to his wife, Ealhswith, along with estates at Wantage and Lambourn. (It is tempting to see in this bequest an acknowl-edgement of the importance of Edington to Alfred's sense of himself – Wantage was the place of his birth, Edington of his greatest victory.) The place remained in royal hands until long afterwards. In the tenth century, royal grants of land at Edington were made to Romsey Abbey.[31] It seems certain, therefore, that Edington was a royal estate centre before and after the battle that was fought there. Although nothing confirming a royal residence has yet been discov-ered, an early medieval spindle whorl has been found in the envi-rons of the village,[32] perhaps implying a settlement of some sort, and the remains of a royal hall may yet lie beneath the modern settlement. This in itself would be enough to explain why this place was chosen as the theatre of battle; a powerful symbol of royal authority, its occupation by either side sent a clear message to the rest of Wessex. However, when taken in combination with the evidence of a resonance both deeper and wider – ancient graves and even older monuments, military assemblies and strategic oversight, and the great geological rift in the land – it seems clear that Edington was a powerful and a fearsome place.

In *Alarms and Discursions*, a compendium of short works published by G. K. Chesterton in 1910, the writer and critic described his own experiences exploring this landscape.

the other day under a wild sunset and moonrise I passed the place which is best reputed as Ethandune, a high, grim upland, partly bare and partly shaggy; like that savage and sacred spot in those great imaginative lines about the demon lover and the waning moon. The darkness, the red wreck of sunset, the yellow and lurid moon, the long fantastic shadows, actually created that sense of monstrous incident which is the dramatic side of landscape. The bare grey slopes seemed to rush downhill like routed hosts; the dark clouds drove across like riven banners; and the moon was like a golden dragon, like the Golden Dragon of Wessex.

As we crossed a tilt of the torn heath I saw suddenly between myself and the moon a black shapeless pile higher than a house. The atmosphere was so intense that I really thought of a pile of dead Danes, with some phantom conqueror on the top of it […] this was a barrow older than Alfred, older than the Romans, older perhaps than the Britons; and no man knew whether it was a wall or a trophy or a tomb […] it gave me a queer emotion to think that, sword in hand, as the Danes poured with the torrents of their blood down to Chippenham, the great king may have lifted up his head and looked at that oppressive shape, suggestive of something and yet suggestive of nothing; may have looked at it as we did, and understood it as little as we.[33]

I don't think that Chesterton was right about Alfred. I think the king knew full well the significance of Edington and its environs: its Bronze Age and Neolithic graves were reused by Alfred's own Saxon ancestors as a burial ground, his royal hall was sited in their shadow. But what Chesterton clearly understood, and was able to express so powerfully, was the sheer drama, the physical presence and the intrusive – almost overpowering – impact of the environment on the imagination. His words are a reminder that landscape has the power to conjure visions and summon the dead back to life, to superimpose the supernatural on the real world and bring history into a concurrent dialogue with the present. What we feel in a given environment – the angle of the rain, the colour of the sky, the 'tilt of the torn heath' – can connect us to the ancient past through a sense of shared feeling and experience. Moreover, these were feelings and emotions that were more potent, more powerful, in Alfred's day than they were in Chesterton's or remain, indeed, in ours.

The Victorians loved Alfred. For the whole of the nineteenth century, and until – at least – the outbreak of the First World War, the Anglophone world (and white English males in particular) had a mania for crediting the West Saxon king with inventing almost everything that people in those days thought was a good idea – from Oxford University to the Royal Navy and from the British Parliament (and its colonial offspring) to the British Empire itself.[34] He was a paragon of chivalry, of learning and wisdom, a Solomon-like figure, imbued with vast reserves of energy and prowess – a reformer of laws and, simultaneously, a conservative upholder of ancient traditions, a defender of the faith and a master of self-restraint, a scholar, a builder, a man of the people, a sufferer, a redeemer, a mighty warrior and 'the ideal Englishman [...] the embodiment of our civilization'.[35] He was, in the words of the great historian of the Norman Conquest, E. A. Freeman, nothing less than the 'the most perfect character in history'.[36]

To illuminate all of the extraordinary contortions, elisions, exaggerations, falsifications, misunderstandings, credulity, hyperbole, political expediency and mischief that collided in the creation of this absurdly hypertrophic idea of kingship would take us on a long detour from our intended destination.[37] However, even though Alfred's greatest achievement may have been the skill with which he publicized his achievements, like most myths his greatness is rooted in a certain amount of truth: for none of it – neither deserved fame nor inflated hero-cult – would have accrued to Alfred had he not found the wherewithal to fight himself out of the corner into which he had been painted in the spring of 878. Even with the knowledge that our view of Alfred derives from the 'authorized' version of his life, the mythic quality of its resurrection narrative lends something truly epic, cinematic in its emotional charge, to the return of the king.

In Alfred's victory over Guthrum at Edington there is something of what Tolkien called 'eucatastrophe', the cathartic joy of a victory attained, against expectation, in the face of horror and despair. In his view, the archetypal eucatastrophe was found in the death and resurrection of Christ, a story that obtained its extraordinary power from its status as what Tolkien called 'true myth' – the entwining, as he saw it, of the strands of history and fairy-tale into the defining cable of truth running through the centre of human experience.[38] It was this that caused him to insist – most famously to C. S. Lewis in discussions which ultimately caused the latter to reject the atheism of his youth – that myths, of all kinds (but 'northern' myths in particular), were not lies: they were echoes of mankind's understanding of the one true myth that shaped all of humanity's creative endeavour. To some degree this was a self-justificatory argument: Tolkien was ever anxious to reconcile his love of myth and fairy-tale – and his own lifelong creation of them – with a profoundly held Catholic faith.[39]

In essence, however, these were not original thoughts, even if Professor Tolkien expressed them in ways which have retained a rare power. G. K. Chesterton himself had made very similar arguments in a public spat with the atheist and political activist Robert Blatchford in 1904.[40] Chesterton had also recognized the mythic potency of Alfred, composing the weird but remarkable *Ballad of the White Horse* in 1911, one year after his disquisition on the floating shade of 'Ethandune'. The *Ballad* comprises 2,684 lines of epic verse that tell the story of the king's return from Athelney to triumph at Edington.[41] It has been described as the high water mark

Alfred the hero, as envisioned by Morris Meredith Williams in 1913

of Victorian Alfredianism, as well as its effective epitaph,[42] and it is hard not to see, in the power it draws from landscape and mythic archetype, a prefiguring of Tolkien's oeuvre – even though the professor, while admiring the 'brilliant smash and glitter' of its language, was characteristically scathing about its merits overall (another demonstration of his tendency to attack more harshly those things which disappointed him than those that simply didn't interest him: 'not as good as I thought [...] the ending is absurd [...] G.K.C. knew nothing whatever about the "North", heathen or Christian').[43]

In the *Ballad*, the action of the battle is transposed to the landscape around the Uffington White Horse – a location which, as we have seen, is much more likely to have been the location of Alfred's battle at Ashdown. But the *Ballad* is not about historical reality; the poem is filled with fictional details and improbable symbolism, designed to emphasize Alfred's Christlike journey from 'death' in exile, to resurrection and apotheosis. It recognizes – or, rather, seeks to revive and recast – the story of these few weeks in 878 as the creation not only of Alfred's personal myth, but of the nation itself, of 'Englishness' and, by extension, of 'Britishness' in its Anglocentric imperial iteration, born in a single moment of transcendent bloodshed that washed away the regional differences and ethnic animus of centuries. Chesterton's three central protagonists, Alfred aside, were an Anglo-Saxon, a Briton and, most anachronistically of all, a Roman – three heroic avatars of what he evidently regarded as the progenitive peoples of (southern) Britain. In his view the Vikings were not part of this heritage:

> The Northmen came about our land
> A Christless chivalry:
> Who knew not of the arch or pen,
> Great, beautiful half-witted men
> From the sunrise and the sea.

Misshapen ships stood on the deep
Full of strange gold and fire,
And hairy men, as huge as sin
With horned heads, came wading in
Through the long, low sea-mire.

Our towns were shaken of tall kings
With scarlet beards like blood:
The world turned empty where they trod,
They took the kindly cross of God
And cut it up for wood.

Chesterton's 'Northmen' are dead-eyed, dim-witted barbarians –
vital and potent, but a force of nature unfeeling as the storm-wind.
They are the primal and impersonal tide against which the quality
of Alfred's humanity could be measured, a mute anvil upon which
the gilt mantle of his greatness could be hammered out and the
shape of the English nation forged. Of such stuff is national mythology built, and Alfred and his descendants themselves ensured that
the events of 878 would be remembered in this light.

But, of course, nothing is ever so simple.

# 12

# THE GODFATHER

And there came to his chrism-loosing
Lords of all lands afar,
And a line was drawn north-westerly
That set King Egbert's empire free,
Giving all lands by the northern sea
To the sons of the northern star.

G. K. CHESTERTON, *The Ballad of the White Horse* (1911)[1]

The priest is too close – the kneeling warrior can see the pores of the man's skin, the wiry hairs that project from his nostrils. The breath comes suddenly, short and sharp amid the low rhythmic babble of unfamiliar words, like the wheeze of a thrall who has spent too long tending the hearth-fire; it is hot and musty, the smell of old wine skins. The kneeling man flinches, a scarred hand flickering to the sword hilt that he knows – all too uncomfortably – is not at his hip. He turns sharply to the side, eyebrows raised. The young man to his right whispers back in the Norse tongue: 'He is driving away evil, so that Christ can enter.' The warrior tenses and narrows his eyes. '*Bolverkr*,' he mutters under his breath, but the priest ignores him and carries on regardless. Salt is placed in the kneeler's hand, and then, suddenly, the priest grasps his nostrils (to remind him, the translator whispers, to stay steadfast while he is still breathing).

The Latin is incessant, hypnotic. Occasionally the warrior nods, or grunts an assent when the translator prompts him, but for the most part he fixes his eyes on the serpent that sprouts from the top of the bishop's staff, imagines it moving, coiling into life, the forked tongue lashing out, hissing … Perhaps, he thinks to himself, this priest is a *seiðmaðr* – a sorcerer. A brief shudder animates the bare flesh of his torso. '*Argr*,' he mouths the word silently, glaring at the bishop with new hostility. But suddenly there is oil being painted on his skin – a cross joining his nipples and running down his breastbone, daubs on his shoulders – and then, before he has a chance to understand what is happening, he is on his feet and King Alfred is beside him, leading him towards a great stone basin, carved all around with spirals and rolling scrolls of foliage, brightly painted.[2] Guthrum gazes into the water that fills it, uncomprehending. The bishop's hand is on his head, pushing him towards the surface – a black mirror in which shards of candlelight dart. He can see his own features looking back, shadowy, his eyes hollowed into pits. Fear begins to twist his guts. He resists, looking to the king, who nods reassuringly.

And then his head is in the water, and all the sound of the chanting and the Latin babble is gone – just a hollow swirl in his ears, and darkness. He rises quickly, water running into his eyes, and he shakes his head like a dog springing from a pool, spray flying from his beard. But as he tries to regain his balance, he is pushed immediately back into the water. For a moment he wonders if he will drown. And then, once again, he is back, choking in the candle-smoke and the fug of incense. Guthrum barely registers the white robe that is hung upon him, or the oil that is tipped over his head; a white cloth is bound around his brow. A conversation is taking place in English between Alfred and the bishop. He doesn't understand it all, but he picks out a name, a name repeated several times as they stare at him: Æthelstan.

After Edington, the Viking army was driven in flight to its encampment (probably at Chippenham). The Vikings were forced to make peace with Alfred, agreeing to vacate West Saxon territory – a promise cemented with hostages and 'great oaths'. It may have been the totality of Alfred's victory that meant that the negotiated peace was less conditional than similar agreements had been in the past. Asser specifically noted that while 'the king should take as many chosen hostages as he wanted' from the Viking army, he would 'give none to them' – the emphasis on Alfred's ability to choose his hostages suggesting that the West Saxons were free to select high-ranking or otherwise valuable individuals from among the Viking ranks. This, apparently, was unprecedented: 'never before, indeed, had they made peace with anyone on such terms'.[3]

Most dramatic of all the gestures made, however, was an agreement that Guthrum, the erstwhile invader of Wessex, would renounce his heathen beliefs and become a Christian. This was a radical proposition – the religious affiliation of a Viking leader in Britain had never before been on the negotiating table – and there must have been many at the time who doubted the intentions of the Viking leadership. Solemn oaths had been made before and broken, hostages sacrificed. So it may have occasioned some surprise when, three weeks later, Guthrum and twenty-nine other senior members of his army presented themselves to Alfred at Aller (3 miles east of Athelney) for baptism.

How deeply Guthrum understood the ritual and symbolism of the baptismal liturgy can never be known – the evocation above is imaginative, based on explanations of the rite written by Alcuin in a letter of the late eighth century – and it is possible that he was a far better-prepared catechumen than I have made him out to be.[4] He had certainly been in contact with Christians – indeed, he probably had several in his army already. But it seems unlikely that the deeper religious symbolism would have meant much to him, and it is an open question how much English – let alone Latin – he would have understood.

The politics, however, would have been crystal clear. Asser and the *Anglo-Saxon Chronicle* explain that Alfred stood as Guthrum's godfather and 'raised him' in Asser's words 'from the holy font of baptism'. In the process, a new name was bestowed upon him, one of unimpeachable Anglo-Saxon probity: Æthelstan. This was an interesting choice for a number of reasons. There had been a King Æthelstan of East Anglia, in the first half of the ninth century, and this may be significant given the territory over which Guthrum would come to rule. But Æthelstan was also the name of Alfred's own eldest brother – the first-born son of King Æthelwulf of Wessex. Æthelwulf had been dynastically fortunate in that his first wife, Osburh, had been exceptionally prone to producing sons. It is an extraordinary fact that every single one of them – five in total – ruled as kings (and their only daughter, Æthelswith, had been queen to the luckless Burhred of Mercia): Æthelbald, king of Wessex (858–60); Æthelberht, king of Wessex (860–5) and Kent (855–66); Æthelred, king of Wessex and Kent (865–71); and, of course, Alfred himself (871–99). Æthelstan, the eldest, had been king of Kent, a junior role while his father reigned as king of Wessex, from 839 until some point in the early 850s when he died.

It had been customary since the reign of Ecgberht for kings of Kent to be members of the West Saxon royal house, sometimes unifying the crowns of Wessex and Kent in the person of a single individual, and sometimes delegating authority to a younger son or brother. By Alfred's reign, this practice was beginning to fizzle out, royal power in Kent becoming part of the standard portfolio of the West Saxon king.[5] In any case, Alfred had no sons (of an appropriate age) or little brothers to placate or promote by offering them inferior kingships (his nephew was altogether another matter, as we shall see). He would, however, have remained well aware of how useful it could be to have a grateful junior kinsman on the throne of a subordinate neighbouring kingdom.

Guthrum, clearly, was no blood relative to Alfred, but kinship could be established in other ways. By standing as Guthrum's godfather, and bestowing on him his new, Christian, name, Alfred was establishing a claim to symbolic paternity. When Guthrum became Æthelstan he had also become Alfred's 'son'. A relationship had been created between the two men that mingled the loyalties of close kinship with the power dynamics of family hierarchy. Assuming, as seems most likely, that it was Alfred who chose the name 'Æthelstan', the choice may have been deliberately intended to cast the relationship between Alfred and Guthrum in the same light as that which had existed between Alfred's father Æthelwulf and his eldest brother Æthelstan: the latter the nominal ruler of a subservient client kingdom, the former the hegemonic West Saxon king, in whose gift lay the thrones of lesser realms.

If the political theatre of Guthrum's baptism were not enough to underscore Alfred's intentions for the post-Edington power dynamic, Guthrum acknowledged Alfred's superior lordship in other ways as well. Alfred had sealed the baptism celebrations by showering Guthrum and his men 'with many excellent treasures'.[6] According to well-established social etiquette, the receiver of gifts – particularly if he had little to offer of commensurate value – was placed in a subservient role. Guthrum, from a West Saxon perspective at any rate, became Alfred's man the moment he took Alfred's gifts.

What, we might ask, were Alfred and Guthrum hoping to achieve by all of this? Perhaps Alfred imagined that – at some stage – he would hold, as Guthrum–Æthelstan's 'father' and overlord, a controlling interest in whatever territory the newly Christian Viking came to rule. If Alfred was thinking along these lines, it suggests that he had reason to expect this outcome. What had the West Saxon king promised to Guthrum? What was it that had brought him to baptism, had convinced him to accept such a one-sided peace deal, to honour the terms of it so faithfully?

In 879, the Viking army moved from Chippenham to Cirencester, where it remained for a year. During this time, a new army of Vikings arrived from overseas, sailing up the Thames with – according to Asser – the intention of linking up with Guthrum's forces upstream. The newcomers made camp at Fulham and dug themselves in. It must have been a tense few months for Alfred and the West Saxons, poised between two Viking armies hovering on the Thames. But winter came, and winter went, and nobody moved. Guthrum, it seems, was mindful of his accord with Alfred and the benefits that his patronage might confer. Whatever the reasoning, it was enough to overcome any temptation to make common cause with these newcomers. In 880 the new Viking army left Fulham and crossed the Channel, wreaking a trail of havoc across France and the Low Countries. Guthrum's forces, meanwhile, decamped from Cirencester and made their way to East Anglia.

When they arrived there, just as Halfdan and his people had earlier done in Northumbria, they 'settled that land, and divided it up'.[7] The next we hear of Guthrum–Æthelstan, he is introduced as a king. Perhaps it was this that Alfred had offered in 878, the prize that had lured the heathen Viking to the baptismal waters; perhaps Alfred, the most powerful Anglo-Saxon king left in Britain, had offered his backing and blessing for Guthrum to claim the East Anglian throne for himself.

We know very little about Guthrum's East Anglian regime, the kingdom over which he ruled for a decade until his death in 890. But what does stand out is how swiftly he seems to have come to terms with the new realities and adapted to them. In the early 880s, new coins were being produced in East Anglia. Like most English coins of the period, they bore the name of the king on one side (the obverse) and, usually, the name of the mint and the moneyer on the other (the reverse). A great many of these coins bore the name of King Alfred, despite the evidence indicating that they had been struck outside Wessex.[8] Wholesale imitation of the coins of other rulers is fairly commonplace among new regimes seeking to establish their own legitimacy, and so it is altogether unsurprising that Guthrum should have taken this approach in getting his own coinage up and running (his moneyers also copied some continental coin types). The coins do, however, give us an indication of how the world looked from the perspective of Guthrum's subjects, and how the new king began to adapt to their expectations: it was Alfred's name that was likely to reassure his subjects that the coinage was legitimate, and Alfred's coinage that was recognized and respected as a means of economic exchange. Equally revealing is the fact that, when Guthrum's name *did* appear on the East Anglian coinage, it appeared as (still copying the design of West Saxon coinage) 'EÐELSTAN REX' – 'King Æthelstan'.

Money is power. Although it is (almost) always an abstracted and symbolic proxy for value, whether it is piles of banknotes or figures moving up and down on digital indices, we understand intuitively that money is bound up tightly with the expression of authority and status. Physical currency embodies and promotes its relationship to state power through the images with which it is encoded, and these convey a host of ideas about the stability of the state, the core symbols of national pride and identity, the strength of the economy, the values of the authority that produces it. Periodic controversy over the personnel selected to decorate modern banknotes demonstrates how important we still feel this to be.

The people of the Viking Age – and the Vikings in particular – often valued coins for their weight as bullion, rather than their face value. But the symbolic qualities of coinage were as readily understood then as they are now. The very power to cause a coinage to be made was a statement in itself – it indicated a willingness, and an ability, to intervene in the means of exchange between people and to regulate the flow of precious metal. It also signalled a desire to engage in behaviours which spoke of elevated political power: all of the coinage of the early medieval period was modelled, to some degree, on the coins produced by Rome, adopted and adapted by the great successor kingdoms that had followed the Empire's demise in the west. Simply having a coinage minted under one's own name was to stake a claim on the legendary and exalted status of Caesar. To mint coins was also to adopt one of the outward trappings of an elite club whose members could consider themselves the heirs of

Rome – the Christian kings of western Europe. This was probably heady stuff for a Viking warlord like Guthrum.

In late 877 he had been one warlord among many, just another Viking chancer plying his bloody business among the surprisingly spongy kingdoms of Britain; by 879 he was the acknowledged king of an ancient realm, baptized by a king anointed by the pope. Of course, being a member of this club also demanded overt Christianity as a condition of membership, and by using his baptismal name (on a coinage also marked with crosses) Guthrum (as Æthelstan) was making sure this message was distributed as widely as possible. Coins were a particularly useful propaganda tool in this regard: nobody could forget who the king was, not when his name was stamped on every new silver penny.[9]

In any case, finding himself the ruler of a kingdom in which the majority of the population were Christian and Anglo-Saxon, Guthrum didn't need to be a Viking Machiavelli to recognize that it would be politic to promote himself as both of these things: if he wanted to be accepted as a legitimate Christian East Anglian king, he would need to *be* a Christian East Anglian. The thoroughness with which new Viking rulers adopted the outward trappings of their adopted kingdom was manifested with the most spectacular irony during the decade after Guthrum's death. In the mid- to late 890s, a new coin was designed and produced that bore the legend 'SC EADMVND REX A' (*Sanctus Eadmund Rex Anglorum*): 'St Edmund, King of the [East] Angles'. Less than a generation after Ivar and Ubbe – the Viking leaders of the *micel here* – had deprived the last native king of East Anglia of his garrulous head, his memory was being celebrated and his cult promoted by the new Anglo-Viking regime.

This wasn't a phenomenon confined to East Anglia. In all of the regions that had fallen under Viking dominance, efforts were under way to create models of authority and cultural compromise that were as indebted to the Anglo-Saxon past as they were to Viking novelty. This was a new world, broken and remade over twenty years of war. But what emerged was not a neatly bifurcated England, split between an Anglo-Saxon south and a Viking north. It was more complicated than that, its identities less clear cut, its politics more tangled, its trajectory uncertain.

> This is the peace which King Alfred and King Guthrum and the councillors of all the English race [*ealles Angelcynnes witan*] and the people who are in East Anglia have all agreed on and confirmed with oaths, for themselves and for all their subjects, both for the living and for the unborn, who care to have God's favour or ours,
>
> 1. First concerning our boundaries: up the Thames, and then up the Lea, and along the Lea to its source, then in a straight line to Bedford, then up the Ouse to Watling Street.[10]

This is how the treaty of Alfred and Guthrum opens. It was made, not in the immediate aftermath of the battle of Edington, but probably at some point between 886 when Alfred took control of London and 890 when Guthrum died.[11] Its first clause is often described as the earliest definition of the southern boundary of what came to be known as the 'Danelaw' – that part of Britain in which Danish laws and customs prevailed from the end of the ninth century. Traditional maps of Viking settlement use this glorified boundary clause to ink a border on to the map of Britain, plotting a great wobbly diagonal from London to somewhere near Wroxeter. The overall implication of such maps is clear enough, even while scholarship demurs: this was a frontier, and beyond it the English-speaking people of Britain had passed into the clutches of a foreign people, to choke under the Danish yoke until liberation came from the south.

But the 'Danelaw', at least in that sense, never existed; there was no great Viking realm stretching from the Thames to the Tyne. For one thing, the treaty of Alfred and Guthrum makes no mention of any such entity. Indeed, the term 'Danelaw' wasn't recorded until the early eleventh century.[12] What the treaty seems primarily concerned with is defining the extent of Alfred's – rather than Guthrum's – practical authority. Firstly, it implicitly recognizes

Alfred's status as the de facto ruler of all those lands that Viking armies had failed to overrun permanently, while Guthrum (Æthelstan), notably described now as 'king', is associated only with the people of East Anglia, the kingdom to which he had taken his army in 880.

Most of the rest of Britain is abandoned to an undefined sphere of influence, the only clear characteristic of which seems to be that this influence did not belong to Alfred. This was nothing new: East Anglia, Mercia and Northumbria (let alone anything further west or north) had never been part of Wessex and had only briefly (and intermittently) fallen under West Saxon influence. They were, however, all areas into which Viking armies had already intruded and assumed a degree of political control. On the other hand, most of the lands south of the treaty border were regions where West Saxon dominance had been acknowledged for decades.

Most, that is, but not all. Mercia, its native rulers broken and dispossessed, had received rough treatment throughout the 870s. Now, by the terms of the treaty drawn up by Alfred and Guthrum, it was carved up with impunity, divided along a diagonal axis, its south-western territories passing into the care of an expanded, 'Greater' Wessex. In practical charge of the Mercian rump at this time was a man named Æthelred. It seems that he had succeeded Ceolwulf as the ruler of (unoccupied) Mercia, but unlike his predecessor was rarely referred to as king. (The Welsh on his western border, whom he mercilessly harassed during the 880s, considered him to be such, but their opinion counted for little in Wessex.)

Instead, Æthelred was generally referred to as 'ealdorman' in West Saxon sources, or else was given the suitably vague title 'lord of the Mercians'. By 883 he had acknowledged his subservience to Alfred, and in 886 was given delegated authority in London, a new West Saxon acquisition that had also once been subject to the Mercian kings (being granted authority over something which had historically been a possession was a particularly direct demonstration of dispossession and reduced status – a bit like a neighbour annexing part of your garden, and then giving you the job of looking after it). He was subsequently married to Alfred's daughter Æthelflæd (becoming, in an echo of the deal with Guthrum, Alfred's 'son' as well as his political subordinate). Whatever ambitions Æthelred may once have had to revive the fortunes of an autonomous Mercia were being rapidly squished by West Saxon power and tied up in clever dynastic entanglements: absorbed by the Alfredian blob.

And so we should recognize that the treaty was never intended to delimit a *Viking* sphere of influence: not one inch of the land that formed the 'Danelaw' was Alfred's to give, and none of it could have been taken away by him even if he had wanted to. It was, rather, a treaty that enlisted the aid of Alfred's godson, Guthrum, in the formalization of West Saxon territorial claims that now included half of Mercia as well as all of the land south of the Thames: a land charter for a Greater Wessex. Alfred would spend the remainder of his reign crafting that nation into something new – an inclusive national identity, expressed most obviously in the formulation of an unprecedented royal style. No longer would Alfred be described, like his predecessors, only as *rex Westsaxonum* or *rex Occidentalium Saxonum* ('king of the West Saxons'); instead, from the 880s onward, he would increasingly be known instead as *rex Anglorum et Saxonum*, or, as Asser has it, *Ælfred Angul-Saxonum rex*: 'Alfred, king of the Anglo-Saxons'.

A sense of what Alfred was hoping to encapsulate is articulated in the *Anglo-Saxon Chronicle* entry detailing Alfred's occupation of London in 886: 'and to him turned all of the English that were not in thrall to Danish men'.[13] Alfred, it is clear, now saw himself as king of all the 'English' – an idea also present in the first lines of the Alfred–Guthrum treaty with its invocation of 'councillors of all the English race [*ealles Angelcynnes witan*]'. The *Angelcynn* – the 'English-kin' – was an elastic description that would allow him and his dynasty to promote a claim to natural lordship over everyone and anyone who was not considered 'Danish' in the former English-speaking kingdoms of Britain. Indeed, in its most grandiose expression, it went even further, encompassing 'all the Christians of the island of Britain'.[14] Clearly, its formulation was politically expedient, creating an artificial homogeneity among the people Alfred now claimed to govern, papering over the annexation of western Mercia and allowing remarkable leeway for future territorial aggrandizement. But it also created something as powerful as it was illusory, an idea that would refuse to go away: it created the idea of a single English people and, by extension, the idea of a natural and contiguous homeland that could be – should be – subject to the authority of a single king. Far from establishing a coherent 'Danish' realm in Britain, the Viking wars and the agreements of Alfred and Guthrum that followed had produced something far more enduring. Alfred and the Vikings had invented England.[15]

This, of course, was just a little England. In the 890s, it comprised only the rump of Mercia and the land south of the Thames. But, in this act of rebranding, Alfred had created a remarkably durable, and elastic, identity. This identity allowed Alfred's descendants to promote the idea (and perhaps they even believed it themselves) that every act of aggression and territorial expansion directed northwards was a 'liberation' of the English rather than the imperial conquest it really was. The translation of Bede's *Ecclesiastical History of the English People* into Old English around the same time can be seen as part of this project – a new emphasis placed by the West Saxon court on shared history, rather than regional differences. Of course, for this to work it was essential that 'Englishness' could be easily and straightforwardly differentiated from anything else. And it is in this context that we should see the creation of the 'Dane' as the catch-all category for 'foreign johnny', bandied about with great liberality and very little specificity in the pages of the *Anglo-Saxon Chronicle*.[16]

Chesterton saw the battle of Edington as a contest for the soul of England, waged between the noble indigenous peoples of Britain and the dead-eyed Viking alien. This, clearly, is also how Alfred,

Asser and the Anglo-Saxon chronicler wanted us to see it – a watershed for the creation of a unified English community. But this was almost certainly not how the battle was seen by the people who fought in it. Alfred's army was led by the ealdormen of the West Saxon shires, but the origins of the personnel who fought for the king are entirely unknown. About Guthrum's army there can be even less certainty, and it is likely that a part of it (perhaps even a large part of it) was comprised, not of people born overseas, but of Mercians, East Anglians and others of British birth. From a West Saxon perspective such people would still have been Vikings – 'Danes' as the *Anglo-Saxon Chronicle* saw them – despite being just as 'British' as those they fought.

This, indeed, may have been the case from a relatively early date throughout Britain. Although we know that the *micel here* did receive outside reinforcements – the 'great summer-fleet' (*micel sumorlida*) that arrived during 870 from overseas and attached itself to the band fighting Alfred and Æthelred in Wessex is a case in point[17] – it is not at all certain that these were adequate to compensate for the casualties incurred over long campaigns, or for the attrition caused by those Vikings who may have cut their losses and returned home to farm and family. It seems likely, therefore, that some 'Vikings' must have had more local origins,[18] and it is not hard to imagine the mechanisms that might have enabled an itinerant army to attract willing recruits. In the first place, there would always have been lordless men, outlaws and exiles, runaway slaves and disinherited sons, all too eager to join a successful war-band and gain a share in the spoils of war. It was still a problem a century and a half later, when Archbishop Wulfstan of York lamented that 'it happens that a slave escapes from his lord and leaves Christendom to become a Viking [*wicing* – a rare contemporary use of the word in Old English]'.[19] If this was happening in the eleventh century, there is little reason to suppose that it was not happening in the ninth.[20]

It is also important to remember that warfare between the Anglo-Saxon kingdoms and their neighbours had long been endemic.

Although the nature of warfare may have changed, to a young Anglo-Saxon warrior with a lust for treasure and adventure, joining a Viking raiding army on a campaign in some other part of Britain would not have seemed too dissimilar to the expeditions mounted by men of his father's or grandfather's generation. Moreover, it is also likely that – in those regions where Viking warlords had established more formal political control – men who had always owed military service of some sort would have continued to feel that their allegiances were local rather than ethnic; such men were likely to have had few qualms about following a 'foreign' king in raids on their neighbours, perpetuating traditions of insular animosity dating back centuries. This tendency would have been magnified if new rulers promised plunder, advancement and security for farms and families – even more so, if they were bright enough to see the value in embracing an English name and the religion of their subjects.

But it was not only the English of the 'Danelaw' who could become Vikings in West Saxon eyes. The fifth and final clause of the treaty of Alfred and Guthrum makes it clear that the possibility of members of Alfred's new *Angelcynn* skipping off to join the 'Danes' was viewed as a real problem: 'And we agreed on the day when the oaths were sworn that no slaves or freemen might go over to the [Danish] army without permission, any more than any of theirs to us.'[21] Indeed, the danger of Alfred's subjects renouncing their West Saxon loyalties may lie behind Alfred's treatment of the Wiltshire ealdorman Wulfhere, who was stripped of his lands for 'leaving without permission';[22] it was not just those at the bottom of society who could be considered an Anglo-Saxon in the morning and a 'Dane' by the afternoon. And if further proof of the flimsiness of these ethnic labels were required, West Saxon dynastic politics would eventually deliver it – in spectacular fashion – on Alfred's death.

# 13

# ROGUE TRADERS

It was a scene of strange incongruity, for in contrast with these
barbaric men and their rough songs and shouts, the walls were hung
with rare spoils that betokened civilized workmanship. Fine tapestries
that Norman women had worked; richly chased weapons that princes
of France and Spain had wielded; armour and silken garments from
Byzantium and the Orient – for the dragon ships ranged far.

ROBERT E. HOWARD, 'The Dark Man' (1931)[1]

In his appraisal of Alfred's later years, Bishop Asser was at pains to stress the frustrating lengths to which the king had gone in his efforts to galvanize his subjects into undertaking works for the good of the realm. It is fairly clear, however, from the bishop's tone in this part of his biography that Alfred had encountered real difficulty in convincing his people that they wanted to spend (or wanted their slaves to spend) their afternoons digging ditches, or raising palisades, or whatever other toil the local reeve had been tasked with delegating. Indeed, when we hear the list of labours that the king required of his people ('cities and towns to be rebuilt [...] others to be constructed where previously there were none'; 'treasures incomparably fashioned in gold and silver at his instigation'; 'royal halls and chambers marvellously constructed of stone and wood'; 'royal residences of masonry, moved from their old position and splendidly reconstructed at more appropriate places by his royal command'), it is no wonder that 'gently instructing' and 'cajoling' soon gave way to 'commanding, and (in the end, when his patience was exhausted) [...] sharply chastising those who were disobedient' and 'despising popular stupidity and stubbornness in every way'.[2]

Evidently, however, all this chastising and despising wasn't always enough, and the king sometimes needed outside intervention in order to convince his subjects of the wisdom of his building programmes. When, according to Asser, Alfred's efforts failed to yield the desired results, and 'enemy forces burst in by land or sea (or, as frequently happens, by both!)',[3] it merely served to teach the people of Greater Wessex a valuable lesson about the unimpeachable wisdom of their king. His wretched subjects 'having lost their fathers, spouses, children, servants, slaves, handmaidens, the fruits of their labours and all their possessions' were probably wasting their time if they thought they could expect much compassion from their spiritual and political leaders: Asser was clear about where to place the blame. The laziness, stubbornness, ineptitude and ingratitude of the people had, in the bishop's eyes, brought affliction down upon their own heads.[4] And, as he approvingly noted, at least those who had 'negligently scorned the royal commands' now 'loudly applaud the king's foresight and promise to do what they had previously refused – that is, with respect to constructing fortresses and to the other things of general advantage to the whole kingdom'.[5]

This is all, of course, the authorized version of events, a narrative constructed to serve the interests of the king. The reality seems to be that Alfred was indeed making practical and long-term changes to the way in which the defence of his kingdom was organized and was also trying hard to overcome resistance to his innovations; it is equally clear, however, that on both counts the king's efforts sometimes failed. (The temptation to blame everyone else for the bungling of executive orders can often be an appealing strategy for a regime and its apologists.) Overwhelmingly, however, whatever the success rates of his projects and the obstacles encountered, what comes across most strongly from Asser's account is the scale of Alfred's ambition: he saw a kingdom ennobled by learning and literacy, adorned with towns and palaces of stone, glittering with treasures of silver and gold. And he wanted to be remembered for it: Asser's biography alone is enough to tell us that Alfred was a man who keenly felt the weight of his own destiny and the desire to preserve its memory.

When he was a small boy, Alfred had travelled to Rome as part of a diplomatic mission, possibly accompanied by his father, possibly by others.[6] While he was there he met the pope who, according to the *Anglo-Saxon Chronicle*, 'hallowed him as king, and took him as his spiritual son'.[7] The questions of when Alfred travelled, who went with him, which pope he met (Leo or Benedict?) and what, precisely, happened when he did, have long been matters of scholarly debate. It is obvious that, from the perspective of West Saxon writers of the 890s, the idea that Alfred was marked for future kingly greatness at such an early age by the heir of St Peter would have been an attractive one to emphasize. It would be wrong, therefore, to take it too seriously – Alfred, after all, still had three older brothers at this stage of his career. However, no matter how faulty his memory and whatever ideas might have been put into the king's head over the years since his meeting with the pope, it would be wrong to assume that Alfred himself did not believe that *something* transcendent, something numinous, had touched him in the holy city. It is likely, indeed, that his experience of Rome affected him deeply.

Imagine the impression it must have left on a boy of five (or eight) whose knowledge of royal and holy splendour began and ended with his father's weather-beaten timber halls and stocky Saxon churches like Winchester Old Minster – impressive, no doubt, in their proper context, but cattle-sheds in comparison with the Pantheon (into which the Old Minster would have fitted several times over) or the mosaic-embellished Basilica of Santa Prassede (completed in the early 820s), let alone the Colosseum, its white marble carcass gleaming in ruinous splendour beneath the Mediterranean sun. If one adds to this the liturgical mystery and material splendour, the carefully cultivated sense of immanent divinity and imperial patrimony that the papacy was uniquely placed to deploy, it becomes difficult to see how the furniture of any sensitive and intelligent young mind could fail to be radically and permanently rearranged. Alfred may well have grown up feeling himself selected for a higher destiny and touched by God, and perhaps some of this lay behind the king's ambitions in education, building works and administrative and military organization: he had seen first hand the legacies that empire could leave, and the role of the divine in animating and motivating their revival.[8] Whatever else, it must have left him with memories – the magical, nostalgia-soaked images of childhood, of an eternal city, shining white and gold, under a sky of endless blue.

One of the most obvious ways in which Alfred's zeal for *Romanitas* manifested itself was in the choice of the 'cities and towns to be rebuilt' and the manner in which 'others [were] to be constructed where previously there were none'.[9] The *urbes* and *oppida* of Roman Britain, long left to wrack and ruin, began to be restored across the West Saxon realm: Bath, Exeter, Winchester and the City of London were slowly restored to the heart of political, economic and social life, their walls repaired, their centres redeveloped. Elsewhere – at Wallingford for example – new proto-urban centres were laid out on a grid that recalled the regular cruciform street plans of Roman towns. Some of the targets for development had already been important places prior to this new phase of consolidation: Malmesbury had been a monastery since the seventh century, Wareham the location of a major church (a minster) and the resting place of King Beorhtric of Wessex, the king whose reign had ushered in the Viking Age in Britain.

But, however motivated Alfred may have been by dreams of civilization (literally, 'city-dwelling'), there is no doubt that the immediate catalyst for this burst of energy was the need to boost the defences of the realm. We have already seen how hard it was in this period of rudimentary siegecraft to dislodge an enemy who had dug himself in – Alfred had experienced this to his own cost at Nottingham, Reading and Exeter – and the need to protect winter stores, people, livestock, property and production had been demonstrated time and time again from the late eighth century onward. Alfred, so it would seem, was not a man to let lessons go unlearned: his would be a kingdom well organized and well fortified, prepared for anything that might threaten it.

At some point between the 880s and the early tenth century, a document was produced, known now as the *Burghal Hidage*.[10] It is a list of around thirty defensible settlements – 'burhs' in Old English (the root of the word 'borough' and the element 'bury' in the names of so many English towns) – of varying origin. Some of them, like Wallingford, were built from scratch; others reused the masonry circuits of dilapidated Roman towns or the earthworks of Iron Age hill-forts, places which had often been neglected for centuries as settlements, but which had retained a powerful grip on the Anglo-Saxon imagination as meeting places, battlefields and the subject of poetry and legend. The purpose of the *Burghal Hidage* was to assess the amount of military manpower required to garrison and maintain each burh according to the length of its defensive circuit and the amount of land from which that manpower could be drawn.[11] More than forts, but not yet true towns, the burhs seem to have been conceived piecemeal in the later years of Alfred's reign and the early years of his son Edward the Elder's in response to the continuing threat of Viking attack from within and without Britain, with the existential threat the *micel here* had posed still fresh in the collective memory. It was, in its primary purpose, a military solution to a specific set of circumstances, a successful one – as Alfred's later reign bore out – and one that his son Edward and daughter Æthelflæd (the lady of the Mercians) continued to roll out in the course of their own bellicose careers.[12]

But burhs also proved to offer a remarkably durable model for imposing, organizing and protecting essential aspects of state governance (such as the minting of coins) in the localities where they were laid out or renewed, as well as providing hubs for manufacture and commerce – places where the inhabitants of the dispersed rural hinterland could exchange agricultural produce for manufactured goods. In this respect, they took over some of the functions that had previously been reserved to monasteries and royal or aristocratic estate centres. As a result, the burhs of the late ninth and early tenth centuries were swiftly on their way to becoming true towns, and though some failed to develop (Eashing, Chisbury, Sashes, the unidentified Eorpeburnan),[13] others were to become (and many still remain) the principal urban centres of the English realm.[14]

In fairness to the rest of Anglo-Saxon England, Alfred and his descendants probably receive too much of the credit for these innovations in urban planning: Mercia seems to have had burhs of its own – at Winchcombe, Hereford and Tamworth.[15] York clearly had defences in 865 (for all the good they did); Thetford, Lincoln and other settlements of East Anglia and the east midlands may or may not have been significantly developed before they fell into Viking hands in the 870s; trading settlements at London, Southampton, Ipswich, Canterbury and York had been in business since the eighth century. But the network of West Saxon burhs was still the most extensive, coherent and ambitious system of planned development in Britain since Roman times, and there can be little doubt that it was principally Viking aggression that had hastened the agglomeration of administrative, ecclesiastical, economic and military functions.

The Vikings, it can be argued, were responsible not just for creating the conditions that gave rise to the nascent English state, but also for the birth of towns and cities, even (or especially) in the parts of southern England that they had never conquered and colonized. They were not, however, merely the unwitting agents of change, catalysts in a chemical reaction in which they themselves remained stable and unaltered. They were, on the contrary, deeply implicated in these changes from the beginning, shaping the outcomes of the socio-economic revolution that their presence had started, their own identities mutating and fusing in the process. The maritime technology and international trading connections that the Vikings brought to Britain were, in this regard, fundamental. So too was the example that they set for the growth of towns. For when Alfred and Edward cast around for the models that their burhs might take, it was not only a dream of Rome that animated the will: closer, more practical, more familiar models already lay close at hand. For the Vikings, from the moment they first stayed over the winter, had been pioneers of the densely settled, bounded and defensible, commercial and administrative hub.

Viking camps had provided a way of life to their inhabitants since the first over-wintering of Viking raiding armies in Britain in the mid-800s. These camps were temporary – at least at first – often adapting structures and defences that were already present (the enclosure at Repton and the camp at Reading are famous examples). But archaeologically the most revealing material in Britain has come from other sites: from Torksey in Lincolnshire and another undisclosed site in north Yorkshire.[16] In Ireland, these Viking winter camps were known as *longphuirt* (singular *longphort*), and several of these camps mutated over time into true urban settlements, the nuclei of what are still Ireland's most populous towns: Dublin, Waterford, Wexford, Limerick and Cork.[17] In England there is little evidence that any camp developed in this way, and when Viking armies turned to permanent settlement it was in places that had at least some pre-existing infrastructure. Nevertheless, the habits developed in places like these – the close-order living, the reliance on local rural communities for food and resources (rather than farming the land directly), the self-sufficiency in craft and manufacture, the provision for shipping, the market economy – translated easily to urban life.

At Torksey, for example, where the *micel here* ensconced itself on a low bluff beside the River Trent over the winter of 872/3, a site of around 65 acres has been discovered through the combined efforts of amateur metal detectorists and professional archaeologists – a sprawling encampment where a large army once lived and transacted its business. And 'business' is the right word, for among the gaming pieces that once marched across wooden boards, only to be lost, perhaps, in the upheaval of the arguments they inspired in drunk and enervated fighting men, were found the tools of craft and industry and the mechanisms of trade. Weaving and smelting, sewing and leatherworking, fishing and woodworking – even the production of imitative coins; this was the self-sustaining business of a proto-town, whose inhabitants were busy with repairs and the provision of essentials: weapons and clothing, ship repairs and sail-cloth, food and tools. And then there are the weights and scales, the coins and the bullion.

More than 350 coins were found at Torksey, including silver pennies of the 860s and 870s struck in England and a large number of copper-alloy 'stycas', a low-value and rather unglamorous Northumbrian coinage of the pre-Viking period. It is these coins that, in great measure, enabled archaeologists to date and identify the encampment as belonging to the *micel here*'s stop at Torksey in 872/3. Crucially, however, it was not only English coins that were discovered. The ground gave up 123 Arabic dirhams, many of them cut into smaller pieces, coins that had once exchanged hands in the streets of Merv (Turkmenistan) or Wasit (Iraq), left to seed the Lincolnshire soil. The dates of these coins, the youngest of which were struck in the late 860s, support the dating of the encampment. But the presence of the fragmentary dirhams is interesting in a number of other ways. Islamic silver coins flowed into Scandinavia in great numbers during the ninth century, travelling up the Russian river-systems towards the Baltic in return for the slaves, furs and amber that poured south. It was this trade that Arab travellers like ibn Fadlan were witnessing when they wrote their accounts of the exotic barbarians they met on the banks of the Volga and elsewhere. The fact that the *micel here* was carrying this coinage in volume, and that some of them were struck later than the arrival of the *micel here* in England, suggests that Viking armies in England remained connected to these sources of silver, even as they kicked their heels on the banks of the Trent. For these venture capitalists of the Viking

Age, the rivers of England and Russia, the sea-roads of the North Sea and the Caspian, were all just byways of one great interconnected network: a world-wide web of slaves and silver.

The fact, however, that the coins were cut into smaller pieces indicates something else significant. For most of the Viking Age, even when Viking rulers were producing coins of their own, a system of economics prevailed across areas of Viking influence that valued precious metal (primarily silver, but also gold and copper alloys) by weight alone. In such a system, silver coins were valuable not so much because they were 'money' but because they represented portable units of precious metal that could be easily melted down and re-formed into other shapes and sizes (as arm-rings, say, or ingots), or broken up into smaller bits as the need arose. And it was not only coins that were tossed into the crucible. Regardless of whether the labour and smithcraft was invested by Anglo-Saxon, Irish or Scandinavian artisans, no work of delicate artistry or imaginative skill, no filigree or niello, enamel or inlay, wire work or beading was safe when the weight of the metal was what mattered: all was there to be melted down or chopped into bits. 'Hack-silver' and, more rarely, 'hack-gold' are commonly found in Viking hoards and settlement sites; both were found at Torksey. Such fragments represent the loose change of a bullion economy, the shrapnel required to top up a large amount or to exchange for lower-value goods. Also present at Torksey are ingots, the result of the melting and re-forming of coins and other objects into bars of precious metal that were easily transported and stored. These provided the raw material for creating new objects, or as convenient building-blocks to be weighed out in a transaction.

The technology of such transactions was also there at Torksey. Dozens of weights were found, many of the 'cubo-octahedral' and 'oblate-spheroid' types that copied the design and weight standards of those encountered in the Islamic world. The latter are colloquially known as 'barrel weights'. The former, with six square and eight triangular faces (imagine a cube with the corners filed down to flat triangular planes), each decorated with a varying number of incised dots, are often known – for obvious reasons – as 'dice weights'. These designs were a visual marker of reliability and, thanks to their incised decoration and distinctive shapes, hard to tamper with.[18] Finally, of course, scales were required, to weigh out silver, to calibrate weights, to measure out loose commodities such as amber, jet, beads or grain. Fragments of a simple balance were recovered from Torksey, but beautifully preserved examples have been found at centres of Viking commerce across the northern world.[19]

Consider, for a moment, what this evidence for trade – at a temporary military encampment unexpectedly thrown up in the Lincolnshire countryside – implies about interactions between Viking armies and local populations. Certainly it suggests that local people were willing to enter into a trading relationship with the *micel here* – the Viking army cannot have been dealing with anyone else, and interaction was probably frequent and associations increasingly familiar. That does not mean, however, that those relationships were symmetrical or respectful ones: trade is not always a happy transaction of goods and services, a mutually beneficial exercise in cultural interchange. It is undeniable that trade has, historically, been one of the greatest drivers of technological innovation, improvements in living standards and the spread of knowledge and ideas. But this is far from being a complete picture: diseases spread faster than knowledge, technology kills as readily as it cures, not all ideas are worth sharing. The history of mercantile adventure, moreover, presents a spectacularly corrupt and bloody carcass: from the infernal horrors of the Belgian Congo to the moral abortion of the Opium Wars, from the mercantile tyranny of the East India Company to the brutality of Amazonian rubber barons, trade has often gone hand in hand with greed, violence and injustice.

It is this tension that makes the signature 'debate' of Viking studies – 'raiders or traders?' – so wearisome and irritating. For what could a Viking army camped on the Trent have had that the local people might have been tempted to buy? The treasures looted from local churches perhaps? The livestock driven from their fields? The grain they had stored against the winter? Their friends? Their families? An account of a Viking army campaigning in France (also during the later ninth century) recorded that they struck camp on an island in the Loire: there they 'held crowds of prisoners in chains', and launched mounted raids to devastate the surrounding countryside. The *Anglo-Saxon Chronicle* makes it plain that Viking camps in Britain disgorged similar raiding parties (it was just such a raid that fell foul of Ealdorman Æthelwulf and the Berkshire *fyrd* in 870). Such raids would have been necessary to provision a large force over winter; but the potential for profiteering from the cruelties inflicted on the locals was ever present. Imagine the misery of a people forced to trade their winter food supplies for their beaten and abused husbands, wives and children, think of them watching blankly as some barbarian measured out the lives of their kin in grain – scales stacked with corn, blood for barley, pigs for people: desperate efforts, in Asser's words, to 'redeem those captured from a hateful captivity'.[20]

Nor was it only human lives that were bartered in this way.

Ealdorman Ælfred and his wife wander through the camp, their cloaks splattered with mud as they stumble on the uneven ground, tripping on tent pegs, skirting the camp-fires. The air thrums with hammers on iron, axes in wood. Away in the distance a wooden pen holds prisoners, shackled and beaten, staring vacantly towards a place that no one else can see. Ælfred and Werburg try not to look at them, terrified of meeting a familiar gaze. As they walk, their own vulnerability radiates from them, turning every foreign word to an insult, distant laughter to cruel jeers. Suddenly, they find the way blocked by a pair of big men, rising suddenly from the low table where they had been seated, pushing dome-shaped pieces of whalebone across a wooden board. They seem to Werburg to leer with undisguised intent, their thoughts as plain as if they had dropped their trousers. Ælfred stammers and waves his hands and eventually they are pointed towards a nearby tent.

Inside, a fat man sits behind a table strewn with silver coins and bullion. Ælfred speaks a little, haltingly, stuttering the words, and a smirking translator – a Northumbrian from his accent – repeats them in Old Norse. A pudgy hand reaches out, to grab the bag of coins that Ælfred offers, spilling them swiftly on to the table. They are gold – coins made long ago, fashioned by the bishops and the old kings of Kent. Surprised, the Viking takes one up and bites down upon it, bends it in his teeth. In the Viking's grimace Ælfred spots the dark grooves that score the man's teeth, blue bands of self-inflicted mutilation; he shudders.[21] The Viking draws a knife and picks up more coins, the point picking and scratching at their surfaces with deft movements born of long practice, like a man gouging the stones from cherries.[22] He grunts, and shovels them on to the pan of a set of scales that hang suspended from a post beside the table. Slowly he places little barrel-shaped weights on to the other side. After a while he looks up, says a few words in Norse. 'Not enough,' the translator sneers.

The tension in the tent rises. The Viking narrows his eyes, looks hard at Werburg and hauls himself upright, reaching out towards her breast. She starts away, Ælfred's hand moving instinctively to his sword hilt. The sound of a weapon unsheathing near the tent door freezes them both, and the hand that had paused in mid-air continues its progress towards the ealdorman's wife, closing around the circular silver brooch she wears on her chest, ripping it suddenly from the fabric. He turns it over in his hands, a silver disc, chased with images of running deer and hounds, the detail limned in black. He tosses it on to the table and the knife comes down, point into the wood and the handle hammered down hard. The brooch splits in one movement, the silver sheared through like hard cheese. The Viking adds half of the brooch to another set of scales, adding weights until he grunts in satisfaction. He bends over to root around in a pile of objects on the floor, retrieving a pile of manuscript pages, tied up in string. Rising red-faced, he tosses them to Ælfred who catches them clumsily, and the couple turn to leave. 'Wait,' comes the voice of the translator. 'Doesn't the lady want her brooch back?'

And they turn, a mangled lump of silver held up in the grinning Viking's fist.

The *Stockholm Codex Aureus* ('the Golden Book') is a copy of the gospels in Latin. The manuscript is a work of art probably produced in Canterbury during the eighth century, glimmering gilded letters and spiral illuminations recalling other famous treasures of the early Anglo-Saxon Church.[23] In the mid-ninth century, however, around a century after the labours of its creators – Ceolhard, Ealhhun, Niclas and Wulfhelm the goldsmith – had come to an end, a new inscription was added:

> + *In the name of our Lord Jesus Christ.* I, Ealdorman Ælfred, and my wife Werburg procured these books from the heathen invading army with our own money; the purchase was made with pure gold. And we did that for the love of God and for the benefit of our souls, and because neither of us wanted these holy works to remain any longer in heathen hands. And now we wish to present them to Christ Church [Canterbury] to God's praise and glory and honour, and as thanksgiving for his sufferings, and for the use of the religious community which glorifies God daily in Christ Church; in order that they should be read aloud every month for Ælfred and for Werburg and for Alhthryth, for the eternal salvation of their souls, as long as God decrees that Christianity should survive in that place. And also I, Ealdorman Ælfred, and Werburg beg and entreat in the name of Almighty God and of all his saints that no man should

be so presumptuous as to give away or remove these holy works from Christ Church as long as Christianity survives there.

Ælfred
Werburg
Alhthryth *their daughter*[24]

The *Stockholm Codex Aureus* was bought back by Ælfred around the time that the first Viking camps are recorded in the *Anglo-Saxon Chronicle* (the first was established at Thanet in 850 – not, we might note, very far away from Ælfred's own shire of Surrey, or from the place – Canterbury – at which the book was probably made and to which it was returned). Of course, we have no idea how this transaction really played out, but it is extraordinary evidence: both for the reality of the Viking acquisition of holy treasures (almost certainly through violence or menaces) and for the fact that Viking armies were trading with local people from the moment they started to maintain a longer-term presence in Britain (if not before).

For all that Viking winter camps like Torksey were superficially 'urban', they would not – in any known case – develop into lasting towns in England. They may have established some of the habits of urban living, may even have given pointers to West Saxon kings about the value of defensible multi-purpose settlements, but they were doomed to be short lived. In little over a generation, however, Scandinavian settlers – whose constituents hailed from overwhelmingly rural communities – had become strongly identified with the control of places which developed, unequivocally, into 'proper' towns, many of which have yielded little or no evidence of prior Anglo-Saxon occupation, and certainly none on a scale or density comparable to the truly urban environments they became.[25] At Thetford, Cambridge, Huntingdon, Bedford, Northampton, Stamford, Leicester, Derby, Nottingham, Lincoln and York, metropolitan life was suddenly beginning to bloom from the withered remnants of defunct Roman garrison forts and old Mercian estate centres, even as the wonky gridirons of the West Saxon burh were being stamped down on to the landscape in a creeping northward expansion.

The interwoven causes and effects of the economic growth that followed the Viking irruption can be difficult to disentangle: the relative weight that is ascribed to the West Saxon state versus Viking entrepreneurship – to determined planning and top-down reforms of currency, law and administration versus the free-wheeling enterprise of an unregulated merchant-warrior class – is, to a certain degree, a matter of preference, subject specialism and, perhaps, personal politics. We certainly shouldn't discount the impact of the new trading connections that Viking armies brought with them, or the redistribution of wealth that their activities had entailed: think of all that Islamic silver, flowing from the Baltic as the human cargo travelled east; imagine the chalices and processional crosses 'liberated' from the treasure houses of the Church, melted into ingots. It must all have provided quite the economic boost.

Unwelcome interactions like the one that Ælfred and Werburg experienced may well have continued to be a feature of British life for some time after the period of Viking settlement began in England. Within the 'Danelaw', however, it is likely that as communities gradually became more integrated and Viking armies more permanently settled, trading relationships would have grown less exploitative, the differences between newcomers and settled communities less sharply delineated. Regional identities, often definitive in this period, would have rapidly swallowed ethnic distinctions as fashions and languages merged and cultural practices homogenized. People whose families had previously thought of themselves as East Anglians or Northumbrians would doubtless have continued to do so. But in eastern Mercia, in the absence of clear royal authority, narrower loyalties would have risen in importance. Mixed communities of Scandinavians and Anglo-Saxons would probably have identified primarily with local places around which the economic aspects of their lives revolved, and to which they increasingly looked for political, spiritual and military leadership, and the same may have been true in parts of East Anglia and Northumbria.[26] This must be partly conjectural, and the evidence – as ever – is thin. But what evidence there is certainly points in this direction, not least the speed with which 'Danish' authority ultimately collapsed in the face of a concerted campaign from the politically unified kingdom to the south.

# 14

# DANELAW

'I will offer thee another course of law, that we go on the holm here at
the Thing, and let him have the property who has the victory.' That
was also the law which Egil spake, and a custom of old, that every
man had the right to challenge another to holmgang, whether he
would defend himself or pursue his foe.

SNORRI STURLUSON(?), *Egil's Saga* (thirteenth century)[1]

Guthrum–Æthelstan died in 890 and was remembered with
something approaching fondness in the *Anglo-Saxon
Chronicle*.[2] Although Viking raids on Wessex had continued
throughout the 880s, and tensions had occasionally flared around
the East Anglian borders, there had been no serious trouble for
Alfred to contend with.[3] This all changed after Guthrum's death,
and Alfred spent several years of the final decade of his own life,
alongside his adult son Edward, engaged in conflict with new waves
of Viking raiders, the most dangerous of whom were a group led by
a warlord called Hæsten, who arrived – fresh from harassing the
Frankish kingdoms – in 892 and gathered fighters from East Anglia
and Northumbria. Once again, Alfred's kingdom was in grave
danger, with Viking armies roaming from Essex to the Severn, and
from the Sussex coast to Chester.[4] But ultimately the Alfred of the
890s was too experienced a warlord to suffer again the indignities
of 878. By 896, the worst of this fresh wave of violence was over,

partly thanks to the king's programme of fortress building and military reforms. Hæsten's army dispersed – some to East Anglia and Northumbria, others back across the Channel – and the Anglo-Saxon chronicler, sounding more than ever like Marvin the Paranoid Android, was able to celebrate the news that 'the raiding-horde, thank God, had not totally and utterly crushed the English.' (The chronicler added, however, as though concerned that this sounded a trifle too upbeat, that 'they were greatly more crushed in those three years with pestilence amongst cattle and men'.)[5]

Alfred died in 899. In the course of his lifetime he had seen Britain irrevocably transformed, and he ended his days as the king of a realm defined in ways that his predecessors could never have imagined. His obituary in the *Anglo-Saxon Chronicle* described him as 'king over all the English race except that part which was under Danish control',[6] a neat summation of the shift which had occurred during his reign – a delimitation of authority which was primarily ethnic rather than territorial. And yet the degree to which those ethnic constructs remained mutable and contestable was dramatically exposed on the king's death.

Alfred was, as we might expect, succeeded by his son Edward, known to posterity as 'the Elder'.[7] Not everyone, however, was happy to see Edward ascend to the throne. Alfred's nephew, Æthelwold, did rather poorly out of Alfred's will, and was evidently disgruntled by the manner in which he had been passed over.[8] The younger (and probably the only surviving) son of Alfred's elder brother, King Æthelred (the man who had prayed so vigorously at the battle of Ashdown in 871), Æthelwold had a decent claim to the West Saxon throne. Instead he had been left with three estates in Surrey, far from the centre of West Saxon power – much less than what even Alfred's obscure kinsman Osferth was to receive.[9] In any case, whatever the rights and wrongs of his grievance, his actions articulated the strength of it without room for ambiguity. With Alfred's body barely cold, he seized the royal manor at Twynham (now Christchurch, Dorset) and then rode to Wimborne (also Dorset), to the burial place of his father King Æthelred, where

– alive to the threat that Edward posed – he 'barricaded all the gates against him, and said that he would live there or die there'.[10]

Edward, for his part, took an army to Badbury Rings, the massive Neolithic hill-fort that dominates the landscape of east Dorset. As political theatre these were striking choices. Whereas Æthelwold had laid claim to his father's resting place, no doubt in an attempt to send a message that emphasized his dynastic claims, Edward's choice of Badbury Rings drew on older and deeper wells of political legitimacy. Whether or not the Anglo-Saxons identified this place (as later generations would) with Mount Badon – the location of the legendary victory of the Britons over the Saxons in the sixth century[11] – the massive earthworks would have spoken in primal terms of power that welled up from another age, the vast earthen ramparts the work of supernatural builders and the mighty kings of old. Not only that, but Badbury was also the hundred meeting place of the district in which it stood: by using it as his fortress, Edward was raising his standard not merely on his dynastic claims, but on an ancient and embedded sense of community, territory and antiquity.

Whether it was this or more pragmatic concerns that eroded Æthelwold's resolve, it swiftly transpired that his nerve was less robust than his rhetoric. Taking with him a nun he had extracted from the convent at Wimborne (whether or not she was a willing accomplice, we shall never know), Æthelwold 'rode away under cover of night and sought out the raiding army in Northumbria',[12] where 'they received him as king and submitted to him'.[13] The *Annals of St Neots*, a later chronicle based (probably) on a lost manuscript of the *Anglo-Saxon Chronicle*, puts this extraordinary moment in even more surprising terms. There Æthelwold, son of Æthelred, son of Æthelwulf, son of Ecgberht, scion of the house of Wessex, is described as *rex paganorum* and *rex danorum*: 'King of the Pagans; King of the Danes'.[14]

\*

Æthelwold has been described as one of the '"Nearly Men" of early medieval Europe'.[15] During the five years that followed his nocturnal flight from Wessex in 899, the ætheling's flame flared brightly, a brief consuming fire. In that flickering red light we can see the dreams of deeds undone, of destiny unfulfilled – a Viking England united by a man thrice begotten of West Saxon kings, trampling the wreckage of his father's realm at the head of a great Anglo-Viking horde. It would not come to pass; Æthelwold's flame would be extinguished in the leeching damp of the East Anglian Fens.

In 902, Æthelwold brought a fleet to Essex and caused the submission of the East Saxon kingdom. Quite where he had come from, whom he had convinced of his regal standing and why they had acquiesced so readily is unknown, but it may be that he managed to convince a substantial faction in the 'Danelaw' that his claim to the West Saxon throne – and the divided loyalties of its aristocracy – meant that the conquest of Wessex was once again a realistic prospect. The submission of Essex would have been a blow to King Edward: Essex had long formed a buffer zone between West Saxon and East Anglian control. Later in 902, Æthelwold made his move, bringing an army out of East Anglia and advancing into English Mercia, raiding and burning as he went, before crossing the Thames at Cricklade in Wiltshire and plundering the region around Braydon. This was a raid, not an attempt at conquest, and Æthelwold swiftly led his army (laden down 'with all that they could grab'),[16] back to East Anglia. But the fact that he had penetrated so far into Wessex unopposed had sent an unmistakable message to his cousin Edward. The reciprocal raid came immediately. Edward raised an army and chased Æthelwold into East Anglia, ravaging territory from the Devil's Dyke (Cambridgeshire) to the River Wissey and the Fens (Norfolk). Edward, however, like Æthelwold, seems to have had little appetite for battle and ordered a retreat. For reasons that remain obscure, however, the men of Kent disobeyed their king and remained in East Anglia.

A measure of Edward's mounting panic (or, perhaps, of his determination to explain what may have been a monumental blunder) is conveyed by the *Anglo-Saxon Chronicle*'s insistence that he dispatched no fewer than seven messengers in his desperation to recall the Kentish contingent. It was to no avail. Æthelwold's armies surrounded the Kentish force at a place called 'the Holme' and a savage battle was fought. The most evocative description was provided by the West Saxon ealdorman Æthelweard, who wrote a chronicle in Latin at some point towards the end of the tenth century:

> They clashed shields, brandished swords, and in either hand the spear was much shaken. And there fell Ealdorman Sigewulf, and Sigehelm, and a part of the Kentish gentry nearly all-inclusive; and Haruc, king of the barbarians, was there let down to the lower world. Two princes of the English, soft of beard, then left the air they breathed ever before, and entered a strange region below the waves of Acheron, and so did much of the nobility on either side. In the end the barbarians were victors, and held the field with exultation.[17]

It was clearly a disaster for the men of Kent, although quite how exultant the barbarians can really have been, considering the apparently ghastly death toll and the demise of their king, is open to question. The 'Haruc' mentioned by Æthelweard was Eohric, king (it is generally assumed) of East Anglia. Perhaps more significant, however, was the detail supplied by the *Anglo-Saxon Chronicle* in its rather more sober (and contemporary) account of the battle: Æthelwold was killed in the fighting.[18]

The Fens – with their vast skies and level horizons, their dykes and waterways, bogs and meres – are an unfriendly environment to those unfamiliar with them: disorientating and alien. At their wildest they can feel like a remnant of a forgotten world, when mammoth and aurochs wandered the wide plains of Doggerland, the lost land that once connected East Anglia with continental Europe – our own Stone Age Atlantis, drowned beneath the North Sea. The Fens are an unending sea of sedges and peat beds – a paradise, as the Somerset Levels once were, for insects and wading birds, amphibians and water mammals. Like the Levels, the Fens were mostly drained long ago and only 1 per cent of the original wetlands, at places like Lakenheath (Suffolk) and Wicken Fen (Cambridgeshire), still survive.[19] This is enough, however, for us to imagine how the region appeared to those who fought and died here a thousand years ago. It would have been an appalling place for a battle, particularly for those who did not know the lie of the land; when lines broke, desperate men would have lost the security of dry land, flummoxed by the blankness of the Fens, floundering into the mire, choking their lives out in the sucking peat bogs.

The name of the place where the battle was supposedly fought – 'the Holme' – is Old Norse in origin, from *holmr* ('small islet', or 'area of dry land set in wetland'). In the midst of the Fens, the meaning is obvious: any raised area of dry land can feel like an island rising from the reed beds. Although *holmr* is a relatively common topographical term in England (with around fifty examples around the country), most of these apply to small, isolated places, and there is no other battlefield of the early Middle Ages in England that is identified with this place-name element.[20] The term, however, had a particular significance in Old Norse literature, where it referred to the idealized location of a type of quasi-judicial knockabout known as the *hólmgang* (lit. 'island-going'), a form of arbitration-by-combat, a settling of differences through formalized and circumscribed violence.

Several accounts describe duels and *hólmgang* fought in Britain. *Flóamanna saga*, for example, tells the tale of the Icelander Thorgils who fought a *hólmgang* in Caithness on behalf of Olaf, the local *jarl*. The most elaborate description of the *hólmgang* ritual is contained in *Kormáks saga*, a thirteenth-century account of the life of the Hiberno-Icelandic skald Kormákr Ögmundarson. The saga describes a weird and highly ritualized event, revealing how it was the 'the law of the *hólmgang*' that a hide should be spread on the ground, 'with loops at its corners. Into these should be driven certain pins with heads to them, called *tjosnur*. He who made it ready should go to the pins in such a manner that he could see sky between his legs, holding the lobes of his ears and speaking the forewords used in the rite called "The Sacrifice of the *tjosnur*". Once this was done, 'Three squares should be marked round the hide, each one foot broad. At the outermost corners of the squares should be four poles, called hazels; when this is done, it is a hazelled field.'

Only after these bewildering preparations had been accomplished could the combat commence:

> Each man should have three shields, and when they were cut up he must get upon the hide if he had given way from it before, and guard himself with his weapons alone thereafter. He who had been challenged should strike the first stroke. If one was wounded so that blood fell upon the hide, he should fight no longer. If either set one foot outside the hazel poles 'he went on his heel', they said; but he 'ran' if both feet were outside. His own man was to hold the shield before each of the fighters. The one who was wounded should pay three marks of silver to be set free.[21]

In reality there is nothing contemporary to suggest that this sort of ritual duel was actually a Viking Age practice, or – if it was – that it was as formal as accounts like the one in *Kormáks saga* describe.

Nevertheless, a number of similar accounts in other sagas, as well as a definition in the *Hednalagen* ('the heathen law'), a fragment of Swedish law written down *c.* 1200 which specifies the conditions under which the *hólmgang* should occur, present a compelling picture.[22] It is possible that, in the militarized and Viking-inflected culture of tenth-century East Anglia, battle could be seen as *hólmgang* on an epic scale – particularly if that battle was considered to be arbitrating a dispute between kinsmen. In this light, the battle of the Holme may have acquired its name as a result of the importation not only of the Old Norse lexicon, but of Old Norse cultural practices as well. And while it was almost certainly not seen in ritualistic terms by those unfortunate enough to fight there, it is entirely likely that it was remembered in those terms afterwards.

It would certainly be no surprise to find that Scandinavian legal concepts were beginning to drift into British syntax and toponymy: everywhere the Vikings had settled in Britain, they were bringing their systems of law and administration with them.

In the wider Viking world, the places set aside for ritual combat seem often to have been located in areas designated for legal or administrative assembly of other kinds. For example, *hólmgang* that took place after deliberations at the Icelandic 'parliament' – the Althing – were fought on an island (ON *holmr*) in the Axewater, the river that cuts through Thingvellir (ON Þingvöllr, 'the assembly plain'), gushing over the rim of the great tectonic rift and surging into white thunder at Öxarárfoss ('Axe-water-fall').[23]

William Morris, visiting Iceland in 1871, recorded his impressions of his arrival at this extraordinary place. The spontaneity of his language reflects the immediacy of the emotional response:

As we ride along (over the lava now) we come opposite to a flat-topped hill some way down the lava stream, and just below it opens a huge black chasm, that runs straight away south toward the lake, a great double-walled dyke, but with its walls tumbled and ruined a good deal in places: the hill is Hrafnabjörg (Raven Burg), and the chasm Hrafnagjá (Raven Rift). But as we turn west we can see, a long way off across the grey plain, a straight black line running from the foot of the Armannsfell right into the lake, which we can see again hence, and some way up from the lake a white line cuts the black one across. The black and the white line are the Almannagjá (Great Rift) and the Öxará (Axe Water) tumbling over it. Once again that thin thread of insight and imagination, which comes so seldom to us, and is such joy when it comes, did not fail me at this first sight of the greatest marvel and most storied place of Iceland.[24]

Thingvellir is rightly famous; it sits amid an alien world, a landscape unlike any other on earth. Like many parts of Iceland, it feels as though it sits at the beginning and ending of time – a place rent and moulded by the primeval forces that stand behind the world, where the 'sun turns black, land sinks into sea; the bright stars scatter from the sky. Flame flickers up against the world-tree; fire flies high against heaven itself.'[25] As has been long remarked, it is easy to see how the crushing waterfalls and grinding glaciers, hot geysers and livid lava flows, and the spectral green corona of the aurora borealis, could have shaped the elemental tenor of the myths that were first given literary form in this unforgiving outpost of the northern world.

The primordial nature of this environment is part of what makes Thingvellir seem such a suitable cradle for the earliest European experiment in representative republican government.[26] One of the most evocative images of the place remains a painting by the English antiquarian W. G. Collingwood, at once a highly observant portrait of the tortured lithics of the primeval geology – the 'curdled lava flows' (to borrow a Morrisian expression) – and an unusually convincing (for its time) reconstruction of the bustle of an Althing in session. Morris, like Collingwood and many more of his Victorian peers, was fascinated by the aspects of representative and communal government that such assemblies embodied. For Morris, the 'doom-rings' and '*thing*-steads' of the sagas seem to have helped him to bridge the intellectual chasm that lay between his romantic old-northernism and the metropolitan socialism by which he was so energized in later life.[27]

*Things* (ON *þing*) had been a ubiquitous element of the legal, political and administrative culture of Scandinavia long before the settlement of Iceland in the mid-ninth century, and not all *things* were great national gatherings like those at Thingvellir. From what we can tell, mostly from later medieval sources, most were regional or local comings-together of heads of families, wealthy farmers, warlords and aristocrats, sometimes under the auspices of a king or *jarl*. Laws were made and disseminated at these gatherings, and

A thing in progress

arbitration was entered into when disputes arose. Criminal matters were also heard and judgements handed down in accordance with the settled laws of the jurisdiction in which the *thing* was held. These laws – with some exceptions – were not written down. This does not mean that they were vague or flimsy or made up on the hoof; quite the opposite. The laws were traditional and cumulative and, like modern legal practice, freighted with precedent and spiced with occasional innovation: maintaining the laws was integral to the life of a community and rich with ancestral tradition and ancient lore. The burden of keeping this knowledge intact rested primarily on the *ars memoriae*, as practised by a single individual – the *lǫgsǫgumaðr*, the 'law-speaker'.[28]

There are a number of place-names in Britain that incorporate the Old Norse *þing* element, most commonly in combination with *völlr* 'plain' (that is, 'the assembly plain' – the same origin as Thingvellir): Tinwald in Dumfries, Dingwall in Ross and Cromarty, Tinwhil on Skye, Tiongal on Lewis (now unlocatable), Tingwall in Orkney, Tingwall in Shetland, Tynwald on the Isle of Man, Thingwall in Lancashire and Thingwall in the Wirral. There are also Thingoe (Suffolk), Thinghou (Lincolnshire) and Thynghowe in

Sherwood Forest, Nottinghamshire (all from ON *þing haugr*, 'assembly mound').[29]

Some of these sites remained in use for centuries. Thynghowe in Sherwood Forest was discovered by amateur historians Stuart C. Reddish and Lynda Mallett who, in 2005–6, came into possession of a document dating to 1816 that described the perambulation of the bounds of the Lordship of Warsop. The local people involved in this expedition gathered at a mound known as Hanger Hill to drink beer and eat cheese and have what sounds like a jolly good time; they did so, apparently, 'according to ancient custom'. Further research revealed that the name Hanger Hill had replaced the old name – Thynghowe – in the seventeenth century. Subsequent exploration of the site revealed parish boundary markers tumbled and choked by undergrowth – ancient standing stones and a Viking meeting place lost to memory, swallowed by the forest for a thousand years.

At Tingwall in Shetland, assemblies were held on an island (a *holm*, in the Old Norse-derived dialect of the islands) in the loch that drives inland from the west. It is an extraordinary place, the hills rising gently on all sides around the water, a sublime natural amphitheatre that cups the setting sun. An account written by a visitor called John Brand, dating to 1701, describes how 'three or four great Stones are to be seen, upon which the Judge, Clerk and other Officers of the Court did sit'. The rest of the assembly gathered on the grassy banks 'at some distance from the Holm on the side of the Loch'. When their cases were to be heard, individuals were called to the island and each crossed the water by a stone causeway 'who when heard, returned the same way he came'.[30] The earliest records of its use date to around 1300, but it is likely that the place was an assembly site from the earliest days of Scandinavian settlement on Shetland.

Tynwald, on the Isle of Man, is the one place in Britain where the Viking past continues to shape the performance – if not the content – of modern law-making. Every year, on 5 July, a representative of the British crown attends a ceremony at Tynwald Hill – the enormous stepped mound, 80 feet in diameter at the base, heavily modified and landscaped over the centuries, that still plays an important role in the tiny devolved government's legislative rituals. There he ascends to declaim the previous year's enacted legislation in English and Manx Gaelic (but not, alas, in Old Norse).[31]

It may be that not all of the *thing* sites in Britain were *new* meeting places established by Vikings in the ninth century; some may have been old local and regional meeting places that came to be known by names and terms introduced by Scandinavian settlers. The same is likely true of the terminology that came to be applied to territorial units in parts of the 'Danelaw'; whereas Anglo-Saxon territories were divided into parcels of land called 'hundreds', by the time of the Domesday Book (1086) these territorial units

Þorgnýr the law-speaker holds forth

were known in large areas of north and west Yorkshire, Nottinghamshire and Lincolnshire as 'wapentakes', from the Old Norse *vápnatak* ('weapon-taking'). The term indicates how weapon-bearing had a direct link to political participation in Viking society. To attend a 'weapon-taking', one obviously had to have weapons to take; the costlier and more elaborate these were, the better to show off one's wealth and status in a highly public forum.

A sense of what weapon-taking was all about can be found in a handful of sources (most of which, in what becomes a tedious refrain for both author and reader, date to long after the Viking Age itself, and are therefore of questionable reliability). The following vignette from *Óláfs saga Helga*, for example, gives an impression of how the intimidating atmosphere of a weapon-bearing assembly could be used to influence authority. Here the venerable Þorgnýr the law-speaker tells the Swedish king how things stand:

'Should you be unwilling to accept what we demand, then we shall mount an attack against you and kill you and not put up with hostility and lawlessness from you. This is what our forefathers before us have done. They threw five kings into a bog at Múlaþing who had become completely full of arrogance like you with us. Say now straight away which choice you wish to take.'

Then the people immediately made a clashing of weapons and a great din.

The king of the Svear to whom this intemperate diatribe was addressed, evidently not fancying his chances, swiftly agreed to 'let the farmers have their way [...] in everything they wanted'.[32]

Such a scene, however improbable we may find the limpness of the Swedish king's authority, evokes in ways otherwise inaccessible how political assembly in a highly militarized society might have felt; it is no wonder that rules of ritual combat should have developed in connection with such events – the potential for violence must have ever simmered at the surface. But, in their essence, such assemblies acted as a means by which royal and aristocratic authority could achieve public legitimacy, a spear-shaking mandate from the warrior class.

After the death of Æthelwold at the battle of the Holme, the early reign of Edward the Elder proved relatively uneventful, although it was clear that tensions between Wessex and the 'Danish' north and east continued to run high; in 906 it was apparently felt necessary to confirm a peace between King Edward and the East Anglians and Northumbrians – with eastern Mercia remaining a contested region. (Indeed, it is utterly unclear who exactly *was* in effective control of this part of eastern Mercia during the four decades between 870 and 910. Coins minted in the name of an 'Earl Sitric' ('SITRIC COMES') at Shelford ('SCELFOR') in Cambridgeshire suggest that effective authority did not necessarily emanate from kings alone, as in fact continued to be the case in Norway. And, as we shall see, when the towns of the 'Danelaw' made peace, they tended to do so one by one, often with named *jarls* offering their submission along with the local communities in which they presumably had some standing.)

The peace of 906 – like so many before – did not hold, although this time it was Edward's kingdom that was the aggressor. In 909, men from Wessex and Mercia 'raided the northern horde very greatly, both men and every kind of property, and killed many of those Danish men, and were inside there [Northumbria] for five weeks'.[33] It is not surprising that the Northumbrians sought retaliation the following year, though the Anglo-Saxon chronicler seems unduly put out by their refusal to see sense, remarking with a slightly indignant tone that 'the-horde in Northumbria broke the peace, and scorned every peace which King Edward and his councillors offered them'.[34] They would have been better advised to take Edward up on his offer.

The campaign started well enough for the Northumbrians. They seem to have wrongfooted King Edward, who had assembled a fleet of a hundred ships, perhaps imagining a waterborne assault in the south; when the Northumbrians started marauding across Mercia, Edward was stuck on a boat off the Kentish coast. But it is clear that, by this stage, the military and defensive innovations that had been implemented by Alfred and continued by Edward were in good working order. It was possible, in a way in which in the past it seems not to have been, for Edward to command (presumably from some distance away) the armies of Wessex and Mercia to rouse themselves swiftly and move against the invaders.[35] Even so, it was nearly too late; the raiding army had already had plenty of time to plunder western Mercia, with doubtless unpleasant consequences for its inhabitants. This, however, may ultimately have been their undoing, for, as they headed back home, 'rejoicing in rich spoil' as the chronicler Æthelweard put it, they became bogged down:

> crossing to the east side of the river Severn over a *pons* to give the Latin spelling, which is called Bridgnorth [Cuatbricge] by the common people. Suddenly squadrons of both Mercians and West Saxons, having formed battle-order, moved against the opposing force. They joined battle without protracted delay on the field of Wednesfield [Vuodnesfelda, 'Woden's Field'];[36] the English enjoyed the blessing of victory; the army of the Danes fled, overcome by armed force. These events are recounted as done on the fifth day of the month of August. There fell three of their kings in that same 'storm' [*turbine*] (or 'battle' [*certamine*] would be the right thing to say), that is to say Healfdene and Eywysl, and Inwær also hastened to the hall of the infernal one [*ad aulam properauit inferni*], and so did senior chiefs of theirs, both jarls and other noblemen.[37]

The three 'kings' whom Æthelweard delights in dispatching to Old Nick are better known by the Anglicized names Halfdan, Eowils and Ingvar; none of them is known from other sources, and no coins (that we know of) were minted in their names. If they truly were somehow joint kings of Northumbria, they have left a remarkably light historical footprint; it may well be that they were simply warlords of a lesser degree (the English sources seem often to exaggerate the quantity of royal blood that was spilled on the edges of Saxon swords). But it is also possible that they were related to the dynasty known in Irish sources as the Uí Ímair – the descendants of Ivar – a Viking clan that had made it big in Ireland and whose founder was the same Ivar the Boneless who, with his brothers, had wreaked such havoc among the kingdoms of Anglo-Saxon England.[38] (Whether or not this is so, it is almost certainly the case that – as we shall see – an influx of Vikings from the Irish Sea had begun to make their presence felt in Northumbria at the beginning of the tenth century, refugees from their expulsion from Dublin in 902.[39])

Whatever the political realities within Northumbria, the battle of Wednesfield (more commonly known as the battle of Tettenhall) marked a watershed.[40] From that moment on, the armies of the 'Danelaw' would never again threaten the peace of southern Britain. Instead, in little over fifteen years, the kings of Wessex would establish themselves as the masters of all England; in time they would be counted the overlords of much of the rest of Britain as well. The details of the campaigns which Edward and his sister Æthelflæd waged against those parts of England that lay beyond the boundary their father had drawn with Guthrum–Æthelstan are known primarily from the accounts provided in the *Anglo-Saxon Chronicle*, including the regional addendum known as the *Mercian Register*.[41] The bald sequence of events these sources present is stark and authoritarian, a drumbeat of inexorable military dominance and fortress building. To string it all together with connective tissue and verbiage would be prolix. I present it here, therefore, in outline – a summary of the history as reported – with the caveat that, as ever, this was how the West Saxons wanted us to remember it: the glorious, inevitable march towards English unity and nationhood – the red ink spilled, a slow pink stain spreading across the map.

In 910, Æthelflæd, the daughter of King Alfred, sister of King Edward and wife of Æthelred, lord of the Mercians, had a fortress built at Bremesbyrig (unidentified, probably in Gloucestershire). In the following year, her husband Æthelred died. Although Æthelflæd assumed most of his authority in Mercia, Edward claimed lordship in Oxford (Oxfordshire) and London. In 912, King Edward constructed two forts at Hertford (Hertfordshire), and one at Witham (Essex), 'and a large portion of the folk who were earlier in the power of Danish men submitted to him'.[42] In 914, armies from Hereford (Herefordshire) and Gloucester (Gloucestershire) defeated a Viking raiding army from Brittany. King Edward ordered defences to be set along the south bank of the River Severn, which stymied Viking raids at Porlock and Watchet (Somerset). The king also constructed twin fortifications at Buckingham (Buckinghamshire), and Jarl Thurcytel and the chief men of Bedford (Bedfordshire) and Northampton (Northamptonshire) pledged their loyalty to the king. In 915, Edward occupied Bedford and constructed a fortress there, while his sister Æthelflæd built strongholds at Chirbury (Shropshire), Weardbyrig (possibly Warbury, Cheshire) and Runcorn (Cheshire). The following year, in 916, the king constructed a stronghold at Maldon (Essex) and 'facilitated' the emigration of Jarl Thurcytel to the continent.

Everyone seems to have been busy in 917. Edward ordered the construction of strongholds at Towcester (Northamptonshire) and Wigingamere (unidentified, possibly Newport, Essex).[43] Viking raids from Northampton, Leicester (Leicestershire) 'and north of there' tried, but failed, to break down the stronghold at Towcester. At the same time, a Viking army from East Anglia built its own fortress at Tempsford (Bedfordshire) and then marched on Bedford, only to be routed by the Bedford militia. Another Viking army from East Anglia besieged Wigingamere, but was unable to capture it and retreated. King Edward's army was, once again, more successful, destroying the Viking fort at Tempsford, killing their king (whoever this may have been), as well as Jarl Toglos and his son, Jarl Manna. Another army raised by Edward from Sussex, Essex and Kent then captured Colchester (Essex), slaughtering the defenders. In response, a Viking army attempted to capture Maldon, but was repelled by the defenders who – with reinforcements – destroyed and routed the erstwhile besiegers.

Presumably demoralized by the way things were going, Jarl Thurferth and his followers, 'together with all the raiding-army which belonged to Northampton, as far north as the Welland', submitted to the authority of King Edward.[44] Taking advantage of this success, Edward restored the defences of Huntingdon (Cambridgeshire), and the local people submitted to his authority. There was more submitting to come: after King Edward had restored the defences at Colchester, the people of Essex and East Anglia swore loyalty to him, and the Viking army at Cambridge (Cambridgeshire) voluntarily adopted King Edward 'as their lord and protector'.[45] To round the year off, Æthelflæd captured Derby (Derbyshire).

In 918 King Edward built a stronghold on the south side of the river at Stamford (Lincolnshire), and the people inhabiting the stronghold on the north bank submitted to the king. Æthelflæd gained the submission of Leicester, but died later that year. Edward did not hesitate to secure his authority over the whole of Mercia, and 'all the race of the Welsh, sought him as their lord'.[46] The king next captured Nottingham (Nottinghamshire) and reinforced its defences, and 'all the people that were settled in the land of Mercia, both Danish and English, turned to him'.[47] In 919 the king ordered a fortress to be built at Thelwall (Cheshire), and in 920 caused fortifications to be built at Nottingham and Bakewell (Derbyshire). This was apparently the final straw: 'And then the king of Scots and all the nation of Scots chose him as father and lord; and [so did] Ragnald and Eadwulf's sons and all those who live in Northumbria, both English and Danish and Norwegians and others; and also the king of the Strathclyde Britons and all the Strathclyde Britons.' For the rest of Britain, enough had finally proved to be enough.

By 920, Edward, king of Wessex, had become – or wished to be perceived as – not only king of all the English south of the Humber, but the overlord of almost everyone who lived beyond it to the north. This went beyond even the claims of Edward's great-grandfather Ecgberht, who had asserted his overlordship of Northumbria in 828. (Perhaps it was an attempt to make good on Alfred's absurd claim to rule over 'all the Christians of the island of Britain'.[48]) However, while there is no doubt that Edward had achieved for his kingdom and his dynasty an unprecedented degree of *imperium* within Britain, quite how realistic the claims of 920 really were remains uncertain; after all, the world to the north of the Mercian border had changed out of all recognition since Ecgberht's time.

# 15

# LAKELAND SAGAS

Coniston Water it is called by the public now-a-days, but its proper
name is Thurston Water. So it is written in all old documents, maps,
and books up to the modern tourist period. In the deed of
1196 setting forth the boundaries of Furness Fells it is called
Thorstancs Watter, and in lawyer's Latin Tiirstini Watra, which
proves that the lake got its title from some early owner whose
Norse name was Thorstein.

W. G. COLLINGWOOD, *The Book of Coniston* (1897)[1]

It is incontrovertible that large parts of Britain were settled by
Scandinavians; the evidence, when taken as a whole, is overwhelming. Nevertheless, not one of the specific questions that one
might wish to pose – how did this settlement happen and where
precisely was it densest; did it start suddenly or gradually; was it
continuous or sporadic; how many people were involved and where
did they come from and were there women and children among
them as well as men? – can be answered satisfactorily.

That does not mean that the subject has been neglected. As one
scholarly duo put it, 'there is in this area such a weight of scholarly
tradition that everything seems to have been said, and firmly
objected to, before'.[2] This is inevitable in cases such as these, where
the evidence itself is weak and contradictory. Consider, for example, the state of archaeological knowledge regarding rural

settlement in Northumbria: the two most frequently mentioned sites that supposedly display evidence of Scandinavian influence in their design and layout are Simy Folds (Co. Durham) and Ribblehead (north Yorkshire). Among a handful of other Scandinavian features, the buildings excavated at both places seem originally to have been furnished with stone benches that ran along the interior walls, features characteristic of the architecture of Viking colonies in the north Atlantic.[3] The size of the Ribblehead farm building also sets it apart from other English buildings of the period, as does its construction method: it has been described as 'a house which undertakes in stone and timber what elsewhere, i.e. in lowland England, was an earthfast timber form'.[4] Such stone-founded homes bear more resemblance to the Viking long-houses of Orkney and Shetland than to the timber halls of Wessex. Even these weak indicators, however, are compromised by the unfortunate fact that we know very little about *pre*-Viking architecture in northern England, and arguments about size, or layout, or building materials are therefore predicated on an absence of evidence; we just don't know for sure how to tell a 'Viking' house from an 'Anglo-Saxon' house.

Instead, scholarly efforts to pinpoint the extent of Viking settlement have turned on place-names and personal names, language and dialect. We have already seen how elements of Scandinavian legal and administrative terminology were imported into parts of Britain, and in certain English regions the vocabulary of the land feels thick with the Viking past, the countryside rumbling away in Old Norse, or at least with a strong accent. These words and names fall heavily like iron on stone, their sharp cadences catching the glimmer of a low northern sun, salt spray jagging off them on the back of a cold wind: 'Garstang' in Lancashire (ON *geirr* + ON *stǫng*, 'spear-post'); 'Grimsby' in Lincolnshire (ON *grims* + ON *bȳ*, 'Grimr's farm'); Micklethwaite in Yorkshire and Cumbria (ON *mikill* + ON *þveit*, 'great clearing'). These are entirely Old Norse words, displacing whatever had preceded them, renaming the land, reimagining the landscape. Elsewhere, however, the Old Norse words are grafted on to an Old English stock – 'Grimstons', for example, abound in the corpus of English place-names (ON *grims* + OE *tūn*, 'Grimr's settlement'), alongside more exotic formulations like 'Brandesburton' (ON *brands* + OE *burh* + OE *tūn*, 'Brandr's fortified settlement'). In addition, the Norse tongue bled into the everyday words which people, especially in the north, still use to frame the world around them: fell (ON *fjall*), beck (ON *bekkr*), tarn (ON *tjarn*), gill (ON *gjel*) …

When Old Norse place-names are plotted on to a map of Britain, they present a pleasing picture, clustering with varying intensity across all the regions where the historical record leads us to expect them, even respecting (more or less) the border of Alfred's treaty with Guthrum. However, satisfying though this may be, it does little beyond apparently confirming that Old Norse-speakers did, indeed, inhabit parts of England at some point in the past. And the closer one looks, more questions than answers arise. Why, for example, are there apparently so many more Old Norse place-name elements in Norfolk than in Suffolk? What is the significance of hybrid place-names as opposed to 'pure' Old Norse ones? Why do the most significant places (by and large) retain their English names? What impact have other, post-Viking, changes to landownership and language had over the 1,100 years since the first Viking settlers arrived? How many Norse-speakers would it have taken to effect linguistic change on this scale and in this way? Did the changes come early (in the ninth century) or accrue over time? Did these Norse-speakers come from Denmark, or from Norway, or from some other outpost of the Viking diaspora – Ireland perhaps or the north Atlantic?

And so it goes on, without any real resolution, the arguments highly technical and the conclusions provisional.[5] The best that can perhaps be said is that, from the late ninth century onwards, changes wrought through migration were affecting the way people spoke and the way they thought – the world shaped and reshaped by words, mental maps reordered in irrevocable ways. These changes can have been effected only by a sizeable number of Norse-speaking immigrants, though the socially dominant position of these migrants may have meant that their language had an impact that was disproportionate to their number.

Cultural changes are evident across the north and east of England. Among the well-to-do community of moneyers who were responsible for minting coins in 'Danelaw' towns during the late tenth and early eleventh centuries, Scandinavian names had become common, if not ubiquitous.[6] In places like Thetford, Lincoln and Norwich they were a minority, the Ascetels and Ulfcetels, Grims and Thorsteins still outnumbered by the Ælfwines, Eadgars and Leofrics. In York, however, the picture was reversed, with Norse names equalling if not outnumbering the English. These changes did not only affect moneyers, and were long-lasting. Less than a century later, in 1086, the Domesday survey for Lincolnshire recorded 240 names of which 140 were Scandinavian.[7] This doesn't mean, of course, that by 1086 three-fifths of the Lincolnshire population were descended from ninth-century Viking settlers, any more than the (relative) abundance of Scandinavian and Scandinavian-inspired jewellery found in that county (and in East Anglia) signifies large-scale migration.[8] Both names and jewellery, however, do strongly suggest that in cultural terms life in those parts of Britain had taken a Viking turn. Affinity for a transmarine North Sea identity was becoming more fashionable from the turn of the tenth century than it had been at any point since the age of Sutton Hoo in the early seventh century, and was arguably edging out (though certainly not extinguishing) other forms of cultural expression.

These trends didn't last for ever, but they were surprisingly durable. The Norman Conquest of 1066 ultimately reorientated English culture decisively, and by the late twelfth century moneyers across England mostly had names like Hugo, Robert, Walter or William. But even as late as the 1180s, during the reign of Henry II (the first Plantagenet monarch), there were moneyers named Rafn, Svein and Thorstein working at Lincoln, and there was still a 'Turkill' (Thorkell) minting coins in York during the reign of

Richard I the Lionheart (r. 1189–99). Although the vogue for Norse names would ultimately die out, there were other changes that could never be undone. As the English language – rapacious omnivore that it is – ruthlessly harvested and absorbed the Scandinavian speech that was introduced to England, it was irrevocably changed by it. Old Norse words in English are not confined to those that we might consider proper to 'Vikings' ('berserk', 'ransack' and 'skull', for example, are all words of Old Norse provenance), but even fundamental linguistic building-blocks like the pronouns 'their' and 'they', and outrageously mundane words like 'husband', 'egg' and 'window', are rooted in the speech of Scandinavian immigrants.[9]

This northern onomasticon was thrilling to an early generation of antiquarians, in particular the place-names that compounded still tangible features of the landscape with Scandinavian personal names. During the nineteenth century, surveys were conducted and beautiful hand-inked maps plotted that conjured the ghosts of the Norse-speaking country-folk, summoning them to reclaim the familiar lakes, farms and fells.[10] Some of these antiquarians, like W. G. Collingwood and Charles Arundel Parker, spun sagas of their own out of the place-names with which they were most familiar, the Cumbrian Lake District becoming a subject of particularly intense study and fascination. Tales like Parker's *The Story of Shelagh, Olaf Cuaran's Daughter* (1909) and Collingwood's *Thorstein of the Mere* (1895) and *The Bondwoman* (1896) are practically forgotten today, the stilted tenor of late Victorian narrative militating against their enduring popularity, but they are fascinating for what they reveal about the intellectual climate in which they were written – as enthusiasm for the Viking past developed in the latter decades of the nineteenth century. For what is so striking about writers like Collingwood is their willingness to marry their romantic attachment to the places, languages and objects of the Viking Age past to the pioneering academic study of them. It was scholarship as both art and science – the attempt to conjure the wonder of a lost world back into existence through the combination of patient study and literary and artistic invocation.[11]

Collingwood, who had been intimately acquainted with the Lake District from an early age (he was born in Liverpool), came to live at Gillhead (Lake Windermere) in 1883. But he had been, and

THORSTEIN OF THE MERE: A SAGA OF THE NORTHMEN IN LAKELAND: BY W. G. COLLINGWOOD.

LONDON: EDWARD ARNOLD,
Publisher to the India Office.

Frontispiece to *Thorstein of the Mere*

remained, closely associated with Coniston; from 1880 he worked as personal assistant to John Ruskin during the long twilight of the latter's life – twenty years during which the great man's powers inexorably dimmed, his mental health failing, his beard growing longer and whiter as his relevance diminished. It was, in Collingwood's own words, a 'very pleasant servitude', often staying one night a week at Ruskin's home, Brantwood, overlooking Coniston Water, the Old Man looming on the far shore. But there can be little doubt of the emotional and practical demands that Ruskin placed on the younger man's shoulders. 'Nobody knows how awful these times are,' he would write of Ruskin's mental degeneration (in 1889, the year before the latter's death).[12] The bond between the two men was a strong one. When Ruskin died, Collingwood designed Ruskin's gravestone (the Ruskin Cross), which stands in the graveyard of St Andrew's Church in Coniston, its elaborate neo-Anglo-Saxon stylings perhaps a more fitting legacy to Collingwood's own life's work than to that of his celebrated patron. Collingwood's own gravestone stands just feet away, modest and plain by comparison, deferential even in death. It is poignant that a man of his talents should be remembered in this way, struggling to break free from a persona as overwhelming as Ruskin's – a young, glittering star, shackled to the orbit of a grotesquely swollen giant, obliterated by the embrace of its sickly dying light.[13]

After Ruskin's death, Collingwood produced a great deal of valuable work; the bibliography of his works – running to seven pages in Matthew Townend's definitive study – speaks for itself. Several of these represented major breakthroughs for early medieval scholarship. His *Northumbrian Crosses of the Pre-Norman Age* (1927), for example – with its meticulously hand-drawn contents, catalogued and described with a breathtaking precision and care born of love – is described by Townend as 'a triumph, a great scholarly achievement, and one that has been enormously influential in the subsequent study of pre-Conquest sculpture'.[14] This was, in many ways, the culmination of Collingwood's antiquarian career – a mature work, published five years before his death in 1932. More remarkable, in some ways, is his much earlier book *Scandinavian Britain*, published in 1908 by the Society for Promoting Christian Knowledge. It has sat on my desk throughout the writing of this book, a reminder that I walk on paths trodden before by others, whose efforts to clear away the brambles and the boulders has made my journey much easier than theirs.[15]

*Scandinavian Britain* was a book years ahead of its time, a fact acknowledged by some[16] but certainly forgotten by most. Its seamless combination of philology, history and archaeology was a pioneering foray into what we would now call inter-disciplinary study, the attempt to liberate evidence from narrow silos and force them to communicate in conjuring an image of the past. There is deep irony in this: what came naturally to Collingwood, the very quality that makes his writing so easy and unforced and his scholarship so lightly worn, has become a subject of protracted theoretical debate and (sometimes heated) argument; I am sure he would have read much modern historical and archaeological theory with bewilderment.[17] For Collingwood, as for many scholars before the creeping professionalization and specialization of the later twentieth century, it would have been entirely natural to muster all of the evidence for the Viking Age that he could access, deploying it on its own merits, without prejudice.

As a result, many of Collingwood's specific conclusions, as well as the overall tenor of his treatment, remain startlingly modern, not least his recognition that Viking identities were surprisingly adaptable to the cultural climates into which they plunged. More obviously dated, though in no way to its detriment, is the physical quality of the first edition – a fine example of early twentieth-century publishing, with its beautiful gilt lettering and a finely drawn fold-out map. This sort of attention to detail was to be a hallmark of the work with which Collingwood was associated, and more often than not it was his own hand that supplied the maps and illustrations: he was a highly skilled draughtsman, and brought his pen to bear on the sculpture of the north, producing some of the earliest accurate surveys of what we might now call Anglo-Scandinavian sculptural style. But he was also more than equal to the task of illuminating fictional and mythological work with lively borders and marginalia, maps and frontispieces – enlivening his scholarly output with artistry, and grounding his imaginative work with observational rigour.

My great-great-great-great-uncle, G. W. Kitchin (1827–1912), had also, like Ruskin, once lived at Brantwood – indeed he was the occupant who vacated the premises immediately ahead of Ruskin's tenure. The two men had a relationship of sorts, Kitchin having once written a long essay entitled 'Ruskin at Oxford' (one of an improbable number of accomplishments and distinctions).[18] Kitchin spent his time at Brantwood in the early 1870s in the employ of the Clarendon Press, proofing the pages of the mighty Cleasby–Vigfusson English–Icelandic dictionary, a monumental work of scholarship which remains a definitive foundation of the study of Icelandic and Old Norse in English. Indeed, Kitchin had been instrumental in supporting Vigfusson's labours during his time at Oxford in the late 1860s.[19] His interest was active and engaged – while working on the proofs he consulted the local antiquarian Thomas Ellwood about the Old Norse antecedents of Cumbrian dialect words – and later he wrote to Ellwood from Denmark (Kitchin's wife Alice was a friend of Queen Alexandra) with the rather outlandish claim that 'a countryman from here [Denmark] and a countryman from that neighbourhood [the Lake District] would, if speaking their respective dialects, be almost able to mutually understand one another'.[20] (One wonders whether, given the rarefied circles in which he moved, Kitchin had all that many conversations with 'countrymen' of either persuasion.)

Some of this interest doubtless originated in his ancestry. His father, Isaac, came from a family of Cumberland 'Statesmen', a class of yeoman-farmers that he praised for 'their independence, their sturdy battle with nature, their simplicity and traditional loyalty'.[21] Kitchin regarded these 'Statesmen' – independent peasant farmers – as parallels to a Norse (or Swiss) 'type', fiercely protective of their freedoms and their rights.[22] They were, in other words, the models for Collingwood's conception of the free Norse farmers who populated fictional works like *Thorstein of the Mere* and, indeed, Collingwood drew direct parallels between these 'Statesmen' and the free farmers (*bóndi*) of Old Norse saga literature. It was a simplistic idea – though a common enough sort of notion in those days – and an appealing one, particularly for antiquarians working in a predominantly local milieu. In its crudest iterations it was articulated in clumsy racial stereotypes offered up as evidence for the longevity of Viking influence. For example, the cleric, writer and conservationist Hardwicke Rawnsley (1851–1920) felt that to 'look at the blue eyes and the fine cut profile and heavy jaws, and large limbs and long arms of the shepherds and farm folk of the dales' is to 'feel that just such were the Norse sea-rangers'.[23]

This sort of thing would be laughable if such ideas had not been manipulated to maleficent ends throughout the twentieth century. Nevertheless, biological descent as an indicator of population movements has, indeed, come to be a viable tool of modern research. South of Cumbria, along the Irish Sea coastline of the Wirral and West Lancashire, maybe half of the male population whose ancestors can be shown to have been present in the region before 1600 have Scandinavian markers in their DNA.[24] What such research cannot show, however, is when or how this genetic material entered a population or the number of *individuals* from which it ultimately derives. It is also selective, ignoring the very many other biological markers that are prevalent in particular communities. More importantly, such research is possible only when it is carried out with relatively large sample sizes, ensuring that results are statistically significant and can be compared meaningfully with other populations. When used in this way, it has the potential to reveal something about the scale of past migrations, even if it remains something of a blunt instrument. Without care, however, it can easily be manipulated to resemble racial bluster – a means to prove (or disprove) a biological connection to a past invested with moral quality or desirable antique glamour: a superiority of the blood.

*

It was turning dark when we arrived in Coniston, and it had just started to rain. We missed the turning. We stopped. I consulted the directions to the cottage provided by the letting company. Turning around we drove back along the darkening street – unfamiliar shop-fronts and strangers in cagoules, wet dogs, impatient local drivers; the rain came down harder. Finally we found it; headlamps catching on the words 'private road', we crossed the cattle grid, feeling the first sickening lurches as the car slumped into the ruts and divots of the unmade road. I started to feel nervous. Safely tucked behind my desk I hadn't thought much about the words 'dirt track'. It had conjured images of a hundred yards of farm track, muddy and bumpy but with a picturesque stripe of greensward rippling down the centre, a touch of bucolic wilderness to signal that the modern world was at our backs – nothing that could threaten defeat.

As we drove on, the gradient increased, until it was clear that the road was taking us into the fells. It soon became apparent that the road was not a road at all. For substantial stretches, the granite bedrock was laid bare beneath us, the bones of the mountain rubbed raw, defleshed by wheels and walkers; and then there were the pools of scree, the carpet of broken slates that poured down from the mountain like a petrified river, the blood of a giant loosed to cover its wounded flanks. I don't really know why we stopped; I think the will just ebbed away. It was the sudden knowledge of having been beaten, the sudden clarity of failure after the adrenaline of panic dies away. But now the car wouldn't move, its sad wheels spinning feebly in the wet sandy gravel. There we were, for a moment, cling-ing like an iridescent beetle to the foothills of the Coniston Old Man, both of us silent, minds blank, despair seeping in.

If three returning walkers hadn't suddenly appeared in the road behind us, all willing to help push the car and endure a muddy splattering and the funk of a tortured clutch, I don't know what would have happened. But they did, and they were, and after a few miserable minutes of grunting and shoving, we were on our way. Finally, tired and dejected, we made it to our lodgings, overlooking the copper mines and the ribbon of silver water that tumbled from the peaks. But up above, glowering down at us, the Old Man was watching. There was no mistaking it. We had been warned.

Almost as soon as we arrived, my wife was struck down with flu. Shuttered in the upstairs room of the cottage, she was not to move beyond the front door until the grim day arrived when she was compelled to drive us both home again. For the rest of the week I watched, increasingly irritated, as a succession of inappropriate hatchbacks bounded up the valley with abandon. On foot I visited the Ruskin Museum, founded by Collingwood in 1901, and the Ruskin Cross, designed by Collingwood in 1900. And every after-noon I sat in the window to write. But always the Old Man was out there watching me, glaring down unmoving, ever changing. I had to climb him. It was inevitable.

'Our first walk is naturally to climb the Coniston Old Man,' declares Collingwood in *The Book of Coniston*: 'It is quite worth while making the ascent on a cloudy day. The loss of the panorama is amply compensated by the increased grandeur of the effects of gloom and mystery on the higher crags.'[25] Everywhere there are delvings and workings, spoil heaps and tunnels, culverts and rush-ing water. Even as I climb, it feels as though the summit recedes, the distances stretching and distorting; the landscape giving up its form grudgingly, revealing its folds and contours one at a time – pain-fully, slowly. I move up under the black-slate crag, the silver-mer-cury water marbling the grey with an endless roar, tumbling down from Low Water above; then up and over the springing turf, past boulders that stud the hillsides, scattered like seeds from the hands of giants, down from Raven's Tor. Suddenly I am up to the rim of Levers Water, the wide cool tarn spreading beneath hunched knots of rock. I skirt the water round to the left and start to climb again. He's always ahead of me, Collingwood, wiry legs poking out from his shorts, a ghost at the bend in the path, always out of reach. A phantom. I picture him like a mountain goat, like the shaggy upland sheep that bound, with terrifying sureness of foot, up and down the mountain paths – a spry old fellow with a bright gleam in his eye, too quick to catch.

'It is here, on a cloudy day when the tops are covered, that the finest impressions of mountain gloom may be found; under the cloud and the precipices a dark green tarn, savage rocks, and tumbling streams; and out, beyond, the tossing sea of mountain forms.'[26]

On the summit ridge, everything changes. Shifting clouds smother the contours, bleaching the landscape, masking the drop. Surrounding peaks loom out of the vapours, hulking leviathans wreathed in mist, no longer chained to the world below but free to crash like icebergs through the fog. The path ahead is bleak and otherworldly, heaped cairns along the path speak of the dead, the horizontal trails of cloud like angry shades, screaming over the mountaintop, voices joined with the howling wind that tears across the peak. Black carrion shapes hover in this twilight kingdom, their wings thrum like propellers overhead.

'The view on a clear day commands Ingleborough to the east, Snowdon to the south, the Isle of Man to the west, and to the north, Scafell and Bowfell, Glaramara and Skiddaw, Blencathra and Helvellyn: and beneath these all the country spread out like a raised model, with toy hills and lakes and villages.'[27]

And then suddenly it clears, and the ghosts are gone. I can see Coniston Water laid out below me, and the fells rising in ranks behind me. And away on the far banks of Coniston Water I can see the house, mere flotsam below the tree line, where Ruskin and Collingwood worked and Kitchin once sat, leafing through proofs from the Clarendon Press; and I know that all of them, every day they were there, raised their eyes from their work to look, up through the great study window, to gaze at the Old Man, unmoving, ever changing, and found me gazing back at them across the water.

# 16

# A NEW WAY

Then, it is well known, good men of the old sort, who could not
abide to see new laws made and old laws undone, took to their
ships and sailed away west. Some of them landed in Iceland;
some went to Orkney, and others wandered about the coasts of
the Irish Sea to find a home; and wherever they could find
shelter and safety, there they settled.

W. G. COLLINGWOOD, *Thorstein of the Mere* (1895)[1]

In *Thorstein of the Mere*, Collingwood gives the account just
quoted in the epigraph of this chapter describing how the eponymous hero's grandfather arrived in Britain – one among the many
Norwegian émigrés supposedly fleeing the autocratic tendencies of
King Haraldr Hárfagri – Harald Finehair (r. *c.* 872–*c.* 932). In
contemporary sources, the extent of Harald's rule and the details of
his life are murky and contradictory in the extreme.[2] In the saga
tradition of the twelfth century and later, by contrast, Harald plays
a pivotal role. He is credited as being the first king to unify the
Norwegian kingdom and thus providing the catalyst for an expansion of Norwegian emigration across the north Atlantic and into
the Irish Sea. The result of this, so the founding mythology runs,
was the establishment of independent colonies on Orkney, Shetland,
Faroe and Iceland, and down the west coast of Scotland towards the
Irish Sea – Viking statelets ruled by (depending on one's view of the

situation) freedom-loving pioneers or belligerent fugitives and outlaws, petty pirate kingdoms of the northern oceans.[3] Indeed, *Orkneyinga saga* describes Harald mounting expeditions to the Northern and Western Isles and the Isle of Man 'to teach a lesson to certain vikings he could no longer tolerate', winning territory for the Norwegian crown in the process.

This version of events is most likely reflective (and supportive) of Norwegian territorial claims of *c.* 1200 when *Orkneyinga saga* was written, rather than an accurate account of what happened some 300 years earlier. The myth of Harald Finehair presents us with a classic example of how complex processes of emigration, cultural compromise and political consolidation could crystallize in legend around particular resonant figures at a much later date.[4] Nevertheless, the extent of Scandinavian influence around the seaways of Britain cannot be disputed. Place-name evidence makes this plain, even if the apparently straightforward patterns we observe mask gaping holes in our understanding of the processes that gave rise to them. Consider, for example, the presence of Irish personal names, Gaelic place-name elements and characteristically Celtic word morphology mixed up with Old Norse in the place-names of north-west England.[5] This could signify the presence of Gaelic- or Brittonic-speaking populations that were later overlaid by, or became subject to, or became influenced by Norse-speaking migrants – a possibility apparently strengthened by Old Norse place-names that seem to single out the presence of Gaelic-speakers in the landscape (for example, Ireby, 'farm of the Irish', in Cumbria). On the other hand it might indicate that some of the migrants themselves were of mixed Norse–Gaelic heritage. Such identities were indeed developing across this zone of cultural interchange.

Nor can the interconnectedness of this maritime world be denied – a world where the sea was a highway that led between strands and inlets, headlands and islets, storms and tides; a world where political authority could often only be provisional and where local chieftains and disparate peoples forged and broke alliances and moulded new identities that shifted and mutated with the ocean currents, or tore like clouds in the wide western sky. We can see this in the violence and insecurity implied by the Viking Age promontory forts of the Isle of Man or the defended settlement at Llanbedrgoch (Anglesey), where the skeletons of four men of Scandinavian origin and one woman were found buried in a ditch, a reminder of the brittleness of life lived on the margins of a world seething with violent profiteering, slave-trafficking and silver. Hoards of coins, arm-rings and bullion, stowed in the earth on Man and Anglesey, speak of the trade that flowed back and forth across the Irish Sea and up and down Britain's western coasts, controlled by the people who built long-houses in the Hebrides at Udal on North Uist and Drimore Machair and Bornais on South Uist, at Braaid and Doarlish Cashen on Man. The same people, possessed of a buccaneering spirit of enterprise, bloody-handed entrepreneurs, ploughed the coastal waters naming the landmarks they passed in their own tongue, the essential vocabulary of a seafaring people; headlands and promontories, islands and bays: Aignish (ON *egg-nes*, 'ridge headland', Wester Ross); Skipnes (ON *skip-nes*, 'ship headland', Coll); Sandaig (*sand-vík*, 'sandy bay', Tiree); Gateholm, Grassholm, Priestholm (all Welsh coast), Steep Holm, Flat Holm (both Bristol Channel), all compounds with ON *holmr* ('islet'); Anglesey, Bardsey, Ramsey – all with ON-*ey* ('island').

At the end of the eighth century, when the first Viking raids fell on the islands of the north, the territories that comprised northern Britain and the Irish Sea made up a diverse and heterogeneous world. There were the ethnically and linguistically British kingdoms of Wales, and the mysterious kingdom of Alt Clud in the region around the Clyde; there was the Gaelic kingdom of Dál Riata, centred on Argyll and the southern Hebrides, and the Pictish kingdom that dominated the highlands and Northern Isles. Of the Isles of Man and Anglesey very little is known, but both seem to have played an important role in trade and travel around the Irish Sea, with mixed Irish, British and perhaps even English populations, some of which were probably transient.[6] Finally, there was the Northumbrian realm, extending to the Forth in the north and west across the Pennines to contest in power with the British-speaking peoples of Wales and Alt Clud.

By the early tenth century, however, after over a century of raiding, disruption, colonization and war, the Pictish kingdom was gone; so too was Alt Clud, at least in its original iteration, its capital of Dumbarton mouldering in ruin on the rock of the Clyde. Dál Riata was no more, its islands overrun, its identity lost. Northumbria was in the hands of Viking kings, and warlords of Scandinavian descent ruled the islands and sea-lanes from the Shetland strands to the Bristol Channel; even the relics of St Columba had been evacuated from Iona 'to escape the foreigners [Gaill]'.[7] When, in 920, Edward the Elder raised his claim as overlord of the Scots, the Northumbrians ('English, Norwegian and Danish') and the Strathclyde Britons (who presumably included many of the former people of Alt Clud), the north had already become a graveyard of lost realms, the course of its history decisively rerouted.

But, as in England, it was out of this chaos and dissolution that new kingdoms and new identities would ultimately arise. Enduring Norse lordships in the Isle of Man and the Hebrides, and in Orkney, Shetland and Caithness, would last as political entities long into the Middle Ages, their distinctive cultural footprints still visible in the present day. Most enduring of all, however, was the reconfiguration of the broken polities of mainland Scotland, the mosaic reassembled from the jumble of tesserae left behind when the Viking tides relented. The colours were the same, but they were combined to make new shapes, and new pictures: what emerged was a kingdom of Alba – the kingdom of the Scots – a 'Scot-land' to mirror the 'Angle-land' coagulating to the south. Unlike England, however, the lack of a detailed historical record of the events that triggered and shaped these upheavals (even one as flawed as the Anglo-Saxon Chronicle and its derivatives) means that scholars are forced to rely more heavily on a patchwork of evidence, including the fragmentary written sources that do survive, and the much larger corpus of archaeological evidence which – though it can tell us an enormous amount about how, where and to what degree Scandinavian culture penetrated and altered the pre-existing communities it encountered – is often equivocal on matters of chronology and causation. Nevertheless, it is still possible to paint an impressionistic picture of what happened over the course of the ninth and early tenth centuries in these northern regions, even if it is painted with a fairly broad brush.

Raids around Britain's northern shores had been occurring from the end of the eighth century onwards, but 839 is the earliest date that we have for an event with significant political ramifications. The *Annals of Ulster* state that the 'heathen [*gennti*] won a battle against the men of Fortriu in which Euganan son of Óengus and Bran son of Óengus and Áed son of Boanta and an almost uncountable number of others fell'.[8] Fortriu is the name given in Irish chronicles for the north-eastern part of what is now mainland Scotland, the region surrounding the Moray Firth – the great violent V-shaped gash that opens the Great Glen to the cold swells of the North Sea. It is a Gaelic rendering of the Roman tribal name Verturiones, and remained the heart of the Pictish kingdom.[9] The ill-starred Euganan (or, to give him his Pictish spelling, 'Wen'), was the Pictish king and Bran was his brother; Áed was king of Dál Riata, apparently at this point allied to the Picts and probably the junior partner in an unequal relationship.[10] Nobody knows who these particular heathens were, nor where the battle took place. Its aftermath is a void of knowledge, the fate and identity of the victors opaque. We can infer, of course, that it was an unhappy day for the supporters of King Wen et al., but that is all. Such are the limits of the historical record in this period, however, that the fact that it was recorded at all argues strongly for its unusual significance. It may even have been, in the words of one of the principal modern historians of the early medieval north, 'one of the most decisive and important battles in British history'.[11]

One reason for this significance is that, like the Viking assaults on Northumbria and East Anglia, the intervention of a raiding army had brought the curtain down on a native dynasty with total, irreversible finality. With the death of Wen and his brother, the line of Wrguist – the family that had risen to the Pictish throne with Onuist I in 732 – was broken. The next king to rule in Pictavia about whom anything is known was of a different ilk. Cinaed son of Alpín (better known to history as Kenneth McAlpin) is popularly imagined as a Gaelic Scot of Dál Riata who conquered the Picts and, in the process, founded the Scottish kingdom. This is a legend, however, with little to support it. Although it is true that he was king in Dál Riata 'two years before he came to Pictavia', Cinaed was probably a Pict.[12] Nevertheless, his reign did mark the beginning of the increasing political and cultural amalgamation of Picts and Gaels. It also, however, coincided with devastating incursions from land and from sea, from foreigners and from neighbours.

At some point during Cinaed's reign (839–58), the Britons of Alt Clud struck back at their erstwhile overlords, burning the Pictish settlement at Dunblane. This was not the end of Cinaed's troubles: also during his reign Vikings 'wasted Pictavia to Clunie and Dunkeld' (probably striking from the mouth of the River Tay).[13] It was in the west, however, that the most fundamental damage was being done. In 847, 'the Northmen', according to the Frankish *Annals of St-Bertin*, 'got control of the islands all around Ireland, and stayed there without encountering any resistance from anyone.'[14] These territories probably comprised (among others) the islands of Tiree, Mull, Islay and Arran and the Kintyre peninsula (as well as, perhaps, the Isle of Man), places which made up the entire seaward side of the Dál Riatan realm; their loss would have broken whatever connections the Gaelic kingdom still maintained across the Irish Sea, leaving the rump that remained little choice but to move towards ever-closer union with the Picts.

In 865 or 866 a Viking named Olaf ('Amlaíb', as rendered in Irish chronicles) arrived in the kingdom of the Picts. He is described in

Irish sources as the son of the king of Laithlind, although since nobody knows what or where 'Laithlind' was supposed to be (other than being somewhere that Vikings emanated from) the information we have is – once again – not entirely helpful. Olaf had been causing chaos in Ireland since the early 850s, and in the reign of King Constantín (Cinaed's nephew), he laid waste to the Pictish kingdom, occupying it for ten weeks 'with his heathens'.[15] Worse, however, was in store for the resurgent Britons of Alt Clud. In 839 they had got stuck into the Picts by burning Dunbar. In 870, however, their own time had come: '*Arx Alt Clud a gentilibus fracta est*,' the Welsh annals report, 'the fortress of Alt Clud was broken by heathens'.[16] The *Annals of Ulster* elaborate, recording that 'Olaf and Ivar, two kings of the Northmen […] besieged that fortress [Alt Clud] and at the end of four months they destroyed and ransacked it.'[17] This was the end for the fortress on Dumbarton Rock; it fell out of use and was mentioned no more. Two years later, Irish chronicles refer – for the first time – to the Britons of Strathclyde, a new political entity already beginning to pupate.

For Olaf's friend Ivar, the breaking of ancient kingdoms had become something of a speciality. We have met this man before: the previous year he had been in East Anglia with his brother Ubbe, separating King Edmund's talkative head from the rest of him. It is possible that he dragged a number of Anglian slaves with him when he sailed north, for in the following year Olaf and Ivar 'returned to Dublin from Britain with two hundred ships, bringing away with them in captivity to Ireland a great prey of English, and Britons and Picts'.[18] Olaf died at Constantín's hands in, probably, 872.[19] In the following year, the Irish chronicles record that 'Ímar [Ivar], king of the *Nordmanni* [Northmen] of all Ireland and Britain, completed his life.'[20] And what a life it had been. Ivar, over the course of his career, had presided over the collapse of Alt Clud, Northumbria and East Anglia, plied his bloody business across Mercia and the kingdoms of Ireland and – probably – all across the other northern realms as well. Whether he was really a 'king' in any sense we would now recognize is immaterial – he had done enough to match the achievements of any number of anointed monarchs – and the 'dynasty of Ivar', the 'Uí Ímair' as they came to be known in Irish sources, were major players across northern and western Britain and Ireland for generations.[21]

The former industrial shipyards of the Clyde are not the first place one might think to look for the remnants of an early medieval kingdom. Since the decline of Britain's shipbuilding industry, starting in the 1950s, Govan has consistently been one of the poorest parts of the United Kingdom: as silence fell on the shipyards of Clydebank, social and economic problems multiplied in Glasgow's brutalist housing estates, exacerbated by disastrous civic planning policies. Today Govan scores below the Glasgow average for employment, educational attainment and life expectancy; it scores more highly for alcohol-related deaths and the proportions (31.5 and 28 per cent respectively in 2016) of people claiming out-of-work benefits and those considered to be 'income deprived'.[22] To put this into perspective, the overall Glasgow figures for poverty and life expectancy are among the worst in the UK.[23] 'It is as if', declared The Economist in 2012, 'a malign vapour rises from the Clyde at night and settles in the lungs of sleeping Glaswegians.'[24] But it was the river that made Govan the greatest shipbuilding powerhouse of the British Empire – in 1900 Govan built a fifth of all new global shipping[25] – and it was the river that turned it into the centre of a durable, and powerful, kingdom of the early medieval world.

I have twice visited Govan Old Church. The first time, as a young PhD student, I was on a field trip organized by the Early Medieval Archaeology Student Symposium (EMASS). I was in Glasgow to give my first ever academic paper, an occasion I had made unnecessarily difficult for myself by consuming prodigious quantities of beer and deep-fried black pudding the night before. I have a dim, and faintly embarrassing, recollection of earnestly lecturing a fellow (Scottish) student on the defects of Scottish nationalism while swaying on a street corner outside a Glaswegian chip shop. My second opportunity to visit the Old Church was undertaken with a group of journalists and others from the British Museum – part of a press trip ahead of the Vikings exhibition of 2014, just before the referendum on Scottish independence.

The church is remarkable for both the antiquity of the setting and the continuity of worship (the current church, dedicated in 1888, is the fourth on this site – there has been a church here since the fifth century), but also for the remarkable collection of early medieval sculpture that is housed within. Such is the quality and quantity of the stonework produced at Govan Old Church that it is now believed likely that the churchyard here was a royal mausoleum for the kingdom of Strathclyde, the successor to the obsolete kingdom of Alt Clud. How this kingdom came into existence, and the ethnic and political dynamics that drove it in its earliest phases are deeply obscure, but there is one clue to what may have been a component of the make-up of this phoenix rising: a rare collection of distinctively Scandinavian-influenced monuments. We had come to see hogbacks.

Hogbacks are most probably gravestones.[26] Not the familiar upright sort, those ubiquitous bedheads for the dead, but more like tomb covers – monuments that once lay lengthwise over the buried corpse below them, perhaps with a standing cross at head or feet.[27] But, unlike recumbent grave slabs and rectangular tombs, hogbacks are, as their name suggests, curvilinear stone edifices, hump-backed and rounded. They are found across the north of England – mostly in Cumbria and Yorkshire – and in Scotland with a famous cluster (five in total) at Govan Old Church. They are curious objects. Examples from Yorkshire, like the ones at St Thomas', Brompton (near Northallerton), are the most endearing, with three-dimensional sculpted bears that cuddle on to the ends of the stones. Most of them are decorated with ropes and cables of Viking-style knots and ring-work, chains of loops and braids incised into the stone. Most, too, have characteristic tegulations that pattern the upper part of the sculpture – overlapping tile-shapes that mean that

Hogbacks at St Thomas', Brompton (drawn by W. G. Collingwood)

hogbacks often resemble armadillos, nervous armoured beasts which might at any minute scuttle off into the shadows when you're not looking (indeed, the animalistic qualities of these objects were not lost on one Govan sculptor, who added an eye and flipper-like feet to his carving, turning it into something that resembles some sort of antediluvian amphibian).

It is the impression of a tiled roof that has led scholars to the understanding that these objects were intended to resemble houses. The Irish and the various peoples of Britain had long traditions of monumental carvings in stone – of crosses in particular – and house-shaped shrines of the type we have encountered before (as Viking loot) were reproduced in stone as tomb covers and as adornments for standing crosses like the early tenth-century Muiredach Cross in Co. Louth, Ireland. But the houses that the hogbacks are modelled on are manifestly unlike these prototypes; they are shingle-roofed and curving like an upturned keel, like the gently bowing roof-lines of the wooden Viking long-house. As we shall see, the idea of the hall as a home for the dead was a powerful concept in the pre-Christian thought-world of the Vikings, and it is certain that such imagery did not vanish from the imagination with any speed. It is, therefore, entirely understandable why Scandinavian settlers on the Clyde would choose this idea to commemorate the dead, even after their conversion to Christianity (which the presence of these stones at an ancient ecclesiastical centre implies). But the result of this impulse was the creation of something unique – a new form of artistic expression that shows how these new communities chose to communicate their sense of themselves to the world around them.

And so, here in Govan, the contradictions of Scottish nationalism feel magnified; few places – from a southerner's perspective – are so unambiguously 'Scottish' as Glasgow. But in the incongruous setting of a strangely severe and massive Victorian neo-gothic church, one can find oneself surrounded by the stonecraft of a people who (if they included a substantial proportion of the surviving Britons of Alt Clud) probably spoke a language closer to Welsh than Gaelic, but among whom dwelt a number of others whose cultural affinities lay with a Scandinavian-infused world, a hybridized Norse–Gaelic culture that was establishing itself all around the Irish Sea. These were people whose own identities were in flux. Hogbacks show us these new identities at the point of their renegotiation. Here were people who saw and embraced traditions of stone carving and house-shaped reliquaries and grave-markers erected in churchyard enclosures and chose these traditions for themselves. But at the same time they were determined to do things in their own way, using their own art-styles, referencing the building styles that were familiar to them. Across northern Britain – from Yorkshire to Cumbria to Clydebank – they were crafting an identity that was distinct: distinct from the communities into which they had intruded, but also from the communities from which they had drifted. Nothing even resembling a hogback exists in Scandinavia.

A classic illustration of what this process meant in cultural terms is found in the transformations that overtook what had hitherto been conservative and ubiquitous accessories. Penannular brooches (open rings that hinge on a long pin, used to secure a cloak at the breast) had for centuries been a typical element of male and female dress in Ireland and the far north and west of Britain. These objects were to play a conspicuous role in defining and reframing identity in the Viking-infused maritime fringes of the west. As tastes and fashions changed with the influx of new people, these brooches swelled to grotesque size as their silver content increased, their bulbous terminals and flat planes chased with decorative interlace and the gaping maws of twisted Viking creatures, or elaborated into thistle-like knobs that announced a new identity taking root. A hoard of such objects, probably gathered together for their weight-value as silver bullion, was recovered from Flusco Pike on Newbiggin Moor near Penrith (Cumbria) over a period of almost two centuries; the first brooch was found in 1795, the second in 1830 and the rest in 1989.[28] The largest of them – the brooch found in 1830 – has a pin that is *c.* 20½ inches in length. There is no way that this can have been a practical object (there are better ways, after all, of fastening a cloak than by using a silver spike weighing a pound and a half). Such objects were intended to communicate the status of their owners, as well as providing a means to carry portable wealth, a vulgar display of power in a society where silver was the crude measure of success.

But perhaps the most direct evidence for this sort of cultural transformation and synthesis can be found in a modification made to an object known, after the place of its finding, as the Hunterston Brooch.[29] Hunterston is over the water from Great Cumbrae where the Firth of Clyde, having turned to the south, broadens out into wider waters around the Isle of Arran. It is not far from Govan, but it is closer to the southern Hebrides – the islands that the *Annals of St-Bertin* described as falling to Viking settlers in the middle of the ninth century. This pre-Viking penannular brooch is, by any standard, an exquisitely wrought piece of jewellery, a Dál Riatan work of art made in around 700, studded with amber gems and wriggling with golden filigree. Any owner of such an object would have fancied himself or herself as quite the business. We do not know for whom or by whom it was originally fashioned, but we do know the name of someone who owned it two centuries after it was made. And we know because the name of its owner was written on the back, scratched into the silver: 'Melbrigda owns this brooch'. Melbrigda is an impeccably Gaelic name and thus not, in itself, surprising. What makes this truly significant is the way in which Melbrigda chose to express his ownership: for the language he used was not Irish, nor even Latin, but Old Norse, and the characters that he scratched were Viking runes.

This, then, was the birth of a new people, a new tick-box on the ethnicity forms of the early tenth century. Call it what you will, Anglo-Danish or Hiberno-Norse, Anglo-Scandinavian, even Cambro-Norse, the implication is the same: British (and Irish) Vikings had become distinct from their Scandinavian counter-parts.[30] And as the example of the hogbacks demonstrates, the way people buried their dead can tell us a lot about how they – or, more accurately, the people who cared for them in life – imagined their place in their world, their connections and their sense of self.

As the ninth century drew to a close, the successors of Cinaed son of Alpín continued to experience pressure brought to bear by Viking raiding armies. We see it only dimly, in the half-light cast by the sporadic notices of chroniclers who were often writing at some remove from the events they laconically describe. At some point during the eleven years after 899, it is recorded that Pictavia was 'wasted' by Vikings, and in 900 Domnall, son of Constantín I, was slain at Dunnottar 'by the heathens'.[31] The notice of his death is a major turning point in British history, for it marks the moment when the kingdom of the Picts slips for ever into the shadows: 'Domnall son of Constantín,' the Irish chronicles relay, 'king of Alba, dies.'[32] Thus a new kingdom was born, quietly and without fanfare. A century after the Viking Age had begun, not a single political entity of what is now Scotland remained radically unaltered: Alt Clud, Dál Riata, the kingdom of the Picts were all gone, to be replaced by an ill-defined kingdom of Strathclyde, a new kingdom of Alba and a wide coastal belt of more or less intensive Scandinavian settlement and political dominance. The new king of Alba, Constantín II, would reign for forty years. The political and cultural changes that occurred over this period would make permanent this burgeoning sense of nationhood, sharpening its identity, hardening its borders and bringing it – inevitably – into conflict with the Viking-infused powers to the south.[33]

# 17

# THE PAGAN WINTER

axe-age, sword-axe, shields are sundered;
wind-age, wolf-age, before the world crumbles:
no man shall spare another

*Völuspá*[1]

She walks away from the fire, eyes glassy, empty as ozone, walking slowly towards the west, into the weak sun and the wind and the cold sea spray and the rain, away from the world. Bare white feet press the black soil and broken turf, climbing the mound, dark and damp – an unhealed wound. The old woman is singing, a cracked calling, like the gulls.

The grave lies open, and she kneels. Thunder breaks out; ash on linden. And harsh voices, men's voices; a dog barks, a horse screams. And screams.

Below the ashes the sleeper sleeps on, sword under soil, spear under stone. Blood steeps the earth, stains the white sand. Ashes close the mound.

Above it all a pillar stands, cut from wood, one eye watching, Facing the sea.

At some point in the tenth century, a man was buried at Ballateare on the Isle of Man.[2] We don't know where he came from, or who his ancestors were, only that he was buried in the manner of the heathen, like a Viking. Dressed in a cloak fastened with a ringed pin, he was laid in a coffin at the bottom of a deep grave. By his side was a sword, its hilt decorated with inlay of silver and copper. It had been broken and replaced in its scabbard. At his feet was a spear. It too had been broken. Around his neck a knife was hung, and a shield placed upon his body. Then the coffin was closed. Spears were placed upon the coffin, their points pointing towards his feet, and the grave was filled with white sand. Above the sand a mound was raised, cut blocks of turf stacked one on top of the other. Later a grave was dug in the top of the mound. A woman was buried there, face down, arms above her head; the top of her head sliced off with a sword. Nothing accompanied her in the grave, but the mound was sealed with the burnt remains of a horse, a dog, a sheep and an ox. A pillar was raised on top.[3] No one can say what the nature of this pillar was. It may have been an elaborate beast-headed carving like one of the five enigmatic objects buried with the Norwegian Oseberg ship,[4] or something like the 'great wooden post stuck in the ground with a face like that of a man' that ibn Fadlan described among the Rūs.[5] However, the presence at Ballateare of what appear to be sacrificial remains chimes with references to the use of wooden posts in the context of other sacrificial offerings.

The ritualized killing of a slave in order that she might accompany her owner in death has been described already, and the Ballateare grave, along with a number of Scandinavian burials, has long been held up as evidence for the killing of humans (as well as animals) in the rituals surrounding the burial of 'Viking' elites.[6] This interpretation of the evidence is not universally accepted, and there are a number of other possible explanations. The most interesting, but the hardest to prove, is the idea that the woman had died before the blow to the head, and that this had been administered after death in order to release the evil spirits trapped inside.[7] It is also possible that the woman buried here was the victim of a judi-cial killing – that is, an execution – rather than a sacrifice, although whether this is a substantive distinction is moot. The association of the graves of criminals with prehistoric monuments, including burial mounds, is well established in Anglo-Saxon England.[8] Such burials are often characterized by the unusual position of the body – often buried face down – as well as by evidence of severe corporal trauma. Sometimes it seems (again, in England) that posts were erected to display parts of the victim, especially the head (the OE phrase *heofod stoccan* – 'head stakes' – occurs sixteen times in English charters).[9] However, the cremated remains of animals that were interred above the woman's body at Ballateare imply that her burial was part of an event that involved multiple killings and buri-als – of animals as well as a human being. Whether or not this woman died to feed the grave, the evidence for elaborate death-theatre is strong and entirely in keeping with the multifarious rites that crowd the mortuary record in the Viking 'homelands'.[10]

One might get the impression, if this were the only sort of evidence we had, that the role of women in the pagan Viking world was an unhappy one, where a likely fate was to be murdered and thrown face down into the grave of a male warrior, one more possession among the other icons of dominance and machismo with which such individuals were wont to be interred. For some women, slaves in particular, such may well have been their fate; but it is also true that such burials are rare and that the evidence for the treatment of women in death was as varied, as enigmatic and often as spectacular as the burial of any male warrior of the age. In fact, the most famous and splendid Viking burial ever discovered – the famous ship burial excavated at Oseberg near Oslo in 1904–5 – contained the bodies of two women, one elderly and the other in late middle age. The ship itself is one of the greatest treasures of the Viking Age, a vessel 70 feet in length, its prow crawling with crea-tures carved in an interwoven chain of sinuous movement. It domi-nated the burial, forming the stage on which the dramaturgy of death was performed and the framework for the earthen mound which eventually submerged it.[11] To see beyond it, however, is to be staggered by what the rest of this mighty tomb once concealed. There is no adequate way to convey in words the quality of the objects that were placed in the grave, their weird beauty, the strange carved faces that peer from the sides of the wooden wagon, or the elaborate three-dimensional beast-head pillars that served no purpose that any scholar has been able convincingly to propose.

But the quantity! This is easier to indicate. I reproduce below the inventory published by the Norwegian Museum of Cultural History:

2 women; 2 cows; 15 horses; 6 dogs; 1 ship; oars; rope; rigging equipment; remnants of sails; 1 hand bailer; 1 anchor; 1 cart; 3 ornate sleighs; 1 work sleigh; 2 tents; 1 framework for a 'booth', with walls of textile; 3 long combs; 7 glass beads, 4 with gold inlay; 2 pairs of shoes; 1 small leather pouch containing cannabis; several dresses and other garments; feather mattress; bedlinen; 2 pieces of flint; 5 animal head posts; 4 rattles; 1 piece of wood, arrow-shaped, approx. 40cm long; 1 round pole with a runic inscription, approx. 2.40m long; 1 leather band, knotted like a tie; 1 burial chamber; 1 approx. 1m long wooden pipe; 1 chair; 6 beds; 1 stool; 2 oil-burning lamps; 1 bast mat; 3 large chests; several smaller chests, boxes and round wooden containers with a lid, used mainly for storing food; 3 large barrels; 1 woven basket; 1 wooden bucket with brass fittings; 1 wooden bucket with a 'buddha' figure; 1 small staved bucket made of yew wood; 3 iron pots; 1 pot stand; several stirring sticks and wooden spoons; 5 ladles; 1 frying pan; 1 approx. 2m long trough; 1 earthenware basin; 3 small troughs; 7 wooden bowls; 4 wooden platters; 10 ordinary buckets (one containing blueberries); 2 work axes; 3 knives; 1 quern-stone; bread dough; plums; apples; blueberries; various woollen, linen and silk textiles; 1 large tapestry; 5 different weaving looms; 1 tablet weaving loom; 1 manual spindle and distaff; various small tools for spinning and textile work; 1 device for winding wool; 2 yarn reels; 2 linen smoothers; 1 smoothing iron; 3 wooden needles; 1

pair of iron scissors; 2 washing paddles; 1 round wooden
container with a lid, used mainly for storing food; 5 balls of
wool; 1 weaving reed; piece of wax; 3 small wooden bowls; 1
small quartz stone; 3 pyrite crystals; 2 slate whetstones; 1 knife
handle; 1 bone comb; 1 small wooden bowl; 18 spades
(probably belonged to the grave robbers); 1 dung fork; 3 grub
hoes; 2 whetstones; 2 awls; 3–5 caskets; 5 wooden pins used to
drape things; 1 horsewhip; 1 saddle; various kinds of harness
fittings; 5 winter horse shoes of iron; several small wooden pegs
for tethering horses; several dog chains of iron; mounts for
several dog collars.[12]

An attentive reader of this list may notice a striking absence. There
is nothing, at all, of silver or gold, no jewellery, no gemstones, no
amber beads or brooches, no pendants, coins or neck-rings, no
gilded bridle mounts or hammered bracteates: none of the things,
in short, that characterize other high-status Scandinavian graves,
male and female, of similar and earlier antiquity. They will also have
noted the presence of '18 spades [which] probably belonged to the
grave robbers'.[13] These were not modern spades; the mound was
disturbed long ago – not long, in fact, after it was closed – and the
absence of precious metal objects is probably attributable to this
ancient tomb-raiding. (Exactly why the grave was disturbed remains
a matter for debate – the scale of the excavation required would
have been difficult to manage covertly and may have been sanctioned in some way. Illicit grave-robbing was, in any case, a risky
business. Later generations of Norse-speakers were fascinated by
the trouble that opened graves could bring down on the heads of
intruders – witting or unwitting.) The extraordinary inventory of
finds from the Oseberg burial thus represents the left-overs, the
picked carcass – the stuff that was too cruddy or too bulky to bother
with. In its pristine condition, the burial chamber of the Oseberg
grave must have been an astonishing sight, its principal occupant a
Nefertiti of the North Sea littoral, buried in a grave to make Sutton
Hoo look like Sutton 'whatever'.

Viking ship burials are known from Britain, though nothing on this scale. Nevertheless, whenever a community chose to treat its dead in this way it represented a very public and conspicuous disposal of wealth: a bit like burying a loved one in a car. Anyone so buried, however modest it may seem relative to the Oseberg burial, was being honoured as an important player within the community. One such man was excavated at Ardnamurchan (Scotland) in 2011; his was the first complete boat burial ever to be found on the British mainland. He was buried with sword, axe, spear and shield, laid out in a boat 16 feet in length; in death, he presents the image of a wealthy and powerful pagan warrior, a warlord of the ocean's edge, equipped to pursue a life of adventure on the dark waters of the hereafter. Other male boat burials have been found in the isles (at Colonsay, Oronsay and Orkney, and on the Isle of Man) and frag-ments of a boat grave – now lost – were found in 1935 at the site of the Huna Hotel in Caithness.[14] At Westness cemetery on Rousay, Orkney, for example, two boat burials were excavated in the 1960s, and the boat graves of men have been found on Man at Balladoole and Knock-e-Dooney. In each case, the boats in which they were interred measured in the region of 13 to 16 feet – the size of the small oared boats that were interred as secondary grave goods in the burial mound of the Gokstad ship in Norway.[15]

It was not only men, however, who were afforded these extrava-gant death rituals in Britain. At Scar on Orkney a woman in her seventies – a fabulously advanced age for the time – was buried in a boat 25 feet long, alongside a man in his mid-thirties and a child.[16] A whalebone 'plaque', a flat board of roughly rectangular shape, with a simple rope-like pattern cut into it at the borders and deco-rative roundels incised into its surface, was set at her feet. At one end, the shape of the board has been carved away to fashion the profile of two bestial heads on sinuous necks, spiralling to confront one another – teeth bared and tongues lolling. It is an iconic image of the Viking Age, but no one knows what objects like this were used for (a similar example can be found in the collection of the British Museum, excavated from another female boat burial in

Norway). They were, however, possessions that not every woman in society could expect to be buried with. Possibly they were emblems of status, a symbol of the magical and religious powers that women in Viking society could wield. The other objects in the grave included the paraphernalia of weaving – spindle whorls and weaving sword, needle-case and shears. The processes and symbolism of weaving were far from mundane – they could, for some Viking women, provide the tools and imagery for hidden and terrible powers.

What is perhaps most important about overtly unChristian burial traditions like these is that they were drawing their material vocabulary from the practices of Viking Age Scandinavia: these were the graves of people and of communities who still felt themselves connected to a homeland from which they had been divorced, and their behaviour implies a desire to maintain a cultural link across space and time. The people who buried their matriarch at Scar were inserting her corpse into a tradition that included the women of the Oseberg burial, claiming for her a shared identity and tapestry of beliefs (the Oseberg burial also contained, on a lavish scale, a battery of equipment related to weaving and textile production). The same can be said of all the 'pagan' Viking graves of Britain – the mound at Ballateare and the cemetery at Westness, the barrow graves of Cumbria and the cremated remains of Heath Wood near Repton among many others.

As the hogbacks demonstrate, however, this conservatism was not to last. From almost the moment they arrived in Britain, new beliefs were shaping the way that the Vikings treated the dead and imagined the afterlife, and evolving identities and political realities were refashioning the way that British 'Vikings' found their place in the world. The old ways were dying fast.

First the snows will come, driving hard from all points of the compass; biting winds, shrill and screeching, bringing the cold that cuts. Thrice the winter comes, three times with no relenting; no spring will come, no summer to follow, winter upon winter, the land swallowed by ice unending. The green shoots will die under the frost, the skeleton trees creaking beneath the weight of snow – the world will fall dim and silent, shadowed in perpetual twilight. 'Fimbulvetr' they will call it, the 'great winter', and few will survive its corpse-grip. Those who do will wish that they had died.

Riding on the back of the ice-wind, sweeping down paths of famine and despair, war will sweep the ice-bound world, violence shattering families, severing oaths – 'brothers will struggle and slaughter each other, and sisters' sons spoil kinship's bonds'. So the prophecy runs. And as the axes rise and fall and all the blood of the earth is emptied out on to virgin snows, a howling will be heard away in the east.

Gods and elves will lament and hold council as their doom unfolds. Yggdrasil, the world tree, will shake and an uproar rumble from Jötunheimr; the dwarves will mutter before their doors of stone. For the time now is short before all bonds are broken, and the wolves of Fenrir's line, the troll-wives' brood, will break free from the Iron Wood and run from the east. And they will swallow down the sun and swallow down the moon, and the heavens will be fouled with blood.

Then the Gjallarhorn will sound, the breath of Heimdallr, watchman of the gods, echoing across the worlds, its blast echoing from the mountains. It shall awaken the gods and the *einherjar* – the glorious dead – and they will assemble and make themselves ready for the final battle, Odin speaking with Mímir's head for final words of counsel. For their foes shall have already arrived and will stand arrayed in dreadful splendour upon the battle plain, the field that runs for a hundred leagues in all directions – a bleak and boundless tundra.

There shall come Loki, father of lies, freed from an age of torments; and with him will stand his terrible children: Fenrir, the wolf, his mouth gaping wide enough to swallow the world, fire spewing from his eyes; and Jormungandr, the world serpent, shall haul his foul coils on to the land, writhing and thrashing, venom gushing. To this place, too, shall the giant Hrym come, he will steer the ship of dead men's nails to this place of reckonings, leading the frost giants on to the battle plain. Last to arrive will be the sons of Muspell, the flaming hordes marshalled by Surt, demon of fire, his shining sword setting all ablaze beneath the riven sky.

And Odin will ride to meet them at the head of his host, gripping the spear, Gungnir, forged by the sons of Ivaldi; and he will wear a helmet of gold and a coat of mail. Thor will be with him and Frey and Tyr and Heimdall, and all those heroes who died in battle and were chosen.

And all will fall.

This was how the Vikings imagined the world would end,[17] shattered in the madness of battle, poured out in the blood of the gods on Vigrid – the 'battle plain'. It would die with the thrashing coils of the serpent, the sun devoured, the earth burned away – choked out in torrents of ice and fire, the way it had begun. The story of *Ragnarök* – the 'doom of the gods' – is recorded in two complete versions, the eddic poem *Völuspá* and a prose account compiled by Snorri Sturluson in the mythological handbook *Gylfaginning*, for which *Völuspá* was the primary source. *Völuspá* means 'the prophecy of the *völva*' – the seeress. It is a prophetic poem delivered to Odin, a telling of the great arc of mythic time, from the world's beginnings in the void to its breaking at *Ragnarök* and its subsequent rebirth. It is the ultimate encapsulation of the knowledge that Odin seeks, the knowledge for which he has sacrificed himself to himself, for which he has given his eye and taken the head of Mímir. It offers cold comfort.

Odin will ride into the jaws of Fenrir and do battle with the wolf; he will face it alone, and that will be the end of him, the All-Father swallowed into the maw of death. Thor will ride beside him, but no help will come from that quarter. Thor will be locked in deadly conflict with Jormungandr and, though he will slay the *wyrm*, he will be poisoned by its venom – staggering nine steps before he too will fall. Frey will die also, cut down by Surt's flaming sword. Tyr, the one-handed god, will go down to Garm – the hound who howls before hell's mouth – and Heimdall and Loki will slay each other.

The ideas contained in *Völuspá*, and rationalized and repeated by Snorri, cannot be attributed with any confidence to the Viking Age itself, but allusions to, and scenes from, the story of *Ragnarök* are found in other poems and fragments.[18] Of these, two of the most dramatic are found carved in Britain, shards of the pagan Viking end of days, frozen in immortal rock.

Thirty-one runestones stand on the Isle of Man, the largest number in any place outside Scandinavia. Like their cousins, they are memorials to the dead (although at least one was erected to salve the soul of a living man) and are defined by the runic carvings – inscribed in the Norse language – that record the names of those lost and those remaining, and the people who raised the stones. (Some also carry inscriptions in Ogham, the vertical Celtic alphabet of hatch-marks used in Ireland and western Britain – a sure sign of a culturally and linguistically mixed population.)[19] They make up roughly a third of all the carved stones of Man, an impressive corpus of sculpture bearing the combined influence of Irish stoneworking traditions and Scandinavian art-styles. They are, stylistically, quite dissimilar to the runestone tradition of the

Viking 'homelands' and are primarily cruciform objects – either high standing crosses, or cross-incised slabs akin to the Christian symbol stones of Pictavia.[20] The inscriptions they carry are, for the most part, fairly mundane, although they do provide a thrilling glimpse of the individuals who peopled Viking Age Man, even if the light that the inscriptions cast on these people is but a fleeting glimmer in the dark.

'Þorleifr the Neck raised this cross in memory of Fiak, his son, Hafr's brother's son,' runs the inscription on the tenth-century standing cross at Braddan Church;[21] 'Sandulfr the Black erected this cross in memory of Arinbjǫrg his wife …' runs another at Andreas Church.[22] Some, like Þorleifr's, hint at premature tragedy ('Áleifr […] raised this cross in memory of Ulfr, his son'),[23] another acknowledges a guilty conscience ('Melbrigði [incidentally, the same Celtic name (albeit spelled differently) as that scratched into the back of the Hunterston Brooch], the son of Aðakán the Smith, raised this cross for his sin …') but concludes with the prideful boast of the rune-carver ('but Gautr made this and all in Man').[24] Sometimes they hint at familial drama and community tensions. A person who identified himself as 'Mallymkun' raised a cross in memory of 'Malmury', his foster-mother. He ends with the sour observation that '[it] is better to leave a good foster-son than a wretched son'. A thousand years later, the rancour still festers in the stone. Other thoughts are snapped off by time and left hanging: 'Oddr raised this cross in memory of Frakki, his father, but …'[25] But what? It is most likely that the missing runes revealed the name of the carver ('but [so-and-so] cut/made this' is a typical formula), but it is impossible to rule out a more personal aside: '… but Hrosketill betrayed the faith of his sworn confederate',[26] runs the truncated inscription on another stone at Braddan Church. Alas, what Hrosketill did – or to whom, or even for what purpose the stone was raised – is lost for ever.

The most famous of the Manx runestones is the fragment of a monument known as 'Thorwald's Cross', found at Andreas Church. It is a slab-type runestone, with its surviving inscription 'Þorvaldr

The eighth-century *Stockholm Codex Aureus*. Comments by ealdorman Ælfred were added in the ninth century above, below and to the right of the illuminated letters

Tingwall: an assembly site on Mainland, Shetland

A hogback stone, carved in the tenth century, from
Govan Old Church, Glasgow

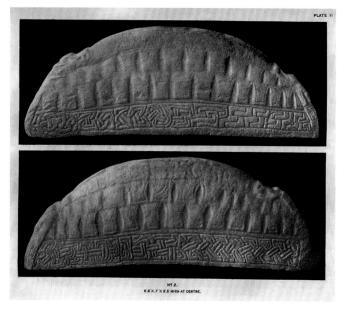

PLATE II

Nº 2.
6.6˝X.7˝X 2.5 HIGH AT CENTRE.

The whalebone plaque from the tenth-century boat burial at Scar, Orkney

Thorwald's Cross, at Andreas Parish on the Isle of Man, depicts – on one side – Odin swallowed by the wolf Fenrir at *Ragnarök*. The other side displays an apparently Christian scene

The Cuerdale Hoard: 90 pounds of buried treasure (only a fraction of the total is shown in this image)

Coins of Viking rulers in England (obverse at top, reverse at bottom ).
From left to right: Guthrum-Æthelstan of East Anglia (reigned *c.*880–90), Siefred of Northumbria (reigned *c.*894–8), Olaf Guthfrithsson of Northumbria (r. 939–41), Sihtric II of Northumbria (reigned *c.*942–3),  Eric 'Bloodaxe' of Northumbria (r. 947–8 and 952–4)

Reconstruction of tenth-century dwellings at Coppergate, York

Northey Island, Essex: a Viking army crossed the causeway (upper right) to fight the Battle of Maldon in 991

The Sanctuary monument at Overton Hill, Wiltshire, erected around 2000 BC, as drawn by William Stukeley in 1723

'Áli had this stone raised in memory of himself. He took Knútr's payment in England. May God help his spirit': so runs the inscription on this runestone in Väsby, Uppland (Sweden)

'Ginna and Toki had this stone set up' reads the runic inscription on this stone, found in 1852 in the graveyard of St Paul's Cathedral, London

A mass grave of over fifty decapitated men, most of them originally from Scandinavia, found near Weymouth in Dorset in 2011

Cnut and his queen, Emma (Ælfgifu), depicted in the pages of the eleventh-century *Winchester Liber Vitae*

raised [this] cross' running down one edge, and a decorative cross on each face, embellished with characteristically Scandinavian ring-chain carvings. In the case of this particular runestone, however, the simple Christian message is complicated by the subject matter to which the carver chose to turn his chisel. On one side of what remains of the stone, cut in relief on the bottom right-hand quadrant left vacant by the cross, is the image of a male, bearded figure with a large bird perched upon his shoulder. A spear is in his hand, its point downwards, thrusting towards the open jaws of a wolf – a wolf that is in the process of devouring him, his right leg disappearing down the lupine gullet. There can be little doubt that this is a depiction of Odin, Gungnir in hand and raven on his shoulder,[27] swallowed by the wolf.

Across the sea from Man, at Gosforth in Cumbria, a tall cross stands in the churchyard of St Mary's, 15 feet of slender masonry with pea-green lichen clinging like sea-scum to the ruddy Cumbrian stone. It seems odd and incongruous, standing there amid the dour eighteenth-century tombstones – like some strange Atlantean pillar recovered from the ocean floor and hauled upright, flotsam from another world. Its carvings are in surprisingly good condition, given the millennium during which it has stood against the elements. The lichen is less ancient than the carvings it obscures. In 1881, Dr Charles Arundel Parker – the obstetrician and part-time antiquarian – and his friend the Rev. W. S. Calverley came to Gosforth 'one dull wet day in the late autumn', when, the two gentlemen had determined, 'the continuous damp and rain of the previous weeks would have softened the lichens which had filled every sculptured hollow'. Happily for them and the condition of their frockcoats, these were days when menial labour was easily to be had. These two learned fellows stood in the churchyard while Dr Parker's coachman, 'up aloft, with a dash of a wet brush to the right and to the left hand scattered the softened mosses'.[28] What he revealed were the triquetrae (interlacing triple-arches) that decorated the cross-head, the final details to be revealed and recorded of a monument that boasts the most comprehensive iconographic depiction of Norse mythology dating to the Viking Age anywhere in Europe.

Many of the scenes that cover the four faces of the shaft of the Gosforth Cross remain open to interpretation, but two in particular stand out. One is the torment of Loki, the punishment inflicted for his part in the death of Baldr and the pivotal event of the mythic cycle that ends with *Ragnarök*. We see him bound in an ovoid cell, a pathetic trussed creature, while his wife Sigyn bends over him to catch the venom that drips from the serpent pressing its diamond head into his face. The other is the depiction of a figure, striding purposefully into the gaping mouth of a beast, one foot upon the lower jaw, one hand reaching to grip the upper, a spear held in the other. Snorri provides the key that enables us to identify this figure as Vidar, son of Odin: 'Vidar will stride forward and thrust one of his feet into the lower jaw of the wolf [...] With one hand he takes hold of the wolf's upper jaw and rips apart its mouth, and this will be the wolf's death.'[29] This is the end of the wolf, Fenrir, but it is not the end of the world. That comes with the final blackening of the heavens and the burning of Yggdrasil, the sinking of the earth into the sea – a return to the primeval void.

In all tellings of the *Ragnarök* story, however, there is a final act, a light to guide us through the darkness. In *Völuspá* it is told with heartbreaking simplicity, the heathen *völva*'s vision of a far green country – a promised land to come:

> She sees rising up a second time
> the earth from the ocean, ever-green;
> the cataracts tumble, an eagle flies above,
> hunting fish along the fell.[30]

There are aspects of this unfolding vision that feel familiar – the 'hall standing, more beautiful than the sun, better than gold', where 'virtuous folk shall live' and 'enjoy pleasure the live-long day' and, in one version of *Völuspá*, the sudden appearance of 'the mighty one down from above, the strong one, who governs everything,'[31]

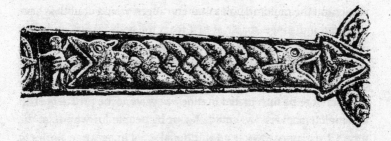

Vidar and Fenrir on the Gosforth Cross

the arrival – as one scholar describes it – 'of Christ in majesty, descending to the earth after the rule of the pagan gods has come to an end'.[32] This Christian coda to the pagan end of days is there at Gosforth as well, more explicitly perhaps than anywhere else. Immediately below the depiction of Vidar's grisly dispatch of Fenrir is a depiction of the crucifixion, the redemptive fulcrum of human history – the event which, in Christian cosmology, ensured safe harbour for the souls of those who embraced its message. It is the symbol of the promise of eternal life, the seal that guarantees that a new world shall rise from the ocean.

It is a supreme irony that the very monuments at Andreas Church and Gosforth which seem to confirm the pagan beliefs written down in a later age also bear witness to their dwindling, their co-option into a new world-view. The old stories were not yet dead at the time these monuments were made, and many of them would never die, living on through the versions written down 300 years after being alluded to in stone. But by this time the stories were no longer (if they ever were) an oppositional belief system, a Viking 'religion' to rival the teachings of the gospel. They were, instead, passing into folklore, becoming tales that could be told without threatening the Christian world-view, complementing it perhaps, explanatory metaphors for the new narratives that were percolating through mixed and immigrant communities. We might imagine that it would, initially, have been easy for a people accustomed to many gods to add another to the throng (or many others – the trinity and the multitudes of saints and angels would doubtless have appeared indistinguishable at first from the gods, ghosts and elves of native belief). Over time, the exclusive nature of the Christian god would have gradually asserted itself, but it cannot have been clear at the beginning. The crosses at Gosforth and Andreas Church can therefore be interpreted in different ways as the products of an incomplete conversion – made for or by people for whom, at the time, Christianity was just an additional set of images and stories to add to the mythological cauldron.

On the other hand, perhaps, these were erudite attempts to juxtapose Christian and pagan images – a means of instructing new converts on the essentials of the Christian faith. For example, although the scene on the reverse of Thorwald's Cross has not been securely interpreted, there is little doubt of its Christian intent: a man wielding a huge cross and a book tramples on a serpent while another Christian symbol, a fish, hovers near by: a triple whammy of Christian symbology. There is room for a little ambiguity here – crosses can easily be mistaken for hammers (indeed, some Thor's-hammer pendants may actually have been intended as crosses, and some deliberately combine cross and hammer on the same object),[33] and Thor was famous as both a fisherman and a fighter of serpents. One thing he was not, however, was bookish, and it is this more than anything else that gives the Christian game away. Although we cannot know for sure, it may be that the missing 'panels' of the complete cross depicted complementary images from pagan and Christian mythology – a sort of pictorial instruction manual to Christianity, the build-it-yourself guide to getting religion with the old myths deployed as the key.

I prefer, however, to see all of this in a different light, to see the *Ragnarök* story as an expression of a melancholy self-awareness, the creative and emotionally profound product of people who could feel the old world slipping away, a poetic response in words and stone to the twilight of an ancient way of life, a twilight of their gods. The *Ragnarök* story brims with sadness and nostalgia, a pagan vision of the future that was alive to the impending extinction of its own world-view in an increasingly homogenized Europe. It is a complex and intellectually involved interplay of hope and defeat, defiance and resignation, an acknowledgement – a recapitulation – of what was already slipping away and a yearning for a new and better world around the corner. For the Viking communities of Britain, that hope lay in the new identities and new ways of being that were being adopted and adapted in different ways across the islands. As the tenth century progressed, old affinities and beliefs began to break down as new political and cultural realities asserted themselves. What it meant to be a 'Viking' in Britain was changing rapidly.[34]

# 18

# THE GREAT WAR

Long was prophesied the time when they will come,
rulers by right of descent taking their possession,
men of the North in a place of honour around them;
in the centre of their van they will advance. [...]
There will be spear-thrusts, a fierce flood.
No friend will spare the body of his enemy.
There will be heads split open, without brains.
There will be women widowed and horses riderless.
There will be terrible wailing before the rush of warriors,
and a multitude wounded by hand before the hosts part.

*Armes Prydein Vawr* (tenth century)[1]

When, in 920, Edward the Elder finally received the submission of the north, Northumbria had been subject to Viking conquest, settlement and rule for half a century. In the years that followed the capture of York by the *micel here* in 866, power in Northumbria appears to have been shared in an untidy fashion among a number of groups, competing or cooperating as circumstances dictated. There were native Northumbrian rulers (Ecgbert I, Ricsige, Ecgbert II), as well as a separate dynasty that retained a power-base at Bamburgh in the north of the kingdom. Then there were the bishops of Northumbria – at Lindisfarne and York – and also, probably, those leaders of the *micel here* who had not gone south with the army to Mercia, East Anglia or Wessex. In 874, however, a new 'big beast' reappeared on the scene: Halfdan, supposed son of Ragnar Loðbrók, and one of the leaders of the army that had captured York in 866, came north from the capture of Repton with an army.[2] He camped on the Tyne, overrunning northern Northumbria before raiding and briefly occupying Pictavia (during the reign of Cinaed's son, Constantín I) and attacking the new kingdom of Strathclyde.[3]

From this point onwards, and particularly from 876 when the *Anglo-Saxon Chronicle* records that Halfdan began to 'share out the land' of Northumbria, men with Scandinavian names began to be recognized as the prime movers in the kingdom, particularly in those territories centred on York.[4] The years that followed saw Halfdan succeeded by a line of Viking kings – Guthfrith, Siefred and Cnut – about whom very little is known. What can be seen, however, is that, like Guthrum–Æthelstan in East Anglia, these were men who outwardly embraced the Christian Church and what is more, the Church – so it would seem – had begun to embrace them back.

A sense of ecclesiastical investment in the way this new royal power was framed can be seen in a remarkable description in the *Historia Sancti Cuthberti* (a history of the see of St Cuthbert, dating from the mid-tenth to mid-eleventh century) describing the circumstances of Guthfrith's elevation to the throne in 877. It is not a very reliable source – neither in general nor within the bounds of the specific anecdote that follows – but it does tell us something about how power was being brokered in the north in those days, about the unlikely accommodations that were being reached. Once again, the discorporate form of our old friend St Cuthbert is on hand, still apparently taking an active interest in British politics, this time appearing:

> by night to the holy abbot of Carlisle, whose name was Eadred, [and] firmly enjoining him as follows: 'Go,' he said, 'across the Tyne to the army of the Danes, and say to them that, if they will

obey me, they are to point out to you a certain boy, Guthfrith, Hardacnut's son […] and at the sixth hour lead him before the whole multitude, that they may elect him king. And at the ninth hour lead him with the whole army on to the hill which is called "Oswiu's down" [Oswigesdune], and there place on his right arm a gold armlet, and thus they all may appoint him as king.'[5]

This, the *Historia* relates, is exactly what Eadred did and, naturally, the Viking army was perfectly happy with this arrangement. Guthfrith was duly made king with 'the great goodwill of the whole multitude'.[6] There are glimpses here, perhaps, of rituals of power being enacted – a glimpse of the royal theatre through which ruler-ship was expressed and validated in the febrile climate of Viking-dominated late ninth-century Northumbria.

Guthfrith ascends the mound, the skies grey and pregnant with rain. A bracing wind is blowing from the west. As the abbot speaks, the syllables of Latin tumble away on the breeze, away from the ears of the uncomprehending multitude who shuffle, cold and confused, their spear-points glinting dully in the leaden light. Dew seeps into woollen cloaks and leather shoes, perfumed with the loamy scent of earth. Some of them know why this place is powerful, but all of them feel it; they know that the dead who sleep under soil have a presence that can touch the living, and this mound is named for a king.[7]

Guthfrith takes the golden ring from the priest. He holds it aloft and a brief shaft of sunlight catches it, burning it for a moment with amber fire. Suddenly a rumble begins, swords on steel rims, ash on linden, a forest thunder. It builds until the hills echo with it, rolling from the fells and dales, crows startled, wheeling from the woods. Guthfrith smiles; he places the ring upon his arm and draws his sword, a silver fish in rapids, dancing in the daylight. A cry of exultation breaks forth, a roar like the falling of trees, rising skyward from a thousand wolfish throats, announcing the birth of a king.

There are fewer reasons to doubt the circumstantial details of the *Historia* than there are reasons to scorn the political and supernatural stories it weaves, and there is the glimmer of truth about the image that the *Historia* obliquely conjures. Taken alongside what we have encountered already of the militarized nature of the body politic – the weapon-waving, the threat and application of violence – we can perhaps see hints of a Viking ceremony of king-making that was a far cry from the democratic fantasies of the Victorian era, where rough but hearty farmers gathered to settle their affairs in straight talk and rough and tumble. Instead, the creation of a new king was probably more like the elevation of a modern tribal warlord, political ascendancy celebrated with the crackle of automatic gunfire, AK-47s discharged recklessly into the sky.

However, the truly revealing part of the *Historia*'s account can be found in Cuthbert's afterthought to Eadred, his injunction that Eadred should also 'say to him [Guthfrith], when he has been made king, that he is to give me the whole territory between the Tyne and Wear'. So, there's the rub: with this line the author of the *Historia* reveals his agenda in telling this (tall) tale – the concern that, right from the outset, the interests of the see of St Cuthbert (that is, the bishopric of Lindisfarne) should be respected and strengthened by future kings of Northumbria. The self-interest, however, was doubtless mutual. Like the unwitting St Edmund, invoked to support the claims of the new East Anglian dynasty, here St Cuthbert – evidently forgetful of the despoliation of his monastery by Guthfrith's putative forebears – was being dragged from his cloud to leave the imprimatur of the Northumbrian Church on a new Northumbrian regime. Church and state had little to lose, and much to gain, by working together to uphold structures of power and privilege.

Guthfrith was buried at York Minster, a very public way to demonstrate the alliance of the new Northumbrian royalty with the Church. Indeed, the kings who followed him – Siefred and Cnut – were, like their East Anglian counterparts, keen to publicize their faith, over-egging the religious iconography of their coinage in a way that has led some to suspect that it was bishops rather than kings who were behind it all.[8] Certain coins of the Northumbrian Cnut, for example, not content with using the patriarchal cross (two crosses for the price of one), also arranged the letters of the king's name at the cardinal points; were they transposed to a human torso, they would be inscribed in the order in which the hand would reach them when marking out the sign of the cross:

Coin of Cnut of Northumbria (*c.* 900–5). The other letters, read clockwise, spell out the word REX ('king')

In addition, the reverse of some of these coins bear the legend 'MIRABILIA FECIT' ('he has done/made wondrous things'), a quotation from Psalm 98 with an obvious double meaning: as much as it celebrated the inscrutable doings of the Almighty, it also implied the power of the king over the means of production. Such innovations in coin design betray an active intelligence and a

sophisticated grasp of Christian symbology and scripture, hinting
– perhaps – at the hand of the Northumbrian Church in shaping the
messages coming from the new Northumbrian court.[9]

These mutual accommodations were driven by primarily political
motives. Future Viking kings of Northumbria were manifestly more
ambivalent about Christian piety, and markedly more concerned
with their own personal power and prestige. In the decades after 900
a new Viking influence came to dominate in Northumbria, one that
originated not with the *micel here* but in the colonies of Ireland and
the west. The coins they issued deployed an entirely new set of
imagery, a deliberate assertion of their distinctive cultural baggage.
Hammers, swords, bows and ravens began to mark out a distinctive
identity for the Viking kings of Northumbria – a defiant dissemina-
tion of martial and mythological symbolism that vied for space with
the cross and the name of St Peter. The most striking of these coins,
issued in the reign of Sihtric (r. 921–7), feature the hammer of Thor
intruding into the inscription itself, the sign of a pagan deity inserted
into the very name of St Peter – a pagan graft on to a Christian

A Northumbrian coin of the 920s. The inscription reads SCI (Sancti: 'Saint')
PETRI ('Peter') MO (Moneta: 'minted [this coin]'). The 'I' of Petri has been
replaced with an upside down hammer

root-stock. It may be that, like the hybrid iconography of the Gosforth and Thorwald crosses, this was a way to bridge a chasm of belief – to encourage a multi-faith population to find common ground (St Peter and Thor were both, after all, famous fishermen) and smooth the path of conversion. But to me it feels like politics: the Viking kings in York needed the support of both the Church and the pagan militarized elite. Coins that combined, however crudely, the symbols of both these camps would have served as a convenient way for kings to demonstrate to the twin pillars of early medieval power that they were both being kept in mind.[10]

In the period immediately after 900, the political situation in Northumbria is plunged into penumbra, a shadow almost as deep as that which cloaks the rest of northern Britain. After Æthelwold's short-lived tenure on the throne (and it is uncertain to what degree he was recognized as 'king of the Danes' in any meaningful sense in Northumbria between 902 and his death in 904), the names of other rulers – Halfdan, Eowils and Ingwær – are known only from the list of 'kings' who died fighting Edward the Elder at Tettenhall in 911. The gloom clears a little, however, with a battle fought at Corbridge (Northumberland) in 918 between an army led by Constantín II of Scotland and a warlord known – in Irish sources – as Ragnall (ON Rögnvaldr; OE Rægnald), the grandson of Ivar.[11]

Ragnall's career, like those of so many other Viking warlords of the tenth century, began in Ireland. In 902, the Viking elite in control of Dublin were driven out by a native Irish coalition led by 'Máel Finnia son of Flannácan, with the men of Brega and by Cerball son of Muiricá, with the Leinstermen; and they abandoned a good number of their ships (and escaped half dead after they had been wounded and broken)'.[12] In the fifteen years that followed, several Viking war-bands seem to have drifted east, looking for new lands and business opportunities. The first to be documented was led by a character called Ingimundr, who was beaten back from

Anglesey by a son of Cadell ap Rhodri, king of Gwynedd (Welsh rulers, unlike almost everyone else in Britain, seem to have been pretty successful at denying the Vikings a significant toehold).[13] After this setback he appeared near Chester where, having first done a deal with King Edward's sister, the redoubtable Æthelflæd of Mercia, he double-crossed the English and attacked the settlement. According to the version written up in the *Fragmentary Annals of Ireland*, Ingimundr's Vikings, thwarted by the town's defences, constructed a roof of hurdles to protect themselves while making a hole in the wall:

> What the Saxons and the Irish who were among them did was to hurl down huge boulders, so that they crushed the hurdles on their heads. What they [the Vikings] did to prevent that was to put great columns under the hurdles. What the Saxons did was to put the ale and water they found in the town into the town's cauldrons, and to boil it and throw it over the people who were under the hurdles, so that their skin peeled off them. The Norwegians' response to that was to spread hides on top of the hurdles. The Saxons then scattered all the beehives there were in the town on top of the besiegers, which prevented them from moving their feet and hands because of the number of bees stinging them.[14]

Perhaps unsurprisingly, having been crushed, scalded and molested by bees, Ingimundr 'gave up the city, and left it'. A good story, certainly. Whether it is true or not is impossible to say, but the town was 'renewed' by Æthelflæd in 907 – probably a reference to the refortification and replanning of the town as a burh.[15]

Ragnall first appears in the written record in 914, where we find him defeating a rival fleet off the Isle of Man.[16] A few years later he appears again, fighting alongside his kinsman Sihtric (another grandson of Ivar) in Ireland. A year after that, he took men from Waterford and went east, to Britain; there he found himself embroiled in conflict with Constantín II at Corbridge. The battle seems to have been indecisive, but Ragnall had evidently done enough to win trust in Northumbria. He was soon having coins minted in his own name at York, and remained in power in Northumbria until his death in 920, the same year in which the *Anglo-Saxon Chronicle* records him acknowledging the overlordship of Edward the Elder.[17] He was succeeded by Sihtric Cáech, his Irish brother-in-arms, who by this point was recognized as king in Dublin. Sihtric vacated that throne in order to take power in Northumbria, leaving Dublin to a further grandson of Ivar, a kinsman named Guthfrith (not to be muddled up with the Guthfrith we have met before). When Sihtric died in 927, this new Guthfrith also briefly acceded to the Northumbrian throne. It seems confusing, and it is. What emerges from all this intra-familial throne-swapping, however, is evidence of the ties – dynastic, political and economic – that were beginning to bind Viking Britain together, an east–west axis linking Northumbria to the Irish Sea.

That Viking war-bands with connections on both sides of the Pennines were operating in northern Britain in the early tenth century is implied by hoards of silver, of which several have been found across the north.[18] The most famous and substantial of these, the Cuerdale Hoard, is perhaps best explained as the war-chest of a large Viking army, the sort of force that might have been traversing the overland routes between York and the Irish Sea. It was discovered in 1840 by workmen repairing the banks of the River Ribble near Preston, Lancashire. One of the men, Thomas Horrocks, recalled his colleague, James Walne, pushing his spade into 'something like lime' and announcing 'at first it was like Cockle shells but immediately swore it was money'. So it was. Once the authorities had involved themselves and divested the workmen of the coins with which they had stuffed their pockets (they were each allowed to keep a single coin), the rest of the hoard was excavated – revealing, in the words of the Duchy of Lancaster's report to the coroner, 'a very large quantity of silver coins [...] besides some bars or Ingots of Silver, Chains, Armlets and Rings or Ring Money and more of the same sort of corroded metal [lead] which was ultimately supposed to have originally formed a box that had contained them'. The hoard was conveyed by wheelbarrow to Cuerdale Hall where it was taken indoors and laid out on the ground – there was so much of it that it 'covered the floor of one of the sitting rooms'.[19]

The hoard is vast, easily the largest Viking Age treasure ever found in Britain. It weighs some 90 pounds, containing around 7,000 coins plus over a thousand silver ingots and fragments of hack-silver. The coins are varied – Anglo-Saxon, Carolingian, Islamic, coins issued by Viking rulers at York and even a number in the name of 'Alwaldus', probably the doomed West Saxon ætheling Æthelwold – and allow the hoard to be dated to *c.* 905–10. Most of them were probably funnelled through York. The hack-silver, however, is dominated by jewellery from the Irish Sea region, and the hoard stands as testament to the connections – and the extraordinary wealth – that was being accumulated by Viking groups exploiting the opportunities that lay between Dublin and York.

In 924 Edward the Elder died. It seems likely that his final years were rather less successful than those leading up to 920 – the *Anglo-Saxon Chronicle*, at least, has not much to say about them, and it is possible that the servile postures supposedly adopted by the other kings and potentates of Britain in 920 were swiftly abandoned as the king began sliding towards the grave. We cannot say for certain. What is clear, however, is that the next king of Wessex – Edward's son Athelstan – would present a highly energetic challenge to all of the powers of the north. In 926 Athelstan married his sister to Sihtric Cáech, king of Northumbria, presumably with the hope of establishing a lasting political alliance and a formal bond of kinship with the Viking ruler and any potential offspring. Any such plans were thwarted however by Sihtric's death the following year. The new Viking claimant to the throne, Guthfrith, didn't last long. Presumably infuriated that his plans had come to naught, Athelstan took the direct approach, throwing Guthfrith out on his ear and burning down a stronghold inside York.[20] It was a defining moment in British history. For the first time, a single king had imposed his rule on the vast bulk of the territory that falls within the boundaries of the modern English nation. If Alfred had invented the idea of England, and Edward had begun to hammer it into shape, it was Athelstan who had drawn it whole from the fire – the first true king of England.[21]

His ambitions were not limited to England, however. In 927, Athelstan called an assembly at Eamont Bridge in Cumbria. In attendance were 'Hywel, king of the West Welsh, and Constantine, king of Scots, and Owain, king of Gwent, and Ealdred, Ealdwulf's offspring, from Bamburgh'. (The rulers of Bamburgh and the territory north of the Tyne seem to have retained a lasting autonomy from the 860s onwards.) Its ostensible purpose was to guarantee peace and forbid 'devil-worship', but the *Anglo-Saxon Chronicle* makes it very clear how Athelstan's power was seen from an English perspective: 'he governed all the kings who were in this island'.[22] This was the least of Athelstan's grandiosity: from 928, the kings of Wales began appearing as witnesses to Athelstan's charters, humiliatingly demoted to *sub-reguli* ('under-kinglets'), and Athelstan himself begins to be styled, not only as 'king of the English', but also, on his coinage, as *rex totius Britanniae*: 'king of all Britain'.[23]

It was doubtless this swollen sense of *imperium* that compelled Athelstan to war with Scotland in 934. We don't know exactly what prompted it,[24] but we can speculate that the Scottish king wasn't living up to the subservient standards Athelstan had set. It was an elaborate business: Athelstan gathered what seems to have been an enormous force, comprising warriors from England as well as allied contingents from Wales under the kings Hywel, Idwal and Morgan. Then 'going towards Scotia with a great army', Athelstan 'subdued his enemies, laid waste Scotia as far as Dunnottar and the mountains of Fortriu with a land force, and ravaged with a naval force as far as Caithness'.[25] The *Anglo-Saxon Chronicle* has a shorter version ('King Athelstan went to Scotland with both a *here* ['raiding army'] and a *sciphere* ['raiding fleet'] and harried across much of it'), the first time 'Scotland' appears in the historical record as a term to describe northern Britain.[26]

Constantín was beaten and humiliated, his son taken as a hostage, treasure extorted.[27] Later in the year, on 12 September 934, he could be found far from home at Buckingham (Buckinghamshire, England), witnessing a charter on behalf of his new master. He appears as a *sub-regulus* – just another little king.

Athelstan had all of the rulers of Britain troop out again the following year to undergo the same sort of abasement they had endured at Eamont Bridge, this time at Cirencester (Gloucestershire), where they were joined by Owain, king of Strathclyde (who may also have been at Eamont Bridge).[28] It was probably getting rather too much to bear for many of them. A Welsh poem composed around this time – *Armes Prydein Vawr* ('The Great Prophecy of Britain'), fantasized about a great pan-British alliance – 'the Cymry and the men of Dublin [...] The Irish of Ireland, Anglesey, and Scotland, the Cornish and the men of Strathclyde' – that would rise up to topple the hated English. Even the 'foreigners of Dublin will stand with us' runs the poem, to force the Saxons to 'pay seven times the value for what they have done, with certain death as payment for their wrong [...] Let blood, let death be their companions.'[29]

But it wasn't all fantasy: war was indeed coming. Olaf Guthfrithsson, the son of the man whom Athelstan had turfed out of York in 927, had been busy securing his own empire, fighting and plundering around Ireland throughout the 920s. By 937 – if not long before – he seems to have secured his power in Dublin, and in that year is referred to in Irish chronicles as 'Lord of the Foreigners', having broken the power of his rival – Amlaíb (Olaf) Cenncairech – at Limerick.[30] The victory seems to have given Olaf the freedom to pursue his father's claim to the Northumbrian kingship, and in that year he left Ireland to enter into an alliance with Constantín, king of Scots (who also seems to have roped in Owain of Strathclyde). They must have imagined that together they would be unstoppable, that they would invade England, take back the lands stolen from them, redeem their honour, trample 'the shitheads of Thanet' (as *Armes Prydein Vawr* calls the English) and leave them 'as food for wild beasts'.[31]

And as the armed men moved through the landscape, the wild beasts – 'corpse sharers, shadow coated' – stalked and followed them, circling overhead, running through woodland, flitting through the dark, expectant of slaughter and the feast to follow: 'the swart raven, horny of beak; the brown eagle of white tail-feather [...] and the silver one, the wolf of the weald'.[32] But it would not be English flesh they feasted on.

No one knows where the battle of Brunanburh was fought, and those who claim to – with any degree of certainty – are overplaying their hand. The problem is that only one place in England – Bromborough in the Wirral – has a place-name that can be definitively shown to derive from the Old English Brunanburh ('Bruna's stronghold'). The Wirral is directly across the water from Dublin, offering secure harbour in the Mersey for a substantial fleet (one source mentions 615 ships). Proximity to the Mercian border would have offered plenty of opportunities for raiding to the south, and overland routes from Lancashire across the Pennines (through the Aire Gap) would have led an army assembled at Bromborough directly to York. However, all of this is complicated by the chronicle of John of Worcester. In his account, Olaf's fleet is described as sailing up the Humber, on the east coast of Britain.

Arguments against John's version hinge on the assumption that it would have been ridiculous for Olaf to have taken his fleet all the way around the north of Britain to reach the other side before landing his army. To attack John's account on this basis, however, is absurd. We have no idea what Olaf did or why he might have done it (perhaps there were reinforcements and mercenaries he hoped to pick up along the way), and, since his objective seems to have been to reassert his claims over the kingship of Northumbria which hinged on control of York, it is perfectly reasonable to suppose that he took a route that brought him as close as possible to his goal. It certainly wasn't beyond the wit of early medieval mariners – only a year earlier, we might recall, Athelstan had dispatched a fleet to harry Caithness, the most north-westerly part of the British mainland. Equally weak is the argument that the reason for John's 'error' in placing Olaf on the Humber is that, because other Viking raids and invasions did indeed come up the Humber, John must have inserted this detail on his own initiative – either because he was confused, or just because it seemed plausible to him (that is, he made it up). It should be obvious that there are methodological problems in disregarding historical records simply because they don't fit a preconceived idea of what 'should' have happened. We just don't know.

What we do know is that the battle, wherever it was fought, shook the nations of Britain. Æthelweard, writing in the late 900s, wrote that 'a huge battle [*pugna immanis*] was fought against the barbarians at Brunandun, wherefore it is still called the "great war" [*bellum magnum*] by the common people'.[33] The *Chronicles of the Kings of Alba* told of the battle of Duin Brunde, 'where the son of Constantine was slain'. The Welsh Annals blankly referred to '*Bellum Brune*' ('the war of Bruin'), almost as if they couldn't bear to repeat the horrid details. The *Annals of Ulster*, however, recalled that 'a great, lamentable and horrible battle was cruelly fought between the Saxons and the Norsemen, in which several thousands of Norsemen, who are uncounted, fell, but their king, Amlaíb [Olaf], escaped with a few followers. A large number of Saxons fell on the other side, but Athelstan, king of the Saxons, enjoyed a great victory'.[34]

It is in the pages of the *Anglo-Saxon Chronicle*, however, that the battle was truly immortalized. In the E manuscript, the scribe simply recorded that 'King Athelstan led an army to Brunanburh'.[35] But it was in the A text that an unknown West Saxon poet went to town. In seventy-four lines of Old English verse, a monument was crafted that celebrated the martial prowess of Athelstan and his brother, the future King Edmund. It invoked the ghosts of the Anglo-Saxon conquerors of old and rubbed defeat in the faces of the other peoples of Britain – a bitter draught they would force down the throats of every idealist who dreamt that, one day, 'the Saxons will sing, "Woe!"'

One day soon the Saxons would indeed sing 'Woe!'; but it would not be this day. Now was the time to sing the triumphal song of a new, self-confident nation. England had been fathered, born and christened – now it had found a voice, and its voice was harsh and crowing. It was, in many ways, a suitable subject for translation by the poet laureate of Victoria's Empire, even if it stands a little at odds with the melancholia that characterizes much else of Alfred Tennyson's poetry:

Athelstan King,
Lord among Earls,
Bracelet-bestower and
Baron of Barons,
He with his brother,
Edmund Atheling,
Gaining a lifelong
Glory in battle,
Slew with the sword-edge
There by Brunanburh,
Brake the shield-wall,
Hew'd the lindenwood,
Hack'd the battleshield,
Sons of Edward with hammer'd brands.[36]

Athelstan's victory at Brunanburh ensured that his status was upheld for the rest of his life, and kept a lid on the simmering cauldron of grievance and aspiration that had given rise to the conflict in the first place. In the longer term, its memory inspired a burgeoning sense of English nationalism. When Athelstan died in Gloucester on 27 October 939, his death was not marked with any great fanfare in the *Anglo-Saxon Chronicle*. The *Annals of Ulster*, however, reported that 'Athelstan, king of the Saxons, pillar of the dignity of the western world, died an untroubled death.'[37] His reign, coinciding with that of Constantín II in Scotland, was pivotal for British history, with new identities crystallizing that would shape the history of the island for centuries.

In the short term, however, the immediate political significance of the battle was limited. The hegemony that Athelstan had established over Northumbria died with him, and the following decade and a half bore witness to one of the periods of intense political insecurity to which the Northumbrian kingdom had long been prone. Olaf Guthfrithsson, the Viking king of Dublin who had been defeated and humiliated at Brunanburh, was quick to take advantage.

# 19

# BLOODAXE

[...] that mighty
maker of men
ruled the land from beneath
his helmet of terror;
In York
the king reigned,
rigid of mind,
over rainy shores.

*Arinbjarnakviða*[1]

Within a year of Athelstan's death, Olaf Guthfrithsson was back in York, claiming power for himself apparently unopposed. He swiftly set about exerting his authority across Northumbria and extending his reach even further south, sacking Tamworth (Staffordshire) and annexing the towns of northern Mercia. This new Viking realm didn't last long, however. Olaf died in 941, possibly during a raid on Tyninghame in Lothian.[2] It was mere months before Athelstan's brother – the new King Edmund – came north to 'liberate' the so-called 'Five Boroughs' (Leicester, Lincoln, Nottingham, Stamford and Derby).

These events are celebrated in a poem in the *Anglo-Saxon Chronicle* which describes the forceful subjection of the 'Danish' population of northern Mercia to the heathen 'Norsemen' – the latter term being used to describe the Dublin-derived Vikings who were now back in power in York.[3] This narrative of unwelcome subjugation may be a fiction of sorts – it seems likely that some, at least, of the folk of northern Mercia would have been perfectly happy (or at least ambivalent) about swapping rule from Wessex with rule from York. But it does point to an interesting perception that was developing in England about the role of 'Danes' in English society. They were still evidently regarded as an ethnically distinct group and retained a distinctive legal status;[4] these 'Danish' English were presumably also distinguishable from the 'English' English by dress or dialect. But, while they were still Danes, they had briefly become – from a certain Anglo-Saxon perspective – 'our Danes'. This paternal attitude to England's immigrant communities was politically expedient in the 940s, but ultimately it would not last. The way a society treats its ethnic minorities can often reveal a great deal about a nation's political priorities and the challenges it faces, and things were no different in tenth-century England – the young nation was soon to be stress-tested to breaking point.

Those calamities, however, lay in the future. More immediately pressing was the bewildering cast of players who now began to agitate for the Northumbrian throne. The chronology of this period is confused (and confusing). Some of the individuals are indistinct to the point of vanishing altogether, and there is general disagreement among historians about the sequence and veracity of the events recorded. Nevertheless, the following paragraphs offer a summary which, if concise and complex, is not, I hope, misleading.

The claim of the West Saxon dynasty over Northumbria was weak. It had never, before the reign of Athelstan, been subject to southern kings, and its people were naturally mindful of their own distinct customs and cultural heritage. Since 866, this sense of Northumbrian particularism had been overlaid by a stratum of Scandinavian settlement and culture which – while it had changed much in the kingdom – had not fundamentally shaken its independence. Significant elements of the old Northumbrian hierarchy had survived – not least its ecclesiastical magnates, particularly the bishops of Lindisfarne and York – and there is a sense in which the Northumbrian elite were willing to accommodate Viking rulers, provided that they were able to offer a bulwark against the imperial ambitions of Alfred's descendants. Naturally, however, the political aspirations and calculations of factions within Northumbria meant that the individuals and dynasties ascendant at any one time could change rapidly, particularly when the political dynamics were being destabilized by the suddenly inflated power of the English kingdom to the south and – to a lesser extent – by the Scottish kingdom to the north.

In the 940s, the simmering potential for chaos seems finally to have bubbled over, precipitated by the deaths in rapid succession of Athelstan and Olaf Guthfrithsson. The secret deals and back-stabbing that resulted can only be seen obliquely in the sources that survive, but the political meltdown that resulted is all too apparent. Olaf Guthfrithsson was replaced as king in York by his cousin, Olaf Sihtricsson (also known as Olaf Cuarán, or Olaf Sandal). This Olaf was the son of Sihtric Cáech who had ruled in York before the previous Olaf's father, Guthfrith. At the same time, however, another son of Guthfrith – Ragnall (OE Rægnald) Guthfrithsson – also seems to have been in Northumbria pressing his father's (and deceased brother's) claim. At some point in all of this, a man called Sihtric (not the same man as the second Olaf's late father) was causing coins to be minted in Northumbria in his name. (The coins are the only evidence of his existence; he is not otherwise mentioned anywhere in the historical record.) According to the *Anglo-Saxon Chronicle*, however, in 944 King Edmund (like many a bemused student of the Viking Age) had had enough of these shenanigans, and 'brought all Northumbria into his power, and caused two kings to flee, Olaf Sihtricson and Rægnald Guthfrithsson.'[5]

Edmund was an energetic ruler, and swiftly got on with giving the people of Cumbria a hard time, ceding territory (possibly won from the kingdom of Stathclyde) to the new Scottish king Malcolm in a diplomatic move presumably intended to normalize relations on the Anglo-Scottish border. (Malcolm succeeded his father, Constantín II, who abdicated in 943, though he lived for another nine years. Constantín was at least sixty-four when he died, but is likely to have been considerably older, and had reigned for forty-three years; the Old English poem, *The Battle of Brunanburh*, set in 937, describes him as *har hilde-rinc* – 'the hoary (that is, old/silver-grey) warrior'. Silver-haired he may have been, but he had managed to outlive his English nemesis, Athelstan, by fourteen years.) Edmund's firm hand did not, however, bring an end to the turmoil in Northumbria. In 946 Edmund also died (stabbed by a chap called Liofa – described by John of Worcester as 'an atrocious robber'[6] – at Pucklechurch in Gloucestershire) and the new English king, Eadred, a younger brother of Athelstan and Edmund, was obliged to extract pledges of allegiance from the Northumbrian worthies. The north, however, had become ungovernable, and in 948 Eadred was heading there again. He had received the news that the Northumbrians, having renounced their oaths to him in 947, had invited another man to be their king.

His was a name to conjure with: Eric, son of King Harald Finehair of Norway, known to us as Eiríkr Blóðøx – Eric Bloodaxe.


The sources for Eric's earlier life in Norway are all late and are frequently contradictory, but all agree that he was a violent and belligerent man. As the idea of the Viking has percolated through the British psyche, Bloodaxe, over the course of the twentieth century, became emblematic of the domestic Viking; never mind that he was (at least nominally) a Christian and that he lived more of his life as a king than as an outlaw. His (nick)name is enough: it presents with effortless economy, with two short, emphatic syllables, the image of the screaming berserker with the wild beard and the bloodstained battle-axe, eyes rolling and mouth frothing with a lust for battle and a mania for death. The explanation for his nickname, however, was not simply the frequent doing of bloody deeds; those were so commonplace during the Viking Age (and not just on the part of 'Vikings') that it can hardly have raised an eyebrow, let alone inspired an epithet. No, what apparently set Eric apart from his peers were cruelty and kin-slaying. The twelfth-century Norwegian historian Theoderic the Monk described him as *fratris interfector* – 'brother-slayer'. When taken together, the range of sources for Eric's life suggest that Eric, alongside his wife Gunnhild (who, we are told, was a wicked, manipulative and beautiful enchantress – a literary trope for which human society apparently has an inexhaustible patience), was responsible for the deaths of no fewer than five of his brothers: five rival sons of King Harald Finehair bumped off in the pursuit of his own ruthless ambition.[7]

That ambition – to succeed his father and become the undisputed king of Norway – was ultimately fulfilled. Eric ruled as king of Norway for three years during his aged father's dotage and two after his death. But his fratricidal tendencies were to pay dividends of another sort. The end of Eric's reign in Norway was brought about by yet another of Harald's many sons – Haakon the Good, also known as Haakon Aðalsteinsfóstri ('Athelstan's foster-son'). Haakon was, according to the Old Norse saga tradition, raised as an Anglo-Saxon prince in the court of King Athelstan. English sources make no mention of this, but it is perfectly plausible. Fostering of this sort among aristocratic families seems to have been common, an accepted way of forging diplomatic and quasi-familial bonds, and the sagas record that Haakon governed Norway in a fashion far more typical of Anglo-Saxon kings than of their Norwegian counterparts.[8] When Haakon, with his legitimate claim to the Norwegian throne and powerful English connections, arrived in Norway, he provided Eric's many enemies with the perfect banner to rally behind. When the inevitable showdown came, Eric didn't even put up a fight.

Instead, Eric fled to England where, according to Snorri Sturluson's *Heimskringla*, he was accommodated by King Athelstan and deputed to rule in Northumbria; from there, it was said, 'he raided Scotland and the Hebrides, Ireland and Bretland, and so increased his wealth'.[9] Most of the Scandinavian sources broadly agree that Eric was active in Northumbria during the 930s. It is certainly possible that he held some sort of power in Northumbria during Athelstan's reign (we know very little about what exactly was happening in the region during this period), and it is also possible that he was involved in the power politics of the 940s; if this was the case, however, English sources make no mention of it. Whatever the truth, and whatever path he had taken to get there, by 948 Eric emerges into the contemporary historical record for the first time as the man chosen by the Northumbrians to be their king. Unfortunately for him, however, like his previous experiments with executive power, Eric's kingship was not an unqualified success. Immediately after he had been invited to take the throne, in 948 a peeved King Eadred sent an army north to show the Northumbrians who was boss, burning down Ripon Minster before heading back south. The Northumbrians, however, presumably on Eric's orders, 'overtook the king's army from behind at Castleford, and a great slaughter was made there'.[10] This, perhaps not surprisingly, displeased Eadred considerably, and proved to be a spectacular political blunder. 'The king became so enraged', the chronicler of the *Anglo-Saxon Chronicle* A text explains, 'that he wanted to raise an army and utterly destroy. When they heard that', the chronicler continues, 'they [the Northumbrian bigwigs] abandoned Eric and compensated King Eadred.'[11] It is a revealing comment, one which strongly indicates where the true backbone of Northumbrian independence lay.

A poem, composed in the tenth century (part of which is reproduced as the epigraph to this chapter), pictures Eric at York, brooding and sinister, his barren soul mirrored in the poet's evocation of the Yorkshire countryside: rain-wracked and storm-weathered. One can imagine him, with panic gripping York as word of the king's rage came north, holed up in his royal hall – taciturn, uncompromising, isolated – waiting for the political realities to come crashing down on his head. It is harder to imagine, however, how the city itself appeared in Eric's day. By the tenth century the Roman walls had been buried under an earthen bank with a corresponding ditch on the outer side, probably with a wooden palisade wall on the top and perhaps equipped with timber gate towers and walkways. There may have been stone towers too – the eleventh-century church tower of St Michael at the North Gate in Oxford was originally a free-standing masonry tower incorporated into the defensive circuit of the burh;[12] it is similar to York's oldest standing building, the eleventh-century tower of the Church of St Mary Bishophill Junior.

However, the vast hulking mass of York Minster, the great gothic cathedral that squats at the centre of the city's web of narrow streets and alleyways, was constructed between the thirteenth and fifteenth centuries (obliterating, in the process, much evidence for earlier churches and other buildings on the site). York Castle, or the surviving part of it (Clifford's Tower), is also a product of the late thirteenth century. Likewise, the walls of the city, though the lower courses in many places retain the Roman masonry, were rebuilt and renovated in stone in the thirteenth and fourteenth centuries before their restoration in the nineteenth.

Thus to the untrained eye it appears – despite the picturesque antiquity of the city – as though nothing of Viking Jorvik remains to be seen. But it's there, fundamental, an endoskeleton of words and roads that the intervening centuries have hung their flesh upon. Nearly all of the roads of York that predate the Norman Conquest are (or were) named with the suffix '-gate', from the Old Norse *gata* ('street'). Often the prefixes – which are sometimes Old English, sometimes Old Norse (often impossible to determine given the similarity of the languages), and sometimes Middle English or modern – provide clues to particular trades or notable characteristics of these places over time: Coppergate, for example, means the street of the wood-turners (that is, cup-makers from ON *koppari*);

Micklegate is the big street ('main street' is a better translation); Goodramgate is the street of Guthrum, a fine Scandinavian name. These roads follow what are almost certainly lines that were set in the ninth or tenth centuries, and the width of the houses and shop-fronts on these thoroughfares still preserves the dimensions of the plots of land that, divided by wattle fencing, were once occupied by the Viking Age townsfolk.[13]

Some of these plots have been excavated, most extensively so at Coppergate in digs carried out between 1967 and 1981. What these revealed was a city that, even as Eric Bloodaxe brooded in his hall, was undergoing an economic boom. Leatherwork and textile production, ironwork and copperwork, cup-making and carpentry, bone- and antler-craft, minting, amber-shaping and glass-recycling were all taking place with high intensity in the tenth-century city, many on an apparently industrial scale: moulds and crucibles for the mass production of jewellery and dies for coin production have been found and the sheer quantity of iron slag and wooden cores from cup- and bowl-making indicates production on a scale far beyond the domestic. Raw and manufactured goods were arriving from overseas – amber from the Baltic, silk from Byzantium, pottery from the Rhineland – and local produce was presumably exported via the same trading connections. Scales and large numbers of weights bear testament to the flourishing market that had developed at this commercial-industrial hub on the River Ouse – a major cog in the engine of North Sea trade.

And the population of York was growing too. Plots were becoming increasingly heavily utilized as the century wore on, more and more of the available space given up to timber buildings until the walls of each unit were almost touching its neighbour on either side. Rubbish pits were dug in backyards over and over again, to accommodate the sewage and the food waste, the industrial by-products and the general detritus. In the most waterlogged parts of the city, near the river, decomposition would have been slow and inefficient, parasites breeding in stagnant meres of mud and excrement. Ground level was rising by up to three-quarters of an inch every year (over the course of the tenth century an increase of between 3 and 6½ feet). The monastic writer Byrhtferth of Ramsay, writing at the end of the tenth century, put the population at 30,000. This may be an exaggeration, but the numbers were still high. Extrapolating from the density of settlement and the number of stray finds (principally of coins and pottery), as well as from the number of turds found preserved in the Viking Age soil, has enabled population estimates to be made in the region of 10,000–15,000, a 500 per cent increase on the population of pre-Viking York.[14] Gut worms were endemic and half of women died before they reached thirty-five (without childbirth to contend with, men could hope to hit fifty if they were lucky). In short, this was a society experiencing all of the typical problems of rapid urbanization: overcrowding, filth, disease, infestation.

It was also a city on the make. By 1066 it was easily the second largest in Britain (after London) and the hammers that smashed out thousands of silver coins in the names of Northumbria's Viking kings were working the city's abundant flow of silver into symbols of royal power and civic prestige. Even without evidence of coin production we would know that the coinage was produced in York from the legend that many of the coins bear: 'EBRAICE' (from 'Eboracum', the Latin name for the city). What is less clear is how much of this hustle and bustle was driven by Scandinavian immigrants and how much by native Northumbrians, or even whether such distinctions were noticed or considered important. The archaeology is equivocal – new trading links with Scandinavia certainly opened up, and new styles of object became fashionable. Shoes in a typically Scandinavian style, for example, started to be manufactured in the tenth century. But, crucially, traditional Northumbrian footwear remained in vogue, indicating that not only the expertise but also the market for both styles remained available and viable.[15] Thus the evidence can be argued from multiple perspectives. The only certainty is that tenth-century York was booming, and Scandinavian contacts and culture were playing a leading role.

Not that this made much difference to the political theatre playing out in the early 950s, except perhaps to raise the stakes for the players involved: York had become an attractive prize to kings of any stamp. The Northumbrians themselves, however, were fickle and – from a southern perspective – incorrigible. In 949 they recalled Olaf Sihtricsson to rule over them, but he didn't last long. In 952 Olaf was out, and Eric was back in.[16] This time, however, Eadred seems to have decided to apply pressure where it really mattered in Northumbria, hauling the archbishop of York to the stronghold at Jedburgh because, apparently, 'he was frequently accused to the king'. Nobody knows what threats and promises the king made to the archbishop there, but in 954 Eric was expelled from York for the second and final time; it can be no coincidence that the archbishop, in the same year, was finally restored to his lands by King Eadred. For the third time in his life, Eric Bloodaxe found himself in political exile.

This time, however, there was to be no comeback.

What is the worth of a king, he wonders, who has been driven out by his own subjects, hunted like a wolf's head over the mountains? He needs ships, and men. Perhaps he will go to Ireland. He doesn't know what welcome he might receive there – perhaps he will find kinsmen among the Dubliners, or someone to whom his name still means something, still carries weight. He is tired, mud-splattered, shoulders hunched, his horse slipping on wet stones in the pass. Turning in the saddle, he looks back at the column of dejected men behind him, fewer now he thinks than when they left York.

'*Niþings*,' he murmurs; 'cowards, oath-breakers.'

He is always looking back: listening for sounds of pursuit, watching for the carrion birds that herald the approach of pursuing armies. But he sees only the grim clouds and the grey land, the stones and the heather, the dull mud; a world rinsed of colour. He pulls his cloak, damp and heavy, tightly around himself, turns towards the wind that drives the rain into his face, and carries slowly on.

It is bleak on Stainmore, treeless and rugged, a high wind-scoured upland that reaches 1,370 feet above sea level; there is no protection up here from the Atlantic weather that comes billowing from the west. When I went there it was foul, a cold driving rain forcing me back into the car to sit miserably in a lay-by on the side of the A66, the busy trunk road connecting Carlisle in the north-west to Catterick in the east, by way of Penrith and Barnard Castle, heavy freight thundering past on its way across the Pennines. A few minutes in the elements were quite enough for me, but for Eric in 954, trying to break west for the sea, there would have been no rest and no respite. Perhaps there would have come a moment up here when he saw the land drop away to the west, the blue fells marching on the horizon, the westering sun dazzling him as it dipped below the slate-grey clouds – a beacon of white light offering the promise of salvation. If it did it might have lightened his heart for a moment – held out the hope of a new life and refuge, an opportunity to find the time and space to plan his political renaissance. Perhaps he saw himself coming back this way, at the head of a glorious host, a king of kings. But perhaps he didn't even make it as far as I did.

It is unclear how Eric died, but it was not from internal parasites. He likely had them (as everyone who spent any time in York probably did), and a perennially itchy arsehole can only have contributed to his bad mood. But the sources, though they differ wildly in most respects, are in agreement on one key issue: that Eric Bloodaxe died a violent death. The Norwegian so-called 'synoptic histories' – *Ágrip af Nóregskonungasögum* ('A Synopsis of the Sagas of the Kings of Norway') and *Historia Norwegiæ* – record a tradition that Eric died raiding in Spain, the least plausible explanation of how he met his end.[17] Other sources agree that Eric died in Britain, but the manner of his death, however, remains far less certain. According to the Anglo-Norman historian Roger of Wendover, 'King Eric was treacherously killed by Earl Maccus in a certain lonely place which is called Stainmore, with his son Haeric and his brother Ragnald, betrayed by Earl Oswulf; and then afterwards King Eadred ruled in these districts.'[18] Oswulf was the quasi-autonomous ruler at Bamburgh in the north of Northumbria, and was to become Earl of Northumbria under Eadred when Eric was dead. In this version of events we can see Eric dying with a dagger between his ribs – bleeding out the last of Northumbrian liberty on a lonely moor, friendless and betrayed, his ertswhile companions turning their mounts back to York to tell Oswulf that the dark deed was done, the last impediment to his own ambition now removed.

The sagas, however, tell a different story; a story of how King Játmundr (Edmund) 'mustered an invincible army and went against King Eiríkr, and there was a great battle [...] and at the end of that day King Eiríkr fell and five kings with him'.[19]

In the Norse mythological cycle, the death of the gods at *Ragnarök* represents the tragic, heroic, final stand of a world doomed to die. Of all the deaths and endings it is the death of Odin that is the most poignant, the one that speaks most clearly to the contradiction at the heart of the human condition. Odin may be the darkest of the gods, but he is also the most like us. He has watched the ebb of time across the ages, the rise and fall of kings and nations, the petty hurts and feeble triumphs of humanity. And despite knowing it to be futile, that ultimately he must fight the wolf and fail, he has prepared carefully for that day, selecting and curating the champions who will fight beside him when the last sun rises over the battle-plain. The *einherjar*, they are called, the glorious dead, doomed to die on earth in battle in order that they may fight again, one last time. It is this bloody-mindedness – the obsessive quest for wisdom though it brings no peace, the desire to gain knowledge of a future that cannot be circumvented, the relentless preparation for a doom that cannot be avoided – that reminds us of our own self-defeating consciousness, the knowledge of mortality that defines our humanity.

The capacity to think, to remember, to dream, to prepare against whatever the future holds – all of it leads inevitably to the only certainty that the universe can provide: that all things fade and all things fail. And yet, like Odin, we struggle on heedless of the long defeat, wading against the tide that one day will overwhelm everything. It was acceptance of this harsh reality that permeated Viking warrior culture, shaping its mentality and appetite for adventure – the willingness to stare death and defeat in the eye, knowing that to carry on is futile and that failure is assured, yet determined to fight on regardless, to struggle until the last breath is spent. It is in that struggle – internal, ethical – that true bravery lies; and there, precisely there, eyeball to eyeball with death unflinching, was the place where legends could be born that might outlast the living.

This desire to be remembered – to secure true immortality in the stories told after death – was the force that drove composition of eulogies and praise-poems, the contemporary material on which so much of our knowledge of Viking kings is ultimately founded. When Eric died, his wife was said to have commissioned a poem that commemorated his life and his deeds. The result, *Eiríksmal*, pictures the arrival of the great king in Valhöll, 'the hall of the slain', to take his place among the *einherjar*, the heroes of the past – with Sigmund and his son Sinfjǫtli – and sit by Odin's side. There he would enjoy the pleasures of the hall that are described in the eddic poem *Grímnismál* and by Snorri in *Gylfaginning*: to feast on the hog Saehrimnir who replenishes his flesh every evening; to fight the endless duels with the other *einherjar*, battling without hurt; to drink the mead that flows unending from the udders of the goat Heidrun, brought by valkyries in gilded cups: a warrior's paradise, filled with all the pleasures of a macho life.[20]

The poem, only the beginning of which survives, is cast as a conversation between Odin, the legendary poet Bragi, Sigmund and Eric himself.

O: 'What kind of dream is this, that I thought that a little before daybreak I was preparing Valhǫll for a slain army? I awakened the *einherjar*, I asked them to get up to strew the benches, to rinse the drinking cups, [I asked] valkyries to bring wine, as if a leader should come. I expect certain glorious men from the world [of the living], so my heart is glad.'

B: 'What is making a din there, as if a thousand were in motion, or an exceedingly great throng? All the bench-planks creak, as if Baldr were coming back into Óðinn's residence.'

O: 'The wise Bragi must not talk nonsense, though you know well why: the clangour is made for Eiríkr, who must be coming in here, a prince into Óðinn's residence. Sigmundr and Sinfjǫtli, rise quickly and go to meet the prince. Invite [him] in, if it is Eiríkr; it is he I am expecting now.'

S: 'Why do you expect Eiríkr rather than other kings?'

O: 'Because he has reddened his blade in many a land and borne a bloody sword.'

S/B: 'Why did you deprive him of victory then, when he seemed to you to be valiant?'

O: 'Because it cannot be known for certain when the grey wolf will attack the home of the gods.'

S: 'Good fortune to you now, Eiríkr; you will be welcome here, and go, wise, into the hall. One thing I want to ask you: what princes accompany you from the edge-thunder [battle]?'

E: 'There are five kings; I shall identify for you the names of all;
I am myself the sixth.'[21]

*Eiríksmal*, unlike the detailed descriptions in *Grímnismál* and *Gylfaginning*, dates to the Viking Age itself. It offers a vivid and immediate depiction of Valhöll and the relationship between Odin, his champions, and his messengers, the *valkyrjur*, the 'choosers of the slain' – the spirits of death and conflict who haunted the battle-fields of the Viking imagination. In the courtly poetry of *Eiríksmal*, valkyries were already undergoing the transformation that would see them become cleaned-up icons of femininity – servile cup-bear-ers and entertainers for the exclusive clientele at Valhöll, the precur-sors of the romanticized visions of nineteenth-century painters and the buxom Wagnerian parodies of popular imagination. But for most Vikings these lesser deities would have been possessed of wilder and more savage personae, terrifying war-spirits with names to chill the soul: Tanngniðr ('teeth-grinder'); Svava ('killer'); Skǫgul ('battle'); Randgniðr ('shield-scraper'); Hjalmþrimul ('helmet-clat-ter'); Geirdríful ('spear-flinger') …[22]

In 954, when the *valkyrjur* came shrieking from the heavens, screaming over the corpse-strewn Stainmore Pass to harvest the souls of the dead and dying, we must picture them coming, not from the clear, crisp skies of Norway or Denmark, nor even from the cold skies above Iceland's ashen peaks, but from the drear, leaden clouds of Yorkshire – come to claim Northumbria's last king.

# 20

# WOLVES

We pay them continually and they humiliate us daily; they ravage
and they burn, plunder and rob and carry to the ship; and lo!
what else is there in all these happenings except God's anger
clear and evident over this nation?

ARCHBISHOP WULFSTAN,
'The Sermon of the Wolf to the English' (1014)[1]

I t was 1006 and the Viking army had come from bases in the Isle
of Wight, riding unopposed through the heart of Wessex – from
Hampshire into Berkshire, from Reading to Wallingford, burning
as they went. There they turned on to the Ridgeway, the path that
so many armies in the past had taken, and travelled east to
Cwichelm's Barrow (a place known today as Skutchmer Knob).
There, the *Anglo-Saxon Chronicle* relates, they prepared for the
showdown they had been promised and 'awaited the boasted
threats, because it had often been said that if they sought out
Cwichelm's Barrow they would never get to the sea'.[2]

The barrow, a Bronze Age burial mound, was the shire meeting
place of Berkshire. It was a place of power and belonging, an
upwelling of the ancient past around which the English organized
their lives and, perhaps, a point of access to their own past.
Cwichelm was a figure of legend, a West Saxon king who, it was
said, had slain 2,045 Britons at a place called Beandun ('Bea's Hill')

in 614 – a warrior ancestor whose blade was sorely needed by the English in the dark days of the early eleventh century. Perhaps there was a belief that the dead king was somehow present, that he slumbered under the mound like Arthur, ready to rise up and drive the enemies of the English to their doom.[3] Perhaps this was the story that the Vikings had heard from their victims as the southern shires burned – a defiant threat spat through blood – that if they dared ride too far, if they probed too deeply into the kingdom's heart, Cwichelm would get them. Or perhaps this was where the muster of Berkshire would assemble, a formidable phalanx of West Saxon warriors ready to stand firm in the presence of their ancient king. Perhaps the Vikings who came here felt a creeping dread as they approached from the west, the dark mound casting long shadows in the wan mid-winter light, skeleton trees clutching at the gloomy threatening skies. They knew that the dead shuffled uncomfortably in their chambered tombs, *draugr* who might hunt the living if awoken by the clumsy or the careless.[4]

But no one came; neither the living nor the dead. It was as though everything had deserted the English – even their ancestors.

The Viking army travelled back along the Ridgeway, west towards Avebury where the path turned towards the south, plunging over the edge of the chalk downs into the Pewsey Vale and the low country that rolls away towards the sea. It was here that the Anglo-Saxons chose to mount their defence, a last bid to halt the Viking horde as it made its way back to the Isle of Wight. Word had travelled, watch-fires flickering up from hill to hill, points of angry flame in the grey December twilight, summoning men from Avebury and Marlborough to follow the herepaths – the army-roads – to muster.

They would have seen and heard the carrion birds first, the tattered black shapes wheeling and cascading over the Ridgeway, their hollow, rasping cries announcing the arrival of the Viking army. Larger birds of prey might have joined them, buzzards or even eagles, circling high above the squalling crows. In the woodland that crept up the hillside from the valley floor to the circle of hoary megaliths where the English waited, other shapes might have been seen, moving furtively among the shadows of the ancient trees: a shaggy pelt, a lupine silhouette, a red eye caught in the pale light of the mid-winter sun.

These animals – the crow and raven, wolf and eagle – have a privileged place in early medieval battle literature. Old English verse records a multitude of sightings of these creatures, almost always in connection with death and violence. *The Battle of Brunanburh* describes how the victorious English 'left behind to divide the corpses the dark-coated one, the black raven, the horn-beaked one, and the dusk-coated one: the white-tailed eagle, to enjoy the carrion, that greedy war-hawk, and that grey beast, the wolf of the weald'. Old Norse skalds also tended to use these 'beasts of battle' in triumphal eulogies to successful warlords. 'Great' kings, like Eric Bloodaxe, were routinely praised as bountiful feeders of wolves and fatteners of ravens:

Battle-cranes swooped
over heaps of dead,
wound-birds did not want
for blood to gulp.
The wolf gobbled flesh,
the raven daubed
the prow of its beak
in waves of red.
The troll's wolfish steed
met a match for its greed.
Eirik fed flesh
to the wolf afresh.[5]

The frequency with which these images were deployed is so high that it has come to be thought of as a 'topos', a conventional poetic device thrown in whenever a poet wanted to signal the anticipation or commemoration of violence. Recent zoological research, however, has demonstrated that there is a strange symbiosis between wolves and corvids in the way in which these eaters of the dead track carrion. Wolf packs will follow the movements of airborne scavengers, using their enhanced perspective to identify easy pickings. Perhaps more surprising is anecdotal evidence which suggests that ravens and wolves are able to recognize and follow groups of armed men. In a modern context this has been interpreted as an environmental adaptation to the probability that humans wielding weapons are a likely predictor for the availability of conveniently pre-killed food (through the by-products of hunting). In the early medieval period, however, the presence of large groups of armed men often meant that killing of a different sort was in the offing.[6]

Overton Hill, near Avebury in Wiltshire, is still an eerie and desolate spot. It lies at a crossroads between two ancient paths: one the track of the Ridgeway that cuts its white furrow across the chalk uplands of southern England for 87 miles through Wiltshire and Berkshire, the other the Roman road from Bath to London, now imperfectly followed by parts of the A4. It is an old landscape. The West Saxons knew the place as *seofan beorgas* – the 'seven barrows' – and the mounds of these ancient tumuli still stud the flat high ground where the roads cross, some of them now smothered with beech stands, giving them the appearance of hairy warts standing out across the closely shaved farmland that surrounds them. There are, in fact, more than seven, most of them Roman or Bronze Age in date, though some were reused in the Anglo-Saxon period for secondary burials: a warrior buried with his shield and spear, a woman buried with her child.[7]

From the Seven Barrows the Anglo-Saxons would have been able to see the strange man-made sugar-loaf hill of Silbury and the great long-barrows of East and West Kennet; most prominent of all, however, was the stone circle at their back. Now known as 'the Sanctuary', the circle was once an impressive monument – two concentric circles of standing stones (the outermost with a diameter of about 130 feet) erected in around 2000 BC, once connected by a long avenue to the enormous stone ring that still stands at Avebury, just over a mile to the north-west.[8] The stones of the Sanctuary now are long gone, blown up in the eighteenth century by the local landowner, but in 1006 it would have stood, ruinous, wind-swept and rime-scoured, an eerie monument to unfathomable antiquity.

It still feels uncanny up on Overton Hill; the landscape is open, exposed, and the wind howls up from the Pewsey Vale, mercilessly driving the clouds overhead. As I walked up the Ridgeway away from the Sanctuary I could see it coming – the brownish veil that smothers the light and blurs the hard edges of things. Rarely have I felt so miserable on a country walk as I did that day, caught in heavy weather at the Seven Barrows. 'There are many pleasanter places', said the one-eyed bagman in Dickens' *Pickwick Papers*, '[…] than the Marlborough Downs when it blows hard; and if you throw in beside, a gloomy winter's evening, a miry and sloppy road, and a pelting fall of heavy rain, and try the effect, by way of experiment, in your own proper person, you will experience the full force of this observation.' It is an ordeal that I have been unwillingly subjected to and can heartily agree that the bagman had the measure of it.

There is no way of knowing what the weather was like on Overton Hill in December 1006, but given the time of year it is unlikely to have been clement. For the English army, waiting in the freezing cold for a Viking host to break the horizon, it would have been a grim place to wait, rain or no. If they still hoped for help from the dead, for some supernatural assistance from the ancient landscape in which they drew their battle-lines, they would once again be disappointed. By the end of the day, the English had been routed from the field, and the Viking host continued its triumphant return to the coast, laden down with plunder.

As they passed the king's capital at Winchester, they jeered at the hapless townsfolk, cowering behind the walls.

*

The events of 1006 were typical of the calamity that befell England between 980 and 1016: a generation of escalating misery during which time Viking armies roamed practically unopposed across the rolling hills of southern England, looting and burning at will. A sense of the scale of the violence can be gauged simply by the number of conflicts recorded, particularly once the eleventh century got under way. Across England, there were (give or take) eighty-eight instances of armed violence recorded in the written record in the thirty-five years up to and including 1016; this compares with fifty-one conflict events recorded over the whole of the preceding eighty years. For the people of southern England, whose experience of Viking incursions had dissipated in the early tenth century, it would have felt as though a forgotten nightmare had dragged itself upright from the mire – a revenant horror, long thought staked and buried, stalking abroad once more.

There are, of course, some issues here about the trustworthiness of the written record – chroniclers sometimes had a vested interest in minimizing or exaggerating the travails of various monarchs – but it is evident that the quarter-century after Eric Bloodaxe's death in 954 had been noteworthy for its stability, its lack of dramatic incident. This seems, in large part, to have been down to the firm grip of one king – a man largely forgotten today, but with a good claim to being one of the most successful and impressive of the Anglo-Saxon kings of England: Edgar *pacificus* – Edgar the Peaceful. It is a name that conjures up images of quiet and contemplation, a just and gentle ruler whose benevolent rule would usher in the golden age of peace and plenty that twelfth-century chroniclers imagined he and his subjects had enjoyed. It was they, however, and not his peers, who conferred the epithet *pacificus* upon him: his contemporaries would take a rather different view.[9]

King Eadred died in 955, one year after seeing his rule extended, formally and finally, to include Northumbria within the English kingdom. He was succeeded by his nephew Eadwig, Edmund's son, but he died in 959 and was succeeded by his brother, Edgar. The most famous achievement of Edgar's reign – and the one incident for which he is chiefly remembered – came towards the end of his life. In 973, he arrived at Chester with – according to the *Anglo-Saxon Chronicle* – his entire naval force, there to meet with the other principal rulers of Britain. Different Norman historians give varying lists of the potentates who were present, but probably among them were Kenneth II of Scotland, Malcolm of Strathclyde, Iago ab Idwal Foel of Gwynedd and Maccus Haraldsson, whom William of Malmesbury called *archipirata* ('arch-pirate') and others referred to as *plurimarum rex insularum* ('king of many islands' – probably Man and the Hebrides).[10] No doubt there were serious and practical issues to discuss – matters of borders and security and the safety of shipping and trade and so on. What Anglo-Norman historians saw fit to record happening there, however, was a most extraordinary spectacle: at least half a dozen of the most powerful men in the islands, cowed into submission by Edgar's majestic presence (or, more likely, the menacing presence of his enormous war-fleet), rowing the English king in a barge down the River Dee. It was a very physical, and very public, demonstration of what it meant to be a 'little kinglet' in Edgar's Britain.

It may be that the way this incident was reported in Anglo-Norman sources was deliberately intended to promote an anachronistic idea of English superiority – issues of insular power dynamics were very much alive in the twelfth and thirteenth centuries and, indeed, have never really gone away. But there is little doubt about who was at the top of the British political food chain in the 970s and, regardless of the details of what took place, it seems likely that the meeting was partly concerned with thrashing out issues of precedence, of putting lands, people and princes into their rightful places; for Edgar seems to have been a king who was obsessed with order. His laws reveal an administration that was determined to regulate and reform – creating nationwide standards of weights and measures and ensuring that coinage was made to uniform standards everywhere it was produced: gone were the idiosyncratic designs of the old Viking kings at York. Edgar's coinage would look and weigh the same, whether it was minted there, or in Exeter,

Chester, Canterbury, Lincoln or Norwich (or anywhere else that coins were made). He was also interested in bringing the whole of his realm into administrative harmony and ensuring that justice was both available and correctly applied. Wessex had long been organized by shires and hundreds, but everywhere else had had different (though perhaps similar) systems of organization. Edgar – perhaps drawing on precedents set by his immediate predecessors – formalized this system, creating new stipulations for the way that courts were held at the hundred (or wapentake in 'Danish' areas) and shire level, making attendance obligatory for the land-holding class.

What really cemented Edgar's legacy, however, was the unprecedented period of peace and stability that England seems to have enjoyed until his death in 975. It was a peace that was achieved to a certain degree at the expense of others: repeated punitive raids into Welsh territory demonstrate that Edgar, despite his nickname, was no pacifist.[11] (Indeed, *pacificus* can be translated as 'Pacifier', just as it can as 'Peaceable' or 'Peaceful'.) It was also a peace paid for through unprecedented investment in the kingdom's naval defences: during his reign the number of English warships, according to later accounts, reached an improbable 4,800,[12] and it is likely that reforms to the manner in which ships and mariners were recruited and obliged to serve the king began during Edgar's reign. It also seems likely that the king's naval power was founded in part on paid fleets of Viking mercenaries. The swelling of English royal authority may have meant that, for some Viking war-bands plying the seas around Britain, the risks of plunder were becoming intolerably high, while at the same time the wealth that the English king commanded may have become an increasingly attractive source of patronage to those prepared to work for him.

All of these achievements added up to what most medieval writers felt constituted a 'Good King': he enforced justice, brought prosperity, upheld the Church and bullied and humiliated all the other (non-English) inhabitants of Britain – especially the Welsh. This was the sort of thing that was guaranteed to ensure a favourable write-up, and indeed his obituary in the D text of the *Anglo-Saxon Chronicle* is largely comprised of effusive praise. And yet, in the eyes of the chronicler – almost certainly Archbishop Wulfstan II of York (d. 1023) – all of his achievements were undermined by the 'one misdeed [...] he practised too widely'. King Edgar, Wulfstan disgustedly reveals, 'loved foul foreign customs and brought heathen habits into this land too firmly, and he enticed outsiders and lured dangerous foreign-folk into this country'.[13]

This censure may have stemmed in part from the pragmatic and conciliatory approach that Edgar adopted. Large parts of his realm had been settled by people of Scandinavian origin for over a century, producing a mixed population whose tastes, trading connections and family ties were as intimately tangled with the wider North Sea world as they were with the populations of Winchester, London or Canterbury. Edgar understood that local interests and national cohesion could be jointly served by recognizing the distinctiveness of local laws and customs in those regions which had become – in Anglo-Saxon parlance – 'Danish'. In his fourth major law code, Edgar promised that 'there should be in force amongst the Danes such good laws as they best decide [...] because of your loyalty, which you have always shown me'.[14] The sudden shift from third to second person feels clumsy when written down, but read out loud at a Northumbrian wapentake or north Mercian *thing*-site, it may have had real dramatic force: that sudden turn to the camera, the steady eye contact that the pronouns imply, delivered a disarmingly direct and personal address from the king exclusively to his Danish subjects.

In some ways, this recognition of a separate and parallel legal tradition stands at odds with Edgar's stated intention (in the same code) to create laws for 'all the nation, whether Englishmen, Danes or Britons, in every province of my dominion'.[15] But, seen more broadly, this limited concession (it does not seem to have overruled all the king's other edicts relating to coinage and administration) can be understood as the product of a keen political intelligence, one that recognized that – in the long term – the cause of national unity was better served by establishing trust and mitigating griev-ance than by lumbering authoritarianism. The result was the real 'Danelaw', a practical solution intended to bring the most reluctant of his new subjects willingly inside his vision for a coherent and cohesive English state.

Attitudes towards strangers in Anglo-Saxon England had not always been kind, but xenophobia seems to have peaked in the late tenth century, perhaps buoyed by the rising sense of English iden-tity that had been growing since the reign of Athelstan but condi-tioned over two centuries of Viking depredations of one sort or another. For his own part, the king seems to have been alive to any threat that such sentiments could pose to the peace of his realm (and his revenues). In 969, 'King Edgar ravaged across all of Thanet,' apparently because the locals had roughed up some Scandinavian traders. Hostility to foreign nationals on England's estuarine outposts has a distressingly long history, but few have responded so robustly as Edgar. According to the Norman historian Roger of Wendover, the king was 'moved with exceeding rage against the spoilers, deprived them of all their goods, and put some of them to death'.[16]

It was presumably this sort of thing that so offended Archbishop Wulfstan. In 975, however, he would doubtless have been relieved to discover that no longer would he have to endure the 'foul foreign customs' that Edgar had so perversely enjoyed. For in that year the king died. He was thirty-one years old. There followed a disputed succession and the short reign of Edgar's son Edward, known as 'the Martyr' – the last of the long line of 'Ed' kings. When Edward died in March 978, he was replaced by his brother Æthelred. The new king was only a boy of twelve, but he came to the throne already in shadow, his people divided in their loyalties: Edward had died, not of natural causes like their father, but at the hands of men loyal to Æthelred, done to death at Corfe (Dorset). Whether the new king was himself complicit in the killing has generally been doubted by historians, but it can have done little to endear those people to him who had supported his brother's claim. Even as stories of Edward's (improbable) sanctity and martyrdom began to spread, so Æthelred's reputation was stained – like Eric's – with fratricide. Little that occurred over the following forty years would help to restore it.

Thirteen years into Æthelred's reign, in 991, a Viking fleet arrived on the River Blackwater in Essex or, as it was known then, the Pant (OE *Pante*). These were not the first Vikings to return to England after Edgar's death; raids are recorded from 980 onwards and continued with little pause thereafter. The crown's authoritarian grip seems to have slackened with mortality and inter-familial strife and it is possible that, distracted by a succession crisis, the English administration had become a less reliable paymaster than it had been in Edgar's day, leaving swarms of unemployed marauders plying the coastal waters. Southampton, Thanet and Cheshire were attacked in 980 (the latter menaced *Norwegenensibus piratis*, according to John of Worcester) and Padstow (Cornwall) in 981. Portland, the scene of the first recorded Viking raid in Britain, was raided in 982, two centuries after the first 'Northmen' had spilled Ealdorman Beaduheard's blood on the Portland strand. In the same year London was burned. In 986 Vikings attacked Watchet (Devon), and in 991 a fleet arrived that harried Folkestone and Sandwich (Kent), before sailing north to assault Ipswich (Suffolk). This fleet – of ninety-three ships – was led by a warlord named in the *Anglo-Saxon Chronicle* as Olaf. Most would agree that that individual can be identified as Olaf Tryggvason, a Norwegian aristocrat who would later – as king – be instrumental in the (often brutal) Christianization of Norway.

Olaf's army was met on the Blackwater by an army led by the Essex ealdorman Byrhtnoth at Northey Island, a chunk of land adrift in the estuary, connected by only a narrow tidal causeway. Seen from above – as no one in 991 could have seen it – the frayed edges of the land are an alien wilderness, a madness of trackless patterns and dark pools, spiral rivulets and twisting gulleys, the rising and falling tidal waters cleansing and hollowing banks and channels, depositing the salts and nutrients that sustain a complex ecology of insects and wading birds; it is a dying landscape – swallowed by the rising waters, obliterated by accelerating climate change. A thousand years ago, the land was higher and Northey Island was closer to the mainland. But it would have presented a similar panorama – mud and water, brine and seabirds, the yellowing marsh-grasses and the cushions of dank moss, a flat and broken vista under an endless sky. The English were assembled on the mainland. Out beyond the flooded causeway, the Viking host stood arrayed on the island, their ships moored across the estuary – a hundred masts jutting from the still water like the ruins of a forest, blasted and drowned in the river waters. And there they stood, facing one another, bellowing their insults across the salt-flats as the gulls wheeled overhead.

We would know very little about what happened at the Blackwater were it not for the survival of an extraordinary poetic fragment, *The Battle of Maldon*, which offers in 325 lines of Old English verse a detailed and dramatic account of what transpired. The poem lacks its beginning and its end, a loss that predates the early eighteenth century, but it is remarkable that the poem survives at all. It formed part of the Cotton library (named after its collector, the MP and antiquarian Sir Robert Cotton, 1571–1631), an enterprise of far-sighted bibliophilia undertaken in the wake of the Dissolution of the Monasteries of the 1530s. Cotton's efforts preserved the Lindisfarne Gospels and the vast bulk of surviving Old English poetic literature, among many other priceless works, but all were nearly lost in 1731 when the building in which the library was preserved – the aptly named Ashburnham House – caught fire. Much was saved – including the badly singed *Beowulf* manuscript, but *The Battle of Maldon* was destroyed. Thankfully, however, the poem had been transcribed in 1724 – less than seven years before the fire. It is this version that now provides the basis of all modern versions of the poem.

Twenty-five lines into the surviving poem, the reader encounters a Viking spokesman shouting his demands across the water, for rings (*beagas*) and speedily sent tribute (*gafol*) to avert the otherwise inevitable killing. The response that the poet places in Byrhtnoth's mouth is the father of all doomed declamations of defiance, words that find their echo in every steadfast utterance delivered throughout England's pugnacious history: the resolve of a proud nation – in the first century of its self-consciousness – to choose death before dishonour. 'Out spoke Byrhtnoth,' the poet proclaims,

> lifted his shield, shook his slim ash spear, held forth with words and, angry and single-minded, gave him answer:
>
> 'Do you hear, sea-wanderer, what this nation says? They will give you spears as tribute, the poison-tipped javelin and ancient swords, those warlike accoutrements which will profit you nothing in battle. Seamen's spokesman, report back again; tell your people much more distasteful news: that here stands a worthy earl with his troop of men who is willing to defend this his ancestral home, the country of Æthelred, my lord's nation and land. The heathens shall perish in battle.'[17]

There would be blood. And yet, to fight across the causeway was impossible; for a proper battle to take place, the Viking army had to be allowed to cross, and this is precisely what Byrhtnoth, on account of *ofermod*, determined to do. This word – 'over-mood' rendered literally into modern English – has stimulated an enormous amount of speculation and learned wrangling over its precise meaning. Tolkien saw it in almost irredeemably negative terms – as hubris, overweening pride and misplaced confidence, a personal flaw that doomed Byrhtnoth, his men and his nation to destruction.[18] Others, however, have stressed the connotations of exceptional courage, unusual reserves of energy and spirit.[19] The ambiguities are obvious – does 'over' in this context imply 'too much' or an exceptional quantity? What, precisely, does 'mood' mean when it is left unqualified? My personal view is that the ambiguity is deliberate, that the poet has chosen to use a term that is essentially an empty vessel, ready to be filled with our own value judgements; all we see is Byrhtnoth, overflowing with spirit, with gusto, with eagerness to go head on with fate – it is up to us, readers or listeners, to judge his motives and his wisdom.

Across the river 'the slaughter-wolves waded, caring not for the water, the Viking war-band; they came west over Pant, bearing shield-boards over bright water and up onto land, linden-wood braced'.[20]

Some have observed the strategic sense of allowing the Viking army to cross; it was perhaps the only opportunity to bring this Viking horde to battle and prevent them from continuing the coastal rampage that had already struck Folkstone, Sandwich and Ipswich.[21] This may be so, although it is worth remembering that this is a poem – a self-consciously literary product – and may not reflect reality with any great accuracy. Its purpose was to emphasize Byrhtnoth's courage, his stoicism and the resolve of his closest followers to stand and die beside him rather than face the ignominy of surrender or retreat.

Byrhtnoth, for all his valiant leadership, was struck down by a spear and died a prolonged Hollywood death – fending off foes until finally slumping to the earth. Some of the English fled the battlefield, the poet ensuring that their names (Godric, Godwine and Godwig) would live for ever in infamy for what was – in reality – probably the wiser path in the circumstances. But wisdom was not what was at stake here: the animating ethic was one of loyalty, even in death, and of the moral courage that the English shared with their Viking enemies – the idea that to face death unflinching, though it came at them up the salt-flats as inevitably as the tide, and to die in heaps around the body of their slain lord was the greatest end to which a warrior could aspire.

The words that the poet gives to the elderly retainer Byrhtwold, steadfast despite Byrhtnoth's demise, echo down the centuries as the unparalleled expression of heroism in defeat, the determination to go down fighting while all around 'fighting men dropped down dead, exhausted by wounds':

'Will shall be harder, hearts the keener, our mettle shall be more
as our strength lessens. Here lies our leader, all hewn down,
goodness on the ground. He has cause to mourn whosoever
from this fight thinks to flee. I am old in life. I will not leave this
place, but I will lie me down by my lord's side, by the man I
think so dear.'[22]

*Maldon* is a better poem than *Brunanburh*, a paean to heroic defeat
that transmits pathos and emotional heft through the bitter-sweet
song of hard-fought failure – sorrow and glory entwine together,
pride and despair. These qualities are nowhere to be found in the
crude triumphalism of *Brunanburh*, its poetic force squandered on
surface glitter and hollow bluster, an English retort to the skaldic
verses prepared for Viking warlords. And for all of the older poem's
proto-nationalism, it is *Maldon* that speaks more deeply and with
greater truth to sentiments that the British have enduringly valued:
that to face one's opponent on a level field and to play the game fairly
– to play with heart and courage no matter the outcome, to fight until
the bitterest of ends – is where true glory resides, worth a thousand
hollow victories or a thousand weaklings sent sprawling in the dirt.

*The Battle of Maldon* was, however, an anachronism even when
it was written, a recapitulation of a heroic ideal that was growing
old, couched in language that harked back to the ideals of a vanished
past – to the sixth-century world of Beowulf, a legendary lost past.
Perhaps this was the poet's intention – to inspire his audience to
hold themselves to a higher standard, to raise their spears in the
face of unfolding calamity, a call to arms to resist the tidal wave of
aggression, whatever the cost: a renewal of the heroic values of Old
England. Now, however, the monsters were real, and the heroes
were dying. As one scholar remarked, 'the poem looks with longing
eyes at a vanished world where heroes could act like heroes' but in
the context of 'a world that was rapidly spinning out of English
control' – passing, as another Old English poet might have put it,
into 'dark beneath the helm of night, as though it had never been'.[23]

*

The *Anglo-Saxon Chronicle* account of what happened at the Blackwater is far less expansive. It does, however, record the death of Byrhtnoth at Maldon (the nearest burh to where the fighting took place). Crucially, it also records another event that took place in the aftermath of the battle – one which would have great ramifications over the fifteen years that followed. '[I]n that year,' the *Anglo-Saxon Chronicle* explains, 'it was decided that tribute [*gafol*] be paid to the Danish men for the great terror they had wrought along the sea coast; that was, at first, ten thousand pounds.' Of course, as previous experience and common sense had shown, the only thing this would bring was time, while providing an incentive for further attacks. And, of course, the attacks kept coming, unending, devastating. And as the years of Æthelred's ill-starred reign progressed, the size of the tribute that was paid got ever larger: £16,000 in 994 and £24,000 in 1002. In 1007, at the end of the campaign with which this chapter opened, £36,000 was paid. In 1012, the English crown handed over £48,000 with an undisclosed sum paid out in 1013. The final sum – an astronomical £72,000 – was agreed, in rather different circumstances, in 1016.[24]

These were vast quantities of silver. A pound represented 240 ordinary silver pennies, and the smallest of these sums – the Maldon tribute of £10,000 – was therefore the equivalent of 2,400,000 coins, each one of which had to be hammered out by hand. For context, this would mean having to multiply all of the coins in the Cuerdale Hoard by a factor of 340 to reach this number. The 1016 tribute – if delivered exclusively in coins – would have amounted to a ludicrous 17,280,000 silver pennies. In truth, there is no reason to assume that the tribute was all handed over in coins – silver in all sorts of forms, and gold as well, would no doubt have been equally welcome, and the higher value of the latter material would have reduced the volume of material accordingly. But these are still massive sums of material wealth – so much, in fact, that the reliability of the *Anglo-Saxon Chronicle*'s figures has been repeatedly called into question.[25] There seems little reason, however, even if the specific figures are suspiciously rounded, to doubt the overall size of these payments: certainly the late Anglo-Saxon state had the administrative and economic machinery to raise and produce coinage on this scale, and huge numbers of Æthelred's coins – more than the number found in England – have been discovered in Scandinavia. Some of them, like those in the hoard of eighty-two pennies found at Tyskegård on the island of Bornholm (Denmark), appear to have been freshly minted and never to have circulated, as though produced in bulk for the express purpose of raising a tribute payment.[26] The impact all these coins had is clear: the design of Æthelred's 'Crux' pennies provided the template for the earliest substantive coinages produced by royal rulers in Denmark, Norway, Sweden and Dublin; the distinctive punky hairstyle with which Æthelred's image is blessed on his 'Long Cross' pennies would go on to distinguish the coin-profiles of Danish kings for decades afterwards.

Perhaps this policy would seem wiser in hindsight had Æthelred's military endeavours met with more success; he certainly seems to have tried – refortifying defences that had dropped out of use and throwing up emergency fortifications at places like Old Sarum and South Cadbury; he also reinvested heavily in the English navy, as his father had before him, and it is from Æthelred's reign that we have the first evidence of 'ship-sokes' – a formalized land-based system of militarized naval obligation. But, no matter what he tried, it seemed always to turn out badly: as the *Anglo-Saxon Chronicle* ruefully put it, Æthelred's ship-army 'achieved nothing, except the people's toil, and wasting money, and the invigoration of their enemies',[27] and the situation wasn't helped by the king's reliance on treacherous and inept councillors, a habit that earned him the sobriquet 'the Ill-Advised' (or more familiarly, and inaccurately, 'the Unready') in accounts written after his death (from OE *unræd*, 'bad-counsel', a play on his name Æthel-ræd, 'noble-counsel').

It has been argued, convincingly, that Æthelred has had a bad press.[28] Certainly the primary source for his reign – the version of the *Anglo-Saxon Chronicle* preserved in the C, D and E manuscripts – was written after his reign had come to an ignominious end, and was composed with a degree of bitter hindsight. There were perhaps few kings who could have weathered the storm that broke on him with greater fortitude. But, for one incident at least, Æthelred deserves all of the opprobrium heaped upon him. In 1002 the king had finally decided (on advice) to arrange a payment of £24,000 to a Viking fleet that had, over previous years, 'raided and burned almost everywhere' across the south-west and into the Wessex heartlands.[29] 'It was in every way a heavy time,' the CDE chronicler sums up, 'because they never left off their fierce evil.'[30] There were, therefore, circumstances around the turn of the millennium that perhaps allow us to understand why the king may have felt under siege and susceptible to the temptation of drastic action. The decree that followed, however, was as indiscriminate as it was ill conceived. Later in 1002, Æthelred ordered that 'all the Danish men who were among the English race were to be killed on Brice's Day [13 November], because it was said to the king that they wished to ensnare his life'.[31]

It is obvious that the order cannot have been intended to apply to everyone who had ever been considered 'Danish' in the wider sense; this would have been an absurd idea and impossible to carry out – especially in the north. It is, in fact, entirely unclear to whom Æthelred intended his order to apply, particularly given the multiplying vagaries of Anglo-Danish ethnicity. The tenor of the command, however, was plain enough. Words spoken by power carry weight, legitimizing impulses that might otherwise be suppressed; Æthelred's order was taken seriously in many parts of England, and was most likely interpreted through whatever local animus most energized his subjects. Edgar's policies of multi-cultural authoritarianism had gone, dissolved in the chaos of the renewed Viking menace that had broken on England from 980. Where his father had once punished harshly those who had infringed the rights of foreign traders, Æthelred exhorted the English to murder their neighbours. And murder them they did.

Excavations at St John's College, Oxford, in 2008 discovered the remains of thirty-seven men aged sixteen to twenty-five whose bodies had been dumped in a ditch; study of the bones suggests that they were hacked to death in the years around 1000, many receiving multiple savage blows. There is no evidence that they had attempted to defend themselves – no wounds to hands or forearms that might have come from recent combat; only scorch marks on the bones. They were probably running away.

A chilling document survives that spells out the realities of ethnic cleansing in Oxford: a charter, dated to 1004, that explains – in a horribly matter-of-fact tone – the need to rebuild the Church of St Frideswide:

> it will be well known that, since a decree was sent out by me
> with the counsel of my leading men and magnates, to the effect
> that all the Danes who had sprung up in this island, sprouting
> like cockle amongst the wheat, were to be destroyed by a most
> just extermination, and thus this decree was to be put into
> effect even as far as death, those Danes who dwelt in the afore-
> mentioned town [Oxford], striving to escape death, entered this
> sanctuary of Christ, having broken by force the doors and bolts,
> and resolved to make refuge and defence for themselves therein
> against the people of the town and the suburbs; but when all the
> people in pursuit strove, forced by necessity, to drive them out,
> and could not, they set fire to the planks and burnt, as it seems,
> this church with its ornaments and its books. Afterwards, with
> God's aid, it was renewed by me.[32]

It has been suggested that the age of the victims, and the evidence of healed prior injuries, implies that the men found at St John's College were fighters, not ordinary townsfolk. But in a violent and militarized society the distinction is hardly a useful one. However one chooses to explain or justify the events of 1002, the image that both documents and archaeology present is a grim one: of people driven in terror to seek refuge in the safest place they could find, barricading themselves within what was probably the largest – if not the only – stone building within reach; shut inside, praying desperately that the sanctity of the space might preserve them. There they would have huddled, listening to the sounds outside – the angry shouts, the thud of wooden beams piled against doors and windows. Perhaps, once the burning had begun, once the heat became unbearable and the smoke robbed them of their breath, once they were blinded and choking and wild with panic, the Danes decided to run – to run through the doors and out into the street, into the light and the clean autumn air, there to be hacked apart by the howling mob.[33]

These were not the glorious battles that the Maldon poet had imagined – nor was this the strong and stable nation that Edgar had worked for. That nation would return, but it would take a new dynasty to restore it: a Danish dynasty – a 'Viking' dynasty.

# 21

# MORTAL REMAINS

King Cnut greets in friendship his archbishops and his diocesan
bishops, and Earl Thorkel and all his earls, and all his people […]
ecclesiastic and lay, in England. And I [Cnut] inform you that I will be
a gracious lord and faithful observer of God's rights and secular law.

'Letter of Cnut to the English' (*c.* 1019–20)[1]

S vein Forkbeard became king of England on Christmas Day
1013. Although his actions seemed to fit the classic Viking
mould of seaborne raiding and extortion, Svein was no mere
chancer. Unlike self-made men such as Guthrum back in the 870s,
Svein Forkbeard was an established figure on the international
stage. The son of Harald Bluetooth, king of Denmark (d. *c.* 985),
Svein had taken the Danish throne from his father in the 980s.
When he conquered England in 1013 he was already a king.

Svein's assaults on England had begun early, in the 990s, and he
had spent two years pillaging the country between 1003 and 1005.
Although he did not lead the assaults that followed throughout the
first decade of the eleventh century – the most devastating of which
fell under the command of a fearsome character known as Thorkell
the Tall – in 1013 he returned with a fleet and, it seems, a clear sense
of purpose. He arrived at Sandwich (Kent), and from there led his
ships northward, prowling the eastern coastline until they reached
the Humber – the gateway to Northumbria. At Gainsborough

(Lincolnshire), the Northumbrians submitted swiftly. Shortly afterwards northern Mercia followed suit and then all the regions north of Watling Street, the old boundary set out in the treaty of Alfred and Guthrum.

When Svein moved south the collapse came quickly, Oxford and Winchester surrendering without a fight. London held firm, its townspeople holding out 'with full battle because King Æthelred was inside'. But it was not enough to avert the disaster hanging over the English king. Briefly thwarted, Svein travelled west, to Bath, where the western nobility submitted to him. This was enough for the remaining English resistance. The Londoners laid down their weapons, pledging themselves to their new lord (because if they did not, the *Anglo-Saxon Chronicle* explains, 'they dreaded that he [Svein] would do them in').[2] Exhausted by a quarter-century of war, England capitulated with a whimper and 'the whole nation had him as full king'.

Æthelred, with his wife Emma and his sons Edward and Alfred, fled across the Channel to his wife's brother, Duke Richard of Normandy (the beginning of an Anglo-Norman dalliance that would have cataclysmic consequences further down the line). For the first time since the Anglo-Saxons had begun to record their own history, no scion of the house of Wessex – indeed, no ruler of any English royal dynasty – wielded power anywhere in Britain.

The invasions of Britain that came from Denmark and Norway in the eleventh century were important – sometimes shattering – events, but they were not the opportunistic raids of stateless warlords. Instead they were campaigns of conquest, led by powerful Christian kings at the head of well-equipped armies, raised and mobilized at the behest of rulers who were vastly more powerful than the Viking warlords of old. As the High Middle Ages began to dawn in Europe, a unified sense of Christian community and an increasingly homogeneous cultural identity – defined by Roman

Christianity, Cistercian monasticism, Latin literacy and Frankish mounted warfare – was beginning to spread from its heartlands in France and Germany to every corner of Europe: from the Irish Sea to the Elbe, and from the Arctic to the Mediterranean. Kings, supported by a powerful military aristocracy and an all-pervasive Church, were becoming ever more powerful, their administrations more sophisticated and better funded. In the new world that was slowly crystallizing there was diminishing space in which the free-booting marauder could operate. For true Vikings of the old school, the late tenth and early eleventh centuries would be a final flourish: their way of life was dying out.

The northern world had also been changing rapidly, the circumstances in Scandinavia that had given rise to the Viking Age gradually evolving out of existence. Where once Scandinavian society had been dominated by local chieftains and tribal identities, the tenth century increasingly saw assertive dynasties and individuals establishing themselves as the ultimate source of secular power in Denmark, Norway and Sweden. In every case the transformation of Scandinavian society had been a long, slow and tumultuous process, one with its roots in the ninth century (if not earlier). Indeed, the disgruntlement and political upheaval the ambitions of kings generated is considered one of the catalysts for the multifarious seaborne phenomena that defined the Viking Age, a spur to the independent and the dispossessed to seek new lands and livings elsewhere.[3] But, by the late tenth century, a measure of enhanced political stability had been, or was close to being, achieved across Scandinavia – in Denmark under the Jelling dynasty from c. 940, in Norway and Sweden towards the end of the century, and in further-flung outposts of the diaspora as well.[4] The development of these kingdoms was not a linear one, and the shape of the future nations was by no means preordained (though geography played a decisive role), but the trajectory was inexorably towards political consolidation. This did not mean that the temptation for individuals to take to the seas in search of plunder and fame was snuffed out – far from it – but a new path had been set.

The earliest, and most dramatic, evidence of this process can be found in Denmark. Denmark was precocious among its Scandinavian peers – a result of its comparatively close relationship with continental (Frankish) European culture, religion and politics. Its kings were relatively swift to experiment with Christianity and coinage, and keen to adopt the ceremonial trappings of Roman-style kingship. Although we know little of the internal affairs of Denmark during the tenth century, the reigns of King Gorm the Old and particularly his son, Harald, seem to have been pivotal. When Gorm died he was buried in a wooden chamber constructed beneath a vast mound at Jelling (Jutland, Denmark), part of a remarkable ceremonial and religious complex that grew up around the burial in the decades after his death.[5] The most celebrated part

The crucifixion face of the Jelling runestone

of this landscape is Gorm's runestone. Erected, ostensibly, to celebrate Gorm's life – an act of filial piety on the part of Harald, his son and successor – it is, in fact, rather more eloquent on the subject of Harald's own hubris.

'King Haraldr', the inscription runs, 'bade that this monument be made in remembrance of Gormr his father and Thyrvé his mother. That', the rune-carver elaborates, is the 'Haraldr who won for himself the whole of Denmark and Norway and who made the Danes Christian'.

Harald Bluetooth, as he came to be known, was staking out his claim not only as the great unifier, but also as the bringer of salvation to his people. To underline his triumphs, both spiritual and earthly, the runestone is decorated with an image of the crucified Christ – not the suffering god, *christus patiens*, broken and lifeless, but a Christ triumphant, *christus triumphans*, with eyes wide open and body unflinching: resolute, heroic, undefeated. This is Christ as the Anglo-Saxons had imagined him in the decades following their own conversion: 'eager to mount the gallows, unafraid in the sight of many […] the great King, liege lord of the heavens'.[6] A suitable deity for warrior kings to embrace.

Harald's reign in Denmark, and more generally the journey of Scandinavia towards the mainstream of European culture, is a fascinating subject which would require another book to do it proper justice. His most visible achievements included the construction of massive circular fortifications in Denmark at Fyrkat and Aggersborg (Jutland), Nonnebakken (Funen), Trelleborg (Zealand) and in what is now Sweden at Trelleborg (Skåne). Although the function is uncertain, the symmetrical planning and impressive defences point to a likely military or part-military rationale – at the very least, they speak of the impressive powers of organization and coercion that Harald wielded in the 980s. Similarly, the construction of a monumental timber bridge across the valley of the River Vejle saw the king preside over the expansion of infrastructure at a pitch of ambition and scale worthy of the Roman Empire; 820 yards of oak-timbered road constructed over the impassable marshlands of the river valley, broad enough at 16 feet in width for two horse-drawn vehicles to pass each other, supported on wooden piles up to 20 feet in length.

Neither the ring-forts nor the bridge seem to have much outlasted Harald, but the elevated idea of royal power they represented was much longer lived. Harald's rule demonstrated and ensured that Danish kings had the power, and now the precedent, to mobilize men and resources on an unprecedented scale. And, while the projects that they pursued were still largely driven by their own private ambitions, it was becoming increasingly difficult to distinguish properly between personal and 'national' agenda: the interests of king and nation were becoming ever harder to disentangle.

This is certainly true of Svein Forkbeard's conquest of England in 1013. The question of what motivated the Danish king's desire for dominion in England remains a live one, and no credible account survives to explain his actions. The *Encomium Emmae Reginae* ('in praise of Queen Emma') – a broadly contemporary history commissioned in the 1040s, blatantly biased in favour of the Danish royal family – provides one possible answer. The *Encomium* suggests that Svein's invasion was prompted by Thorkell the Tall's decision, in 1012, to enter King Æthelred's service as a mercenary after several years of terrorizing the English kingdom (earlier in the same year, Thorkell had been in charge of a group who had murdered Ælfheah, the archbishop of Canterbury, at Greenwich – beating him to death with an axe handle after pelting him with 'bones and the heads of cattle').[7] This is possible – Thorkell was cutting an increasingly impressive figure in the early eleventh century, and Svein may well have seen him as a potential rival. But the *Encomium* is not a trustworthy source, and this part reads like a post hoc rationalization. Instead, Svein's invasion was probably driven by opportunism. He was well aware of England's impressive economic potential relative to his own kingdom. He had seen first hand the wealth that English kings were able to rustle up when they needed to – he himself had been a beneficiary. He also knew full well how militarily enfeebled England had become – he had wielded the axe himself on many an occasion. When the time came for Svein's hostile takeover, the Danish king knew that he was pushing on an open door: behind it lay power and riches that dwarfed any returns that his own people could provide.

However, he did not have long to enjoy his new kingdom. Five weeks after becoming king of England, in early February 1014, Svein Forkbeard dropped dead. The cause of death remains a mystery, but by the twelfth century Anglo-Norman writers had hit upon a picturesque legend to account for what – at the time – must have seemed miraculous. As the chronicle of John of Worcester tells it, King Svein was busy carousing with his retinue of Danish warriors when he caught sight of a menacing armed figure approaching – a figure that no one but the king could see. 'When he [Svein] had seen him,' John explains, 'he was terrified and began to shout very noisily, saying "Help, fellow-warriors, help! St Edmund is coming to kill me!" And while he was saying this he was run through fiercely by the saint with a spear, and fell from the stallion on which he sat, and, tormented with great pain until twilight, he ended his life with a wretched death on 3 February.'[8] St Edmund, the East Anglian king martyred by Ivar and Ubbe in 870 (and memorialized in the East Anglian coinage of the early 900s), had appeared like Banquo to wreak his belated revenge.

This, I suppose, was reckoned to be a sort of poetic justice after more than two centuries of Viking harassment. If it is truly what contemporaries believed, however, the comfort it offered was short lived. Æthelred was restored to the throne, it being generally decided by the English magnates that 'no lord was dearer to them than their natural lord', but not before they had extracted a promise from him to 'govern more justly than he did before'.[9] And maybe that would have been the end of it – the English lords even promising to forswear Danish kings once and for all – had it not been for the fact that Svein's son, Cnut, was still in England. And he was showing scant sign of wanting to go home.

*

Cnut's campaign in England began in brutally defiant fashion. He sailed to Sandwich with the hostages provided to his father, put them ashore and had their hands and noses cut off. From that point onward, matters proceeded much as they had in the past. Æthelred once again stumped up tribute (£21,000 according to the *Anglo-Saxon Chronicle*), and once again it failed to deter the attacks. Cnut's armies menaced the coast of England and raided into Wessex, while at the same time exploiting the political divisions that Æthelred's calamitous reign had failed to heal. The situation was, once again, spiralling out of control. Only Æthelred's death would halt the decay and, probably much to the relief of many, he finally died after a short illness on St George's Day (23 April) 1016. As the CDE chronicler unnecessarily reminded his readers, the king ended his days 'after great labour and tribulations in his life'.[10] It was the end of a protracted (and briefly interrupted) reign of thirty-eight years. It had been an uncomfortable time for all of his English subjects: Britons, Anglo-Saxons and Danes alike.

The man who replaced him, his son Edmund who according to the *Anglo-Saxon Chronicle* earned the sobriquet 'Ironside' for 'his bravery',[11] was – from what little is known of him – a rather different proposition. Unlike his father, who hardly ever seems to have taken personal command of English armies, Edmund was a hands-on warlord. He immediately set about raising armies (as he had in fact tried to do, unsuccessfully, during his father's decline) and led them into battle with tireless, relentless, resolve. The year 1016 proved to be a bruising year for everyone. Edmund beat Cnut at Penselwood (Somerset), and a clash at Sherston (Wiltshire) – though bitterly contested – ended inconclusively. Shortly afterwards, Edmund's army drove the Danes away from London and defeated them again at Brentford (Middlesex) and Otford (Kent). It must have seemed that England finally had the champion it needed. But Edmund was to make a mistake in the aftermath of this last victory that would ultimately undo much of his good work. At a gathering at Aylesford (Kent) – perhaps in a fit of *ofermod* – he was reconciled with the Mercian ealdorman Eadric Streona – Eadric the Acquisitor.

Eadric Streona is the principal villain of eleventh-century England. Crowning a multitude of other reported perfidies (which included murder, pillage, appropriation of church lands and property, treachery, oath-breaking and obstruction, as well as a good proportion of the *unræd* whispered into King Æthelred's earhole), Eadric defected to Cnut's army in 1015 – despite his earlier marriage to Æthelred's daughter Edith. He apparently embraced Cnutism with a convert's zeal: according to John of Worcester, during the battle of Sherston, Eadric:

> cut off the head of a certain man called Osmear, very like King Edmund in face and hair, and raising it aloft he shouted, saying that the English fought in vain: 'You men of Dorset, Devon, Wiltshire, flee in haste, for you have lost your leader. Look, I hold here in my hands the head of your lord, King Edmund. Flee as fast you can.'
>
> When the English perceived this they were appalled, more by the horror at the action than by any trust in the announcer.[12]

If true (and it may well not be), this was pretty appalling stuff. Nevertheless, whatever his crimes, it seems that Edmund decided at Aylesford that it was better to keep Eadric close than leave him outside the tent. It was probably a sound policy – had Eadric been left in the cold he could well have rejoined Cnut or else followed an agenda all of his own; Edmund certainly didn't need a powerful loose cannon threatening his supply chain and his home front. In hindsight, however, it is easy to agree with the E chronicler's verdict that there 'was not a more ill-advised decision [*unræd geræd*] than this was',[13] and ultimately Edmund probably wished that he had acted otherwise. When the decisive battle came – at a place called 'Assandun' (probably Ashingdon in Essex, but possibly Ashdon in the same county), 'Ealdorman Eadric', the *Anglo-Saxon Chronicle* wearily relates, 'did as he had often done before, and was the first to start the flight with the Magonsæte [the people of western Mercia]; thus he betrayed his royal lord and all the English people.'[14] The description of the battle provided in the *Encomium* is more vivid, if rather less reliable. The Encomiast has Eadric announce: 'Let us flee, oh comrades, and snatch our lives from imminent death, or else we shall fall forthwith, for I know the hardihood of the Danes.' The Encomiast also repeats the belief – apparently current at the time, and no less believable now – that 'he did this not out of fear but in guile; and what many assert is that he had promised this secretly to the Danes in return for some favour'.[15]

Despite its pro-Cnut bias, the *Encomium* gave a respectful account of King Edmund's deeds. The words attributed to him are heroic ('Oh Englishmen, to-day you will fight or surrender yourselves all together. Therefore, fight for your liberty and your country, men of understanding') and his actions valiant ('he advanced into the midst of the enemy, cutting down Danes on all sides, and by this example rendering his noble followers more inclined to fight').[16] The fighting, according to the *Encomium*, lasted from morning until after darkness fell. 'And if the shining moon had not shown which was the enemy, every man would have cut down his comrade, thinking he was an adversary resisting him, and no man would have survived on either side, unless he had been saved by flight.'[17] English history now hinged on the outcome of this one battle. A decisive victory for Edmund – particularly one that led to the death of Cnut – would have changed the course of history. But, in the end, 'the English, turning their backs, fled without delay on all sides, ever falling before their foes, and added glory to the honour of Knútr [Cnut] and to his victory'.[18] The exhausted Danish warriors, 'rejoicing in their triumph, passed the remainder of the night amongst the bodies of the dead'. When morning came, they stripped the vanquished of their arms and weapons, but left the bodies where they lay – a carrion feast for the 'beasts and birds'.[19]

Cnut's own poets summed up this victory in a few concise words of praise, the conquest of a nation boiled down to a vision of dark wings fluttering over a field stained black with blood:

'Mighty king, you performed a feat under shield at Assatún(ir); the blood-crane [raven] received dark carrion.' Cnut had won back his father's briefly held throne. The human cost – for the English and the Danes alike – had been terrible.

Runestones stud the Scandinavian countryside, the vast majority in Sweden. Irregular grey monoliths, jutting from the grass like crooked teeth, many still stand in the open air, defying time and weather as the world changes round them. Cut with knotted serpents and angular runes, they frequently carry the sign of the cross, the unmistakable branding of the increasingly ubiquitous faith of the northern world. These are not the exotic remnants of a pagan age, but monuments of the new world that was forming in the early eleventh century, memorials to those who died in the age of Cnut. Of all the stones that are known today, a group of thirty are referred to as the 'England runestones', monuments whose inscriptions make explicit reference to the exploits of these late-period Vikings in England, giving names to the people who helped to shape eleventh-century Britain.[20] Some refer to the payments received by individuals – a record of the wealth that was wrung from the English in those brutal years. Áli, for example, was evidently a forward planner: he 'had his stone raised in memory of himself. He took Knútr's payment in England. May God help his spirit.'[21] Perhaps he invested some of his new-found silver in this shameless act of self-promotion.

Other inscriptions are even more specific, setting in stone particular events that are chronicled in English sources. A stone at Yttergärde in Uppland (Sweden), erected by two men called Karse and Kalbjörn in memory of their father, Ulf, records that 'Ulf has taken three payments in England. That was the first that Tosti paid. Then Thorkell paid. Then Cnut paid.'[22] 'Tosti' was probably a man identified by Snorri as Sköglar-Tosti, father-in-law to both Svein Forkbeard and the Swedish king, Eric the Victorious.[23] 'Thorkell' was Thorkell the Tall, whose exploits deprived the English of £48,000 in 1012. Cnut, of course, needs no explanation.

It was men like Ulf who were the beneficiaries of England's years of pain.

More rarely, runic inscriptions provide a glimpse of the Scandinavians who died in Cnut's England: 'Sveinn and Þorgautr made this monument in memory of Manni and Sveini,' an inscription on a stone in Scania (Sweden) runs. 'May God help their souls well. And they lie in London.'[24] Stunning archaeological evidence for the presence of an eleventh-century migrant community in London was discovered in 1852 in the graveyard of St Paul's Cathedral. A stone, decorated in the Scandinavian Ringerike style with an elaborate backwards-turning beast, once painted in colours of red, white and black, carries a runic inscription down one edge: 'Ginna and Toki had this stone set up.' For whom, we will never know. The gravestone can be seen now in the Museum of London, beside a display of the Viking axes that have been dragged from the stinking mud of the River Thames at low tide – the debris scattered where wave after wave of violence had broken, crashing on the walls of the city that held out until the bitter end.

Most of the Scandinavians who died in England, however, remain nameless, though the manner of their deaths is sometimes laid horribly bare. In 2009, during the initial stages of the construction of the Weymouth Relief Road in Dorset, a grave was discovered on the downs. The skulls were found first, a pile of yellowing husks, forty-seven heads tossed haphazardly into a pit. The bodies were found later, fifty-two headless corpses heaped naked one upon the other – a charnel tangle of ribs and femurs jutting from the earth. Analysis of the remains revealed that the heads had been hacked off with swords. The killing had been hard work – many hands and blades had laboured over it, often it had taken multiple blows to sever the vertebrae, and sometimes the aim of the killers had been poor or hasty, shearing through skulls and faces, blood staining the white chalk in crimson torrents. It would have taken hours. The five heads that were missing from the grave might well have been the only memorial for these men – taken and rammed on to wooden stakes (*heofod stoccan*) and set up to watch sightlessly from the hills.

Analysis of the skeletal remains revealed that all of the people who died here were men, aged mostly between their teens and early adulthood, and that they had died in the years around 1000. Only five of them might have grown up in Britain, the rest came from Scandinavia and the Baltic, from Iceland, Russia and Belarus, from the Arctic and the sub-Arctic, from every corner of the Viking North. They had come to Britain and they had died in England, though what had brought them here, and who did this to them, remains a mystery. The men who died were not professional fighters – their bones show no evidence of wounds gained and healed, of the stresses and strains of a life of battle. Some in fact seem to have suffered from debilitating illness and disability. Perhaps these were people who came to England to seek their fortune, tempted by the silver they had seen flowing north, by stories of adventure and the weakness of the English, lured by the runestones that boasted of payments in the service of famous and mighty lords. All they found was death.[25]

The identities of these people will never be known, but someone, somewhere, must have grieved for them. A sad stone in Norway records that 'Arnsteinn raised this stone in memory of Bjórr his son who died in the retinue when Knútr attacked England.'[26] Perhaps Bjórr was a hardened warrior who came to grief in the thick of battle; or perhaps he was a mere boy, hacked to death before his adventure even began.

Edmund survived the battle of Assandun long enough to negotiate a peace with the victorious Danish king. They may have fought again in the Forest of Dean (depending on how a skaldic reference to a battle at Danaskógar is interpreted),[27] but all sources agree that the parties then met for talks at a place called Olanige ('Ola's Island') near Deerhurst in Gloucestershire. According to a later tradition, the two kings were transported to this island in the River Severn where they engaged in single combat – a royal *hólmgang* to determine the fate of the kingdom. However improbable it may seem, there is no way of knowing whether anything like this really happened. I like to imagine that it did – the two great warriors slugging it out alone, as though two and a quarter centuries of conflict and compromise had been distilled down to this single scene: the young kings of Wessex and of Denmark, the Anglo-Saxon and the Dane, wrestling for the soul of England as the olive-green waters passed slowly by. Whatever the reality, a settlement was ultimately reached. Tribute payment was agreed (the astronomical figure of £72,000 was collected in 1018), oaths were made and hostages were given by both sides. And Edmund was to keep his throne, retaining his familial lands and rule over Wessex; Cnut was to receive Mercia (as well as, presumably, East Anglia and Northumbria). England, so recently assembled, was to be partitioned once more.

That was the idea. As things turned out, however, the details proved academic. Edmund died on 30 November 1016, the third English king (including Svein) to have died in two years. In 1017 'King Cnut succeeded to the whole kingdom of England.'[28] Edmund's sudden and unexplained death has always smelled suspicious. If it wasn't murder, it was certainly convenient for Cnut. A later tradition, first recorded by the Norman historian Henry of Huntingdon in the early twelfth century, had Edmund suffering an unseemly end, shot up the arse with a crossbow while enthroned upon the privy.[29] It is, happily for Edmund's posthumous dignity, unlikely to be true.

Cnut's first actions as king were probably the most radical of his reign. He divided England into four great earldoms that corresponded to the four ancient realms of Wessex (which he governed directly himself, at least to begin with), Mercia (which was given, briefly, to Eadric Streona), East Anglia (given to Thorkell the Tall, who had reconciled with Cnut in 1015) and Northumbria (which was put under the authority of the Norwegian, Eric Hákonarson). The title 'earl' (OE *eorl*) was an Anglicization of the Old Norse title *jarl*, and it was introduced into English at this time, a new rung of power between the existing English nobility and the king. Cnut also took the opportunity to raise the enormous tax agreed at Olanige, crush a number of dissenting English noblemen, and – in what may have been a more popular move – have Eadric Streona killed at London and thrown over the city wall. This was done, according to the *Encomium*, in order that 'retainers should learn from this example to be faithful, not faithless, to their kings'.[30]

Cnut would rule England until his death in 1035, and his sons Harald and Harthacnut until 1042. For the twenty-five years that the Knýtlinga (the house of Cnut) ruled England, the latent Scandinavian influences – already so prominent in the north and east of the country – became a part of mainstream English culture. During those years, England would lie at the heart of a North Sea empire that swelled to include Denmark, Norway and parts of Sweden, and exert claims of lordship over the Norse-speaking communities of the Northern and Western Isles of Britain. Old Norse was spoken at the royal court at Winchester, Scandinavian warlords ruled as earls in what had once been Anglo-Saxon kingdoms, and Scandinavians could have runestones raised to them in the graveyard of St Paul's Cathedral. Objects like the gilded bronze brooch found in Pitney in Somerset – hardly an epicentre of Viking settlement – demonstrate the convergence of late Scandinavian and Anglo-Saxon art-styles in places that may have experienced little direct contact with speakers of Old Norse before the reign of Cnut. Likewise, a remarkable monument stone from Bibury in Gloucestershire was carved in the Ringerike style, leonine faces on weird twisting necks sprouting from its base like flowers seeking the sun.

Even after the West Saxon dynasty had been restored in the person of Edward the Confessor, many of these influences remained deeply entrenched. England's last 'Anglo-Saxon' king, Harold Godwineson, had a Norse name (Haraldr) and a Danish mother, as did his brothers Tostig, Svein and Gyrth. Even the great double-handed axes, wielded to devastating effect by so many English warriors in the Bayeux Tapestry's telling of the battle of Hastings, were a Scandinavian import – horse-killing weapons developed in Denmark to stop the Frankish cavalry that was increasingly dominating the continent.

And yet it was at this moment, at the very zenith of Scandinavian influence and power in England, that the Vikings as they had been would begin to fade away.

In some ways, Cnut was the most awesome Viking of them all – a Danish king whose longships bound together a maritime empire through fear and force, and whose skalds composed bloodthirsty eulogies about his victories – just as his ancestors had done. But, in other, perhaps more important ways, Cnut was not a Viking at all. A Danish aristocrat like his father, Cnut was king of England before he was ever a king in Scandinavia (he became king of Denmark in 1018 and of Norway in 1028), and he spent considerable time in Britain. He was emphatically Christian, and in his laws, his coinage, his self-depiction and his generosity to the Church, he presented himself as the quintessential Anglo-Saxon king. He made a point of reconfirming the laws of Edgar and even married the late King Æthelred's queen, Emma – it was at the behest of their son Harthacnut (king of England, 1040–2) that her *Encomium* was later written.[31]

The *Liber Vitae* of New Minster and Hyde Abbey is a book, produced at the beginning of the 1030s, which records donations to the New Minster at Winchester, the church built by Edward the Elder, and which housed the bones of his father, King Alfred. Among its pages is an extraordinary illustration – produced while the king and queen were still alive – of Cnut and Emma presenting an enormous altar cross to the New Minster. Christ and St Peter hover overhead, and an angel places a crown upon Cnut's brow. He stands on the altar steps, at the threshold of the Middle Ages, looking every inch the ideal monarch of a new era. The heathen warlords of the ninth and tenth centuries had gone, and although Scandinavians would continue to bother the British Isles for a century or more, there would be no going back. The world had moved on.

When he died, Cnut was buried at the Old Minster, the venerable church that the New Minster had been constructed to replace. He had earlier, in an expression of a curious affection that Cnut seems to have held for his one-time rival, had the remains of King Edmund Ironside translated there in 1032. Harthacnut, his son by Emma, was buried there in 1042, and his long-lived wife Emma in 1052. In the church next door, separated by a few feet, lay King Alfred and his wife, Ealhswith, their sons Edward (the Elder) and Æthelweard, and Edward's son Ælfweard. For years the house of Wessex and the house of Cnut slumbered on in their separate mausolea – similar but distinct, separated by walls and clear green grass. But as the centuries passed and the old churches tumbled, to be replaced by the great gothic cathedral that still stands in Winchester, the royal tombs were moved – Alfred's family to the monastery at Hyde, and Cnut's family along with a number of others (including Edmund and, perhaps, the tenth-century King Eadred) to the cathedral where they would lie alongside the remains of Anglo-Saxon bishops and Norman princes for hundreds of years.

There they remained until 1642, when soldiers fighting for the Parliamentary army in the English Civil War broke into the cathedral. These men, 'for whom nothing is holy, nothing is Sacred, did not stick to profane, and violate these Cabinets of the dead, and to scatter their bones all over the pavements of the Church'. The stained-glass windows 'they brake to pieces, by throwing at them, the bones of Kings, Queens, Bishops, Confessors and Saints'.[32] In 1661, in an attempt to remedy the chaos, 'the bones of princes and prelates scattered by sacrilegious barbarism' were 'brought together again mixed up' and deposited in the chests that still sit atop the walls of the choir.[33] Subsequent investigations in the late eighteenth and nineteenth centuries revealed total disorder: a hopeless jumble of mortal remains.

New DNA research offers the slender possibility of bringing some sense to it all. But for the time being the puzzle remains unsolved, a physical expression of what England by the end of the eleventh century had become. Anglo-Saxons and Danes, hopelessly muddled together in death, impossible now to tell apart.

# EPILOGUE

The death of the second of Cnut's sons, Harthacnut, in 1042 and the re-establishment of the house of Wessex (in the person of Edward the Confessor) by no means spelled the end of Scandinavian Britain or, indeed, of the Viking Age.

In the north and west, particularly in the island strongholds of Orkney, Shetland, Man and the Hebrides, Viking lordships endured and prospered long into the Middle Ages, exerting a decisive influence on Scottish history for centuries. The Lords of the Isles (Man and the Western Isles) remained independent from Scotland until 1266 (there was a brief period of direct rule from Norway in the late eleventh century that followed the intervention of King Magnus Barefoot). The earldom of Orkney – the polity established in Caithness and the Northern Isles through Scandinavian settlement from the ninth century onwards – was even longer lived; Orkney and Shetland remained a part of the kingdom of Norway until 1467 and 1468 respectively. But, no matter how vitally entangled this northern fringe of Britain was with Scandinavian politics, or how deeply penetrated by Scandinavian culture, language and people, these lordships only emerge into historical view in the late eleventh century, their origins and their development obscure.[1]

The earldom of Orkney, in particular, presents something of a conundrum. The eradication of almost all traces of pre-Scandinavian (Pictish) place-names, language and material culture on the islands has given rise to a suggestion that the settlement of these

North Sea outposts was carried on a wave of genocidal migration. Others have stressed the absence of secure chronology, the uncertainties of earlier population size and density, the many centuries of continuing migration and influence from Scandinavia. The evidence is equivocal, though the pride the islanders take in their Viking heritage remains palpable. For these parts of Britain, as for much of England, the Viking Age never really ended. Nobody packed up their battle-axes and Thor's-hammer amulets and went 'home'. These Viking Age immigrants may have imported new ideas and new identities, making accommodations of various kinds with their neighbours, but they were – certainly by the eleventh century – as British as anyone else in these islands.

Scandinavian raids also continued, though they remained the province of kings rather than freebooters. The failed invasion of England in 1066 by the Norwegian king Harald Harðráði ('Hard-ruler') was only one of many. In 1069, in the aftermath of the Norman conquest of England, the Danish king Svein Estridsson (r. 1047–76) captured York in alliance with the last viable member of the West Saxon dynasty (Edgar the Ætheling). William the Conqueror paid him to go away. (In 1075 he came back again for a quick pillage.) Svein's grandson, Cnut IV (r. 1080–6), was keen to keep up this national pastime, and readied a fleet to invade England in 1085. His people were less enthusiastic, however, and refused to serve; when he tried to round them up a second time they chased him into a church and stabbed him to death. Even in the mid-twelfth century, Scandinavian kings sometimes felt the temptation to harass the shores of Britain. The Norwegian king Eystein Haraldsson (r. 1142–57) led a fleet that menaced Orkney, Scotland and northern England in the 1150s during the reign of King Stephen.

Should these be considered Viking raids? Perhaps they should, although – in the end – all attempts to define the limits of the Viking Age dissolve into fruitless semantic arguments. What is perhaps better to acknowledge is that, by the twelfth and thirteenth centuries, the literary idea of the Viking – the image that would shape and colour perception of the Age until the present – was being born, both in Iceland's saga literature and in fanciful Anglo-Norman tales like that of Havelok the Dane. The creation of literary tropes and fantastical tales depended, to some degree, on a critical distance from the world these works sought to describe. It was a past that had become safe to romanticize precisely because it was over.

The Vikings had changed Britain, that is without doubt. But Britain had also changed the Vikings – transforming them until it seemed that they were gone for ever. One of my goals has been to undermine the monolithic form they take in popular representation, to show them as more susceptible to the influence of their environments and of the people and ideas they encountered. But the Vikings were also a vital force: agents of change who transformed the world they moved through, even if they sometimes lost themselves in the process, emerging only as shadows, as figures of legend to be put back together in new shapes. It has also been my goal to share the stunning legacy of their world, to illuminate to those who may never have encountered it the breadth and depth of the footprint that they have left in Britain, and to allow their story to serve as a reminder that culture, identity and ethnicity are often more complex and contestable than we might imagine.

I have also tried to steer a course that, though it recognizes the debt we owe to Viking culture and the impact of these events and processes on British history, does not diminish the strangeness of the people who fashioned the Viking Age. They were not 'just like us': there is more to being human than using coins or wearing shoes, and mundane things do not readily reveal how people felt, thought and dreamt. But we can still stand where they stood, and feel the grass under our feet and know that they felt it, and taste the sea-breeze on our tongues and know that they tasted it. And when we wait by the shoreline, with the sun dipping like blood into the west and the breakers crashing on the strand, we can still hear their voices singing with the tide, the grinding of keels on the shingle.

# TIMELINE

| | |
|---|---|
| **786–802** | In the reign of the West Saxon king Beorhtric, Vikings arrive by sea at Portland in Dorset and kill his reeve. |
| **793** | Vikings attack the monastery at Lindisfarne in Northumbria. |
| **794–5** | Vikings attack monasteries in northern Britain and Ireland. |
| **837** | Ireland suffers numerous Viking raids. |
| **838** | A Cornish army and its Viking allies are defeated at Hengestdun (Cornwall) by the West Saxon king Ecgberht. |
| **847** | Vikings overrun the islands of north-western Britain and the Irish Sea. |
| **850** | For the first time, Vikings spend the whole winter in Britain (on the island of Thanet in the Thames Estuary). |
| **865** | A Viking army, bigger than any seen before, arrives in East Anglia. It is known to people at the time as the 'great heathen horde'. |
| **865–6** | The Vikings lay waste to the Pictish realm. |
| **866** | The great heathen horde captures York, the capital of Anglo-Saxon Northumbria. |
| **867** | The two rival kings of Anglo-Saxon Northumbria are killed in battle by the Vikings at York. |
| **870** | King Edmund of the Anglo-Saxon kingdom of East Anglia is killed by the great heathen horde. Dumbarton |

Rock, the capital of the British kingdom of Strathclyde, is destroyed by Vikings from Dublin and its king taken prisoner.

**c.870**   Vikings begin to dominate Orkney, Shetland and other parts of the Atlantic coast of northern Britain.

**871**   King Æthelred of the Anglo-Saxon kingdom of Wessex, with his brother Alfred, fights the Vikings to a stalemate at the battle of Ashdown (now in Oxfordshire).

**873**   Repton (Derbyshire), the capital of Anglo-Saxon Mercia, is occupied by the great heathen horde and the Mercian king, Burhred, is driven into exile.

**876**   The great heathen horde occupies the Anglo-Saxon kingdom of Northumbria and begins to share out the land. Its leader, Halfdan, becomes the first in a series of Viking kings of Northumbria.

**878**   A Viking army led by Guthrum occupies Wessex and drives King Alfred into hiding at Athelney in Somerset; King Alfred returns to defeat Guthrum at the battle of Edington in Wiltshire. Guthrum accepts Christianity and the new name Æthelstan, becoming Alfred's godson.

**880**   Guthrum–Æthelstan withdraws to East Anglia with his army, where he becomes king.

**899**   Alfred dies and is succeeded as king of Wessex by his son, Edward 'the Elder'. Alfred's nephew, Æthelwold, flees to Northumbria in order to raise an army against his cousin.

**900**   Domnall, king of Alba (Scotland), is killed by Vikings at Dunnottar.

**902**   Æthelwold is killed in battle in East Anglia at the battle of the Holme. The Viking rulers of Dublin are expelled by the Irish. A Viking war-band led by Ingimundr is driven from Anglesey by Cadell ap Rhodri, king of Gwynedd.

**910**   An alliance of Anglo-Saxons from Wessex and Mercia destroy a large Viking army at the battle of Tettenhall (near Wolverhampton).

| | |
|---|---|
| **910–20** | King Edward, with the help of his sister Æthelflæd, conquers East Anglia and Mercia and is recognised as overlord of all northern Britain. |
| **917** | The Vikings return to rule in Dublin. |
| **927** | Edward's son, King Athelstan, conquers Viking Northumbria, creating a unified kingdom of England for the first time. |
| **937** | King Athelstan crushes an alliance of Scots, Vikings and the Britons of Strathclyde at the battle of Brunanburh in northern England. |
| **939** | King Athelstan dies and is succeeded by King Edmund. An independent Viking kingdom of Northumbria is restored under King Olaf Guthfrithsson. |
| **942** | King Edmund takes control of five important towns formerly under Viking domination: Leicester, Lincoln, Nottingham, Stamford and Derby. |
| **954** | The last independent Viking king of Northumbria – Eric Bloodaxe – is expelled from York and killed. |
| **970s** | The Viking rulers of the Isle of Man increase their power around the Irish Sea. |
| **981** | Vikings raid Southampton, and for the next thirty-five years Viking attacks on England become increasingly serious. |
| **991** | A Viking army attacks Essex, defeating an English army at the battle of Maldon and killing the East Anglian ealdorman Byrhtnoth; the English pay the Vikings £10,000 to go away. |
| **994** | The English pay the Vikings £16,000 to go away. |
| **1002** | The English pay the Vikings £24,000 to go away. |
| **1007** | The English pay the Vikings £36,000 to go away. |
| **1012** | The English pay the Vikings £48,000 to go away. |
| **1013** | Svein Forkbeard, king of Denmark, conquers the whole of England. |
| **1014** | Svein Forkbeard becomes king of England. He dies five weeks later. |

**1016**   Edmund 'Ironside' becomes king of England on the death of his father Æthelred ('the Unready'), and fights a series of battles against Svein Forkbeard's son, Cnut; King Edmund dies in November and Cnut becomes king of England.

**1018**   King Cnut raises £72,000 from his English subjects.

**1035**   King Cnut dies.

**1042**   Cnut's son, King Harthacnut, dies. The English crown passes back to the West Saxon dynasty and Æthelred's son, Edward ('the Confessor'), becomes king.

**1066**   Harald 'Hard-ruler' Sigurdsson, king of Norway, invades England and is defeated and killed at Stamford Bridge (Yorkshire) by an army led by the English king, Harold Godwineson. Two weeks later Harold is killed at the battle of Hastings.

# ABBREVIATIONS
# AND PRIMARY
# SOURCES

## Note on the *Anglo-Saxon Chronicle*

Citations from and references to the manuscripts of the *Anglo-Saxon Chronicle* have made use of the editions published under the general supervision of David Dumville and Simon Keynes (see individual volumes below), with reference to the translated editions produced by Dorothy Whitelock and Michael Swanton: D. Whitelock (ed. and trans.), *The Anglo-Saxon Chronicle: A Revised Translation* (1961, Eyre & Spottiswoode); M. Swanton (ed. and trans.), *The Anglo-Saxon Chronicles* (2001, 2nd edition, Phoenix Press). Where a reference to the *Chronicle* is given in the notes simply as *ASC*, the material cited is common to all manuscripts (the 'core' text); otherwise, references specify the manuscript by letter when information is restricted to one or more versions.

## Note on Irish Chronicles

Thomas Charles-Edwards has reconstructed and translated the joint stock of a putative 'Chronicle of Ireland' (*CI*) to the year 911 from annals surviving in a variety of manuscripts, principally the *Annals of Ulster* and the Clonmacnoise group (*Annals of Tigernach, Annals of Clonmacnoise, Chronicum Scotorum*), with some additions from the *Annals of Innisfallen, Annals of the Four Masters* and the *Fragmentary Annals*: T. Charles-Edwards (ed. and trans.), *The*

*Chronicles of Ireland* (2006, Liverpool University Press). I have relied on this edition for translations from these texts until 911. Beyond this date, I have relied on the translations published online by University College Cork: *Corpus of Electronic Texts* (CELT) [http://www.ucc.ie/celt/published/T100001A/]

*AC* – *Annales Cambriae*; J. Morris (ed.), *Nennius, British History and the Welsh Annals* (1980, Phillimore)

*AClon* – *Annals of Clonmacnoise* (see 'Note on Irish Chronicles' above)

*AFM* – *Annals of the Four Masters* (see 'Note on Irish Chronicles' above)

*AI* – *Annals of Innisfallen* (see 'Note on Irish Chronicles' above)

Alfred-Guthrum – 'The Treaty of Alfred and Guthrum'; S. Keynes and M. Lapidge (eds and trans.), *Alfred the Great: Asser's 'Life of King Alfred' and Other Contemporary Sources* (1983, Penguin)

*APV* – *Armes Prydein Vawr*; J. K. Bollard (ed. and trans.), in M. Livingston (ed.), *The Battle of Brunanburh: A Casebook* (2011, University of Exeter Press), pp. 155–70, with notes pp. 155–69 and commentary pp. 245–6

*ASC* – *Anglo-Saxon Chronicle* (see 'Note on the *Anglo-Saxon Chronicle*' above):

    A – J. M. Bately (ed.), *The Anglo-Saxon Chronicle: A Collaborative Edition, vol. 3. MS. A* (1986, Brewer)

    B – S. Taylor (ed.), *The Anglo-Saxon Chronicle: A Collaborative Edition, vol. 4. MS. B* (1983, Brewer)

    C – K. O'Brien O'Keeffe (ed.), *The Anglo-Saxon Chronicle: A Collaborative Edition, vol. 5. MS. C* (2001, Brewer)

    D – G. P. Cubbin (ed.), *The Anglo-Saxon Chronicle: A Collaborative Edition, vol. 6. MS. D* (1996, Brewer)

    E – S. Irvine (ed.), *The Anglo-Saxon Chronicle: A Collaborative Edition, vol. 7. MS. E* (2004, Brewer)

    F – P. S. Baker (ed.), *The Anglo-Saxon Chronicle: A Collaborative Edition, vol. 8: MS. F* (2000, Brewer)

*ASN* – *Annals of St Neots*; D. N. Dumville and M. Lapidge (eds), *The Anglo-Saxon Chronicle: A Collaborative Edition, vol. 17. The annals of St Neots with Vita prima Sancti Neoti* (1985, Cambridge: Brewer)

*ASPR – Anglo-Saxon Poetic Records*; G. P. Krapp and E. V. Dobbie (eds), *The Anglo-Saxon Poetic Records: A Collective Edition*, 6 vols (1931–53, New York: Columbia University Press) [ota.ox.ac.uk/desc/1936]

*AU – Annals of Ulster* (see 'Note on Irish Chronicles' above)

*Beowulf – ASPR*, volume 4

BM – British Museum registration number

*Boethius* – Boethius, *Consolatio Philosophiae*; J. J. O'Donnell (ed.), *Boethius: Consolatio Philosophiae* (1984, Bryn Mawr College)

*Brunanburh – The Battle of Brunanburh* (*ASPR*, volume 6)

*BVSC* – Bede, *Vita Sancti Cuthberti*; B. Colgrave (ed. and trans.), *Two Lives of Cuthbert* (1940, Cambridge University Press)

*c. – circa* ('around')

*CA* – Æthelweard, *'Chronicon' of Æthelweard*; A. Campbell (ed. and trans.), *The Chronicle of Æthelweard* (1962, Thomas Nelson & Sons)

Canmore ID – Reference number to the Scottish database of archaeological sites, monuments and buildings [https://canmore.org.uk/]

*CASSS* – Corpus of Anglo-Saxon Stone Sculpture [http://www.ascorpus.ac.uk/index.php]

*CC* – John of Worcester, *Chronicon ex Chronicis*; R. R. Darlington (ed.), P. McGurk (ed. and trans.) and J. Bray (trans.), *The Chronicle of John of Worcester* (1995, Clarendon Press)

*CKA* – *Chronicle of the Kings of Alba*; B. T. Hudson (ed. and trans.), 'Chronicle of the Kings of Alba', *Scottish Historical Review* 77 (1998), pp. 129–61

*CS* – *Chronicon Scottorum* (see 'Note on Irish Chronicles' above)

*Deor – ASPR*, volume 3

DR – Denmark (geographical reference; runestones)

*EE* – Geffrei Gaimar, *Estoire des Engleis*; I. Short (ed. and trans.), *Gaimar: Estoire des Engleis/History of the English* (2009, Oxford University Press)

*Egil's Saga* – B. Scudder (ed. and trans.), 'Egil's Saga', in Ö. Thorsson (ed.), *The Sagas of Icelanders* (2000, Penguin), pp. 3–185

*EHD* – *English Historical Documents*; D. Whitelock, *English Historical Documents 500–1041, Vol. 1* (1979, 2nd edition, Routledge)

*Elene* – *ASPR*, volume 2

*Enc.* – *Encomium Emmae Reginae*; A. Campbell (ed. and trans.) with S. Keynes (ed.), *Encomium Emmae Reginae* (1998, Cambridge University Press)

*Ex.* – Gildas, *De Excidio Britanniae*; M. Winterbottom (ed. and trans.), *Gildas: The Ruin of Britain and Other Works* (1978, Phillimore)

*FA* – *Fragmentary Annals* (see 'Note on Irish chronicles' above)

*FH* – Roger of Wendover, *Flores Historiarum*; H. O. Coxe (ed.), *Rogeri de Wendover Chronica; sive, Flores Historiarum* (1841–2, Sumptibus Societatis); translated passages in *EHD*

*Finnsburg* – *The Fight at Finnsburg* (*ASPR*, volume 6)

*GD* – Saxo Grammaticus, *Gesta Danorum*; P. Fisher (trans.) and K. Fries-Jensen (ed.), *Saxo Grammaticus: The History of the Danes, Book I–IX. Volume I* (1979, Brewer)

*Genesis* – *ASPR*, volume 1

*GH* – Adam of Bremen, *Gesta Hammaburgensis ecclesiae pontificum*; F. J. Tschan (ed. and trans.), *History of the Archbishops of Hamburg-Bremen* (2002, Columbia University Press)

*GRA* – William of Malmesbury, *Gesta Regum Anglorum*; R. A. B. Mynors, R. M. Thomson and M. Winterbottom (eds and trans.), *William of Malmesbury: Gesta Regum Anglorum* (1998, Oxford University Press)

*Grímnismál* – A. Orchard, *The Elder Edda: A Book of Viking Lore* (2011, Penguin), pp. 38–41

*Gylfaginning* – Snorri Sturluson, 'Gylfaginning'; J. L. Byock (ed. and trans.), *The Prose Edda* (2006, Penguin), pp. 9–79

*HA* – Henry of Huntingdon, *Historia Anglorum*; D. Greenway, *Henry, Archdeacon of Huntingdon: Historia Anglorum/The History of the English People* (1996, Oxford Medieval Texts)

*Hávamál* – A. Orchard, *The Elder Edda: A Book of Viking Lore* (2011, Penguin), pp. 15–39

HB – *Historia Brittonum*; J. Morris (ed. and trans.), *Nennius, British History and the Welsh Annals* (1980, Phillimore)

HE – Bede, *Historia Ecclesiastica Gentis Anglorum*; D. H. Farmer (ed. and trans.) and L. Sherley-Price (trans.), *Ecclesiastical History of the English People* (1991, Penguin)

*Heimskringla I* – Snorri Sturluson, *Heimskringla*; A. Finlay and A. Faulkes (eds and trans.), *Heimskringla Volume I: The Beginnings to Óláfr Tryggvason* (2011, Viking Society for Northern Research)

*Heimskringla II* – Snorri Sturluson, *Heimskringla*; A. Finlay and A. Faulkes (eds and trans.), *Heimskringla Volume II: Óláfr Haraldsson* (The Saint) (2014, Viking Society for Northern Research)

*Helgakviða Hundingsbana fyrri* – A. Orchard, *The Elder Edda: A Book of Viking Lore* (2011, Penguin), pp. 117–25

HR – Symeon of Durham, *Historia Regum*; T. Arnold (ed.), *Symeonis Monachi Opera Omnia* (2012 [1885], Cambridge University Press); translated passages in *EHD*

HSC – *Historia Sancti Cuthberti*; *EHD* (6)

*Krákumál* – B. Waggoner (ed. and trans.), *The Sagas of Ragnar Lodbrok* (2009, The Troth)

*Lokasenna* – A. Orchard, *The Elder Edda: A Book of Viking Lore* (2011, Penguin), pp. 83–96

*Maldon* – *The Battle of Maldon* (*ASPR*, volume 6)

*Maxims II* – *ASPR*, volume 6

N – Norway (geographical reference; runestones)

NMR – National Monument Record number (Historic England) [http://pastscape.org.uk]

NMS – National Museum of Scotland registration number

OE *Boethius* – The Old English *Boethius*. S. Irvine and M. Godden (eds), *The Old English Boethius with Verse Prologues and Epilogues Associated with King Alfred* (2012, Harvard University Press)

*Orkneyinga saga* – H. Palsson and P. Edwards, *Orkneyinga Saga: The History of the Earls of Orkney* (1981, Penguin)

*PSE* – Abbo of Fleury, *Passio S. Eadmundi*; F. Hervey (ed. and trans.), *Corolla Sancti Eadmundi: The Garland of Saint Eadmun d King and Martyr* (1907, E. P. Dutton)

r. – regnal dates

*Ragnarssona þáttr* – B. Waggoner (ed. and trans.), *The Sagas of Ragnar Lodbrok* (2009, The Troth)

*Ragnars saga Loðbrókar* – B. Waggoner (ed. and trans.), *The Sagas of Ragnar Lodbrok* (2009, The Troth)

*RFA* – *Royal Frankish Annals*; B. W. Scholz (ed. and trans.), *Carolingian Chronicles: Royal Frankish Annals and Nithard's Histories* (1970, Ann Arbor)

*Rígsthula* – A. Orchard, *The Elder Edda: A Book of Viking Lore* (2011, Penguin), pp. 243–9

Rundata – Scandinavian Runic-text Database [http://www.nordiska.uu.se/forskn/samnord.htm/?languageId=1]

S – Charter number in P. H. Sawyer, *Anglo-Saxon Charters: An Annotated List and Bibliography* (1968, Royal Historical Society) [esawyer.org.uk]

s. a. – *sub anno* ('under the year')

Sö – Södermanland, Sweden (geographical reference; runestones)

*Thrymskvida* – A. Orchard, *The Elder Edda: A Book of Viking Lore* (2011, Penguin), pp. 96–101

U – Uppland, Sweden (geographical reference; runestones)

*VA* – Asser, *Vita Ælfredi Regis Angul Saxonum*; S. Keynes and M. Lapidge (eds and trans.), *Alfred the Great: Asser's 'Life of King Alfred' and Other Contemporary Sources* (1983, Penguin)

Vg – Västergötland, Sweden (geographical reference; runestones)

*VKM* – Einhard, *Vita Karoli Magni*; S. E. Turner (ed. and trans.), *Einhard: The Life of Charlemagne* (1880, Harper & Brothers)

*Völuspá* – A. Orchard, *The Elder Edda: A Book of Viking Lore* (2011, Penguin), pp. 5–15

*VSG* – Felix, *Vita Sancti Guthlaci*; B. Colgrave (ed. and trans.), *Felix's Life of Saint Guthlac* (1956, Cambridge University Press)

*Wanderer* – *ASPR*, volume 3

# NOTES

1. *Wanderer*, lines 101–5

**Preface**
1. J. Jones, 'Vikings at the British Museum: Great Ship but Where's the Story?', *Guardian* (4 March 2014) [http://www.theguardian.com/artanddesign/2014/mar/04/vikings-british-museum-ship-story]
2. In recent years, spectacular Viking hoards have been discovered in Galloway (2014), at Lenborough, Buckinghamshire (2014) and at Watlington, Oxfordshire (2015)
3. The recently launched 'Viking Phenomenon' project, for example, directed by Professor Neil Price at the University of Uppsala, is a ten-year programme with a budget of approximately six million US dollars. [http://www.arkeologi.uu.se/Research/Projects/vikingafenomenet]

**Chapter 1: Outsiders from Across the Water**
1. *Beowulf*; trans. S. Heaney, *Beowulf: A New Translation* (1999, Faber), pp. 9–10
2. *ASC* D, *sub anno* 787
3. *ASN*
4. *CA*, p. 27
5. *ASC* D s.a. 787
6. *CC* s.a. 787
7. *EHD*, line 20
8. Although the poem's story is set in a vaguely defined legendary epoch (seemingly the fifth century), it was written in Old English (and presumably in England) at some point between the seventh and the eleventh centuries. The manuscript in which the received form of the poem survives – the Nowell Codex – dates to around the year 1000, and attempts to refine the dating of an earlier archetype remain highly controversial. A recent survey of the issues can be found in L. Neidorf (ed.), *The Dating of Beowulf: A Reassessment* (2014, Boydell & Brewer)
9. *Beowulf*, lines 237–57; trans. Heaney (1999)
10. Gildas, *De Excidio Britanniae* (*Ex.*)

11. It should be noted that some recent research has proposed dates earlier than Offa's reign for some sections of the dyke. It also remains unclear what should and should not be considered part of the continuous structure. The most detailed review of the evidence can be found in K. Ray and I. Bapty, *Offa's Dyke: Landscape & Hegemony in Eighth-Century Britain* (2016, Oxbow)

12. *ASC* s.a. 796

13. R. Bruce-Mitford, *The Sutton Hoo Ship-Burial, Volumes 1–3* (1975–1983, British Museum Press); M. Carver, *Sutton Hoo: A Seventh-Century Princely Burial Ground and Its Context*, report of the Research Committee of the Society of Antiquaries of London 69 (2005, British Museum Press)

14. The principal source, aside from the *ASC*, is the *Annales Cambriae* ('the Welsh Annals') abbreviated henceforth as *AC*

15. The Ordovices (Gwynedd), Demetae (Dyfed), Silures (Gwent), and Cornovii (Powys); see T. Charles-Edwards, *Wales and the Britons: 350–1064* (2013, Oxford University Press), pp. 14–21

16. R. Bartlett, *The Making of Europe: Conquest, Colonization and Cultural Change 950–1350* (1993, Penguin)

17. M. Carver, *Portmahomack: Monastery of the Picts* (2008, Edinburgh University Press)

18. *Beowulf*, lines 255–7

19. Mercian diplomas S134, 160, 168, 177, 186, 1264 (792–822)

20. C. Downham, '"Hiberno-Norwegians" and "Anglo-Danes": Anachronistic Ethnicities and Viking-Age England', *Mediaeval Scandinavia* 19 (2009), pp. 139–69

## Chapter 2: Heart of Darkness

1. *The Holy Bible, King James Version* (1769, Cambridge Edition); [*King James Bible Online*, 2017. http://www.kingjamesbibleonline.org]

2. *Gylfaginning*, ch. 49 (own translation)

3. This, and the subsequent extracts, are taken from the Old English boundary clause of a charter dated to 808 describing a grant of land at North Stoke, Somerset from the West Saxon king, Cynewulf, to the monks of St Peter's Minster (S265)

4. All these creatures, and many others, are mentioned in Old English charter-bounds. A survey of some of the beastly entities that occur in Old English place-names more generally can be found in papers by John Baker ('Entomological Etymologies: Creepy-Crawlies in English Place-Names') and Della Hooke ('Beasts, Birds and Other Creatures in Pre-Conquest Charters and Place-Names in England'), both of which appear in M. D. J. Bintley and T. J. T. Williams (eds), *Representing Beasts in Early Medieval England and Scandinavia* (2015, Boydell & Brewer)

5. There are many examples of parishes in England where this tradition is maintained or has been revived – a notable, and high-profile, beating of the bounds takes place at the Tower of London (http://blog.hrp.org.uk/blog/beating-the-bounds/); it is not possible, however, to determine if any of these traditions have been consistently performed from the early medieval period

6. D. Adams, *The Hitchhiker's Guide to the Galaxy* (1979, Pan Books)

7. Recent books have increasingly addressed the cultural aspects of map-making, including Alastair Bonnett's *Off the Map* (2015, Aurum Press) and Jerry Brotton's *A History of the World in Twelve Maps* (2013, Penguin)

8. P. D. A. Harvey, *Mappa Mundi: The Hereford World Map* (2010, Hereford Cathedral)

9. *Genesis*, lines 103–15

10. *Beowulf*, lines 102–4

11. Ibid., line 710

12. On wolfish imagery in Britain and Scandinavia see A. Pluskowski, *Wolves and the Wilderness in the Middle Ages* (2006, Boydell & Brewer)

13. *Beowulf*, lines 1358–9

14. *VSG*, pp. 104–5

15. Irmeli Valtonen discusses the cartographical material and the classical tradition of a monstrous north in her *The North in the Old English Orosius: A Geographical Narrative in Context*, Mémoires de la Société Néophilologique de Helsinki LXXIII (2008, Société Néophilologique): 'Thule' was first mentioned by Pytheas (330–320 BC), Hyperborea by Hecateus in the sixth century BC, with some references even earlier

16. *VSG*, pp. 104–5

17. Visio S. Pauli in Blickling Homily XVI, translated by Andy Orchard in *Pride and Prodigies: Studies in the Monsters of the Beowulf Manuscript* (1995, 2nd edition, University of Toronto), p. 39

18. Jude S. Mackley, *The Legend of St. Brendan: A Comparative Study of the Latin and Anglo-Norman Versions* (2008, Brill), p. 85

19. By the thirteenth century at any rate; *Gylfaginning*, ch. 49

20. E. Christiansen, *The Northern Crusades* (1997, Penguin), p. 76

21. *ASC* DE s.a. 793

22. One of a number of islands around a dozen miles to the south-east of Lindisfarne

23. *BVSC*, ch. 17

24. *VSG*, ch. XXX

25. Alcuin's letter to Ethelred, *EHD* (193)

26. See, in general, J. Palmer, *The Apocalypse in the Early Middle Ages* (2014, Cambridge University Press)

27. Alcuin's letter to Higbald, *EHD* (194) (Accusing the survivors of an atrocity of having brought it all on themselves through their lifestyle choices, before berating them for defending themselves inadequately, is a form of sanctimony not new to the modern age.)

28. Alcuin's letter to Ethelred, *EHD* (193)

29. See, for example, D. Bates and R. Liddiard (eds), *East Anglia and Its North Sea World in the Middle Ages* (2015, Boydell & Brewer); S. P. Ashby, A. Coutu and S. Sindbæk, 'Urban Networks and Arctic Outlands: Craft Specialists and Reindeer Antler in Viking Towns', *European Journal of Archaeology* 18.4 (2015), pp. 679–704

30. Alex Woolf, 'Sutton Hoo and Sweden Revisited', in A. Gnasso, E. E. Intagliata, T. J. MacMaster and B. N. Morris (eds), *The Long Seventh Century: Continuity and Discontinuity in an Age of Transition* (2015, Peter Lang), pp. 5–18; M. Carver, 'Pre-Viking Traffic in the North Sea', in S.

McGrail (ed.), *Maritime Celts, Frisians and Saxons* (1990, CBA Research Report 71), pp. 117–25

31. *HE* I.15 (Sherley-Price; Farmer)
32. Valtonen, *The North in the Old English Orosius*, Chapter 3
33. For foundational work on the genealogies, see K. Sisam, 'Anglo-Saxon Royal Genealogies', *Proceedings of the British Academy* 39 (1953), pp. 287–348 and D. Dumville, 'Kingship, Genealogies and Regnal Lists', in P. W. Sawyer and I. N. Wood (eds), *Early Medieval Kingship* (1977, Leeds University), pp. 72–104
34. Alcuin's letter to Higbald, *EHD* (194)
35. J. T. Koch, 'Yr Hen Ogledd' in J. T. Koch (ed.), *Celtic Culture: An Historical Encyclopedia*, Vol. III (2006, ABC-CLIO); J. E. Fraser, 'From Ancient Scythia to the Problem of the Picts: Thoughts on the Quest for Pictish Origins' in S. T. Driscoll, J. Geddes and M. A. Hall (eds), *Pictish Progress: New Studies on Northern Britain in the Early Middle Ages* (2011, Brill)

## Chapter 3: Mother North

1. R. E. Howard, 'The Dark Man', *Weird Tales* (December 1931)
2. The Gjermundbu helmet is now in the Norwegian Historical Museum in Oslo (http://www.khm.uio.no/english/visit-us/historical-museum/index.html)
3. 'Sermon of the Wolf to the English', *EHD* (240)
4. The best work on this subject has been published by Judith Jesch: for a clear overview of the meaning of the word 'Viking', see *The Viking Diaspora* (2015, Routledge); detailed analysis can be found in *Ships and Men in the Late Viking Age: The Vocabulary of Runic Inscriptions and Skaldic Verse* (2001, Boydell & Brewer)
5. J. J. North, *English Hammered Coinage*, Vol. 1 (1994, Spink), p. 175
6. There are quite a few names of moneyers (individuals responsible for the production of coinage and whose names are frequently recorded on their coins) that fall into this category. Brandr can mean both 'fire' and 'sword' in Old Norse, for instance. (A particularly intriguing example – though not a Norse name – is that of Matathan Balluc. His first name is Gaelic, and he may have been part of the Norse–Irish community that linked York and Dublin in the tenth and eleventh centuries. His second name, however, is the Old English word 'Bollock'. We will never know whether he possessed impressive testicular attributes in the figurative or the literal sense or, indeed, whether the use of the singular was deliberately significant.) However, many of the most famous 'Viking' epithets – 'Skull-splitter', 'Bloodaxe', 'Hard-ruler' and so on – were first recorded in Icelandic literature written down long after the end of the Viking Age
7. Preserved in *Egil's Saga*, and attributed to Egil Skallagrimsson (*c.* 950); translation by J. Jesch in *Viking Poetry of Love and War* (2013, British Museum Press), p. 53
8. Rundata (Vg 61)
9. There is some evidence to suggest that Old Norse speakers also recognized this commonality among themselves – several medieval sources refer to the *Dansk tongu* in terms that indicate that this was a language spoken by Icelanders, Norwegians and Swedes as well as by Danes (Jesch, *Diaspora*)

10. These connections – particularly the link between Jacob Grimm's linguistic revelations and the ethno-archaeological approaches of the early twentieth century are delineated in I. Wood, *The Modern Origins of the Early Middle Ages* (2013, Oxford University Press)

11. The German archaeologist, Gustaf Kossina, is perhaps the central figure of culture-historical theory. His influence on Nazi archaeology and racial theory tainted his legacy in post-war Europe, and more nuanced – and less obviously racist – approaches were pioneered by a new generation of British post-war archaeologists following the lead of pioneers such as Vere Gordon Childe. In many parts of the world, however, these habits of thought have been dying hard and in some cases have sprung back into life, generally where they are underpinned by resurgent nationalist sentiment and/or supported by the state. The former communist republics of Eurasia are notable examples. For an example of the chilling influence of the Russian state in Viking studies, see Leo S. Klejn's paper, 'Normanisn and Anti-Normanism in Russia: An Eyewitness Account', in P. Bauduin and A. Musin (eds), *Vers l'Orient et Vers l'Occident: Regards croisés sur les dynamiques et les transferts culturels des Vikings à la Rous ancienne* (2014, Presses Universitaires de Caen), pp. 407–17

12. P. Geary, *The Myth of Nations: The Medieval Origins of Europe* (2001, Princeton University Press) is a classic debunking of this sort of thing

13. R. M. Ballantyne, *Erling the Bold: A Tale of the Norse Sea-Kings* (1869)

14. J. Parker, *England's Darling: The Victorian Cult of Alfred the Great* (2007, Manchester University Press)

15. C. G. Allen, *The Song of Frithiof, Retold in Modern Verse* (1912, Hodder & Stoughton), with illustrations by T. H. Robinson; R. Wagner [trans. M. Armour], *The Rhinegold & The Valkyrie* (1910, William Heinemann) and *Siegfried & The Twilight of the Gods* (1911, William Heinemann) with illustrations by A. Rackham

16. Adapted from the text of the 2 June 1941 meeting of Nasjonal Samling at Borre, as given by Lise Nordenborg Myhre in 'Fortida som propaganda Arkeologi og nazisme – en faglig okkupasjon', *Frá haug ok heiðni* 1 (1995)

17. Ibid.; see also B. Myhre, *The Significance of Borre* in J. M. Fladmark (ed.), *Heritage and Identity: Shaping the Nations of the North* (2002, Routledge)

18. J. Graham-Campbell, *Viking Art* (2013, Thames & Hudson), pp. 48–81

19. B. Myhre, 'The Significance of Borre' in J. M. Fladmark (ed.), *Heritage and Identity: Shaping the Nations of the North* (2002, Routledge)

20. On the novelty of nationalism see Ernest Gellner, *Nations and Nationalism* (2006, 2nd revised edition, Wiley-Blackwell)

21. In Wodehouse's *The Code of the Woosters* (1938, Herbert Jenkins), Bertie Wooster famously unleashes the following put-down: 'The trouble with you, Spode, is that because you have succeeded in inducing a handful of halfwits to disfigure the London scene by going about in black shorts, you think you're someone [...] You hear them shouting "Heil Spode!" and you imagine it is the Voice of the People. That is where you make your bloomer. What the Voice of the People is saying is: "Look at that frightful ass Spode, swanking about in footer bags! Did you ever in your puff see such a perfect perisher!"'

22. J. R. R. Tolkien, letter to his son Michael (45). H. Carpenter (ed.), *The Letters of J. R. R. Tolkien* (2006, 8th edition, HarperCollins), No. 45, pp. 55–6

23. R. Paulas, 'How a Thor-Worshipping Religion Turned Racist', *Vice* (1 May 2015) [https://www.vice.com/en_us/article/how-a-thor-worshipping-religion-turned-racist-456]

24. P. Sawyer, *The Age of the Vikings* (1975, 2nd revised edition, Hodder & Stoughton)

25. Neil Price points the way to this darker, weirder Viking in his introduction ('From Ginnungagap to the Ragnarök: Archaeologies of the Viking Worlds') to M. H. Eriksen, U. Pedersen, B. Rundtberger, I. Axelsen and H. L. Berg (eds), *Viking Worlds: Things, Spaces and Movement*, as well as more generally in his wider oeuvre

26. J. Trigg, *Hitler's Vikings: The History of the Scandinavian Waffen-SS: The Legions, the SS-Wiking and the SS-Nordland* (2012, 2nd edition, The History Press)

## Chapter 4: Shores in Flames

1. This Old Irish poem was written into the margins of a manuscript copy of a grammatical treatise (*Institutiones Grammaticae*) by the sixth-century author Priscian of Caesarea (http://www.e-codices.unifr.ch/en/list/one/csg/0904). The manuscript, and the marginalia, date to the middle of the ninth century. Translation from R. Thurneysen, *Old Irish Reader* (1949, Dublin Institute for Advanced Studies), translated from the original German by D. A. Binchy and O. Bergin

2. *AI*; s.a. 795; *ASC* DE s.a. 794; *AU* s.a. 802, 806; *FH* s.a. 800; *HR* s.a. 794

3. *AU* s.a. 795, 798, 807; *AI* s.a. 798

4. BM 1870,0609.1

5. M. Redknapp, *Vikings in Wales: An Archaeological Quest* (2000, National Museum of Wales Books); M. Redknapp, 'Defining Identities in Viking Age North Wales: New Data from Llanbedrgoch' in V. E. Turner, O. A. Owen and D. J. Waugh (eds), *Shetland in the Viking World* (2016, Papers from the Proceedings of the Seventeenth Viking Congress Lerwick), pp. 159–66

6. M. Carver, *Portmahomack: Monastery of the Picts* (2008, Edinburgh University Press), p. 3

7. Ibid.

8. NMS X.IB 189 (http://www.nms.ac.uk/explore/stories/scottish-history-and-archaeology/hilton-of-cadboll-stone/). Where exactly the stone originally stood is unknown but, by the 1660s, it lay somewhere in the immediate vicinity of its replica. See Sian Jones' paper '"That Stone Was Born Here and That's Where It Belongs": Hilton of Cadboll and the Negotiation of Identity, Ownership and Belonging', in S. M. Foster and M. Cross (eds), *Able Minds and Practised Hands: Scotland's Early Medieval Sculpture in the 21st Century* (2005, Society for Medieval Archaeology), pp. 37–54. Martin Carver's paper in the same volume ('Sculpture in Action: Contexts for Stone Carving on the Tarbat Peninsula, Easter Ross', pp.13–36) draws out the wider context

9. The earliest symbol stones may date to the late fourth century. Iain Fraser (ed.), *The Pictish Symbol Stones of Scotland* (2008, RCAHMS) provides a

good introduction. Adrian Maldonado's review of the aforementioned volume in the *Scottish Archaeological Journal*, 30.1–2, pp. 215–17 is a handy guide to the main literature on the subject. The papers in Foster and Cross (eds), *Able Minds and Practised Hands*, provide multiple perspectives

10. A surviving example is the slab that still stands in the churchyard at Eassie near Glamis (Canmore ID 32092). Cf. the fate of the Woodwray cross-slab (Iain Fraser, '"Just an Ald Steen": Reverence, Reuse, Revulsion and Rediscovery' in Foster and Cross (eds), *Able Minds and Practised Hands*, pp. 55–68)

11. Fraser, '"Just an Ald Steen"', p. 62; Carver (*Portmahomack*) gives alternative possibilities, and the true motivations of whoever broke the stones are irrecoverable

12. Carver, *Portmahomack*; the individuals were respectively carbon-dated to 680–900 and 810–1020

13. In fact, there is good evidence that activity at Portmahomack continued for centuries after this incident, a traumatic moment in the life of a settlement, but not its death-knell. What does seem to have changed is the focus of activity on the site (Carver, *Portmahomack*, pp. 136–48)

14. Lord Smith was appointed by the then Prime Minister David Cameron in 2014 to oversee the devolution commitments made by the government during and after the Scottish Referendum of the same year

15. What seems to have been a gaming board was found among the slates (Carver, *Portmahomack*, p. 47)

16. The slate is now housed at Bute Museum (http://www.butemuseum.org. uk/1061-2/). Technically it is two objects: the image is split between two fragments of what was originally one slate

17. C. Lowe, 'Image and Imagination: The Inchmarnock "Hostage Stone"', in B. B. Smith, S. Taylor and G. Williams (eds), *West over Sea: Studies in Scandinavian Sea-Borne Expansion and Settlement Before 1300* (2007, Brill), pp. 53–6

18. M. Blindheim, 'The Ranuaik Reliquary in Copenhagen: A Short Study' in J. B. Knirk (ed.), *Proceedings of the Tenth Viking Congress, Larkollen* (1985, Universitetets Oldsaksamlings Skrifter), pp. 203–18. Egon Wamers gives a sense of the quantity of Irish and British metalwork that made its way to Scandinavia in this period: E. Wamers, 'Insular Finds in Viking Age Scandinavia and the State Formation of Norway' in H. B. Clarke, M. Ní Mhaonaigh and R. Ó Floinn (eds), *Ireland and Scandinavia in the Early Viking Age* (1998, Four Courts Press); also A. M. Heen-Pettersen, 'Insular Artefacts from Viking-Age Burials from Mid-Norway. A Review of Contact between Trøndelag and Britain and Ireland', *Internet Archaeology* 38 (2014) [https://doi.org/10.11141/ia.38.2]

19. As Snorri tells it, at the end of the world 'the ship Naglfar loosens from its moorings. It is made from the nails of dead men, and for this reason it is worth considering the warning that if a person dies with untrimmed nails he contributes crucial material to Naglfar, a ship that both gods and men would prefer not to see built': *Gylfaginning*, 51

20. The word most often used to describe Vikings in Irish chronicles is *gennti* ('gentiles'). Charles-Edwards gives the original word in his translation – I have substituted 'heathen' here and throughout; *AU* s.a. 824

21. J. Jesch, *Women in the Viking Age* (1991, Boydell & Brewer), pp. 45–6
22. Other possibilities include the translation of relics guarded by a warrior retinue, although the composition doesn't seem to support this (one would expect the relics and their bearer to have been the absolute focal point of any such scene); another possibility is that the stone depicts a scene from the life of St Patrick – his abduction by Scottish raiders in the sixth century given an anachronistic treatment *c.* 800. If this is the case, it is probably inspired by or modelled after contemporary events and still therefore reflective of the dangers facing monastic communities at that time. There is no certainty that the warriors depicted are necessarily Vikings, but the broadly known circumstances of its creation and certain details of the ship (the combination of sail and oars) imply that this is the case (see Lowe, 'Image and Imagination')
23. Ibn Rusta, c. 913, translated in P. Lunde and C. Stone, *Ibn Fadlān and the Land of Darkness: Arab Travellers in the Far North* (2012, Penguin), p. 126
24. Ibn Fadlan, describing events of 921–2; Lunde and Stone, *Ibn Fadlān and the Land of Darkness*, p. 53
25. Peter Frankopan, *The Silk Roads: A New History of the World* (2015, Bloomsbury)
26. *AU* s.a. 821; 831; 836
27. Research is under way, and will form part of the research outputs of the Viking Phenomenon project at Uppsala University (http://www.arkeologi.uu.se/Research/Projects/vikingafenomenet/). See also A. Lawler, 'Vikings May Have First Taken to Seas to Find Women, Slaves', *Science* (15 April 2016)
28. S. Brink, 'Slavery in the Viking Age'; S. Brink with N. Price (eds), *The Viking World* (2008, Routledge), pp. 49–56
29. *Rígsthula*, verses 12–13
30. D. A. E. Pelteret, *Slavery in Early Mediaeval England: From the Reign of Alfred Until the Twelfth Century* (2001, Boydell & Brewer)
31. *AU* s.a. 836

## Chapter 5: Beyond the North Waves

1. R. Kipling, *Puck of Pook's Hill* (1906, Macmillan)
2. See Chapter 21
3. *Capitulatio de partibus Saxoniae* ('Ordinances concerning Saxony'). See D. C. Munro, *Selections from the Laws of Charles the Great* (2004 [original printing 1900], Kessinger Publishing)
4. Similar fears had been shared by at least some English-speaking peoples, although by the end of the eighth century these had been eroded, forgotten, replaced and transformed by two centuries of Christian mission. See papers in M. Carver (ed.), *The Cross Goes North: Processes of Conversion in Northern Europe, AD 300–1300* (2003, Boydell Press)
5. One of the Saxon tribal leaders – Widukind – had sought sanctuary among the Danes after Charlemagne's early victories, returning in 782 to foment rebellion. The *Royal Frankish Annals* claim that the Danevirke was built new in 808; archaeological investigation has shown, however, that its first stages date to the sixth century and that it was reinforced from the mid-eighth century onward: A. Pedersen, 'Monumental Expression and

Fortification in Denmark in the Time of King Harald Bluetooth', in N. Christie and H. Herold (eds), *Fortified Settlements in Early Medieval Europe: Defended Communities of the 8th–10th Centuries* (2016, Oxbow), Chapter 6

6. *RFA* s.a. 804
7. *RFA* s.a. 808
8. C. B. McClendon, *The Origins of Medieval Architecture: Building in Europe, A.D. 600–900* (2005, Yale University Press), pp. 105–28
9. *Codex Carolinus* 81 (Ibid., p. 112); *VKM*, 26
10. *RFA* s.a. 810
11. For an overview of the Carolingian context see R. Hodges, *Towns and Trade in the Age of Charlemagne* (2000, Bloomsbury Publishing)
12. G. S. Munch, O. S. Johansen and E. Roesdahl (eds), *Borg in Lofoten. A Chieftain's Farm in North Norway* (2003, Tapir Academic Press)
13. S. Ratke and R. Simek, 'Guldgubber: Relics of Pre-Christian Law Rituals?' in A. Andrén, K. Jennbert and C. Raudvere (eds), *Old Norse Religion in Long-Term Perspectives: Origins, Changes, and Interactions* (2006, Nordic Academic Press), pp. 259–64
14. N. Price, 'Belief and Ritual' in G. Williams, P. Pentz and M. Wemhoff (eds), *Vikings: Life and Legend* (2014, British Museum Press), pp.162–95
15. J. Story, *Carolingian Connections: Anglo-Saxon England and Carolingian Francia, c. 750–870* (2003, Ashgate)
16. B. Myhre, 'The Beginning of the Viking Age – Some Current Archaeological Problems', in A. Faulkes and R. Perkins, *Viking Revaluations* (1993, Viking Society for Northern Research), pp. 192–203; Myrhe's arguments are rather more subtle and plausible than they are often presented in the work of others
17. With the exception of the kingdom of Bhutan (which, to the country's inexplicably unique credit, uses a measure of 'gross national happiness' (GNH) to judge the success of its domestic policies)
18. *Gododdin*
19. *Maxims II*, lines 21–8, p. 514
20. 'Kennings' are poetic allusions, used in both ON and OE verse, that provided poets with an endless number of ways to describe things and concepts, often using mythological references or deeply symbolic language. These examples, and their provenances, can be found amongst the eighteen kennings for 'generous ruler' listed in the database of *The Skaldic Project* (http://skaldic.abdn.ac.uk)
21. J. Jesch, 'Eagles, Ravens and Wolves: Beasts of Battle, Symbols of Victory and Death', in J. Jesch (ed.), *The Scandinavians from the Vendel Period to the Tenth Century* (2002, Boydell & Brewer), pp. 251–71
22. T. Earle, *How Chiefs Come to Power: The Political Economy in Prehistory* (1997, Stanford University Press); in some tribal societies – including, possibly, the small kingdoms of early medieval Britain – the potentially apocalyptic outcomes of spiralling violence and rapacity were forestalled by the evolution of ritualized warfare, confined to certain seasons and locations and hedged around with mutually understood norms and rules of engagement. This, of course, only really works if everyone is playing the same game. One of the reasons why Viking attacks in Britain and elsewhere

were reported with such horror and alarm was perhaps in part because they didn't know the rules (or, if they did, chose not to play by them); G. R. W. Halsall, 'Playing by Whose Rules? A Further Look at Viking Atrocity in the Ninth Century', *Medieval History*, 2.2 (1992), pp. 3–12; T. J. T. Williams, *Landscape and Warfare in Early Medieval Britain* (2016, unpublished PhD thesis)

23. This, essentially, was the thrust of the 2014 British Museum exhibition and its accompanying publication, G. Williams et al. (eds), *Vikings: Life and Legend*

## Chapter 6: The Gathering Storm

1. *Finnsburg*, lines 5–12

2. We should, however, bear in mind that the record we have of these years is far from being complete – there are, for example, no surviving chronicles produced in Mercia or East Anglia that provide an independent insight into what was going on in these regions, and the West Saxon chronicle only records what its compilers in the late ninth century wanted their readers to remember. There are, in fact, hints that unrecorded coastal raids did occur in Kent (at least), and possibly before the killings in Portland took place. A synod attended by Offa of Mercia in 782 includes provision for an expedition against pagans arriving in ships in Kent and Essex. Susan Kelly (ed.), *The Charters of St Augustine's Abbey, Canterbury, and Minster-in-Thanet*, Anglo-Saxon Charters 4 (1995, Oxford University Press), no. 15

3. It is worth considering that twenty-nine years prior to the publication of this book the Soviet Union was still an apparently permanent feature of the geopolitical scene

4. *ASC* F s.a. 798

5. *ASC* s.a. 813 (F s.a. 815)

6. *ASC* s.a. 823

7. *HA*, iv.29

8. *ASC* s.a. 832; Ships dated to the ninth century and excavated in Norway can be reliably estimated to have had crews of between 40 (the Oseberg ship) and 66 (the Gokstad ship); see T. Sjøvold, *The Viking Ships in Oslo* (1985, Universitetets Oldsaksamling); G. Williams, *The Viking Ship* (2014, British Museum Press). For an introduction to debates regarding the size of ninth-century armies see G. Halsall, *Warfare and Society in the Barbarian West, 450–900* (2003, Routledge)

9. *Elene*, lines 99–123; prose translation of Old English verse by S. A. J. Bradley, *Anglo-Saxon Poetry* (1982, Everyman), p. 168

10. See Halsall, *Warfare and Society*, for the messy reality of early medieval combat; sixty-four shields were excavated with the Gokstad ship, and may have been made specifically for display during the burial rites; they were hung outwards along the gunnels of the ship, thirty-two per side: Sjøvold, *The Viking Ships in Oslo*, p. 58

11. There is a degree of mystery surrounding this object – despite its obvious quality, it seems to have been discarded or hidden, deposited in a pit on a domestic workshop plot in Viking York. The circumstances under which it was disposed of remain obscure; D. Tweddle, *The Anglian Helmet from 16–22 Coppergate* (1992, Council for British Archaeology)

12. J. W. Binns, E. C. Norton, D. M. Palliser, 'The Latin Inscription on the Coppergate Helmet', *Antiquity* 64.242 (1990), pp. 134–9

13. G. Williams, 'Warfare & Military Expansion' in G. Williams et al. (eds), *Vikings: Life and Legend*, pp. 76–115; S. Norr, 'Old Gold – The Helmet in *Hákonarmál* as a Sign of Its Time', in S. Norr (ed.), *Valsgärde Studies: The Place and Its People, Past and Present* (2008, Uppsala), pp. 83–114

14. *ASC* s.a. 833. The literature concerning the nature of military obligation in Anglo-Saxon England is vast. For an introduction to the key themes and literature see R. Lavelle, *Alfred's Wars: Sources and Interpretations of Anglo-Saxon Warfare in the Viking Age* (2010, Boydell & Brewer), and for an influential overview R. P. Abels, *Lordship and Military Obligation in Anglo-Saxon England* (1988, University of California Press)

15. T. J. T. Williams, *Landscape and Warfare in Early Medieval Britain*

16. *ASC* s.a. 835

17. P. C. Herring, *The Archaeology of Kit Hill: Kit Hill Archaeological Survey Project Final Report* (1990, 2nd edition, Cornwall Archaeological Unit)

18. Herring, *The Archaeology of Kit Hill*, p. 141; D. L. Prior, 'Call, Sir John, first baronet (1732–1801)', *Oxford Dictionary of National Biography* (2004, Oxford University Press)

19. M. Peake, *Titus Groan* (1946, Eyre & Spottiswood), p. 1

20. Herring, *The Archaeology of Kit Hill*. It is easy to imagine the voice of David Jason: 'Deep inside this picturesque hill, somewhere in the sleepy countryside of Cornwall, Baron Silas Greenback, the world's most villainous toad, is plotting to detonate a massive nuclear warhead …'

21. This sort of tautology is a remarkably common occurrence in British place-names. Multiple linguistic layers – Celtic, Latin, Old English, Old Norse, Norman French – have resulted in older word elements (having lost their original sense) being combined with newer words with similar meanings: for example, Eas Fors waterfall on the Isle of Mull ('waterfall' [*eas*, Gaelic] + 'waterfall' [*fors, foss*, ON] + waterfall [ModE]) or Breedon on the Hill, Leicestershire ('hill' [*bre*, Brittonic] + 'hill' [*dun*, OE] + 'on the hill' [ModE]).

22. T. J. T. Williams, '"For the Sake of Bravado in the Wilderness": Confronting the Bestial in Anglo-Saxon Warfare', in Bintley and Williams (eds), *Representing Beasts*, pp. 176–204

23. T. J. T. Williams, 'The Place of Slaughter: The West Saxon Battlescape' in R. Lavelle and S. Roffey (eds), *The Danes in Wessex* (2016, Oxbow), pp. 35–55; T. J. T. Williams, *Landscape and Warfare in Early Medieval Britain*

## Chapter 7: Dragon-Slayers

1. A. Lang, *The Red Fairy Book* (1906, Longmans, Green and Co.)

2. *ASC* BCDE s.a. 851; *CA* adds 'on Thanet', *VA* and *CC* suggest Sheppey

3. *FH* s.a. 844

4. *ASC* s.a. 839; 851 (C s.a. 853)

5. All s.a. 837; 838; 839; ADEF s.a. 840 (C s.a. 841); s.a. 851 (C s.a. 853)

6. *ASC* s.a. 848

7. *ASC* s.a. 850 (C s.a. 853); Either the burial mound of a man called Wicga, or a mound infested with 'wiggling' things (Baker, 'Entomological Etymologies')

8. *ASC* s.a. 851 (C s.a. 853). The location of Aclea is unknown, although Ockley in Surrey is a plausible candidate

9. For a sceptical and comprehensive analysis of feuding in Anglo-Saxon England, see J. D. Niles, 'The Myth of the Feud in Anglo-Saxon England', *Journal of English and Germanic Philology* 114 (2015), pp. 163–200

10. G. Williams, 'Viking Camps in England and Ireland' in G. Williams et al. (eds), *Vikings: Life and Legend* (pp. 120–1) is a useful introduction to the subject of Viking camps

11. B. Orme, *Anthropology for Archaeologists* (1981, Cornell University Press), p. 196

12. G. Halsall, 'Anthropology and the Study of Pre-Conquest Warfare and Society', in S. C. Hawkes (ed.), *Weapons and Warfare in Anglo-Saxon England* (1989, Oxford University Committee for Archaeology), pp. 155–78; T. J. T. Williams, 'The Place of Slaughter'

13. Halsall, 'Playing by Whose Rules?'

14. It should be noted, however, that – as I have argued elsewhere – the impression of novelty may be a product of the increased detail present in the source material from the ninth century onward: T. J. T. Williams, 'The Place of Slaughter' and *Landscape and Warfare in Early Medieval Britain*

15. This was normally a reference to Slavic people, but may have referred to any European transported eastward as a slave: Lunde and Stone, *Ibn Fadlān and the Land of Darkness*, p. 222, n. 2

16. Ibn Rusta, *c.* 913, translated in Lunde and Stone, *Ibn Fadlān and the Land of Darkness*, p. 126

17. *EHD* (13.1); R. Abels, 'The Micel Hæðen Here and the Viking Threat', in T. Reuters (ed.), *Alfred the Great: Papers from the Eleventh-Centenary Conferences* (2003, Ashgate), pp. 269–71; T. J. T. Williams, 'The Place of Slaughter'

18. See Chapter 13

19. G. Williams, 'Raiding and Warfare', in Brink with Price (eds), *The Viking World*, pp. 193–203

20. L. Abrams, 'The Conversion of the Danelaw' in J. Graham-Campbell, R. Hall, J. Jesch and D. N. Parsons (eds), *Vikings and the Danelaw: Select Papers from the Proceedings of the Thirteenth Viking Congress* (2001, Oxbow), pp. 31–44; cf. D. M. Hadley, 'Conquest, Colonization and the Church: Ecclesiastical Organization in the Danelaw', *Historical Research* 69, pp. 109–28

21. 'Dore, Whitwell Gap and the River Humber' (*ASC* ABCD s.a. 942); G. Rollason, *Northumbria, 500–1100: Creation and Destruction of a Kingdom* (2003, Cambridge University Press), p. 26

22. *ASC* s.a. 827; S. Keynes, 'Bretwalda or *Brytenwalda*', in M. Lapidge, J. Blair. and S. Keynes (eds), *The Blackwell Encyclopaedia of Anglo-Saxon England* (2008, 8th edition, Wiley-Blackwell), p. 74

23. *ASC* s.a. 867

24. Rollason, *Northumbria*, pp. 192–8

25. All these behaviours are attested to in one way or another in Anglo-Saxon England. Farting in the general direction of the enemy could be one part of the defiant warrior's arsenal; when in 1068 William the Conqueror turned up at Exeter expecting the town's surrender, he was roused to particular

wrath towards the 'irreverent' defenders because 'one of them' – according to the twelfth-century historian William of Malmesbury – 'standing upon the wall, had bared his posteriors, and had broken wind, in contempt of the Normans [*GRA*, b.III]'; in 1006, a Viking army had jeered at the cowering townsfolk of Winchester (*ASC* CDE s.a. 1006), and the display of severed heads seems to have been commonplace in Anglo-Saxon judicial culture: A. Reynolds, *Anglo-Saxon Deviant Burial Customs* (2009, Oxford University Press)

26. *ASC* s.a. 867 (C s.a. 868); *VA*, 27
27. *Ragnarssona þáttr* ('The Tale of Ragnar's Sons'); *Ragnars saga Loðbrókar* ('The Saga of Ragnar Loðbrók'); *Krákumál* ('The Song of Kraka'); *Gesta Danorum* ('Deeds of the Danes') by Saxo Grammaticus (*GD*)
28. *Jarl* is an Old Norse word designating a nobleman – roughly analogous to the OE *ealdorman*
29. Saxo Grammaticus, in perhaps the earliest version of this tale, recounts that there were several serpents given to Þóra, and that they roamed wild over the land, burning and poisoning with their foul breath; *GD*, book IX
30. *Krákumál*, verse 1
31. *Beowulf*, lines 2312–20; trans. Heaney, p. 73
32. *Beowulf*, lines 2275–7; trans. Heaney, p. 72
33. *Maxims II*, lines 26–7
34. *Maxims II*, lines 28–9
35. *Völuspá*, verse 66
36. J. R. R. Tolkien, 'The Monsters and the Critics' [1936], in C. Tolkien (ed.), *The Monsters and the Critics and Other Essays* (1997, HarperCollins), p. 12; *Beowulf*'s dragon is undeniably a model for the depiction of Smaug the Golden in Tolkien's *The Hobbit*, originally published by George Allen & Unwin in 1937
37. The most complete version of the story is told in the late thirteenth-century Old Norse *Völsunga saga*, but it is also told in poetic form in a number of related – so-called 'eddic' – poems compiled together in the Icelandic Codex Regius: J. L. Byock (trans.), *The Saga of the Volsungs: The Norse Epic of Sigurd the Dragon Slayer* (1999, 2nd edition, Penguin); A. Orchard, *The Elder Edda: A Book of Viking Lore* (2011, Penguin)
38. C. E. Doepler, *Der Ring des Nibelungen: Carl Emil Doeplers Kostümbilder für die Erstaufführung des Ring in Bayreuth* (2012 [1889], Reprint-Verlag Leipzig); see also R. Wagner [trans. M. Armour], *The Rhinegold & The Valkyrie* (1910, William Heinemann) and *Siegfried & The Twilight of the Gods* (1911, William Heinemann) with illustrations by A. Rackham
39. J. R. R. Tolkien, 'On Fairy Stories' [1947], in C. Tolkien (ed.), *The Monsters and the Critics and Other Essays*, p. 135
40. E. Magnússon and W. Morris (trans.),*Völsunga Saga: The Story of the Volsungs and Niblungs, with certain Songs from the Elder Edda* (1870, F. S. Ellis)
41. J. R. R. Tolkien, *The Legend of Sigurd and Gudrún* (2009, HarperCollins)
42. G. B. Shaw, 'William Morris as I Knew Him', Introduction to May Morris, *William Morris: Artist, Writer, Socialist*, vol. 2 (1936, Blackwell), p. xxxvii
43. 'Letter 216' in N. Kelvin (ed.), *The Collected Letters of William Morris*, volume 1 (1984, Princeton University Press), p. 205

44. *Beowulf*, in what is clearly intended as a foreshadowing of events to come, refers to the Sigurd legend directly, although the poem substitutes Sigurd's father Sigemund in the role of dragon-slayer; lines 873–99

45. G. Williams et al. (eds), *Vikings: Life and Legend* (pp. 120–1), p. 88; Tatarstan is a Russian republic with its capital at Kazan

46. Rundata (Sö 101; Sö 327); see V. Symons, '*Wreoþenhilt ond wyrmfah*: Confronting Serpents in *Beowulf* and Beyond' in Bintley and Williams (eds), *Representing Beasts*, pp. 73–93

47. The Manx stones are as follows: Maughold 122; Andreas 121; Jurby 119; Malew 120; they are identified by the name of the parish in which they were found and the catalogue number assigned in P. M. C. Kermode, *Manx Crosses or The Inscribed and Sculptured Monuments of the Isle of Man From About the End of the Fifth to the Beginning of the Thirteenth Century* (2005 [1907], Elibron Classics). See also S. Margeson, 'On the Iconography of the Manx Crosses' in C. Fell, P. Foote, J. Graham-Campbell and R. Thomson (eds), *The Viking Age in the Isle of Man* (1983, Viking Society for Northern Research). The English stone cross-shaft is designated in *CASSS* as Halton St Wilfrid 1, 2, 9 and 10

48. *Ragnars saga Loðbrókar*

49. R. McTurk, *Studies in Ragnars saga loðbrókar and Its Major Scandinavian Analogues* (1991, Society for the Study of Medieval Languages and Literature)

## Chapter 8: Eagles of Blood

1. *Hávamál*, 144

2. One of Ragnar's sons is named as Hvitserk ('Whiteshirt') in *Ragnarssona þáttr*; this may have been an alternative name for the individual named Halfdan and identified as a brother of Ivar and Ubbe in the *Anglo-Saxon Chronicle*: *ASC* All MSS s.a. 878 (C s.a. 879)

3. *Ragnarssona þáttr*

4. *GD*, book IX; a similar version appears in *Ragnars saga Loðbrókar*

5. M. Townend, 'Knútsdrápa', in D. Whaley (ed.), *Poetry from the Kings' Sagas 1: From Mythical Times to c. 1035* (2012, Brepols), p. 649

6. R. Frank, 'Viking Atrocity and Skaldic Verse: The Rite of the Blood-Eagle', *English Historical Review* XCIX.CCCXCI (1984), pp. 332–43

7. Ibid., p. 337

8. Ibid.

9. Ibid., p. 337

10. *GH* IV.26; The translated passage is taken from A. Orchard, *Dictionary of Norse Myth and Legend* (1997, Cassell), p. 169

11. O. Sundqvist, *An Arena for Higher Powers: Ceremonial Buildings and Religious Strategies in Late Iron Age Scandinavia* (2015, Brill), pp. 110–15

12. Archaeological interventions have discovered evidence for buildings underlying the cathedral church at Gamla Uppsala; these are no longer believed to belong to the temple described by Adam of Bremen; see A. M. Alkarp and N. Price, 'Tempel av guld eller kyrka av trä? : markradarundersökningar vid Gamla Uppsala kyrka', *Fornvännen* 100:4 (2005), pp. 261–72

13. Analysis of the excavated material has cast doubt on whether the human remains should be considered part of the evidence for sacrificial ritual – they seem to have been grouped together and show fewer signs of weathering than the animal bones, implying that they were buried earlier. This research also emphasized the presence of butchery marks on many of the animal bones – including the bones of several brown bears – implying that the animals were killed and cut up before being deposited at the tree (although none of this rules out the possibility that they were suspended from the tree in pieces, or butchered after having been taken down). O. Magnell and E. Iregren, 'Veitstu Hvé Blóta Skal? The Old Norse blót in the light of osteological remains from Frösö Church, Jämtland, Sweden', *Current Swedish Archaeology* 18 (2010), pp. 223–50; see also Price, 'Belief and Ritual' for a wider discussion of the evidence of cult sites

14. Lunde and Stone, *Ibn Fadlān and the Land of Darkness*, p. 48

15. Ibid., p. 162

16. A. E. Christensen and M. Nockert, *Osebergfunnet IV: Tekstilene* (2016, Kulturhistorisk Museum, Universitetet i Oslo)

17. *Orkneyinga saga*, 8; the story is repeated by Snorri in *Heimskringla*, probably drawing on the saga: 'Haralds saga ins Hárfagra', chapter 30 (*Heimskringla I*)

18. N. Price, *The Viking Way: Religion and War in Late Iron Age Scandinavia* (2002, Uppsala University), pp. 100–7

19. *Völuspa*, 28

20. *Hávamál*, 138–9

21. *ASC* s.a. 867

22. 'Ynglinga saga', chapter 8 (*Heimskringla I*)

23. 'Hákonar saga góða', chapters 13–14 (*Heimskringla I*)

24. *CC* s.a. 868, pp. 282–5; also *ASC* All MSS s.a. 868 (C s.a. 869)

25. Halsall, *Warfare and Society*, p. 223

26. It once adorned the walls of the king's palace at Nineveh (in modern Iraq), but can now be seen at the British Museum in London (a fact for which the whole world should be grateful since the remains of Nineveh were systematically obliterated by Islamic extremists in 2015)

27. The Vikings, according to the poem *De bellis Parisiacæ urbis* [or *Bella Parisiacæ urbis*] by the Parisian monk Abbo, may have used some sort of rock-lobber during the siege of Paris in 886, though his account is exaggerated in a number of details (N. Dass (ed. and trans.), *Viking Attacks on Paris: The Bella Parisiacae Urbis of Abbo of Saint-Germain-des-Prés* (2007, Peeters Publishers); Halsall, *Warfare and Society*, p. 225)

28. *ASC* C s.a. 917

29. *CC* s.a. 868, pp. 282–5; *ASC* s.a. 868 (C s.a. 869)

30. We should, however, be slightly cautious about accepting the *ASC* at face value here; Mercia produced no independent chronicle for this period, and the only guide to events is provided by the Wessex-produced *ASC* compiled in the following decades. The reality of West Saxon involvement may have been far more complex and ambiguous than the *ASC*'s version allows

31. *ASC* s.a. 870 (C s.a. 871)

32. Beornwulf (*ASC* s.a. 823; *CC* s.a. 823) and Ludeca (*ASC* s.a. 825; *CC* s.a. 825)

33. *PSE*, V
34. *PSE*, X
35. It is likely, however, that Viking chiefs did indeed play central roles in cult practice. For an introduction to the issues see O. Sundqvist, 'Cult Leaders, Rulers and Religion' in Brink with Price, *The Viking World*, pp. 223–6
36. *PSE*, XIII
37. *PSE*, XIV
38. R. Pinner, *The Cult of St Edmund in Medieval East Anglia* (2015, Boydell & Brewer)
39. The mystery of the Holy Trinity is among the most baffling and incomprehensible aspects of Christian theology. Vatican attempts at clarification cannot always be judged wholly satisfactory (http://www.vatican.va/archive/ccc_css/archive/catechism/p1s2c1p2.htm)

## Chapter 9: Wayland's Bones

1. W. Camden, *Britannia*, 'Barkshire', 12: P. Holland (trans.), D. F. Sutton (ed.) (2004 [1607], The University of California): http://www.philological.bham.ac.uk/cambrit/
2. Thomas Hughes, *Tom Brown's School Days* (1857, Macmillan), pp. 11–13
3. The quote is attributed to Vladimir Ilyich Ulyanov (Lenin), but he never seems to have used these precise words. He is, however, recorded saying: 'we [...] must probe with bayonets whether the social revolution of the proletariat in Poland had ripened': R. Pipes (ed.), *The Unknown Lenin: From the Secret Archive* (1996, Yale University Press). In 1975, the American columnist Joseph Alsop wrote: 'The Soviets [...] merely follow Lenin's advice to probe with bayonets any situation that looks mushy, withdrawing only when the bayonets meet steel' (J. Alsop, 'Post-Vietnam Assessment is Intense and Painful', *Sunday Advocate* (18 May 1975), p. 2-B, col. 2)
4. *VA*, 35–6
5. *VA*, 35–6. No evidence for any major earthworks of this period have yet been discovered at Reading (J. Graham-Campbell, 'The Archaeology of the "Great Army" (865–79)', in E. Roesdahl and J. P. Schjødt (eds), *Beretning fra treogtyvende tværfaglige vikingesymposium* (2004, Aarhus Universitet), pp. 30–46). It is possible that the defences were hastily built, perhaps utilizing buildings and timbers that were already present. If so, this might explain the reluctance of the Viking army to place much faith in the defences
6. *ASC* s.a. 871 (C s.a. 872)
7. *VA*, 35–6, p. 78
8. *EE*, 2953–71; Geoffrey is a little difficult to evaluate as a historian of this period; although his *Estoire des Engleis* (1135–7) contains details that are not preserved anywhere else (and he would have had few reasons to invent them), he also had a habit of including obviously fantastical material and was writing many centuries after the event
9. *ASC* s.a. 871 (C s.a. 872); *VA*, 37–9
10. *VA*, 37–9; Asser is probably mistaken about the death of Sidroc the Old – according to the *ASC* he had been killed at Englefield
11. A number of suggestions have been made. See, for example, P. Marren, *Battles of the Dark Ages* (2006, Pen & Sword Books), pp. 118–21

12. F. Wise, *A Letter to Dr Mead Concerning Some Antiquities in Berkshire: Particularly Shewing that the White Horse, which Gives Name to the Vale, is a Monument of the West-Saxons, Made in Memory of a Great Victory Obtained Over the Danes A.D. 871* (1738, Oxford)

13. Ibid., p. 23

14. Hughes, *Tom Brown's School Days*, p. 13

15. Ibid., p. 7

16. M. Gelling, *The Place-Names of Berkshire*, volumes I and II (1973; 1974, English Place-Name Society, volumes 49/50)

17. It is also possible that battles were not fought at these places at all, that these might simply have been the royal manors closest to where the fighting took place, and therefore useful geographical markers that everyone – especially the king – would have recognized

18. S288

19. S524

20. O. S. Anderson, *The English Hundred Names: The South-Western Counties* (1939, University of Lund), pp. 14–15

21. G. B. Grundy, 'The Ancient Highways and Tracks of Wiltshire, Berkshire, and Hampshire, and the Saxon Battlefields of Wiltshire', *Archaeological Journal* 75 (1918), pp. 69–194

22. NMR: SU 28 NE 4

23. It is also, incidentally, nearer to how it would have appeared to J. R. R. Tolkien when he visited the place with his family in the 1930s – one of a number of sights near Oxford to which the professor drove in his Morris Cowley (named 'Jo'), charging around the countryside in a manner which his biographer Humphrey Carpenter described as 'daring rather than skilful'. H. Carpenter, *J. R. R. Tolkien: A Biography* (2002 [1977], HarperCollins), p. 39

24. The phrase appears in a boundary clause, in a charter of King Eadred (r. 946–55) dated to 955 (S564); the phrases 'Wayland's Smithy' and 'Wayland Smith' may or may not have something to do with the choice of the name 'Waylon Smithers' for the subservient assistant to Springfield power-plant owner Monty Burns. If this is a deliberate joke, the relevance is not altogether clear. It has been suggested that the choice of name may be an ironic inversion of macho stereotypes, the violent, rapey manual labourer becomes, in Mr Smithers, an effete, homosexual personal assistant. I think it's a push, but who knows? The creators of *The Simpsons* have never – so far as I am aware – made any comment on the matter. M. S. Cecire, 'Wayland Smith in Popular Culture' in D. Clarke and N. Perkins, *Anglo-Saxon Culture and the Modern Imagination* (2010, Boydell & Brewer), pp. 201–18

25. Wise, *Letter to Dr Mead*, p. 37

26. Wise also asserted that the tomb was the burial place of the Viking king Bacsecg, a claim for which he offers no supporting evidence whatsoever and which is, needless to say, total bunk. This is not to say, however, that important Vikings were never interred beneath impressive monuments, as the following chapter elaborates

27. *Boethius* II.7; OE *Boethius* XIX. The works traditionally believed to have emanated from Alfred's circle are summarized in S. Keynes and M.

Lapidge, *Alfred the Great: Asser's 'Life of King Alfred' and Other Contemporary Sources* (1983, Penguin), p. 29. Alfred's personal input has, however, been questioned in recent years, especially by Malcolm Godden (M. Godden, 'Did King Alfred Write Anything?', *Medium Ævum* 76 (2007), pp. 1–23). The noun *faber* in Latin means 'smith'; it is uncertain whether Alfred is being playful or erroneously literalistic in his translation of the Latin proper name Fabricius

28. C. R. Peers and R. A. Smith, 'Wayland's Smithy, Berkshire', *The Antiquaries Journal : Journal of the Society of Antiquaries of London* 1 (1921), pp. 183–98

29. N. G. Discenaza, 'Power, Skill and Virtue in the Old English *Boethius*', *Anglo-Saxon England* 26 (1997), pp. 81–108

30. *Beowulf*, line 907; *Deor*, lines 1–13

31. *Völundarkvida*, verse 34

32. Price, 'From Ginnungagap to the Ragnarök: Archaeologies of the Viking Worlds', p. 7

33. Sigmund Freud, 'The Uncanny' (trans. Alix Strachey), in S. L. Gilman (ed.), *Sigmund Freud: Psychological Writings and Letters* (1995, Continuum), pp. 126, 142; see also G. Moshenska, 'The Archaeological Uncanny', *Public Archaeology* 5 (2006), pp. 91–9 and 'M. R. James and the Archaeological Uncanny', *Antiquity* 86.334 (2012), pp. 1192–1201

34. *ASC* s.a. 871 (C s.a. 872)

35. Ibid.

## Chapter 10: Real Men

1. *CC* s.a. 850

2. *ASC* s.a. 872 (C s.a. 873)

3. *ASC* s.a. 873 (C s.a. 874)

4. *ASC* s.a. 874 (C s.a. 875)

5. W. J. Moore, *The Saxon Pilgrims to Rome and the Schola Saxonum* (1937, University of Fribourg)

6. St Wystan's churchyard is also notable as the resting place of the extraordinarily multi-talented C. B. Fry (1872–1956). His career took in football, rugby, athletics, acrobatics, politics, writing, publishing, broadcasting, teaching and, above all, cricket. One can't help but think that had Fry been around in 874, the Vikings would have found themselves batting on a very sticky wicket

7. R. I. Page, *Norse Myths* (1990, British Museum Press), p. 35

8. *Gylfaginning*, 21

9. *Thrymskvida*, verse 8; Freya was the goddess of love, sex and fertility: she was frequently an object of desire among gods, giants, elves and dwarves: Orchard, *Dictionary*, p. 48

10. *Thrymskvida*, verses 15–17

11. Ibid., verse 31

12. Page, *Norse Myths*, p. 14

13. P. M. Sørensen, *The Unmanly Man: Concepts of Sexual Defamation in Early Northern Society* (1983, Odense University Press)

14. In general, D. Wyatt, *Slaves and Warriors in Medieval Britain and Ireland, 800–1200* (2009, Brill), pp. 206–14; Sørensen, *The Unmanly Man*, pp. 76, 83

15. Ibid., pp. 17–18, 80, 82, 111; see also, for example, the planned rape of a man and his wife by the hero of *Guðmundar saga dýra* (Wyatt, *Slaves and Warriors*, pp. 211–12)

16. *Helgakviða Hundingsbana fyrri*, verses 37–43

17. *Lokasenna*, verse 24

18. S. W. Nordeide, 'Thor's Hammer in Norway: A Symbol of Reaction against the Christian Cross?', in Andrén et al., *Old Norse Religion in Long-Term Perspectives*. A. S. Gräslund, 'Thor's Hammers, Pendant Crosses and Other Amulets' in E. Roesdahl and D. Wilson (eds), *From Viking to Crusader: The Scandinavians and Europe 800–1200* (1992, Nordic Council of Ministers)

19. J. Staecker, 'The Cross Goes North: Christian Symbols and Scandinavian Women' in M. Carver (ed.), *The Cross Goes North*, pp. 463–82

20. DR 110, DR 209, DR 220, Vg 150; Tentative: Sö 140

21. *Thrymskvida*, verse 30

22. S. Degge, 'An Account of an Humane Skeleton of an Extraordinary Size, Found in a Repository at Repton in Derbyshire ...', *Philosophical Transactions* 35 (1727–8), pp. 363–5; M. Biddle and B. Kjølbye-Biddle, 'Repton and the "Great Heathen Army", 873–4', in Graham-Campbell et al. (eds), *Vikings and the Danelaw*, pp. 45–96

23. Degge, 'An Account of an Humane Skeleton'

24. R. Bigsby, *Historical and Topographical Description of Repton* (1854)

25. J. Richards et al., 'Excavations at the Viking Barrow Cemetery at Heath Wood, Ingleby, Derbyshire', *The Antiquaries Journal* 84 (2004), pp. 23–116; cf. Biddle and Kjølbye-Biddle, who suggested – largely on account of the apparent stature of a number of the male skeletons – that many of the later bones were of Scandinavian origin, and were the recovered bones of earlier deceased members of the Viking army. In February 2018, new research was published which indicated that the age of the bones in the mass grave are consistent with a single act of deposition in the late ninth century, a result which has been taken to be supportive of the interpretation advanced by the original excavators (see C. Jarman, M. Biddle, T. Higham and C. Bronk Ramsey, 'The Viking Great Army in England: New Dates from the Repton Charnel', *Antiquity* 92.361 (2018), pp. 183–99)

26. According to the thirteenth-century *Chronicon Abbatiae de Evesham*, King Cnut had the relics of Wystan moved to Evesham in the early eleventh century (J. Sayers and L. Watkiss (eds and trans.), *Thomas of Marlborough: History of the Abbey of Evesham* (2003, Clarendon Press)); this is suspicious, however, on a number of levels (How did Wystan's relics survive the Viking takeover? What was the nature of the relics moved by Cnut, and how can we be sure they ever belonged to Wystan? Did Cnut ever move anything to Evesham, or did the monks of Evesham simply need a credible provenance for whatever mouldy old bones they had decided could usefully be attributed to an obscure saint? And so on)

27. If he can be equated with the Imair of the Irish chronicles, Ivar the Boneless had been active in the Irish Sea, on and off, during the 850s, 860s and 870s: C. Downham, *Viking Kings of Britain and Ireland* (2007, Dunedin). The *Annals of Ulster* record his death as 873, the year the *micel here* came to Repton. The tenth-century English chronicler Æthelweard states that he died in 870, but implies that his death came in England. *Ragnars saga*

*Loðbrókar* claims that he was buried in Northumbria under a barrow (see Biddle and Kjølbye-Biddle, 'Repton', pp. 81–4)

28. 'Ynglinga saga', chapter 8 (*Heimskringla I*)
29. Ibn Fadlan; Lunde and Stone, *Ibn Fadlān and the Land of Darkness*, p. 51
30. Ibid., p. 53
31. Although ibn Fadlan recounts that a poor man was also burned in a small boat, and modest boat burials are known from Britain and Scandinavia; ibid., p.4
32. Ibid., p. 54
33. Although it is the diversity of Viking burial practice – as we have already begun to see – that is perhaps its most defining characteristic. N. Price, *Odin's Whisper: Death and the Vikings* (2016, Reaktion Books); also Price, 'Belief and Ritual'
34. *ASC* s.a. 876

## Chapter 11: The Return of the King

1. G. K. Chesterton, *Ballad of the White Horse* (2010 [1911], Dover Publications), Book I
2. *VA*, 53
3. *Beowulf*, lines 102–4
4. *VA*, 92; see also the explanatory notes to the text in Keynes and Lapidge, *Alfred the Great*
5. Ibid.
6. *VA*, 55
7. *ASC* s.a. 874; *VA*, verse 48
8. *ASC* A s.a. 877; the events are also mentioned in all other versions of the *ASC* s.a. 877 (C s.a. 878) and *VA*, 49
9. Ibid.
10. *CA*, p. 42
11. *VA*, 52; see also *ASC* s.a. 878 (C s.a. 879)
12. *HSC*, 16
13. L. Simpson, 'The Alfred/St Cuthbert Episode in the Historia de Sancto Cuthberto: Its Significance for mid-Tenth Century English History' in G. Bonner, D. W. Rollason and C. Stancliffe (eds), *St Cuthbert, His Cult and His Community to AD 1200* (2002, Boydell & Brewer), pp. 397–412
14. *HSC*, 12–13
15. *ASC* s.a. 878 (C s.a. 879); *ASN* s.a. 878, p. 78; *VA*, 54, pp. 83–4 ; *CA*, p. 43; *EE*, 3144–56
16. Geoffrey Gaimar later claimed that his body was interred at a place called 'Ubbelawe' ('Ubbe's barrow') in Devon (*EE*, 3144–56)
17. *ASC* s.a. 878 (C s.a. 879)
18. *ASN*, s.a. 878
19. Lavelle, *Alfred's Wars*, pp. 55–106; J. Baker and S. Brookes, *Beyond the Burghal Hidage: Anglo-Saxon Civil Defence in the Viking Age* (2013, Brill), pp. 199–208; Halsall, *Warfare and Society*, pp. 40–133
20. Anglo-Saxon riddles could be surprisingly suggestive. For example, Riddle 44 in the *Exeter Book* is translated into prose by S. A. J. Bradley (*Anglo-Saxon Poetry*, p. 379) as follows: 'A curiosity hangs by the thigh of a man, under its master's cloak. It is pierced through in the front; it is stiff and hard

and it has a good standing-place. When the man pulls up his own robe above his knee, he means to poke with the head of his hanging thing that familiar hole of matching length which he has often filled before.' Riddles 25 and 45 are also notoriously rude: all are translated by Bradley; see also K. Crossley-Holland, *The Exeter Book Riddles* (1993, Penguin) [the solution to Riddle 44 is 'Key']

21. The story of Finn and Hengest is told in two Old English poems, *Beowulf* and a fragment known as 'the Fight [or Battle] at Finnsburgh' (*ASPR* 6); it is a tale of divided loyalties, betrayal and revenge. The episode was discussed by Tolkien in a series of lectures, published after his death as 'Finn and Hengest: The Fragment and the Episode' (2006 [1982], HarperCollins)

22. For Anglo-Saxon beacon systems see D. Hill and S. Sharpe, 'An Anglo-Saxon Beacon System', in A. Rumble and D. Mills (eds), *Names, Places & People* (1997, Paul Wathius), pp. 97–108, and extensive discussion in Baker and Brookes, *Beyond the Burghal Hidage*

23. *VA*, 55–6

24. Baker and Brookes, *Beyond the Burghal Hidage*, pp. 186–7; J. Baker, 'Warrior and Watchmen: Place Names and Anglo-Saxon Civil Defence', *Medieval Archaeology* 55 (2011), pp. 258–9

25. Anderson, *The English Hundred Names: The South-Western Counties*, p. 152

26. P. H. Robinson, 'The Excavations of Jeffery Whitaker at Bratton Camp', *Wiltshire Archaeological and Natural History Magazine Bulletin* 25 (1979), pp. 11–13

27. A. L. Meaney, *A Gazetteer of Early Anglo-Saxon Burial Sites* (1964, Allen & Unwin), p. 266

28. *Beowulf*, lines 3137–49

29. T. J. T. Williams, 'The Place of Slaughter'; the place-name Edington (Eðandun) may have been used by the chronicler to suggest a reference to Alfred's grandfather Egbert and his achievements at Ellendun in 825, a victory that prefigured Alfred's own in establishing a greater West Saxon sphere of control (the alliteration, rhyme and equal syllabic count of the two place-names may also have helped to foster the comparison)

30. S290

31. Alfred's Will is translated in Keynes and Lapidge, *Alfred the Great* (pp.173–8); S1508; S765

32. NMR ST 95 SW 38

33. G. K. Chesterton, *Alarms and Discursions* (1910, Methuen)

34. Parker, *England's Darling*

35. Ibid., p. 195, n. 16

36. E. A. Freeman, *The History of the Norman Conquest of England*, 5 vols (1867–79, Clarendon Press), p. 51

37. See especially Parker, *England's Darling*, but also S. Keynes, 'The Cult of King Alfred the Great' in *Anglo-Saxon England* 28 (1999), pp. 225–356 and B. Yorke, *The King Alfred Millenary in Winchester, 1901* (1999, Hampshire County Council)

38. T. Shippey, *The Road to Middle-Earth: How J.R.R. Tolkien Created a New Mythology* (2005, 2nd edition, HarperCollins)

39. Shippey, *Road to Middle-Earth*, pp. 222–31; Tolkien, *On Fairy-Stories*; H. Carpenter, *The Inklings: C.S. Lewis, J.R.R. Tolkien, Charles Williams and their Friends* (2006, 4th edition, Harper Collins), pp. 42–5

40. G. K. Chesterton, 'The Blatchford Controversies' [1904], in D. Dooley (ed.), *The Collected Works of G.K. Chesterton*, vol. 1(1986, Ignatius Press)

41. Chesterton, *Ballad of the White Horse*

42. Parker, *England's Darling*

43. Carpenter (ed.), *The Letters of J.R.R.Tolkien*, No. 80, p. 92

## Chapter 12: The Godfather

1. G. K. Chesterton, *Ballad of the White Horse* (2011 [1911], Dover Publications), Book VIII

2. An example of a mid-ninth-century Anglo-Saxon font survives at Deerhurst (Gloucestershire). R. Bryant, *Corpus of Anglo-Saxon Stone Sculpture: Vol. X, The Western Midlands* (2012, Oxford University Press), pp. 161–90

3. *VA*, 46, p. 85

4. E. Dümmler (ed.), *Epistolae Karolini Aevi*, vol. 2 (1895, Berlin), nos 134 and 137; J. H. Lynch, *Christianizing Kinship: Ritual Sponsorship in Anglo-Saxon England* (1998, Cornell University Press)

5. It is possible, however, that Alfred's son Edward was promoted to a 'kingship' – perhaps of Kent – later on; a charter which includes both Edward and Alfred lists him as *rex* on a Kentish charter's witness list (Alfred is designated *rex Saxonum*); Keynes, 'The Control of Kent', *Early Medieval Europe* 2.2 (1993), pp. 111–31

6. *VA*, 56; *ASC* s.a. 878 (C s.a. 879)

7. *ASC* s.a. 880 (C s.a. 881)

8. The evidence is fairly complex, but relates to the naming of moneyers unknown at established southern mints, die links between 'Alfred' coins and others, and the maintenance of a different weight standard. See M. A. S. Blackburn, 'Presidential Address 2004. Currency under the Vikings. Part 1: Guthrum and the Earliest Danelaw Coinages', *British Numismatic Journal* 75 (2005), pp. 18–43

9. G. Williams, 'Kingship, Christianity and Coinage: Monetary and Political Perspectives on Silver Economy in the Viking Age', in J. Graham-Campbell and G. Williams, *Silver Economy in the Viking Age* (2007, Left Coast Press), pp. 177–214

10. Alfred-Guthrum, 1

11. Keynes and Lapidge, *Alfred the Great*, p. 171 (although the dating of the treaty is open to revision: G. Williams, *pers. comm.*)

12. D. Hadley, *The Vikings in England: Settlement, Society and Culture* (2006, Manchester University Press), pp. 31–3; P. Kershaw, 'The Alfred-Guthrum Treaty: Scripting Accommodation and Interaction in Viking Age England', in D. M. Hadley and J. D. Richards (eds), *Cultures in Contact: Scandinavian Settlement in England in the Ninth and Tenth Centuries* (2000, Brepols), pp. 43–64

13. *ASC* s.a. 886 (C s.a. 887)

14. Alfred-Guthrum, 'Prologue'

15. Kershaw, 'The Alfred-Guthrum Treaty'; P. Foote, 'The Making of Angelcynn: English Identity before the Norman Conquest', *Transactions of the Royal Historical Society*, 6th Series, 6 (1996), pp. 25–49
16. Ibid. See also Downham, '"Hiberno-Norwegians" and "Anglo-Danes"'
17. *ASC* s.a. 871 (C s.a. 872); *VA*, 40
18. The large quantities of 'Anglo-Saxon' material culture at a Viking camp like Torksey might even be evidence of this (see following Chapter 13)
19. 'Sermon of the Wolf to the English', *EHD* (240)
20. Ibid.
21. Alfred-Guthrum, 5
22. S362; B. Yorke, 'Edward as Atheling', in N. J. Higham and D. H. Hill (eds), *Edward the Elder, 899–924* (2001, Routledge), pp. 25–39

## Chapter 13: Rogue Traders

1. R. E. Howard, 'The Dark Man', *Weird Tales* (December 1931)
2. *VA*, 91
3. *VA*, 91
4. Nor was it any use bothering the king's ear with humiliating apologies, for – as Asser helpfully pointed out – 'what use is their accursed repentance, when it cannot help their slaughtered kinsfolk, nor redeem those captured from a hateful captivity, nor even occasionally be of use to themselves who have escaped, since they no longer have anything by which to sustain their own life?'; *VA*, 91
5. Ibid.
6. *VA*, 8, 11; see also the notes in Keynes and Lapidge, *Alfred the Great*, pp. 232, 234; the issues around Alfred's interactions with the pope are discussed in J. Nelson, 'The Problem of King Alfred's Royal Anointing', *Journal of Ecclesiastical History* 18.2 (1967), pp. 145–63
7. *ASC* A s.a. 853; this was evidently a good lesson in the political advantages that could be gained by turning powerful aquaintances into one's 'sons'
8. S. Irvine, 'The Anglo-Saxon Chronicle and the Idea of Rome in Alfredian Literature', and D. Hill, 'The Origins of Alfred's Urban Policies', in T. Reuter (ed.), *Alfred the Great* (2003, Ashgate), pp. 63–77; pp. 219–33
9. *VA*, 91
10. It only acquired that name in 1897 thanks to the intervention of the great legal scholar Frederic William Maitland: *Domesday Book and Beyond. Three Essays in the Early History of England* (1897, Cambridge University Press); D. Hill, 'The Burghal Hidage – the Establishment of a Text', *Medieval Archaeology* 13 (1969), pp. 84–92
11. The relationship of burhs to the territory that sustained them is drawn out in the greatest detail by Baker and Brookes, *Beyond the Burghal Hidage*; see also papers in D. Hill and A. Rumble (eds), *The Defence of Wessex: The Burghal Hidage and Anglo-Saxon Fortifications* (1996, Manchester University Press)
12. S. Keynes, 'Edward, King of the Anglo-Saxons', in N. J. Higham and D. H. Hill (eds), *Edward the Elder, 899–924* (2001, Routledge)
13. N. Brooks, 'The Unidentified Forts of the Burghal Hidage', *Medieval Archaeology* 8.1 (1964), pp. 74–90
14. J. Haslam (ed.), *Anglo-Saxon Towns in Southern England* (1984, Phillimore)

15. S. R. Bassett, 'The Middle and Late Anglo-Saxon Defences of Western Mercian Towns', *Anglo-Saxon Studies in Archaeology and History* 15 (2008), pp. 180–239

16. G. Williams (ed.), *A Riverine Site Near York: A Possible Viking Camp, and Other Related Papers* (forthcoming); M. A. S. Blackburn, 'The Viking Winter Camp at Torksey, 872–3', in M. A. S. Blackburn (ed.), *Viking Coinage and Currency in the British Isles* (2011, Spink), pp. 221–64; D. Hadley and J. D. Richards, 'The Winter Camp of the Viking Great Army, AD 872–3, Torksey, Lincolnshire', *The Antiquaries Journal* 96 (2016), pp. 23–67

17. P. Wallace, *Viking Dublin: The Wood Quay Excavations* (2015, Irish Academic Press); I. Russell and M. F. Hurley (eds), *Woodstown: A Viking-age Settlement in Co. Waterford* (2014, Four Courts Press)

18. I. Gustin, 'Trade and Trust in the Baltic Sea Area during the Viking Age', in J. H. Barrett and S. J. Gibbon (eds), *Maritime Societies of the Viking and Medieval World* (2016, Oxbow), pp. 25–40

19. Some of the most spectacular finds come from the Danish trading site of Hedeby, near the modern town of Schleswig in Germany; an introduction can be found in V. Hilberg, 'Hedeby: An Outline of Its Research History' in Brink with Price, *The Viking World*, pp. 101–11

20. *VA*, 91

21. Viking skulls from Gotland and Dorset have been found that display evidence of deliberate dental modification – horizontal striations filed into the tooth enamel of the front incisors; the purpose was presumably aesthetic; C. Arcini, 'The Vikings Bare Their Filed Teeth', *American Journal of Physical Anthropology* 128 (2005), pp. 727–33; L. Loe, A. Boyle, H. Webb and D. Score (eds), *'Given to the Ground': A Viking Age Mass Grave on Ridgeway Hill, Weymouth* (2014, Dorset Natural History and Archaeological Society)

22. Deliberately bent coins are a relatively common feature of silver coins in Viking hoards, as are those with evidence of what is known as 'nicking' and 'pecking' (deliberate gouges on the surface of the metal); all are methods of testing the purity of the silver: see, for example, M. Archibald, 'Testing' in J. Graham-Campbell (and contributors), *The Cuerdale Hoard and Related Viking-Age Silver and Gold from Britain and Ireland in the British Museum* (2013, 2nd edition, British Museum Press), pp. 51–63

23. R. Gameson (ed.), *The Codex Aureus: An Eighth-Century Gospel Book: Stockholm, Kungliga Bibliotek, A. 135* (2001, Rosenkilde and Bagger)

24. Trans. University of Southampton [http://www.southampton.ac.uk/~enm/codexau.htm]

25. Certainly, the concept of the trading settlement (emporium) was no novelty: Scandinavia had several, and they would continue to develop throughout the tenth century until the largest of them (Hedeby, Birka etc) took on major significance for North Sea economy and the wealth of Scandinavian monarchies – but this was little different to the situation that had pertained in the Anglo-Saxon kingdoms when the Vikings had arrived (D. Skre, 'The Development of Urbanism in Scandinavia' and sub-papers, in Brink with Price, *The Viking World*, pp. 83–145)

26. G. Williams, 'Towns and Identities in Viking England', in D. M. Hadley and L. Ten Harkel (eds), *Everyday Life in Viking-Age Towns: Social Approaches to Towns in England and Ireland, c.800–1100* (2013, Oxbow), pp. 14–34

## Chapter 14: Danelaw

1. *Egil's Saga*, 68
2. 'And Guthrum, the northern king, whose baptismal name was Æthelstan, died; he was King Alfred's godson, and he lived in East Anglia and was the first to settle that land.' *ASC* A s.a. 890
3. See R. Abels, *Alfred the Great: War, Kingship and Culture in Anglo-Saxon England* (1998, Routledge) and Lavelle, *Alfred's Wars*
4. *ASC* s.a. 893–7
5. *ASC* s.a. 897
6. *ASC* A s.a. 901
7. This epithet was coined in the late tenth century by Wulfstan the Cantor to distinguish him from Edward the Martyr; the proliferation of Edwards in royal nomenclature later led to the adoption, from 1215, of a numbering system for Edwards. This, however, started at the number one, with Edward I, disregarding the three – including Edward the Confessor – who had preceded him. The complex science of Edwardology gave medieval historians all sorts of bother: see M. Morris, *A Great and Terrible King: Edward I and the Forging of Britain* (2008, Hutchinson), pp. xv–xvi
8. 'The Will of King Alfred' in Keynes and Lapidge, *Alfred the Great*, pp. 173–8; R. Lavelle, 'The Politics of Rebellion: The Ætheling Æthelwold and West Saxon Royal Succession, 899–902', in P. Skinner (ed.), *Challenging the Boundaries of Medieval History: The Legacy of Timothy Reuter* (2009, Brepols)
9. 'The Will of King Alfred' in Keynes and Lapidge, *Alfred the Great*, pp. 173–8
10. *ASC* s.a. 901
11. Attributed to Ambrosius Aurelianus by Gildas and Bede, but to Arthur in British sources of the ninth century. *Ex.* 26.1; *HE* i.16; *HB*, 56; E. Guest, *Origines Celticae*, Vol. II (1883), pp. 186–93
12. *ASC* A s.a. 901
13. *ASC* D s.a. 901
14. *ASN*
15. Lavelle, 'The Politics of Rebellion'
16. *ASC* A, D s.a. 905
17. *CA*, p. 52
18. The other soft-bearded prince was presumably Beorhtsige, son of Beorhtwulf – whom the *ASC* describes as ætheling (prince). It may be, as some have argued (see Lavelle, 'Politics of Rebellion'), that this Beorhtwulf was a scion of the dispossessed royal house of Mercia, a possibility which puts rather a different complexion on the whole affair; one could quite readily frame the rebellion as armed resistance to a tyrannical and overreaching West Saxon regime: an attempt to restore the pre-878 geopolitics of Britain
19. An initiative that took off in 2001 – the Great Fen project – aims to recreate a much more substantial tract of fen habitat over the next fifty years (http://www.greatfen.org.uk/about/introduction)

20. M. Gelling and A. Cole, *The Landscape of Place-Names* (2014, 3rd edition, Stamford)

21. *Kormáks saga*, chapter 10 (translated by W. G. Collingwood and J. Stefánsson, *The Saga of Cormac the Skald* (Viking Club, or Society for Northern Research), pp. 65–7)

22. Olav Bø, 'Hólmganga and Einvigi: Scandinavian Forms of the Duel', *Medieval Scandinavia* 2 (1969), pp. 132–48

23. T. S. Jonsson, 'Thingvellir as an Early National Cente' in O. Owen (ed.), *Things in the Viking World* (2012, Shetland Amenity Trust), pp. 42–53

24. W. Morris, '1871 and 1873 Journeys to Iceland' in M. Morris (ed.), *The Collected Works of William Morris*, vol. 8, p. 77

25. *Völuspá*, 57, p. 13

26. J. Byock, 'The Icelandic Althing: Dawn of Parliamentary Democracy', in J. M. Fladmark (ed.), *Heritage and Identity: Shaping the Nations of the North* (2002, Donhead), pp. 1–18

27. A. Wawn, *The Vikings and the Victorians* (2000, Boydell), pp. 277–9

28. *Lǫgsǫgumaðr*: the law-speaker was an elected elder/local bigwig whose role was to memorize local law, preside over the *thing* and impose its judgements

29. O. Olwen, 'Things in the Viking World – An Introduction' in Olwen (ed.), *Things*, pp. 4–29; G. Fellows-Jensen, 'Tingwall: The Significance of the Name' in D. Waugh and B. Smith (eds), *Shetland's Northern Links: Language and History* (1996, Scottish Society for Northern Studies), pp. 16–29

30. B. Smith, 'Shetland's Tings', in Olwen (ed.), *Things*, pp. 68–79

31. A. Johnson, 'Tynwald – Ancient Site, Modern Institution – Isle of Man', in Olwen (ed.), *Things*, pp. 104–17 (see also: https://www.thingsites.com/thing-site-profiles/tynwald-hill-isle-of-man)

32. 'Óláfs saga Helga', chapter 80 (*Heimskringla II*)

33. *ASC* A s.a. 909

34. *ASC* A s.a. 911

35. See Baker and Brookes, *Beyond the Burghal Hidage* for the development of Anglo-Saxon civil defence

36. Now a village/suburb on the outskirts of Wolverhampton (West Midlands)

37. *CA*, p. 53

38. Downham, *Viking Kings*

39. Ibid. The sources for this period are woefully inadequate, and the historical arguments surrounding the Uí Ímair are complex

40. D. Horowitz, *Notes and Materials on the Battle of Tettenhall 910 AD, and Other Researches* (2010, self-published)

41. A separate set of annals that provides additional specifics relating to Æthelflæd's remarkable military leadership, later inserted in the C manuscript of the *ASC*

42. *ASC* A s.a. 912

43. J. Haslam, 'The Location of the Burh of Wigingamere – Reappraisal', in A. R. Rumble and A. D. Mills (eds), *Names, People and Places* (1977, Watkins), pp. 114–18

44. *ASC* A s.a. 921

45. *ASC* A s.a. 921

46. *ASC* A s.a. 922
47. *ASC* A s.a. 922
48. *VA*, I, see also Keynes and Lapidge, *Alfred the Great*, p. 225

**Chapter 15: Lakeland Sagas**
1. W. G. Collingwood, *The Book of Coniston* (1897, Titus Wilson)
2. L. Abrams and D. N. Parsons, 'Place-names and the History of Scandinavian Settlement in England' in J. Hines, A. Lane and M. Redknapp (eds), *Land, Sea and Home: Proceedings of a Conference on Viking-Period Settlement* (2004, Northern Universities Press), p. 380
3. D. Coggins, K. J. Fairless and C. E. Batey, 'Simy Folds: An Early Medieval Settlement Site in Upper Teesdale. Co. Durham', *Medieval Archaeology* 27 (1983), pp. 1–26; D. Coggins, 'Simy Folds: Twenty Years On' in J. Hines et al. (eds), *Land, Sea and Home*, pp. 326–34; A. King, 'Post-Roman Upland Architecture in the Craven Dales and the Dating Evidence' in Hines et al. (eds), *Land, Sea and Home*, pp. 335–44 (see also the broader discussion in Hadley, *The Vikings in England*, pp. 81–144)
4. King, 'Post-Roman Upland Architecture', p. 340
5. Dawn Hadley (*The Vikings in England*, pp. 99–104) provides an excellent overview of the issues and literature
6. See, for example, the names of moneyers working during the reign of Æthelred (R.978–1013, 1014–1016); J. J. North, *English Hammered Coinage*, Vol. 1 (1994, Spink), pp. 162–7
7. K. Leahy and C. Paterson, 'New Light on the Viking Presence in Lincolnshire: The Artefactual Evidence' in Graham-Campbell et al. (eds), *Vikings and the Danelaw*, pp. 181–202
8. J. F. Kershaw, *Viking Identities: Scandinavian Jewellery in England* (2013, Oxford University Press)
9. J. Geipel, *The Viking Legacy: The Scandinavian Influence on the English Language* (1975, David and Charles); see also S. D. Friðriksdóttir, *Old Norse Influence in Modern English: The Effect of the Viking Invasion* (2014, unpublished BA dissertation, University of Iceland) [http://skemman.is/stream/get/1946/17234/40268/1/Old_Norse_Influence_in_Modern_English.pdf]
10. M. Townend, *The Vikings and Victorian Lakeland: The Norse Medievalism of W. G. Collingwood and His Contemporaries* (2009, Cumberland and Westmorland Antiquarian and Archaeological Society), p. 67
11. A. Wawn, 'The Spirit of 1892: Saga-Steads and Victorian Philology', *Saga-Book of the Viking Society* 23 (1992), pp. 213–52; M. O. Townend, 'In Search of the Lakeland Saga: Antiquarian Fiction and the Norse Settlement in Cumbria', in D. Clark and C. Phelpstead (eds), *Old Norse Made New: Essays on the Post-Medieval Reception of Old Norse Literature and Culture* (2007, Viking Society for Northern Research); Wawn, *The Vikings and the Victorians*, pp. 308–9
12. Townend, *The Vikings and Victorian Lakeland*, pp. 33–4
13. For his part, Collingwood seems to have felt no sadness at his eclipse, though it was noted by contemporaries (Townend, *The Vikings and Victorian Lakeland*, pp. 44–5)
14. Ibid., p. 258

15. My own first-edition copy of *Scandinavian Britain*, I recently discovered to my great delight, is *ex libris* Robert Eugen Zachrisson, the famous Swedish philologist and place-name scholar: he signed the flyleaf in 1924 and, at some point, added a personalized bookplate. Zachrisson was responsible for a good deal of pioneering work on, among other things, the etymology of English place-names (including their Norse origins) and the Norman influence on modern English pronunciation; he is chiefly remembered today, however, for an ingenious attempt to overhaul the spelling of English with a system which he called Anglic. Although at the time it received considerable support, with reports (in Anglic) noting that 'leeding eduekaeshonists and reprezentativz of the Pres, who hav been prezent at korsez givn in Stockholm and Uppsala, hav testified that Anglic is a moest efektiv meenz of teeching English to forinerz', it was – perhaps mercifully – doomed to fail. A sage voice in the *Spectator*, commenting approvingly on these initiatives, observed in 1931 that 'Language can be, and often is, the greatest obstacle to thought, and nowhere is this truer than in thinking about language itself.' There may be something in that, but it was not, thankfully, enough to overcome the 'instinct of every educated man [...] to rise in revolt against any attempt to interfere with a custom sanctified by long usage' (A. Lloyd James, 'Anglic: An International English', *Spectator*, 14 August 1931, p. 7: http://archive.spectator.co.uk/article/15th-august-1931/7/anglic-an-international-english)

16. Townend, *The Vikings and Victorian Lakeland*, p. 157

17. For the tenor of the debate see, e.g., D. Austin, 'The "Proper Study" of Medieval Archaeology', in D. Austin and L. Alcock (eds), *From the Baltic to the Black Sea: Studies in Medieval Archaeology* (1990, Routledge), pp. 9–42; G. R. W. Halsall, *Cemeteries and Society in Merovingian Gaul: Selected Studies in History and Archaeology, 1992–2009* (2010, Brill), pp. 49–88

18. Kitchin exemplifies in many ways the late Victorian churchman and antiquary. His improbable list of accomplishments is a record of his talents, but also serves as an indicator of the excellent connections and oodles of free time that his position in society afforded. He was a fellow of the Society of Antiquaries and a member of the British Archaeological Society, to whom he delivered learned disquisitions on (among other things) the font at Winchester Cathedral and 'The Burial-place of the Slavonians' at North Stoneham Church in Hampshire; he was dean of Winchester Cathedral (from 1883) where he contributed significantly to the restoration of the reredos, and was later dean of Durham Cathedral (from 1894) and chancellor of Durham University (from 1908) until his death in 1912; he wrote the popular hymn 'Raise High the Cross' as well as a three-volume history of France and a biography of Pope Pius II; as a young man in 1863 he was private tutor to Frederik, Crown Prince of Denmark (later crowned King Frederik VIII). He also, and probably this is the least interesting of all his many achievements despite being the one for which he is most remembered, fathered Xie Kitchin, the favourite child-muse of Charles Lutwidge Dodgson, aka Lewis Carroll; indeed, he was himself photographed by Dodgson and the result can be found in the archives of the National Portrait Gallery. A copy of the same likeness hangs on the wall

of my study: I am contemplating his magnificent mutton-chops even as I type

19. Wawn, *The Vikings and the Victorians*, p. 128; Townend, *The Vikings and Victorian Lakeland*, p. 52

20. Townend, *The Vikings and Victorian Lakeland*, pp. 189–90; M. Townend, *Language and History in Viking Age England: Linguistic Relations between Speakers of Old Norse and Old English* (2002, Brepols Publishers)

21. G. W. Kitchin, 'The Statesmen of West Cumberland' in *Ruskin in Oxford, and other Studies* (1904, John Murray), p. 56; Isaac Kitchin, my great-great-great-great-grandfather, was born in Cumberland and educated at St Bees Theological College

22. When Kitchin spoke of the 'love of liberty and simple independence, bred in the blood of men of mountain regions' he was also, of course, including himself in this blood-borne character portrait (Ibid.)

23. Quoted in Townend, *The Vikings and Victorian Lakeland*, p. 192

24. D. Griffiths, *Vikings of the Irish Sea* (2010, Oxbow), p. 23

25. W. G. Collingwood, *The Book of Coniston*, pp. 1–7

26. Ibid.

27. Ibid.

**Chapter 16: A New Way**

1. W. G. Collingwood, *Thorstein of the Mere* (1895, Edward Arnold), p. 1

2. C. Krag, 'The early unification of Norway' in K. Helle, (ed.), *The Cambridge History of Scandinavia, Volume I: Prehistory to 1520* (2003, Cambridge University Press), pp. 184–9

3. e.g. 'Haralds saga ins hárfagra', chapter 19 (*Heimskringla I*)

4. Krag, 'The early unification of Norway'

5. Griffiths, *Vikings of the Irish Sea*, p. 51

6. K. A. Hemer, J. A. Evans, C. A. Chenery, A. L. Lamb, 'No man is an island: Evidence of pre-Viking Age migration to the Isle of Man', *Journal of Archaeological Science* 52 (2014), pp. 242–9; Charles-Edwards, *Wales and the Britons*, pp. 14, 148–52

7. *AU* s.a. 878

8. *AU* s.a. 839

9. A. Woolf, *From Pictland to Alba, 789–1070* (2007, Edinburgh University Press), pp. 9–10

10. Ibid., p. 66

11. Ibid.

12. Ibid., pp. 93–8

13. *CKA*

14. *The Annals of St-Bertin*, s.a. 847; J. Nelson (ed. and trans.), *The Annals of St-Bertin* (1991, Manchester University Press)

15. *CKA*; *AU* s.a 866

16. *AC* s.a. 870

17. *AU* s.a. 870

18. *AU* s.a. 871

19. *CKA*; Woolf, *From Pictland to Alba*, p. 109

20. *AU* s.a. 873

21. Downham, *Viking Kings*

22. Glasgow Community Planning Partnership, *Govan Area Partnership Profile 2016* (2016, Glasgow City Council) [https://www.glasgow.gov.uk/councillorsandcommittees/viewSelectedDocument.asp?c=P62AFQDNT1Z3DN0GUT]

23. K. Goodwin, 'The Glasgow Effect', *Guardian* (10 June 2016) [https://www.theguardian.com/cities/2016/jun/10/glasgow-effect-die-young-high-risk-premature-death]

24. 'No City for Old Men', *The Economist* (25 August 2012) [http://www.economist.com/node/21560888]

25. A. Campsie, 'Everything You Need to Know About Clyde Shipbuilding', *Scotsman* (30 March 2016) [http://www.scotsman.com/heritage/people-places/everything-you-need-to-know-about-clyde-shipbuilding-1-4086097]

26. I say probably, because, as others have observed, none have survived in their original settings: H. Williams, 'Hogbacks: The Materiality of Solid Spaces' in H. Williams, J. Kirton and M. Gondek (eds), *Early Medieval Stone Monuments: Materiality, Biography, Landscape* (2015, Boydell & Brewer)

27. J. T. Lang, 'Hogback Monuments in Scotland', *Proceedings of the Society of Antiquaries of Scotland* 105 (1976), pp. 206–35

28. See, for example, the largest of the brooches, BM 1909,0624.2; Graham-Campbell, *The Cuerdale Hoard*, contains considerable detail on the contents of the hoard and its protracted recovery

29. NMS X.FC 8 [http://www.nms.ac.uk/explore/stories/scottish-history-and-archaeology/hunterston-brooch/]

30. The Irish of the tenth century had their own word for this phenomenon: *Gallgoídil* ('foreigner Gaels'); see Downham, '"Hiberno-Norwegians" and "Anglo-Danes"'

31. *CKA*

32. *AU* s.a. 900; *CS* s.a. 900

33. The development of the Scottish nation is a complex subject to which this book cannot hope to do justice; for the fullest narrative treatment, see Woolf, *From Pictland to Alba*

## Chapter 17: The Pagan Winter

1. *Völuspá*, v. 45 (author's translation)

2. There's no point searching for it – it was flattened after excavation in 1946 to facilitate the progress of farm traffic

3. For discussion of the burial see: http://skaldic.abdn.ac.uk/db.php?table=mss&id=22110&if=myth; see also Wilson, *Vikings in the Isle of Man*

4. These are often, mistakenly, assumed to have been used as the figureheads of ships. Five such pillars accompanied the occupants of the Oseberg burial into the grave-mound, and we can presume therefore that they had some purpose in the most elaborate Viking death theatre. Handles at the base of the posts would have allowed these objects to be attached to another object – what, why or precisely how is unknown

5. Lunde and Stone, *Land of Darkness*, pp. 47–8

6. H. E. Davidson, 'Human Sacrifice in the Late Pagan Period of North-Western Europe' in M. O. H. Carver (ed.), *The Age of Sutton Hoo: The Seventh Century in North-Western Europe* (1992, Boydell Press), pp. 331–40

7. Griffiths, *Vikings of the Irish Sea*, pp. 81–3

8. Reynolds, *Anglo-Saxon Deviant Burial*

9. Ibid.

10. Price, 'Belief and Ritual'

11. Price, *The Viking Way*

12. The list of objects is adapted from that published by the Norwegian Museum of Cultural History [http://www.khm.uio.no/english/visit-us/viking-ship-museum/exhibitions/oseberg/in-the-grave.pdf]

13. [http://www.khm.uio.no/english/visit-us/viking-ship-museum/exhibitions/oseberg/in-the-grave.pdf]

14. Canmore ID 9383

15. Sjøvold, *The Viking Ships in Oslo*

16. The story of the discovery of the grave is dramatic in itself, involving a race against time by archaeologists, bracing themselves against the dire Orkney storms that sweep off the Atlantic in the autumn; Graham-Campbell, *Vikings in Scotland: An Archaeological Survey* (1998, Edinburgh University Press), pp. 138–40; see also http://www.orkneyjar.com/history/scarboat/

17. Broadly speaking: as ever, the details are contradictory and late

18. C. Abram, *Myths of the Pagan North: The Gods of the Norsemen* (2011, Bloomsbury), pp. 157–68

19. Maughold (I) [202A]; Kirk Michael (III) [215]; individual Manx runestones are identified by the parish in whch the stone was found, followed by the individually assigned number of the stone within that parish. The Rundata reference is provided in square brackets

20. This is not to say that Scandinavian runestones never feature carved crosses – they frequently do – but the style and form of these monuments is usually very different

21. Braddan (IV) [193A]

22. Andreas (II) [184]

23. Ballaugh [189]

24. Andreas (I) [183]

25. Braddan (III) [191B]

26. Braddan (II) [191A]

27. The twin ravens Huginn ('thought') and Muninn ('memory') were key attributes of Odin; see, esp., *Gylfaginning* 38

28. W. S. Calverley and W. G. Collingwood, *Notes on the Early Sculptured Crosses, Shrines and Monuments in the Present Diocese of Carlisle* (1899, Titus Wilson); C. A. Parker, *The Ancient Crosses at Gosforth and Cumberland* (1896, Elliot Stock)

29. *Gylfaginning* 51

30. *Völuspá* 59, p. 13

31. *Völuspá* 65, p. 14

32. Abram, *Myths of the Pagan North*, p. 165

33. Price, 'Belief and Ritual'

34. Abram, *Myths of the Pagan North*

## Chapter 18: The Great War

1. *APV*, lines 14–17, 115–20
2. Halfdan didn't last long according to the *HSC*. In punishment for his depredations 'he began to rave and stink so badly that his whole army drove him from its midst'
3. *ASC* s.a. 875; see also *CKA* and Woolf, pp. 111–12
4. *ASC* s.a. 875
5. *HSC*, ch. 13
6. Ibid.
7. Oswiu of Northumbria (r. 640–70) was the king whose reign can be said to have ushered in that kingdom's Golden Age. It was Oswiu who had killed (against all expectations) the notorious pagan king of Mercia, Penda, in the battle of the Winwæd in 655 – an act which had made him the most powerful man in Britain and overturned the last bastion of non-Christian belief on the island. During his reign he had also presided over the Synod of Whitby (664), a meeting which formally brought religious observance into line with Roman practice, and Northumbria firmly into the orbit of the mainstream religious–political–intellectual circles of post-Roman Europe. For any king to be proclaimed at a place named Oswiu's Hill would have been to make an unmistakable political statement and, indeed, we may well wonder if this place had a long association with the public acknowledgement of kingship in Northumbria; see also discussion and references in Hadley, *The Vikings in England*, pp. 37–41
8. Hadley, *The Vikings in England*, pp. 44–54
9. Ibid.; Blackburn, *Viking Coinage*; G. Williams, 'Kingship, Christianity and Coinage'
10. G. Williams, 'Kingship, Christianity and Coinage'
11. This identification has at times been contested, see Downham, *Viking Kings*, pp. 94–6
12. *AU* s.a. 902
13. *AC*; *FA*
14. *FA* s.a. 907; see also Lavelle, *Alfred's Wars*, pp. 230–3
15. Hadley, *The Vikings in England*, p. 177
16. *AU* s.a. 913
17. *AU* s.a. 917; *ASC* s.a. 924
18. J. Graham-Campbell, *The Viking-Age Gold and Silver of Scotland, AD 850–1100* (1995, National Museums of Scotland); Graham-Campbell, *Cuerdale*
19. T. Hugo, 'On the Field of Cuerdale', *Journal of the British Archaeological Association* 8 (1853), pp. 330–5; Graham-Campbell, *Cuerdale*, pp. 21–37
20. *ASC* D, s.a 926, *ASC* E s.a 927; *GRA* 1.3
21. Woolf, *From Pictland to Alba*, p. 158; *EHD* (104)
22. *ASC* D s.a. 926
23. North, *English Hammered Coinage*
24. Woolf, *From Pictland to Alba*, pp. 164–6
25. *HR*
26. *ASC* D s.a. 934; Woolf, *From Pictland to Alba*, p. 161, n. 73
27. *CC* s.a. 934
28. *GRA* 1.3

29. *APV*, lines 132, 143, 162
30. *AFM* s.a. 937
31. *APV*, lines 40, 60
32. *Brunanburh*, lines 61–5; M. Alexander (trans.), *The Earliest English Poems* (1991, Penguin), p. 97
33. According to Æthelweard, writing in the late tenth century; *CA*, p. 54
34. *CKA*; *AC* s.a. 938; *AU* s.a. 936
35. *ASC* E, s.a. 937
36. A. Tennyson, 'The Battle of Brunanburh', lines 1–14 in C. Ricks (ed.), *The Poems of Tennyson* III (1987, Longman), pp. 18–23
37. *AU* s.a. 939

## Chapter 19: Bloodaxe

1. *Egil's Saga*, 80, v.4 (p. 159)
2. *The Chronicle of Melrose*, s.a. 941; J. Stevenson (ed. and trans.), *A Mediaeval Chronicle of Scotland: The Chronicle of Melrose* (1991 [reprint of 1850s edition], Llanerch)
3. *ASC* A s.a. 942
4. See Chapter 20
5. *ASC* A s.a. 944
6. *CC* s.a. 946
7. G. Williams, *Eirik Bloodaxe*
8. Ibid.
9. 'Hakonar saga góða', chapter 3 (*Heimskringla I*)
10. *ASC* D s.a. 948
11. *ASC* A s.a. 948
12. M. Shapland, *Buildings of Secular and Religious Lordship: Anglo-Saxon Tower-nave Churches* (2012, unpublished PhD thesis, UCL)
13. R. Hall, *Viking Age England* (2004, The History Press), p. 283; R. Hall, 'York', in Brink with Price (eds), *The Viking World*, pp. 379–84; Hadley, *The Vikings in England*, pp. 147–54; the full Coppergate excavations are published in twenty-one volumes by York Archaeological Trust
14. Hall, 'York', p. 376
15. Q. Mould, I. Carlisle and E. Cameron, *Leather and Leatherworking in Anglo-Scandinavian and Medieval York* (2003, CBA/York Archaeological Trust)
16. Olaf ended his days as a monk on Iona, not the retirement one might imagine for a Viking king – it shows how much the cultural compass had shifted since the Viking Age began
17. G. Williams, *Eirik Bloodaxe*
18. *FH* I
19. 'Hakonar saga góða', chapter 4 (*Heimskringla I*); note that the saga names King Edmund (Játmundr), although Eadred was the reigning English king at the time
20. *Grímnismál*, verse 36
21. Slightly adapted from R. D. Fulk, '(Introduction to) Anonymous, Eiríksmál' in D. Whaley (ed.), *Poetry from the Kings' Sagas 1: From Mythical Times to c. 1035* (2012, Brepols), p. 1003
22. Price, *The Viking Way*

## Chapter 20: Wolves

1. 'Sermon of the Wolf to the English', *EHD* (240)
2. *ASC* CDE s.a. 1006
3. No Anglo-Saxon remains have been found, although the former use of the mound as a Bronze Age burial mound has been confirmed: A. Sanmark and S. J. Semple, 'Places of Assembly: New Discoveries in Sweden and England', *Fornvännen* 103. 4 (2008), pp. 245–59
4. The walking dead appear frequently in Old Norse literature, most famously in *Grettis saga*: see G. A. High (trans.) and P. Foote (ed.), *The Saga of Grettir the Strong* (1965, Dent)
5. *Egil's Saga*, 61, v.11 (p. 116)
6. T. J. T. Williams, 'For the Sake of Bravado in the Wilderness'; E. M. Lacey, *Birds and Bird-lore in the Literature of Anglo-Saxon England* (2013, unpublished PhD thesis, UCL), pp. 114–19
7. T. J. T. Williams, 'Landscape and Warfare in Anglo-Saxon England and the Viking Campaign of 1006', *Early Medieval Europe* 23 (2015), pp. 329–59
8. The stones replaced an even older timber monument; J. Pollard, 'The Sanctuary, Overton Hill, Wiltshire: A Re-examination', *Proceedings of the Prehistoric Society* 58 (1992), pp. 213–26. J. Pollard and A. Reynolds, *Avebury: The Biography of a Landscape* (2002, Tempus)
9. *CC*
10. This Maccus may conceivably have been the man who ended King Eric's life in 954: there is no way to be certain. More importantly, this reference represents the first time that a kingdom of the isles is mentioned in contemporary records. A political entity that brought together the Scandinavian-settled territories of north-western Britain and the Irish Sea was coming into view for the first time
11. Lavelle, *Alfred's Wars*
12. *CC*; *FH*
13. *ASC* D s.a. 959; in the twelfth century, William of Malmesbury helpfully elaborated on Wulfstan's sentiments by explaining how the English had picked up the despicable foreign habits of drunkenness from the Danes, effeminacy from the Dutch and ferocity from the Germans (*GRA*)
14. *EHD* (41)
15. Ibid.
16. *FH*
17. *Maldon*, lines 46–56; trans. Bradley, *Anglo-Saxon Poetry*
18. J. R. R. Tolkien, 'The Homecoming of Beorhtnoth Beorhthelm's Son' in *The Tolkien Reader* (1966, Ballantine)
19. Neil Price, in a personal communication to me, suggested the old-fashioned word 'vim' – a particularly apposite approximation
20. *Maldon*, lines 96–100
21. Halsall, *Warfare and Society*, p. 183
22. *Maldon*, lines 312–19
23. J. D. Niles, 'Maldon and Mythopoesis', *Mediaevalia* 17 (1994), pp. 89–121; *Wanderer*
24. Other, smaller sums were dished out on an ad hoc basis; S. Keynes, 'The Historical Context' in D. Scragg (ed.), *The Battle of Maldon AD 991* (1991, Blackwell), p. 100

25. See J. Gillingham, '"The Most Precious Jewel in the English Crown": Levels of Danegeld and Heregeld in the Early Eleventh Century', *English Historical Review* 104 (1989), pp. 373–84 and 'Chronicles and Coins as Evidence for Levels of Tributes and Taxation in Late Tenth and Eleventh Century England', *English Historical Review* 105 (1990), pp. 939–50

26. J. C. Moesgaard, 'The Import of English Coins to the Northern Lands: Some Remarks on Coin Circulation in the Viking Age based on New Evidence from Denmark', in B. J. Cook, G. Williams and M. Archibald (eds), *Coinage and History in the North Sea World, c. AD 500–1250: Essays in Honour of Marion Archibald* (2006, Brill)

27. *ASC* CDE s.a. 999

28. S. Keynes, 'The Declining Reputation of King Æthelred the Unready' in D. Hill (ed.), *Ethelred the Unready: Papers from the Millenary Conference* (1978, BAR), pp. 227–53; L. Roach, *Æthelred* (2016, Yale University Press)

29. *ASC* A s.a. 1001

30. *ASC* CDE s.a. 1001

31. *ASC* CDE s.a. 1002; A. Williams, '"Cockles amongst the Wheat": Danes and English in the Western Midlands in the First Half of the Eleventh Century', *Midland History* 11 (1986), pp. 1–22

32. *EHD* (127); S909

33. A. M. Pollard, P. Ditchfield, E. Piva, S. Wallis, C. Falys and S. Ford, '"Sprouting like Cockle amongst the Wheat": The St Brice's Day Massacre and the Isotopic Analysis of Human Bones from St John's College, Oxford', *Oxford Journal of Archaeology* 31 (2012), pp. 83–102

## Chapter 21: Mortal Remains

1. *EHD*, 48

2. *ASC* CDE s.a. 1013

3. T. Lindkvist, 'Early Political Organisation: Introductory Survey' in K. Helle (ed.), *The Cambridge History of Scandinavia, Volume 1: Prehistory to 1520* (2003, Cambridge University Press)

4. See chapters by I. Skovgaard Petersen ('The Making of the Danish Kingdom'), C. Krag ('The Early Unification of Norway'), M. Stefánsson ('The Norse Island Communities of the Western Ocean'), T. Lindkvist ('Kings and Provinces in Sweden') in Helle (ed.), *The Cambridge History of Scandinavia*

5. A. Pedersen, 'The Royal Monuments at Jelling' in G. Williams et al., *Vikings: Life and Legend*, pp. 158–60

6. *The Dream of the Rood* (*ASPR* 2); Alexander, *Earliest English Poems*, p. 87

7. *ASC* CDE s.a. 1012

8. *CC* s.a. 1013, p. 477

9. *ASC* CDE s.a. 1014

10. *ASC* CDE s.a. 1016

11. *ASC* D s.a. 1057

12. *CC* s.a. 1016, pp. 487–9

13. *ASC* E s.a. 1016

14. *ASC* D s.a, p. 152

15. *Enc.* 10; pp. 24–7

16. Ibid.; pp. 26–7

17. Ibid.
18. Ibid.
19. *Enc.* 11; pp. 28–9
20. They carry, in fact, some of the earliest uses of the term 'England' to be found anywhere, proof that the concept of England had become sufficiently concrete by the eleventh century to be common currency outside Britain (Jesch, *Ships and Men*, pp. 70–7)
21. U194
22. U344; see discussion in S. B. F. Jansson, *Swedish Vikings in England: The Evidence of the Rune Stones* (1966, UCL)
23. Jansson, *Swedish Vikings in England*, pp. 12–13
24. DR337
25. Loe et al., *Given to the Ground*
26. N 184
27. M. O. Townend, *English Place-Names in Skaldic Verse* (1998, English Place-Name Society), p. 31
28. *ASC* CDE s.a. 1017
29. *HA*, vi. 13, pp. 360–1
30. *Enc.* ii.15; *CC* s.a. 1017
31. In addition to a previous wife, an English noblewoman named Ælfgifu
32. M. Biddle and B. Kjølbye-Biddle, 'Danish Royal Burials in Winchester: Cnut and his Family' in Lavelle and Roffey (eds), *The Danes in Wessex*, pp. 231–2
33. Ibid., p. 232

## Epilogue

1. B. E. Crawford, *The Northern Earldoms: Orkney and Caithness from AD 870 to 1470* (2013, Birlinn); Woolf, *From Pictland to Alba*, pp. 275–311

# FURTHER READING

## The Vikings and Viking Age Scandinavia

S. Brink with N. Price (eds), *The Viking World* (2008, Routledge)

J. Graham-Campbell and G. Williams, *Silver Economy in the Viking Age* (2007, Left Coast Press)

K. Helle (ed.), *The Cambridge History of Scandinavia, Vol. 1: Prehistory to 1520* (2003, Cambridge University Press)

J. Hines, A. Lane and M. Redknapp (eds), *Land, Sea and Home: Proceedings of a Conference on Viking-Period Settlement* (2004, Northern Universities Press)

J. Jesch, *Ships and Men in the Late Viking Age: The Vocabulary of Runic Inscriptions* (2001, Boydell & Brewer)

J. Jesch, *The Viking Diaspora* (2015, Routledge)

N. Price, *The Vikings* (2017, Routledge)

P. Sawyer (ed.), *Oxford Illustrated History of the Vikings* (1997, Oxford University Press)

B. B. Smith, S. Taylor and G. Williams (eds), *West over Sea: Studies in Scandinavian Sea-Borne Expansion and Settlement Before 1300* (2007, Brill)

G. Williams, P. Pentz and M. Wemhoff (eds), *Vikings: Life and Legend* (2014, British Museum Press)

### *Myths and Beliefs*

C. Abram, *Myths of the Pagan North: The Gods of the Norsemen* (2011, Bloomsbury)

A. Andrén, K. Jennbert and C. Raudvere (eds), *Old Norse Religion in Long-term Perspectives: Origins, Changes, and Interactions* (2006, Nordic Academic Press)

N. Price, *The Viking Way* (2017, 2nd edition, Oxbow)


## Vikings in Britain and Ireland

J. Carroll, S. H. Harrison and G. Williams, *The Vikings in Britain and Ireland* (2014, British Museum Press)

C. Downham, *Viking Kings of Britain and Ireland* (2007, Dunedin)

J. Graham-Campbell (and contributors), *The Cuerdale Hoard and Related Viking-Age Silver and Gold from Britain and Ireland in the British Museum* (2013, 2nd edition, British Museum Press)

K. Holman, *The Northern Conquest: Vikings in Britain and Ireland* (2007, Signal Books)


### *England*

J. Graham-Campbell, R. Hall, J. Jesch and D. N. Parsons (eds), *Vikings and the Danelaw: Select Papers from the Proceedings of the Thirteenth Viking Congress* (2001, Oxbow)

D. M. Hadley, *The Vikings in England: Settlement, Society and Culture* (2006, Manchester University Press)

D. M. Hadley and J. D. Richards (eds), *Cultures in Contact: Scandinavian Settlement in England in the Ninth and Tenth Centuries* (2000, Brepols)

R. Hall, *Viking Age England* (2004, The History Press)

R. Lavelle and S. Roffey (eds), *The Danes in Wessex* (2016, Oxbow)


### *Scotland*

B. Crawford, *Scandinavian Scotland* (1987, Leicester University Press)

J. Graham-Campbell, *Vikings in Scotland: An Archaeological Survey* (1998, Edinburgh University Press)

A. Woolf, *From Pictland to Alba, 789–1070* (2007, Edinburgh University Press)

### Western Britain and the Irish Sea

D. Griffiths, *Vikings of the Irish Sea* (2010, Oxbow)

M. Redknapp, *Vikings in Wales: An Archaeological Quest* (2000, National Museum of Wales Books)

D. Wilson, *Vikings in the Isle of Man* (2008, Aarhus University Press)

### The Viking Revival

D. Clark and C. Phelpstead (eds), *Old Norse Made New: Essays on the Post-Medieval Reception of Old Norse Literature and Culture* (2007, Viking Society for Northern Research)

M. Townend, *The Vikings and Victorian Lakeland: The Norse Medievalism of W. G. Collingwood and His Contemporaries* (2009, Cumberland and Westmorland Antiquarian and Archaeological Society)

A. Wawn, *The Vikings and the Victorians* (2000, Boydell)

A full bibliography of all literature cited in this book can be accessed at tjtwilliams.com

# ILLUSTRATION CREDITS

## Integrated

p. 50 Norwegian propaganda for the SS by Harald Damsleth, 1940–5

p. 55 Engraving of the Hilton of Cadboll stone by Charles Carter Petley, 1812 (*Wikimedia Commons*)

p. 118 Snorri Sturluson, as imagined by the artist Christian Krohg, 1899 (*Wikimedia Commons*)

p. 177 Alfred the hero, as envisioned by Morris Meredith Williams, 1913 (*Photo © Historical Picture Archive/Corbis/Corbis via Getty Images*)

p. 219 A thing in progress, Halfdan Egedius, 1899 (*Wikimedia Commons*)

p. 221 Þorgnýr the law-speaker holds forth; Christian Krohg, 1899 (*Wikimedia Commons*)

p. 234 Frontispiece to *Thorstein of the Mere*, drawn by W. G. Collingwood, 1895

p. 251 Hogbacks at St Thomas', Brompton, drawn by W. G. Collingwood, 1927

p. 269 Vidar and Fenrir on the Gosforth Cross; Julius Magnus Petersen, 1913 (*Wikimedia Commons*)

p. 276 Coin of Cnut of Northumbria, *c.*900–5 (*© Gilli Allan, 2017*)

p. 277 A Northumbrian coin of the 920s (*© Gilli Allan, 2017*)

p. 326 The crucifixion face of the Jelling runestone; Julius Magnus Petersen, 1869–71 (*from Peder Goth Thorsen, De danske runemindesmærker, 1879, National Museum of Denmark*)

## Plate sections

A ninth-century gravestone from the monastery at Lindisfarne (*Photo by CM Dixon/Print Collector/Getty Images*)

The late-tenth-century Gjermundbu helmet (© *2017 Kulturhistorisk museum, UiO/CC BY-SA 4.0*)

A lead weight, adapted from a piece of ecclesiastical metalwork (© *The Trustees of the British Museum*)

The Inchmarnock 'hostage stone' (© *Headland Archaeology (UK) Ltd*)

The reconstructed Viking Age long-house at Borg, Lofoten (*Hemis/ Alamy Stock Photo*)

The Gokstad Ship, built *c.*890, now housed in Oslo (© Thomas J. T. Williams)

The Coppergate Helmet, a Northumbrian helmet forged between 750 and 775 (*courtesy of York Museums Trust: http:// yorkmuseumstrust.org.uk/CCBY-SA4.0*)

Sigurd pierces the body of the dragon Fáfnir from beneath on a runestone from Ramsund, Södermanland (Sweden) (*robertharding/Alamy Stock Photo*)

Ivar and Ubbe setting sail for England (*Photo by Fine Art Images/ Heritage Images/Getty Images*)

Wayland's Smithy in *c.*1900 (*Photo by Henry Taunt/English Heritage/ Arcaid/Corbis via Getty Images*)

The village of East Lyng, attached to the Isle of Athelney (© *Historic England Archive*)

A reconstruction of the Viking camp at Repton (© *Compost Creative*)

An Anglo-Saxon font at Deerhurst in Gloucestershire (*Colin Underhill/Alamy Stock Photo*)

The early medieval crypt of St Wystan's Church at Repton (*Heritage Image Partnership Ltd/Alamy Stock Photo*)

A reconstruction of the Viking camp at Torksey (© *Compost Creative*)

The eighth-century *Stockholm Codex Aureus* (*Art Collection 3/Alamy Stock Photo*)

Tingwall: an assembly site on Mainland, Shetland (© *Thomas J. T. Williams*)

A hogback stone from Govan Old Church, Glasgow (*Glasgow University Library, Special Collections*)

The whalebone plaque from the tenth-century boat burial at Scar, Orkney (*World History Archive/Alamy Stock Photo*)

Thorwald's Cross, at Andreas Parish on the Isle of Man, depicts – on one side – Odin swallowed by the wolf Fenrir at *Ragnarök*. The other side displays an apparently Christian scene (*Photographs by CM Dixon/Print Collector/Getty Images*)

The Cuerdale Hoard (© *The Trustees of the British Museum*)

Coins of Viking rulers in England (© *The Trustees of the British Museum*)

Reconstruction of tenth-century dwellings at Coppergate, York (© *York Archaeological Trust*)

Northey Island, Essex (© *Terry Joyce; Creative Commons Attribution Share-alike license 2.0*)

The Sanctuary monument at Overton Hill, Wiltshire, erected around 2000 BC, as drawn by William Stukeley in 1723 (*Chronicle/Alamy Stock Photo*)

The inscription on a runestone in Väsby, Uppland (Sweden) (*Berig, Wikimedia Commons*)

Stone found in 1852 in the graveyard of St Paul's Cathedral, London (*Granger Historical Picture Archive/Alamy Stock Photo*)

A mass grave of over fifty decapitated men, most of them originally from Scandinavia, found near Weymouth in Dorset in 2011 (© *Oxford Archaeology*)

Cnut and his queen, Emma (Ælfgifu), depicted in the pages of the eleventh-century *Winchester Liber Vitae* (© *British Library Board. All Rights Reserved/Bridgeman Images*)

# INDEX